Volume 1
THE ENVIRONMENT
- Prof. Dato' Dr Sham Sani
  Universiti Kebangsaan Malaysia

Volume 2
PLANTS
- Dr E. Soepadmo
  Forest Research Institute of Malaysia (FRIM)

Volume 3
ANIMALS
- Prof. Dr Yong Hoi Sen
  Universiti Malaya

Volume 4
EARLY HISTORY
- Prof. Dato' Dr Nik Hassan Shuhaimi Nik Abdul Rahman
  Universiti Kebangsaan Malaysia

Volume 5
ARCHITECTURE
- Chen Voon Fee
  Architectural Consulting Services

Volume 6
THE SEAS
- Prof. Dr Ong Jin Eong and Prof. Dr Gong Wooi Khoon
  Universiti Sains Malaysia

Volume 7
EARLY MODERN HISTORY
[1800–1940]
- Prof. Dr Cheah Boon Kheng
  Universiti Sains Malaysia (retired)

Volume 8
PERFORMING ARTS
- Prof. Dr Ghulam-Sarwar Yousof
  Universiti Malaya

Volume 9
LANGUAGES AND LITERATURE
- Prof. Dato' Dr Asmah Haji Omar
  Universiti Pendidikan Sultan Idris

Volume 10
RELIGIONS AND BELIEFS
- Prof. Dr M. Kamal Hassan and Dr Ghazali bin Basri
  International Islamic University Malaysia and
  World Council of Muslims for Interfaith Relations

Volume 11
GOVERNMENT AND POLITICS
[1940–2006]
- Prof. Dato' Dr Zakaria Haji Ahmad
  Universiti Kebangsaan Malaysia

Volume 12
PEOPLES AND TRADITIONS
- Prof. Dato' Dr Hood Salleh
  Universiti Kebangsaan Malaysia

Volume 13
THE ECONOMY
- Prof. Dr Osman Rani Hassan
  Universiti Pendidikan Sultan Idris

Volume 14
CRAFTS AND THE VISUAL ARTS
- Datuk Syed Ahmad Jamal
  Artist

Volume 15
THE MALAY SULTANATES
- Datuk Prof. Emeritus Dr Mohd Taib Osman and
  Prof. Emeritus Dato' Dr Khoo Kay Kim
  Universiti Malaya

Volume 16
SPORTS AND RECREATION
- Tan Sri Dato' Seri (Dr) Ahmad Sarji bin Abdul Hamid
  President, Malaysia Lawn Bowls Federation

THE ENCYCLOPEDIA OF MALAYSIA

PEOPLES AND TRADITIONS

The Encyclopedia of Malaysia was first conceived by Editions Didier Millet and Datin Paduka Marina Mahathir. The Editorial Advisory Board, made up of distinguished figures drawn from academic and public life, was constituted in March 1994. The project was publicly announced in October that year, and eight months later the first sponsors were in place. In 1996, the structure of the content was agreed; later that year the appointment of Volume Editors and the commissioning of authors were substantially complete, and materials for the work were beginning to flow in. By late 2006, 12 volumes were completed for publication. Upon completion, the series will consist of 16 volumes.

The Publishers wish to thank the following people for their contribution to the first seven volumes:
Dato' Seri Anwar Ibrahim,
who acted as Chairman of the Editorial Advisory Board;
and
the late Tan Sri Dato' Dr Noordin Sopiee
Tan Sri Datuk Augustine S. H. Ong
the late Tan Sri Zain Azraai
Datuk Datin Paduka Zakiah Hanum bt Abdul Hamid
Datin Noor Azlina Yunus

EDITORIAL TEAM

Series Editorial Team

PUBLISHER
Didier Millet

GENERAL MANAGER
Charles Orwin

PROJECT COORDINATOR
Marina Mahathir

EDITORIAL DIRECTOR
Timothy Auger

PROJECT MANAGER
Martin Cross

PRODUCTION MANAGER
Sin Kam Cheong

DESIGN DIRECTORS
Annie Teo
Yusri bin Din

EDITORIAL CONSULTANT
Vivien Stone

EDITORS
Azrina Abdul Karim
William Citrin
Kiri Cowie
Shoba Devan
Fong Min Yuan

ASSISTANT EDITOR
Lee Li Lian

DESIGNERS
Muamar Ghadafi bin Ali
Theivani A/P Nadaraju

Volume Editorial Team

EDITOR
Shoba Devan

CONSULTANT EDITORS
Prof. Dato' Dr Zainal Kling
Assoc. Prof. Dr Soo Kim Wah

DESIGNERS
Theivani A/P Nadaraju

ILLUSTRATORS
A. Kasim Abas
Chai Kah Yune
Jacky Chin
Lim Joo
Tan Hong Yew
Wong Lek Min

SPONSORS

The Encyclopedia of Malaysia was made possible thanks to the generous and enlightened support of the following organizations:

- DRB-HICOM BERHAD
- MAHKOTA TECHNOLOGIES SDN BHD
- MALAYAN UNITED INDUSTRIES BERHAD
- MALAYSIA NATIONAL INSURANCE BERHAD
- MINISTRY OF EDUCATION MALAYSIA
- NEW STRAITS TIMES PRESS (MALAYSIA) BERHAD
- TRADEWINDS CORPORATION BERHAD
- PETRONAS BERHAD
- UEM WORLD BERHAD
- STAR PUBLICATIONS (MALAYSIA) BERHAD
- SUNWAY GROUP
- TENAGA NASIONAL BERHAD
- UNITED OVERSEAS BANK GROUP
- YAYASAN ALBUKHARY
- YTL CORPORATION BERHAD

PNB GROUP OF COMPANIES
- PERMODALAN NASIONAL BERHAD
- NCB HOLDINGS BERHAD
- GOLDEN HOPE PLANTATIONS BERHAD
- SIME DARBY BERHAD
- MALAYAN BANKING BERHAD
- MNI HOLDINGS BERHAD
- PERNEC CORPORATION BERHAD

Published by Archipelago Press *an imprint of* Editions Didier Millet Pte Ltd
121, Telok Ayer Street, #03-01, Singapore 068590
Tel: 65-6324 9260 Fax: 65-6324 9261 E-mail: edm@edmbooks.com.sg

First published 2006

Editions Didier Millet, Kuala Lumpur Office:
25, Jalan Pudu Lama, 50200 Kuala Lumpur, Malaysia
Tel: 03-2031 3805 Fax: 03-2031 6298 E-mail: edmbooks@edmbooks.com.my
Websites: www.edmbooks.com • www.encyclopedia.com.my

Colour separation by United Graphic Pte Ltd
Printed by Star Standard Industries (Pte) Ltd
ISBN 981-3018-53-4

CONTRIBUTORS

Abdullah Ahmad
Institut Kajian dan Ekonomi

Prof. Dr Leonard Y. Andaya
University of Hawaii

Poline Bala
Universiti Malaysia Sarawak

Dr Baharun Azhar bin Raffia'i
Prime Minister's Department (retired)

Joseph Blandoi
SALCRA

Dr Michael E. Boutin
Summer Institute of Linguistics

Dr Cheu Hock Tong
National University of Singapore (retired)

Dr Daniel Chew
Sarawak Development Institute (retired)

Assoc. Prof. Dr Chia Oai Peng
Universiti Malaya

Ipoi Datan
Sarawak Museum

Assoc. Prof. Dr Julie Edo
Universiti Malaya

Prof. Dr Ghulam-Sarwar Yousof
Universiti Malaya

Dr Sarjit Singh Gill
Universiti Putra Malaysia

J. M. Gullick
Historian

Prof. Dr Heng Pek Koon
American University

Prof. Dr Hood Salleh
Universiti Kebangsaan Malaysia

Prof. Dr Jayum Anak Jawan
Universiti Putra Malaysia

Judeth John Baptist
Sabah Museum

Antonio Kahti Galis
Miri Municipal Council

Dr Peter M. Kedit
Tokyo University of Foreign Studies

John Wayne King
Summer Institute of Linguistics (retired)

Jayl Langub
Universiti Malaysia Sarawak

Rita Lasimbang
Kadazandusun Language Foundation

Dr Lee Kam Hing
Star Publications (Malaysia) Berhad

David Ling
Public relations consultant

Dr Herman Luping
Lawyer

Prof. Dr Kenneth McPherson
La Trobe University
Fellow, University of Heidelberg

Manimaran Subramaniam
Universiti Malaya

Prof. Emeritus Dr Mohd Taib Osman
Universiti Malaya

Prof. Dr Mohamad Yusoff Ismail
Universiti Kebangsaan Malaysia

David Moody
Summer Institute of Linguistics

Stella Moo-Tan
Sabah Museum

Dr Mustaffa Omar
Universiti Kebangsaan Malaysia

Prof. Dr Muhamad Muda
Universiti Institut Teknologi MARA

Dr Colin Nicholas
Coordinator, Centre for Orang Asli Concerns

Leo Mario Noeb
Ministry of Social Development, Sarawak

Assoc. Prof. Norani Sidek
Universiti Institut Teknologi MARA

Dr Ong Puay Liu
Universiti Kebangsaan Malaysia

Dr Ong Seng Huat
Xiao-en Cultural Endowment (Kuala Lumpur)

Peter Phelan
La Salle Organisation, Malaysia

Assoc. Prof. Dr Jacqueline Pugh-Kitingan
Universiti Malaysia Sabah

Prof. Dr R. Rajakrishnan
Asian Institute of Medicine, Science and Technology

Prof. Dr M. Rajantheran
Universiti Malaya

Rashid Esa
Orang Asli cultural specialist

Dr Rashila Ramli
Universiti Kebangsaan Malaysia

Patricia Regis
Ministry of Tourism, Culture and Environment, Sabah

James Ritchie
Journalist

Richard Robless
Selangor and Federal Territory Eurasian Association

Ruhanas Harun
Universiti Malaya

Assoc. Prof. Dr Sue Russell
Biola University

Dr Salfarina Abdul Gapor
Universiti Sains Malaysia

Prof. Dr Clifford Sather
University of Helsinki

Ding Seling
Education officer (retired)

Prof. Shamsul Amri Baharuddin
Universiti Kebangsaan Malaysia

Prof. Emeritus Dr S. Singaravelu
Universiti Malaya

Prof. Dr Kobkua Suwannathat-Pian
Universiti Tenaga Nasional

Prof. Dr Tan Chee-Beng
The Chinese University of Hong Kong

Dr Wan Hashim Wan Teh
Member of Parliament

Assoc. Prof. Dr Danny Wong
Universiti Malaya

Prof. Dr Zainal Kling
Universiti Malaya

Prof. Dr Zuraina Majid
Universiti Sains Malaysia

THE ENCYCLOPEDIA OF
MALAYSIA

Volume 12

PEOPLES AND TRADITIONS

Volume Editor
Prof. Dato' Dr Hood Salleh
Universiti Kebangsaan Malaysia

ARCHIPELAGO PRESS

Contents

Baba-Nyonya couple in traditional bridal dress.

Previous page: Malay boys.

Half title page: Bidayuh woman, Sarawak.

Chitty boys, Melaka.

Malaysia's multiethnic population

The peoples of Malaysia are descended from a multitude of immigrant communities from virtually every direction since ancient times. Traditional demographic distribution, economic pursuits, cultural heritage and languages have been affected by modernization and development; despite this, the various ethnic groups continue to manifest distinct social and cultural identities.

Perlis	('000)
Malays	185.6
Chinese	21.8
Other Malaysians	6.4
Indians	2.8
Other Bumiputera	0.7
Total	217.3

Kelantan	('000)
Malays	1369.4
Chinese	52.0
Other Malaysians	14.3
Other Bumiputera	12.1
Indians	4.0
Total	1451.8

Terengganu	('000)
Malays	935.6
Chinese	25.8
Other Bumiputera	3.2
Other Malaysians	2.7
Indians	2.1
Total	969.4

Kedah	('000)
Malays	1363.3
Chinese	255.4
Indians	124.3
Other Malaysians	28.7
Other Bumiputera	3.3
Total	1775.0

Penang	('000)
Chinese	626.4
Malays	587.3
Indians	145.4
Other Malaysians	6.0
Other Bumiputera	5.0
Total	1370.1

Perak	('000)
Malays	1153.7
Chinese	678.2
Indians	279.3
Other Bumiputera	52.7
Other Malaysians	8.0
Total	2171.9

Pahang	('000)
Malays	959.8
Chinese	229.6
Other Bumiputera	66.9
Indians	65.5
Other Malaysians	9.0
Total	1330.8

Selangor	('000)
Malays	2330.1
Chinese	1307.0
Indians	625.6
Other Bumiputera	66.4
Other Malaysians	48.2
Total	4377.3

Federal Territory of Kuala Lumpur	('000)
Malays	614.2
Chinese	610.4
Indians	157.8
Other Malaysians	19.3
Other Bumiputera	14.0
Total	1415.7

Negeri Sembilan	('000)
Malays	507.5
Chinese	224.8
Indians	142.3
Other Bumiputera	12.9
Other Malaysians	4.1
Total	891.6

Melaka	('000)
Malays	424.8
Chinese	189.8
Indians	42.9
Other Bumiputera	8.3
Other Malaysians	4.8
Total	670.6

Johor	('000)
Malays	1595.9
Chinese	987.3
Indians	199.0
Other Bumiputera	37.8
Other Malaysians	18.9
Total	2838.9

LEFT: Young Indian Hindus taking offerings to the temple.

FAR LEFT: Orang Asli hunting with blowpipes.

Men beating traditional Malay *rebana ubi* drums.

Kite-flying remains a popular pastime among the Malay population of Kelantan and Terengganu.

Chinese shops, decorations and people, Melaka.

Population growth in Malaysia since Independence

Population of the Malay Peninsula (1957) ('000)

Malays	2802.9
Chinese	2333.8
Indians	696.2
Others	404.6
Orang Asli	41.3
Total	6278.8

Population (1960)

Sabah	('000)	Sarawak	('000)
Dusun	145.2	Dayak Laut	237.7
Chinese	104.5	Chinese	229.2
Bajau	55.8	Malays	129.3
Kedayan	31.3	Dayak Darat	57.7
Indonesian	24.8	Melanau	44.7
Murut	22.1	Kenyah	8.1
Orang Sungei	15.1	Kayan	7.9
Sulu	11.1	Kedayan	7.2
Bisaya	10.1	Murut	5.2
Sino-native	7.4	Punan	4.7
Tidong	4.4	Indonesian	3.2
Illanun	3.9	Bisaya	2.8
Malays	1.6	Kelabit	2.0
		Other Indigenous	0.1
Others	16.9	Others	4.9
Total	454.2	Total	744.5

Population of Malaysia (2004)* ('000)

Malays	12,893.6
Chinese	6074.7
Other Bumiputera**	2808.1
Indians	1806.8
Other Malaysians	304.4
Non-Malaysian citizens	1693.8
Total	25,581.4

* Estimated figures.

** Other Bumiputera includes the Orang Asli and the indigenous groups of Sabah and Sarawak.

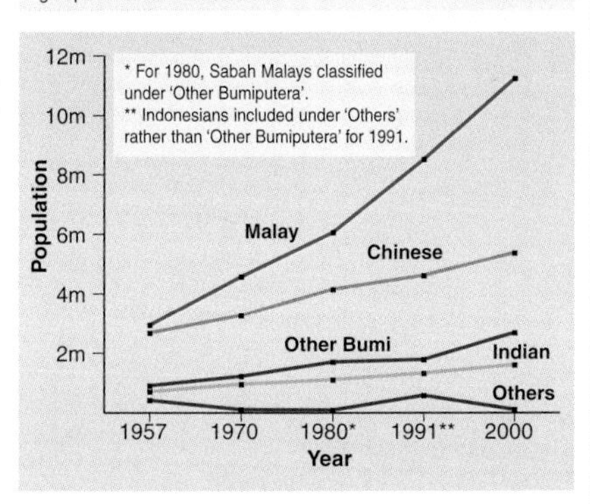

Source for all statistics: Department of Statistics. Population figures for each state are estimated figures for 2004.

South China Sea

Sulu Sea

Federal Territory of Labuan ('000)

Malays	30.0
Other Bumiputera	20.9
Chinese	10.2
Other Malaysians	20
Indians	0.8
Total	63.9

Sabah ('000)

Kadazandusun	514.4
Other Bumiputera	421.7
Bajau	381.5
Malay	330.6
Chinese	277.3
Others	127.4
Murut	94.0
Indian	10.7
Total	2157.6

Kota Kinabalu

BRUNEI

KALIMANTAN

Sulawesi Sea

Sarawak ('000)

Iban	657.7
Chinese	578.7
Malay	505.8
Bidayuh	181.3
Other Bumiputera*	128.8
Melanau	124.3
Others	4.6
Indian	4.3
Total	2185.5

* Includes the Orang Ulu.

Iban in traditional attire.

Kadazandusun performing the Magavau ritual to invoke the rice spirit as part of the harvest festival.

Introduction

Malaysia is a nation of tremendous ethnic diversity. The multicultural nature of the population—often described as rojak *(a spicy mixed salad)—goes back a long way, to the earliest habitation of the Peninsula. Since then, there have been continuous waves of immigrants from virtually all directions. Over time, increasing inter-ethnic contacts and influences have resulted in a polyglot nation of ethnicities, religions, cultures and traditions. This volume introduces the various ethnic groups that call Malaysia home—described by anthropologists, historians and other specialists—and captures the essence of the traditions and cultural manifestations of these communities.*

From right: a Malay, a Chinese and an Indian, sharing a meal at a typical traditional coffee shop.

Far right: Children from various ethnic groups ride together on a trishaw, once a common mode of public transport.

Below: The *miring* (appeasing the spirits) ceremony is a fundamental aspect of the Iban *gawai* (festival).

A cosmopolitan nation

The Malaysian population is made up of over 70 distinct ethnic groups, some with their own internal variations and sub-groups which add to the complex social and cultural mosaic. The earliest inhabitants of the country were the Orang Asli (aborigines)—who are linked to the Hoabinhians of the Middle Stone Age—and the indigenous groups of Sabah and Sarawak, followed by the Malays. Traders from China, India, Sumatra and Java visited the Malay Archipelago from at least the 5th century CE, bringing with them Buddhist and Hindu influences, while Islam was introduced in the 14th century. Traders in later centuries established settlements in the Malay Peninsula. Indeed, cosmopolitan communities are believed to have existed in the Peninsula since the earliest recorded times. The Melaka sultanate (c. 1400–1511) during its heyday represents an early example of the multiculturalism that now prevails.

During the colonial period that began with the Portuguese defeat of Melaka in 1511 and was followed by periods of Dutch and British colonization, a second wave of foreigners, mainly from South Asia and China, arrived in the Peninsula. So too did Western influences. In 2006, in addition to the main ethnic groups, there are spread throughout the country people from South and East Asia, Javanese, Acehnese, Mandailing, Banjarese, Filipinos, Thais, Myanmars, and Chams among others. There are also the mixed races such as the Eurasians and the Chinese Peranakan (or Baba), and there are many intermarriages. The fluid ethnic and cultural environment contributes to the intriguing cosmopolitan character of the nation, as cultural assimilation through intermarriage and conversion to other faiths continue to blur ethnic boundaries and produce new 'hybrids', whose appearance, including the much-touted 'Pan-Asian' look, often belies their mixed racial backgrounds.

Social and cultural montage

The religious, artistic and cultural traditions found in Malaysia are symbolic of the varieties of peoples who populate the country. These traditions underscore the social and cultural identity of each community, and are manifested in their dress, food, worldview, festivals and customs, some of which are centuries old. Indigenous beliefs and traditions have been affected by incoming influences from the north, south, east and west, while some imported traditions have been localized. Throughout the nation's history, inter-ethnic and cross-cultural interaction has resulted in acculturation, assimilation and syncretization. Indeed, some new traditions have resulted from religious accommodation, while others are fusions that have evolved over time.

Royal Malay wedding in Terengganu, 1920s.

Senoi Orang Asil making a trap while hunting in Pahang.

Collectively, the traditions of the various ethnic groups form a national heritage. At the same time, each of the groups continues to observe time-honoured practices, and it is these, in a sense, that are the defining characteristics of the respective communities. For instance, the Malay concept of *semangat* (meaning soul or vital energy) is a pervasive influence on Malay life. Although an animistic concept founded on ancient faiths and folk belief systems, it is manifested in modern-day Malay life and the Malay language, and Malay literature is imbued with it. The Chinese, too, are identified with their distinctive traditions, such as scholarly traditions, clan traditions, filial piety and traditions of managing businesses. Among the indigenous hunter-gatherer groups, such as the Orang Asli of the Peninsula and the Penan of Sarawak, the physical environment has shaped their beliefs, lifestyles and culture. These are but some instances of traditions that have endured and are enlivened in a contemporary environment.

Cultural dancer performing at Dataran Merdeka, Kuala Lumpur.

Modernization and traditions

Much of the cultural and historical knowledge of the indigenous communities in the Peninsula, Sabah and Sarawak has been preserved and passed down the generations by way of oral tradition. Unsurprisingly, storytelling and song have been affected by the modernization of Malaysian society since the late 20th century, as well as by neglect and lack of interest, invariably resulting in the erosion or loss of some traditions. Religious and secular influences, too, have had an impact on the practice of rites and rituals which stem from beliefs that are rooted in the land, the seasons and the supernatural. With an increasing number of indigenous communities turning from traditional animist beliefs to Christianity, Islam and other institutionalized religions, many practices are being abandoned. Traditional practitioners and keepers of old customs are diminishing in number, with few among the younger generation interested in taking over. In addition, urbanization and industrialization have given an enhanced importance to science and technology, which is reflected in the curricula of educational institutions.

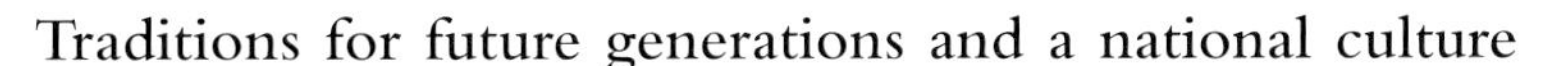

Lundayu wedding procession, Sabah.

Traditions for future generations and a national culture

A shift in focus from Western to Asian traditions has, however, taken place in some of the public universities, resulting in traditional performing and visual arts being introduced into the curricula. This augurs well for the documentation and preservation of age-old indigenous traditions. There have also been initiatives to preserve traditions which are considered manifestations of the ethnic and cultural identities of the respective communities. Cultural associations, conscious that the use of traditional vernacular languages has been eroded by the extensive use and promotion of the national language, Malay, promote their vernacular languages through books, music and songs. Ethnic identity is promoted through the use of traditional costumes, dances and cultural practices at festivals and other celebrations. The revitalization of cultural traditions has been partly due to the growth of cultural tourism. However, the danger is that efforts to develop a national culture in the interests of tourism are resulting in a synthetic fusion. Some traditions, such as the indigenous dances of Sabah and Sarawak, and even some indigenous customary practices, have been re-created as tourist attractions, altogether neglecting the traditional context.

A history of migration

Artefacts from prehistoric times denote the presence of early cultural influences in the region. Indian, Chinese, Greek, Egyptian, Arab and Persian records include references to contact with the Malays. Bustling trade encouraged by its unique maritime location enhanced the diversity of nationalities found in the Malay Archipelago. During the 19th and 20th centuries, there was a great influx of Chinese and Indian labour, which contributed to the ethnic make-up of the country.

Through the ages

The use of stone tools and a hunting-gathering economy were characteristics of the area during the Palaeolithic era, while the Neolithic period saw a semi-nomadic lifestyle and the beginnings of farming and the use of pottery. Bronze and iron artefacts appeared during the Metal age, heralding the development of occupational specialization and intra-regional trade and exchange. The variety of burial methods employed, including the storage of remains in jars, canoes and boats, as well as mound and slab burials, testifies to the diversity of peoples and societies stretching back to prehistoric times.

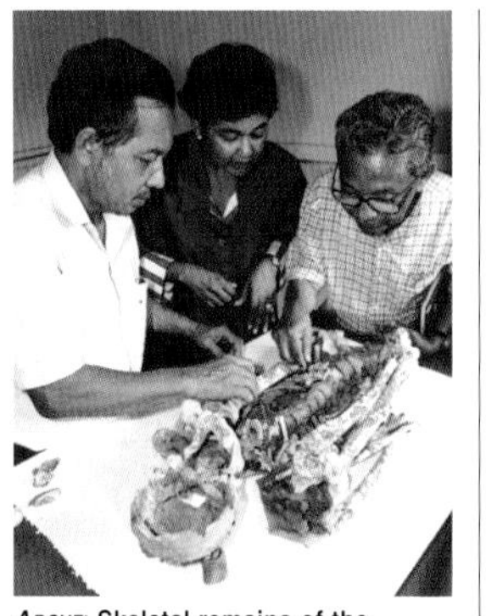

Above: Skeletal remains of the 11,000-year-old Perak Man, found in Lenggong, Perak, in 1991.

Top: 1000-year-old rock carvings discovered near Santubong in Sarawak.

Early cultural contacts

Significant from unrecorded times to the early 14th century (prior to the emergence of Melaka) are the phases of occupation and influence of Hinduism and Buddhism. This period also witnessed the development of intra-regional and international trade, reinforced by the country's position as a link between the Indian Ocean and the South China Sea. Trade brought with it cultural exchanges, and artefacts discovered include vimana-mandapa style temple remnants dated between the 11th and 13th centuries CE. Other artefacts providing clues of the cultures and traditions at the time include Sung and Yuan Dynasty wares and Thai, Indo-Chinese, and Middle Eastern wares such as glass and beads. This period also saw the emergence of early Malay kingdoms and port kingdoms which were entrepôts for international trade.

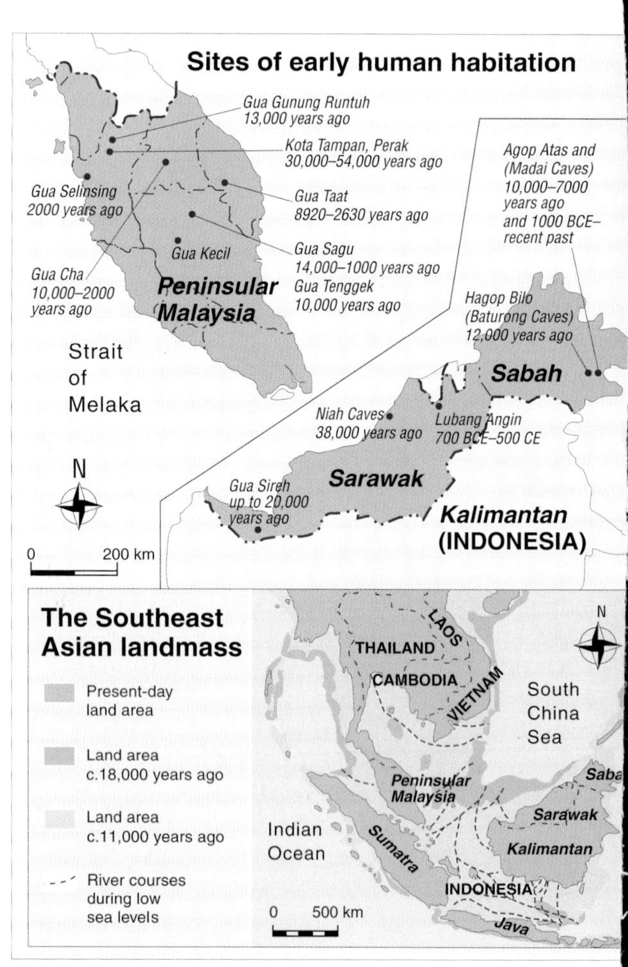

The Melaka Sultanate

The trade in spices brought lucrative fortunes and inspired the search to find a sea route to the East from Europe. Thus, Melaka grew to be not only a pivotal trade emporium because of the accommodating policies of its ruler, but managed to hold at bay the great powers in Asia such as China, Ayutha (Siam) and Java (Majapahit). Although Melaka as a Malay-Muslim kingdom (1403–1511 CE) was preceded by other kingdoms such as Samudra-Pasai or Perlak on the east coast of Sumatra by a century, it was Melaka that came to be regarded as the fount of Malay-Muslim identity and development which characterized the Malay Archipelago from the 14th to 19th centuries. At the same time, Melaka was able to bring into its sphere of influence the neighbouring states in the Peninsula, the east coast of Sumatra, and the west coast of Borneo.

Immigration timeline

Palaeolithic era

100,000–7000 BCE

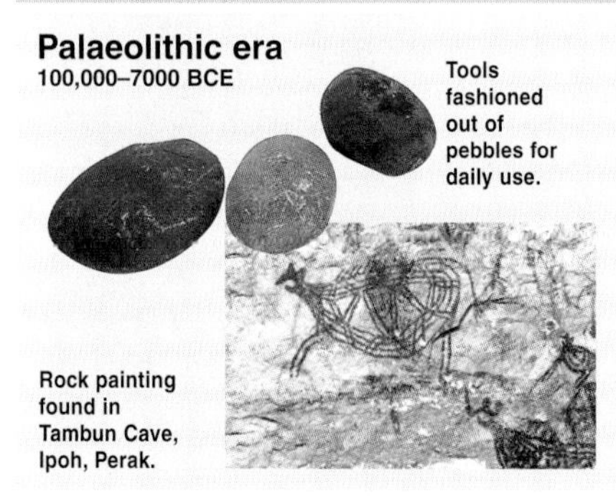

Tools fashioned out of pebbles for daily use.

Rock painting found in Tambun Cave, Ipoh, Perak.

Neolithic period

7000–4000 BCE

Above: Neolithic burial unearthed in Kelantan.

Right: Pottery, earthenware and more polished tools indicate progress.

Metal age

4000 BCE–500 CE

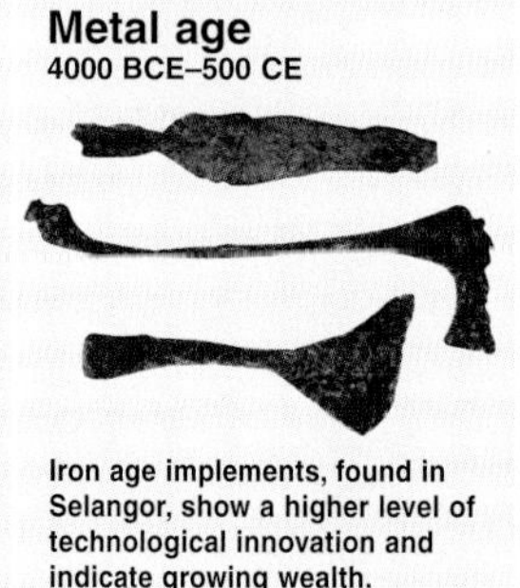

Iron age implements, found in Selangor, show a higher level of technological innovation and indicate growing wealth.

Hindu and Buddhist Influence

500–1400 CE

Vimana-mandapa tomb-temple (above) in the Bujang Valley, Kedah, and bronze statuette (right), 52.5 cm, found in Jalong, Perak.

The arrival of the Europeans

The earliest Europeans in Southeast Asia before the 16th century were merchants, followed by missionaries. In the early 16th century, the Portuguese captured Melaka, occupying it from 1511 until 1643 when they were ousted by the Dutch, while the English succeeded in a 1824 treaty to keep the Dutch out of the Malay Peninsula and northern Borneo.

With the Portuguese occupying Melaka, the Catholic faith established a foothold through missionary endeavours (for instance, the work of Francis Xavier). The Dutch and English introduced Protestantism wherever they established trading factories, but evangelism was not their priority. The succeeding Portuguese, Dutch and English occupations of Melaka (and other parts of the Malay Peninsula) each left edifices such as churches, forts, city halls and club houses. While there was no European migration as most of the Portuguese, Dutch and English factors and traders were temporary residents, they left a legacy of sizeable communities of Portuguese mestizos, Dutch and English Eurasians in Melaka. Traditionally, the British employed the indigenous Malays as policemen, scribes and clerks when they colonized the other Malay states in the Peninsula in the 19th century.

The colonial era

By 1919, the entire Malay Peninsula had been brought under the following British-created political units: the Straits Settlements (formed in 1826 comprising Melaka, Penang, Province Wellesley and Singapore), the Federated Malay States (created in 1896 and consisting of Perak, Selangor, Pahang and Negeri Sembilan), the Unfederated Malay States (formed in 1919 from the northern states of Perlis, Kedah, Kelantan and Terengganu) and Johor (incorporated into British Malaya in 1914). These divisions served to highlight the fact that the British Resident and Adviser wielded true political clout. The two main commodities of the colonial economy were tin and rubber and to reap the benefits of these ventures, Chinese and Indian immigrant labour were imported.

While economic and social differentiation was maintained by policy, the necessity to train English-educated local individuals led to the creation of English schools patronized by the sons of leading families of each of the ethnic groups, while the rest of the population were sent to vernacular schools, government English schools and missionary schools. Graduates from these prestigious schools formed an elite which crossed ethnic boundaries and came to form the nucleus of leaders in independent Malaya.

A polyglot city: Melaka in the 15th century

Melaka grew rapidly following the founding of the sultanate in 1403, soon developing into a thriving entrepôt with a diverse population. The *Sejarah Melayu* (Malay Annals), commissioned in 1612, describes the cosmopolitan life of the Melaka Sultanate in the 15th century. Indian merchants, both Muslim and non-Muslim, feature particularly prominently in the narrative, as do the Arabs. The Indian merchants are described as wealthy, and involved in activities at the court of the Sultan of Melaka. The Arab merchants, too, were influential; one even commanded the palace coup of Raja Kasim (later Sultan Muzaffar Shah) against his half-brother, Sultan Abu Shahid. Another Arab resident, the *Sejarah Melayu* informs, helped to diffuse Siam's intended attack on Melaka with his mystical power.

The Annals also mention Melaka's contact with the Chinese and Sultan Mansur's marriage to a Chinese princess. As for people from elsewhere in the Malay World, the *Sejarah Melayu* mentions the Javanese, Bugis, the peoples of Sumatra, and those from Patani, as well as a host of others.

Above: For much of the 15th century, Melaka was the most prosperous trading city in Southeast Asia, attracting maritime traders from all corners of coastal Asia.

Below: Map of Asia by Sebastian Munster, 1540. Melaka ('Malaqua'), which remained an important strategic and trading centre long after the sultanate fell in 1511, is the only location marked on the Malay Peninsula.

Melaka
1400–1511 CE

The Cultural Museum in Melaka purports to be a replica of the palace of the Sultan of Melaka, as recorded in the *Sejarah Melayu* (Malay Annals).

The Portuguese and the Dutch
1511–c. 1800 CE

Chromolithograph from a drawing of a sea battle between the Spanish and the Portuguese in the Strait of Melaka, dated 1606.

British administration
c. 1800–1941 CE

The British High Commissioner with Terengganu Sultan Zainal Abidin III, in 1909. Malay kingdoms existed simultaneously with the colonial system.

Ethnic diversity

Malaysia's population is a complex web of over 70 distinct ethnic groups, each with its own variations. The ethnic, religious and cultural variety reflects the nation's history and strategic geographical location. Situated at the crossroads between the East and the West, Malaysia has for centuries attracted foreign rulers, traders and travellers. Immigrants have settled in the country since the earliest recorded times, underscoring the heterogeneity of the contemporary population.

Multiethnic performers in traditional costumes line up prior to taking part in a cultural performance in Kuala Lumpur.

Mah Meri Orang Asli at Pulau Carey, Selangor.

Ethnic and cultural variety

The major ethnic groups in the country are the Malays, Chinese and Indians. The Malays and other indigenous peoples of the country are termed Bumiputera ('sons of the soil') and they constitute approximately 61 per cent of the total population, The Chinese make up about 24 per cent of the population, and the Indians, seven per cent. The Bumiputera are a heterogeneous group, and are made up of different ethnic groups such as the Malays, the Orang Asli, and the indigenous peoples of Sabah and Sarawak. Among the Malays, who form the largest community in the country, there are ethnic sub-groups which originate from different parts of Indonesia, including the Minangkabau, Acehnese, Javanese, Madurese and Bugis.

The multi-ethnic society of present-day Malaysia was largely created during the era British administration, particularly in the late 19th and early 20th centuries. Large numbers of Chinese and Indian migrants were brought into the country to work in the mining industry and the plantations respectively. The Chinese are differentiated along dialect lines and their provincial origins in China. The Indian community is differentiated as well, comprising many ethnic sub-groups reflecting their place of origin and language.

The populations of Sabah and Sarawak are made up of no fewer than 70 ethnic groups, of whom at least 50 are considered indigenous. The main indigenous groups—in Sabah, the Kadazandusun, Bajau, Murut, and in Sarawak, the Iban, Bidayuh and Melanau—each has its own customs, expressions, beliefs and languages.

Penan elder, Ulu Baram, Sarawak.

Adding to the multi-ethnic milieu are several minority groups, each with distinct social and cultural identities. The Baba, Chitties and the people of Portuguese-descent of Melaka, as well as the Jawi-Peranakan of Penang, are among the oldest groups of foreign origin in Malaysia and represent remarkable instances of cultural fusion. There are also small communities established by more recent migrants from various parts of Asia.

The various ethnic groups have their own social, cultural and religious heritage. Most of the world's great religions—Islam, Christianity, Buddhism and Hinduism—are found in the country. Malay culture, which forms the core of the national culture, has been enriched by Arabic, Indian and other foreign elements, as well as by the animistic traditions. At the same time, the cultures of the immigrant communities have undergone changes and have become localized, particularly in traits such as dress, language and food. The indigenous cultures of Sabah and Sarawak, on the other hand, have not undergone drastic transformation under foreign pressures, although modernization, development and religious influences have had an impact on the practice of some traditions.

A heterogeneous society

Malaysians live in harmony and accept the principle of sharing political and economic power, yet the cultural lives of the people generally remain confined to their respective ethnic groups. While cultural and religious differences tend to perpetuate the heterogeneous nature of the population, shared values and a willingness among the communities to participate in one another's festivals creates an identity that is based not on one culture, but on multiculturalism. Indeed, the government encourages multiculturalism as a means of fostering national unity in this plural society. There is no policy of assimilating minorities and their cultures into the majority and mainstream culture, unlike the policy in some neighbouring countries. Neither is there a policy to impose the cultural dominance and hegemony of the majority group on the minority groups, especially since the latter groups are themselves inheritors of great cultures and civilizations.

Although Malay is the national language, languages of the other ethnic groups such as Mandarin, Tamil, Iban and Kadazandusun are taught in schools and used in public life. Newspapers are printed in Malay, English, Chinese, Tamil and Kadazan.

Rungus lady, Sabah.

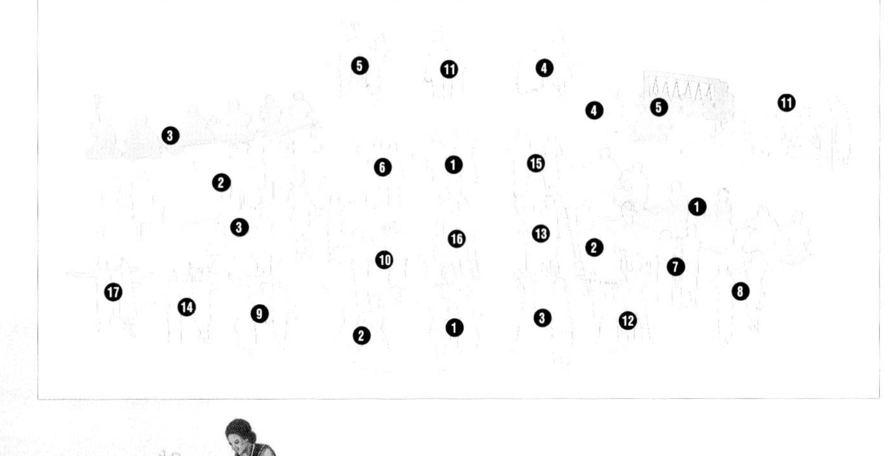

Ethnic groups of Malaysia

1. Malays
2. Chinese
3. Indians
4. Orang Asli
5. Iban
6. Bidayuh
7. Melanau
8. Kelabit and Lun Bawang
9. Kayan and Kenyah
10. Other Orang Ulu groups, including Kajang, Bisaya, Penan, Kejaman, Sekapan, Lahanan, Punan Bah, Seping, Bemali, Beketan, Berawan, Buket, Lisum, Punan Busang, Saiban, Sihan, Tabun, Tring, Tagal, Tanjong, Kanowit and Tatau.
11. Kadazandusun, including Kadazan, Dusun, Lotud, Kwijau, Bisaya, Rungus, Dumpas, Mangkaak, Minokok, Maragang and Kadayan.
12. Bajau
13. Murut
14. Coastal and island groups of Sabah, including Suluk, Iranun, Tidong, Belabak, Bonggi, Kagayan and Ubian.
15. Orang Sungai of Sabah, including Labuk Kadazandusun, Tombonuwo, Makiang, Kolobuan, Sinabu, Rumanau, and Dusun Segama, Abai Sungai, Ida'an, Dumpas and Paitan.
16. Others, including Eurasians, Chinese Peranakan, Chitties, Nepalese, Sino-natives, Cocos Islanders, Thais, Myanmars, Indonesians, Filipinos, Japanese, Koreans and Europeans.
17. Papar Kadazandusun.

National unity

Malaysia has a distinct multi-ethnic composition with a variety of ethnic groups professing different religious and cultural beliefs. This poses a challenge to the Malaysian government to maintain the peace and stability necessary for prosperity. By way of testimony to the government's success, for the greater part of the years since achieving Independence in 1957, Malaysians have been able to live together in harmony. This has been due largely to policies that foster unity whilst taking into account the historical, political, economic and social dimensions.

Schoolchildren participating in the National Day parade, Putrajaya.

Historical background

The struggle that led to Independence for the country proved to be one of the first steps in forging unity between the various ethnic groups. The three major ethnic groups—the Malays, Chinese and Indians—were each represented by a dominant political party. These were able to form a coalition called the Alliance composed of three parties: the United Malays National Organisation (UMNO), the Malayan Chinese Association (MCA) and the Malayan Indian Congress (MIC). As a united voice, the Alliance gained the confidence of the British and was able to advance the campaign for Independence. Between 1957 and 1969, under the premiership of Tunku Abdul Rahman Putra, the country began to charter its own destiny.

Unity through politics

The Federal Constitution is a document that promotes unity and guarantees basic human rights for all citizens. It also guarantees that each citizen is allowed to practise his or her own religion. Furthermore, all citizens above the age of 21 have the right to vote at elections. The three branches of government—the Executive, Legislature and Judiciary—work in tandem to uphold the principles stated in the Constitution.

Since Independence, there have been 11 general elections. The Alliance, and from 1974 the Barisan Nasional (National Front), has won each of them. However, the riots that occurred after the 1969 general election forced the government to introduce new policies to reduce the economic disparity between the main ethnic groups. Furthermore, it had to rethink the framework of inter-ethnic cooperation. After 1969, the Alliance was expanded to include more political parties. A new coalition, the Barisan Nasional, was formed to replace the Alliance in 1974 and in 2006 comprised 14 political parties.

Pro-independence rally in Kuala Lumpur, 1955.

The formation of Malaysia in 1963 brought together the Peninsula, Sabah and Sarawak, and posed additional challenges to the government, particularly in forging unity among the various ethnic groups as both Sabah and Sarawak are extremely culturally diverse. The government was aided in overcoming these challenges by the unity of the parties that comprise the Barisan Nasional.

Bridging socioeconomic differences

One of the main reasons for the occurrence of the riots in 1969 was the economic imbalance between the three main ethnic groups. Therefore, when the New Economic Policy (1971–90) was developed, it had as its two main objectives the eradication of poverty and the redressing of economic disparities between the ethnic groups. This 20-year plan envisioned the redistribution of wealth such that the indigenous people, known as 'Bumiputera', would own 30 per cent of all equity by the year 1990. The Bumiputera were also to be given preference in terms of access to education, employment and economic subsidies.

Socio-cultural harmony

The government actively promotes unity through the *Rukunegara* (National Ideology), the creation of the National Education Policy, and the emphasis on social interaction programmes. At the same time, the people are advised to accommodate and accept each other's religion and culture.

Multi-ethnic neighbourhoods facilitate interaction amongst people of different backgrounds.

National Service was implemented in 2003, with thousands of youths conscripted each year. One of the major aims of the programme is to enhance unity among the country's multi racial communities.

The *Rukunegara* consists of five principles that are meant to guide the citizens in their interaction with one another and with the state. They are: belief in God; loyalty to King and country; the supremacy of the Constitution; the rule of law, and good morality and ethics.

The National Education Policy was formulated in 1971. Certain key points in this policy have a direct bearing on creating unity among the young. These include the usage of the Malay language as the medium of instruction, a standard school curriculum and compulsory primary education for all.

The implementation of Malay as the national language brought forth many debates. The government sees the language as a unifying factor among citizens. On the other hand, some sections of society see the move as denying the growth of the various other cultures and languages. Despite the differences in opinion, Malay has grown into a language which is widely used, not only for day to day communication, but also within the technical and business sectors. However, the government has also recognized the need to enhance the use of English in the school system in order to make Malaysians more confident in their dealings in the modern globalized world. In addition, the government created the National Education Fund to be accessed by students from all ethnic groups.

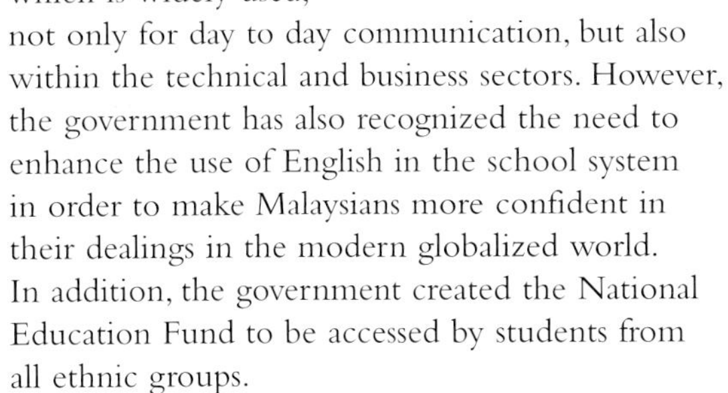

Large corporations often produce advertisements reflecting upon, and promoting, national unity, especially to coincide with the anniversary of Independence.

Social interactive programmes to promote integration include the Rukun Tetangga (RT) or neighbourhood watch patrol. The RT was introduced in 1975 as a self-help scheme where residents in designated residential areas would look after their own safety and welfare. The concept was expanded in 2001 to include social outreach efforts at specific target groups such as disabled persons, single mothers and drug addicts. The RT plays an important role in intervening and mediating when social issues arise between neighbours of different ethnicity. Some RT areas have also set up kindergartens to introduce early education and promote interaction between children of different ethnic backgrounds. In other residential areas, residents' associations as well as social and recreation clubs are encouraged to promote neighbourliness.

Respect for each other's religions and customs constitute a key element in fostering unity amongst the people. As a mark of respect for the different religions in the country, public holidays are given to all citizens. In this way, all Malaysians can join in the celebration of the various religious and cultural festivals. 'Open houses' (where one's home is visited by all races) are held so that the spirit of unity through diversity is strengthened. Most importantly, the ability to be tolerant of one another has been the hallmark of peace in Malaysia.

Co-curricular activities are promoted through the school system and by many non-governmental organizations. Activities such as cross-country runs, outdoor camps and various sports are seen as avenues to promote unity, especially among the younger generation. Many organizations such as the Boy Scouts, Girl Guides, Red Crescent and St John's Ambulance have members from diverse economic and ethnic backgrounds.

The media

The media, too, plays an important role in promoting unity in Malaysia. As a source of information for the public, the print, audio-visual and electronic media actively promote unity by enlightening people regarding the diverse cultural and religious aspects of the various ethnic groups. Songs on unity such as *Muhibbah* (Unity), *Jalur Gemilang* (Our Flag) and *Tanah Air ku* (My Homeland) are often highlighted on television and the radio.

LEFT: The Malaysian custom of 'open house' during festivals such as Chinese New Year reflects the willingness of people of different ethnic backgrounds to accept and participate in each other's culture.

BELOW: Celebrating Deepavali with friends from other ethnic groups.

Demographics

Malaysia has seen a huge increase in its population over the last 200 years. Initially fuelled by migration—of Chinese to tin-mining areas and Indians to the rubber plantations in the late 19th and early 20th centuries—and the creation of new villages and land development schemes in the mid-1900s, the major source of growth is now natural increase. Increasing urbanization, together with its attendant factors of industrialization, housing development and the growth of cities, is the most distinct trend since Independence.

Population growth and composition

By 1911, the population of the Peninsula was 2.4 million, rising to 2.9 million in 1921 and 3.8 million in 1931, equivalent to an annual growth rate of 2.7 per cent. Between 1931 and 1947, total population further increased from 3.8 to 4.9 million.

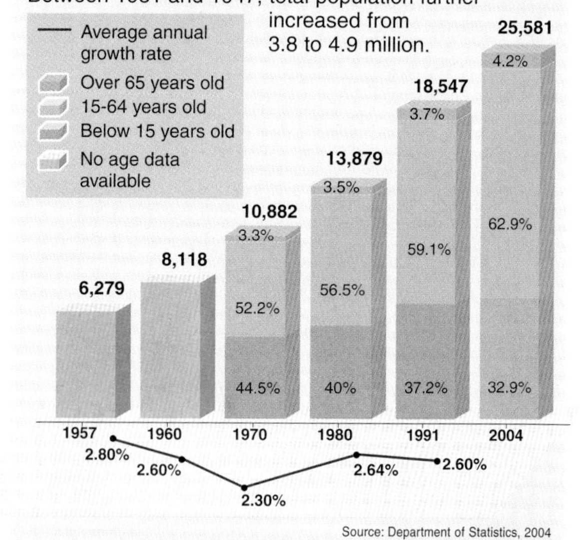

Celebrating National Day. At current growth rates, the size of the Malaysian population—at over 25 million in 2004—is expected to double by 2030.

Life expectancy

Year	Life expectancy
2004	73.2 years
2000	72.6 years
1991	71.3 years
1980	68.4 years
1970	63.6 years
1957	54.6 years
1947	45.7 years

Early population and its distribution

Until 1800, the Malay Peninsula was very sparsely populated, with probably no more than 250,000 inhabitants. These consisted almost entirely of Malays, mainly found in coastal villages, and urban settlements were few. The interior regions were devoid of population apart from a few thousand aborigines now known as Orang Asli.

By 1850, the population had grown to approximately 550,000, confined mainly to rural areas. Approximately 30,000 of these were non-Malays, primarily Chinese immigrants who worked as tin miners, and settled mainly in the main urban centres in the west of the Peninsula, especially in Perak, Selangor and Negeri Sembilan.

In 1874, through the Pangkor Treaty, British participation in the affairs of the Malay states gave rise to an increase in the immigration of mainland Chinese, Malays from elsewhere in the Malay Archipelago, and Indian workers, as a result of the opening up of tin mines and rubber plantations. Mining villages sprang up along the foothills on the west coast, and developed into major towns.

The combined immigration of Malays (from what is now Indonesia), Chinese and Indians in the late 19th century and early decades of the 20th century led to a rapid increase in the population, particularly during the economic prosperity of the 1920s. However, the following decade the rate of population increase slowed.

Post-war growth

After World War II, natural increase—the excess of births over deaths—in an increasingly settled population became the most important determinant of population size, rather than immigration. A significant development as a result of the Emergency (1948–60) was the resettlement of almost a million rural dwellers, mainly Chinese, in more than 600 New Villages.

Rapid population growth occurred until Independence in 1957. This was primarily due to a sharp decline in mortality as a result of improved living conditions and advances in medical technology. Fertility among all ethnic groups rose, and family size increased as a result of improvements in health.

In Sabah and Sarawak, prior to World War II, population flowed freely in and out. As a result, the rate of population growth was greatly influenced by migration. Since the formation of Malaysia in 1963 and the implementation of laws restricting immigration, migration has had little effect on the growth rate, the main factor—as in the Peninsula—being natural increase. The population density of Sabah and Sarawak remains considerably lower than Peninsular Malaysia, with concentrations occurring only along the coasts of Sabah and in Sarawak riverine settlements. The birth rate in Sabah and Sarawak increased steadily from 1945 until the late 1960s, after which it dropped sharply. However, in comparison with the Peninsula, the average birth rate in the two states remains high, which can be attributed to better health services.

The population of Malaysia grew between 1970 and 1991 as a result of both immigration and natural increase. The rise in the average growth rate since 1980 is, however, attributed to the increase in the net inflow of foreign migrants.

Shifts in population distribution in the Peninsula in the post-Independence period were influenced

Slow population growth from 1931–1947

The slow rate of population growth after 1931 can be attributed to four main factors. First, a considerable emigration of Chinese tin miners and Indians contract labourers back to their respective countries, as a result of unemployment arising from the global economic depression during the 1930s.

Second, the Aliens Enactment 1933 improved the Chinese gender ratio, which paved the way for natural increase to become important in the future with the increased reproductive potential of the Chinese community. Third, a ban on emigrant labour to other British territories, including Malaya, was imposed by India in 1938.

As a result of World War II the birth rate declined, whilst the death rate increased due to lack of food and tropical diseases.

by several factors, the most important of which were new land development schemes and urbanization associated mainly with the creation of industrial estates close to major towns. The integrated Federal Land Development Authority (FELDA) scheme initiated by the government in 1956 resulted in the resettling of 40,000 settlers or about 220,000 people, mostly Malays, by 1978. They were concentrated in three states—Pahang, Johor and Negeri Sembilan. As most FELDA settlers were typically young couples with children, their presence brought about a higher rate of natural increase of population in the state.

Rapid industrialization resulted in an increase of urban areas from 125 in 1991 to 170 in 2000. The urban population grew from 34 per cent of total population in 1980 to 51 per cent in 1991, and 62 per cent in 2000. The rural population, meanwhile, decreased from 66 per cent of the total population in 1980 to 39 per cent in 2000.

As a result of urbanization, housing development in urban areas increased at an annual rate of 8.7 per cent between 1980 and 1991, and at 6.3 per cent between 1991 and 2000, with the number of houses built increasing from 828,000 in 1980 to 2.1 million in 1991 and 3.6 million in 2000. In comparison, rural housing recorded a far lower annual growth rate, of one per cent between 1980 and 1991 and 0.3 per cent between 1991 and 2000, with the number of dwellings built increasing from 1.8 million in 1980 to 2.1 million in 2000.

Determinants of population growth

Changes in the annual population growth rate since World War II have largely depended on changing trends in fertility, mortality and urban migration.

Since 1947, the crude death rate in Peninsular Malaysia has declined steadily, reaching 4.6 per 1000 in 2004. The decline is attributed to advances in medical technology to control and eradicate communicable diseases, improved sanitation and nutritional standards, higher literacy levels, as well as improved public administration.

The census

The first censuses were undertaken in the Straits Settlements of Penang (1801), Malacca (1826) and Singapore (1824). By 1860, 11 counts had been taken in Penang and ten in Melaka. However, the statistics produced from these were unreliable and not comprehensive.

The first modern census was taken in Penang and Malacca in 1871 and another in 1881. Information gathered included basic data on sex, age, and race as well as more detailed data on houses, occupation and geographical areas based on a simple town–country division. In 1891, the first census was undertaken in the Federated Malay States, comprising Selangor, Perak, Negeri Sembilan and Pahang, in addition to the third census of the Straits Settlements, followed by similar censuses in 1901.

A census enumerator gathering data at an Orang Asli settlement in 1957.

Population statistics for Peninsular Malaysia were made available for the first time in 1911, following a census of the Unfederated Malay States of Perlis, Kedah, Kelantan, Terengganu and Johor, the Federated Malay States and the Straits Settlements. The 1911 census additionally included questions relating to birthplace, religion, occupation and industry. In 1921, a combined population census for Peninsular Malaysia and Singapore was undertaken, with a similar decennial census in 1931. A census planned for April 1941, however, was abandoned as a result of World War II. After the war, a census was immediately executed, and completed in 1947. Another was taken in 1957. Following the formation of Malaysia in 1963, a census was held in 1970, covering for the first time both Peninsular Malaysia and the East Malaysian states of Sarawak and Sabah. Censuses were subsequently held in 1980, 1991 and 2000.

Problems and challenges of conducting the census

Besides problems of under-enumeration due to logistical factors such as communications and transportation, there are also problems related to ethnic classification. Due to the ethnic diversity, the major ethnic groupings in Peninsular Malaysia, Sabah and Sarawak differ in classification. Since the 1991 census, efforts have made to standardize all ethnic classifications to produce an integrated set of ethnic groupings.

The decline in the birth rate can be attributed to a number of factors, such as the increasing age of marriage, the changing marital status of the population, as well as family planning. Opportunities for education, particularly among women, have delayed marriage among the population as better-educated women generally marry later and have fewer children. The proportion of the population getting married below 20 years also declined, from 36 per cent in 1970 to 12 per cent in 1988.

Urbanization has also contributed to the decline in birth rate. Between 1974 and 1994, the mean number of children born to married women aged 15–49 years declined sharply in urban areas from 3.7 to 2.9 compared with 4.3 to 3.8 in rural areas.

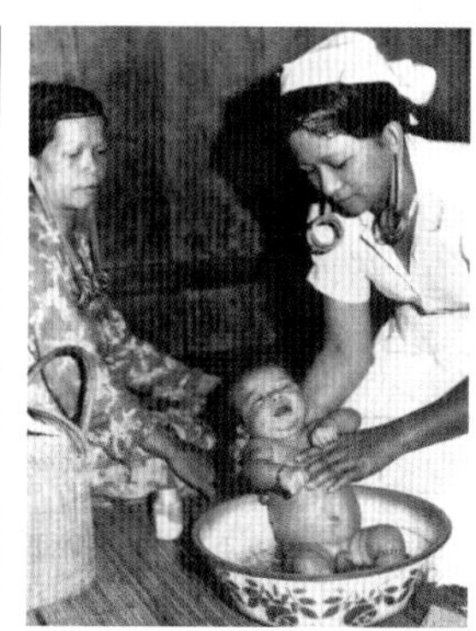

Kayan midwife in Sarawak, 1950.

Recent demographics

Population age structure

The reduction in the proportion of the population aged below 15 years since 1980 can be attributed to a decline in fertility, whilst increases in the proportion of the population aged 65 years and above have been brought about by an increase in life expectancy. The proportion of the population in the working age group between 15 and 64 years also increased between 1980 and 1991, suggesting a net inflow of foreign migrants. The increase in the median age from 17.4 years in the 1970s to 23.6 years in 2000 is in line with the decline in fertility and increase in life expectancy.

Gender balance

In Malaysia, as in most countries, there are more males than females. Of the total population in year 2004, 13 million were males compared with 12.6 million females, giving a ratio of 103 men for every 100 women. However, variations and significant changes in the sex ratios were noted across the various states. Johor, Negeri Sembilan, Pahang, Sabah, Sarawak, Selangor, Terengganu, Kuala Lumpur and Labuan have more males than females. In Kedah, Kelantan, Melaka, Perak, Perlis and Penang, females have outnumbered males since the 1980s, due to the continuous migration of males to other states for employment.

Household size

Across the nation, household size declined from an average of 4.92 persons per household in 1991 to 4.47 persons in 2004. Not surprisingly, small households were found in more urbanized and developed states such as Kuala Lumpur (4.18), Selangor (4.25) and Penang and Perak (4.30). In Sabah, the average household size was 5.13 persons while in Kelantan and Terengganu it was 5.02 persons.

Immigrants

The growth in the population between 1992 and 2001 was not only the result of natural increase, but of the inflow of foreign migrants as well. The number of foreign migrants increased from 78,243 in 1992 to 106,374 in 2001.

Distribution of the population

Considerable changes occurred in the relative size of the population in each state between 1991 and 2000, although the population of all states registered an increase. The increase in the population of Sabah was the result of a a relatively high rate of natural increase combined with a large inflow of foreign migrants from neighbouring countries. Net in-migration from other states contributed to the high growth rate in Selangor.

1. Hari Raya Aidilfitri celebrations in the kampong. The festival is a time for Malays to visit their families and friends.

2. Chinese worshippers praying at a temple.

3. Indian Hindus carrying pots of milk (*palkodam*) to the temple as offerings.

4. Eurasian famly at the Portuguese Settlement, Melaka.

5. Bhangra folk dance performed by Punjabi men.

6. Melaka Chitty newly-weds. The Chitties are Straits-born Indians, descended from 16th century traders from India.

7. Young Chinese drummers at National Day celebrations.

8. Malay women bearing traditional wedding gifts of boiled eggs on trays of glutinous rice.

9. Chinese Peranakan (Baba-Nyonya) women helping a bride with her traditional wedding robes and adornments.

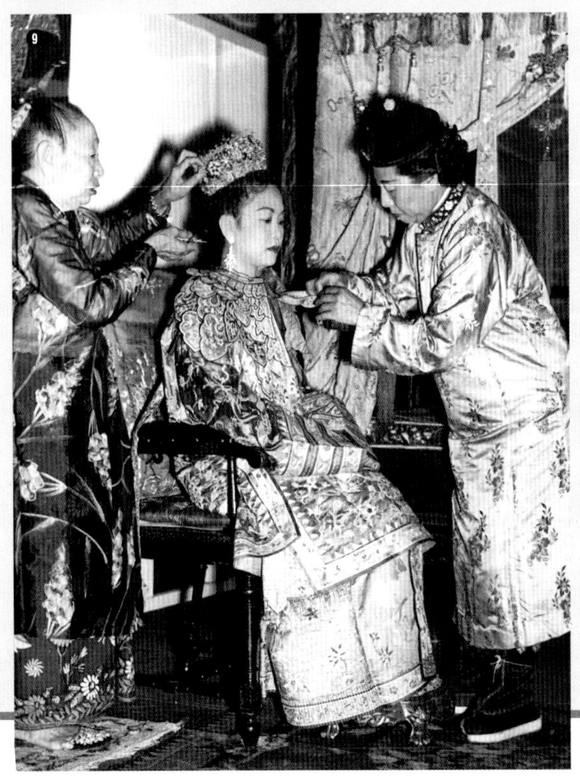

PENINSULAR ETHNIC GROUPS

Ethnicity in Peninsular Malaysia is multifarious and to some extent can only be defined in terms of religion, language, custom and geographical place of origin. A diverse population comprising Orang Asli, Malays, Chinese, Indians, Thais, Eurasians and people of many other ethnic origins makes for a unique Malaysian lifestyle.

The Malays, Chinese and Indians respectively comprise the major population groups. The Malays constitute over 53 per cent of the country's population. Whilst they are a homogenous people socially and culturally, being almost totally Muslim and practising Malay culture, differences exist between Malay sub-ethnic groups of various territorial locations in terms of *adat* (customary) practices, and lineage and kinship systems. Most of the Malay sub-ethnic groups comprising the Javanese, Bugis, Minangkabau, and several other groups, are descendants of inter-island migrants within the Malay Archipelago who settled in the Peninsula as long ago as the early Malay kingdoms. Since the late 1980s massive migration has taken place from all over Indonesia, in search of economic livelihood. Some have acquired permanent resident status and citizenship.

The Chinese and Indians are associated with the geographical origins of their forebears. While Chinese dialect associations remain to this day, dialect differences are no longer a serious consideration in inter-group interactions. Like the Chinese, the Indian population is highly differentiated internally.

The minority groups in the Peninsula include the Portuguese-descended population of Melaka, whose origins date back to the 16th century; and the Thais of Kedah and Kelantan. Since Independence in 1957, other migrants have been accepted into the country, including the Nepalese, some of whom were former Gurkha military personnel employed by the British administration to fight communism in the country; the Chams of Vietnam and Cambodia; and the Rohingya of Myanmar.

Malaysians have generally adapted to the idea of being citizens of the country in spite of their diverse origins and the safeguarding of their primordial identities. Inter-ethnic interactions are encouraged through the national celebration of major ethnic festivals and religious festivities. The whole idea of ethnic and cultural diversity has been regarded as enriching rather then differentiating for all citizens. Cultures and traditions are respected, celebrated and adapted by the various communities to foster an inclusive Malaysian identity. This demonstrates the racial harmony and tolerance that exists in the cultural melting pot that is Malaysia.

Perak Temiar Orang Asli playing nose flutes.

The Orang Asli: Origins, identity and classification

The Orang Asli (aborigines) are indigenous to Peninsular Malaysia, and are believed to have occupied the land as early as 25,000 years ago. The early Orang Asli mostly lived in remote communities within specific geographical areas. They identified themselves by their ecological niche—which they called their customary or traditional land—and with which they developed a close affinity. Much of their culture and spirituality was derived from this close association with their environment. In present day Malaysia they are recognized as Bumiputera ('sons of the soil').

Three generations of Orang Asli at their family home.

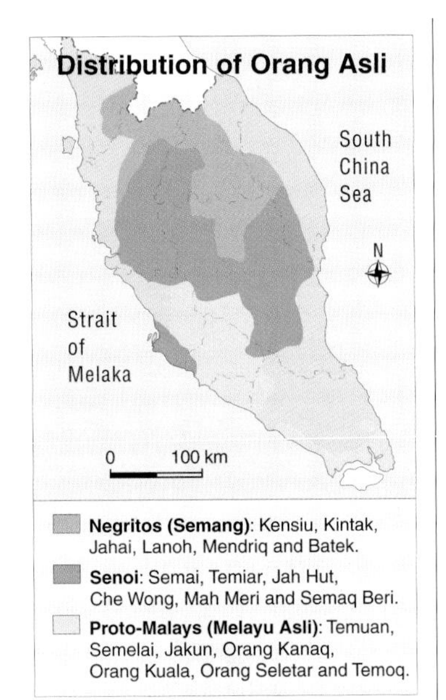

Population of Orang Asli (2000)

Negritos	**4,494**
Senoi	**73,166**
Temiar	23,074
Semai	38,574
Other Senoi	11,518
Proto-Malays	**56,115**
Jakun	23,896
Temuan	21,381
Semelai	5,937
Other Proto-Malay	4,901
Total	**133,775**

Source: Census 2000, Department of Statistics

Origins and demographics

With a total population of 133,775 in 2000, the Orang Asli comprise at least 19 sub-groups, distinguished into three categories—Negritos, Senoi and Proto-Malays—based on physical characteristics, linguistic affinities and cultural practices.

Negritos

Also known as Semang, the Negritos are the oldest group—and the smallest—constituting just over 3 per cent of the Orang Asli population. They are believed to have been in the Malay Peninsula for at least 25,000 years, although current archaeological evidence links the Negritos to the Hoabinhians who lived between 8000 BCE and 1000 BCE during the Middle Stone Age. The present-day Negritos are the descendants of these early Hoabinhians, who were largely nomadic foragers, living in one location as long as the food supply was able to sustain the community. Today, however, many of the Negritos live in permanent settlements in the central, northern and eastern regions. Customarily, some groups enter the forest for varying lengths of time, such as during the fruit season, to practise opportunistic foraging, or to extract forest products, such as rattan and gaharu, for sale. Such activities have often caused them to be labelled nomadic and to be considered the more economically backward of the Orang Asli groups. Their languages belong to the Aslian family of Mon-Khmer languages.

Rock art by the Negritos found at Tambun Cave in Perak. The charcoal drawings are dated 1899.

Senoi

The largest Orang Asli group are the Senoi, constituting about 54 per cent of the population. They are a Mongoloid people, and are descendants of both the Hoabinhians and the Neolithic cultivators who entered the Malay Peninsula from the north around 2000 BCE. They speak Austro-Asiatic languages of the Mon-Khmer sub-group, which reflects their ancient connection with mainland Southeast Asia. Mainly swidden cultivators who in the past depended on the forest for their subsistence, many Senoi today have taken to permanent agriculture, managing their own rubber, oil palm or cocoa farms. Some are employed as skilled and unskilled workers in the private and public sectors, and a small number are professionals. They live mainly on the slopes of the main Titiwangsa Range.

Proto-Malays

The Proto-Malays (also known as Aboriginal Malays or Melayu Asli) make up about 43 per cent of the Orang Asli population, and live mainly in the

Right: Orang Asli man displaying jungle produce.

Below: Orang Asli woman and children, 1959.

Physical characteristics of Orang Asli sub-groups

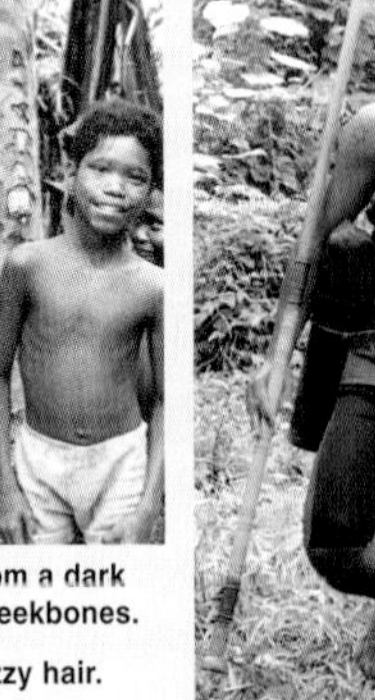

1. The Negritos are generally small in stature (1.5 metres or less), dark-skinned (varying from a dark copper to black), with typically woolly or frizzy hair, broad noses, round eyes and low cheekbones.
2. The Senoi are slightly taller than the Negritos, with lighter skin, and wavy rather than frizzy hair.
3. The Proto-Malays are the tallest and most heavily built of the three groups. Their skin is darker than the Senoi but lighter than the Negritos, and their hair is smooth and straight.

southern half of the Peninsula. While prehistoric recordings in the south are almost non-existent, it is generally accepted that between 2000 and 3000 years ago, the southerly groups encountered the sea-faring peoples from Borneo and the Indonesian islands. Some of these Orang Asli who traded with Austronesian speakers assimilated with them, hence the term Proto- (or early) Malay is used to refer to them. Their languages remain archaic variants of the Malay language (with the exception of the Semelai and Temoq languages that have links to the Senoic languages). The Proto-Malays are very settled peoples, engaged mainly in permanent agriculture or in riverine and coastal fishing. Many of them are wage earners and some are in entrepreneurial and professional occupations.

TOP LEFT: **Orang Asli community hall in Selangor, 1960s.**

TOP RIGHT: **Orang Asli receiving health education from the Red Cross (later Red Crescent) in Melaka in the 1950s. All matters concerning the Orang Asli are the responsibility of the Department of Orang Asli Affairs (Jabatan Hal Ehwal Orang Asli).**

ABOVE: **Orang Asli queuing to register at the National Registration Office in Bentong, 1949.**

Changes in classification and nomenclature

Since the 16th century the Orang Asli have been referred to by anthropologists and administrators by a variety of terms. Some of these terms were descriptive of their abode, such as Orang Hulu (people of the headwaters), Orang Darat (people of the hinterland), and Orang Laut (people who live by the sea). Other terms described their perceived characteristics, such as Besisi (people with scales), and Mantra (people who chanted). Some were derogatory, such as Orang Liar (wild people), Pangan (eaters of raw food), Orang Mawas (ape-like people), and Orang Jinak (tame or enslaved people).

Towards the end of the British administration there were attempts to categorize the various Orang Asli groups into homogeneous ones. Those in the south were frequently referred to as Jakun, while those in the north were called Sakai, and at times these terms were used interchangeably. With time, Sakai—a term despised by the Orang Asli even today for its derogation and its allusion to backwardness and primitivism—came to be used as a generic term for all the Orang Asli groups, and was used interchangeably with the English equivalent, aborigines.

It was during the Emergency of 1948–60 that the administration realized that a more correct and positive term was necessary if they were to win the hearts and minds of the Orang Asli (and so win the war against the communist insurgents). Realizing that the insurgents were able to get the sympathy and support of the indigenous inhabitants in the forest, partly by referring to them as 'Orang Asal' (original people, from the Arabic 'asali'), the administration in turn adopted the next closest term, 'Orang Asli' (literally 'natural people', but now taken to mean 'original people' as well). It also became official policy that the Malay term be used even in the English language. However, this administrative fiat was not enough to forge a common identity among the Orang Asli, and they did not immediately accept the term or identify with it.

Orang Asli in Selangor in the 1890s.

Legally, an Orang Asli is defined in the Aboriginal Peoples Ordinance 1954, revised 1974, as a member of an aboriginal ethnic group (either by blood descent or by adoption), who speaks an aboriginal language and who habitually follows an aboriginal custom and belief.

This definition can pose problems for the Orang Asli, in terms of efforts to integrate them into mainstream Malay society. Furthermore, given that the foundation of the Orang Asli's culture and spirituality lies in their continued ownership of their traditional homelands, the loss of these ecological niches affects the integrity and survival of the Orang Asli as a people. While the Orang Asli are recognized as Bumiputera (sons of the soil), they do not enjoy the special status enjoyed by the other Bumiputera communities, namely the Malays and the natives of Sabah and Sarawak.

Identification during the Emergency

Copper discs were issued to the Orang Asli from 1948 to 1960, during the Emergency, for identification purposes. Different designs on the discs denoted different groups and the sex of the holder, but no names were inscribed.

1

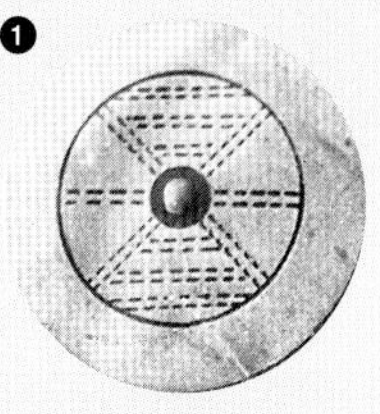

2

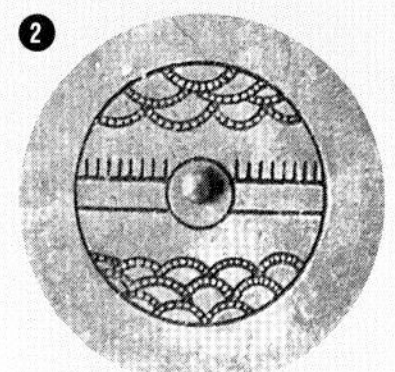

3

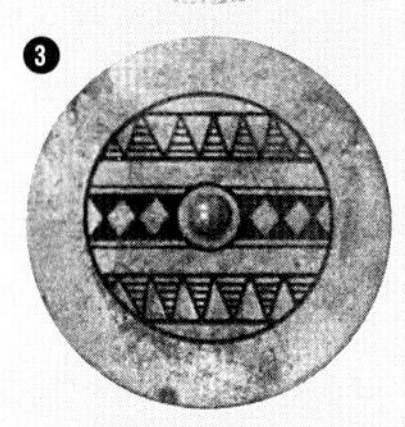

4

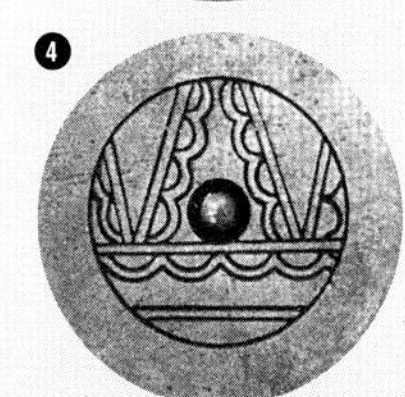

Discs (1) and (2) were for Temiar males and females respectively; and (3) and (4) were for Semai males and females respectively.

A scene from the 1930s film *Timeless Temiar*, showing Orang Asli shooting rapids near Gerik, in Perak.

Orang Asli beliefs and value systems

The belief systems of the Orang Asli are among the oldest religions in Asia. Based on animism, these systems share the view that every creature is imbued with spirits, and that a supernatural world inhabited by spirits affects order in the secular world and the well-being of man. Religion forms the basis of the Orang Asli's values and social mores, which constitute the bedrock of indigenous laws that maintain unity within the communities and ensure the survival of their culture.

ABOVE: The Mah Meri and Jah Hut honour the spirits annually with a day-long feast and *sewang* (dance rituals), known as Hari Moyang and Hari Bes, respectively. Food and tobacco are placed in small woven baskets atop a seashore temple for the spirits.

RIGHT: The shaman (*tok jenang*, in yellow clothing) conducts the ceremony, and enters a state of trance when possessed by the spirits (*moyang* or *bes*).

Offerings for the spirits.

Peruman, creator in the Jah Hut pantheon.

Gods, spirits and demons

While Orang Asli beliefs systems have common themes and structures, they do not share a common bureaucratic or governing structure that creates adherence to an exclusive order or authority. As such Orang Asli religions differ in their teachings and the rituals conducted. These belief systems subscribe to the existence of a supernatural world inhabited by gods and a multitude of spirits ranked according to significance, with the creators at the top, and predatory spirits at the bottom. In the Orang Asli cosmology, the supreme creator is aided by other gods, spirits and demons. Good spirits perform a variety of services, from helping the community cope with life on earth to assisting the dead in their journey after life. Evil spirits are known variously, for example, as *sitan, hablis, najis* and *bes* (Jah Hut), *bas* (Che Wong) and *nyaniik* (Semai).

The names accorded to the spiritual beings vary among the Orang Asli groups, as do their rituals, such as those commemorating ancestors, as well as healing or cleansing rites. Some groups, such as the Batek (a sub-group of the Negritos) and the Semai and Temiar (sub-groups of the Senoi), also believe that supernatural beings play a role in maintaining order on earth. The supernatural tiger, for instance, is believed to punish those who insult or mock weaker animals, or misuse certain plants. In addition, the Senoi and the Proto-Malays believe in *keramat*, a category of deities who serve as guardians of a particular area or a large rock, river estuary, lake or mountain.

Adat and social mores

Adat (customary law) is central to the Orang Asli way of life. As a mechanism of social control, it is vital for ensuring harmony and unity in the communities. Derived from religion and indigenous ideas of natural laws, *adat* law, however, can be ignored if a compromise is reached among members in a dispute that better serves community interests and unity. Values that promote and reinforce unity among Orang Asli communities include communal interest, respect for privacy and property, honouring promises, and sharing of food. Communal interest is developed by working together in almost all aspects of community life, including rituals. Cooperation is necessary in the building of ritual structures, and in

Gods and deities in the Orang Asli pantheon

Group	Supreme gods	Gods and deities
Negrito (Batek)		Gobar (thunder god; governs human behaviour), Potew (guardian tigers), Naga' (snake deity), Tohan (creator deity), Cemroy (fruit deity).
Senoi (Semai)	Nyenang (creator)	Maklikat (assists Nyenang), Hala' Asal Jaja' Bidat, Mai Dengri' (land guardians).
Senoi (Semaq Beri)	Tohan (creator and protector)	Nabi Adam (assists Tohan), Hawa (Nabi Adam's wife), Karei (Tohan's helper), Dewa-dewi, Orang Halus and Bidadari (angels).
Senoi (Jah Hut)	Peruman (creator)	Allah-ta-alla, Ibrahil, Sarafil, Nukereh and Musapil (God's messengers); Datok Nenek Nenek Moyang, Melaikat or Bahalak, Rang Pengabis Rang Pengalih, Bujiang Hitam, Kelamut, Dangku Dangka, Bungsu Lirang (ancestor guardians).
Proto-Malays (Jakun)	Tuhan Atas and Tuhan Bawah (creators)	Dewa
Proto-Malays (Semelai)	Tohan (creator)	Nabi (prophets), Qadam and Nagak (govern human behaviour).

ABOVE: A shaman (*tok jenang*) performing a ceremonial ritual.

RIGHT: Part of a Mah Meri worship house, believed to be about 200 years old, on Carey Island, Selangor. Fronting the structure are statues of tigers—guardian spirits of the house—and the *moyang gadeng*—guardian spirit of the mountains, seas, rivers, caves and villages.

Healing ritual

The Jah Hut and Mah Meri believe that sickness is caused by evil spirits known as *bes* (Jah Hut) and *moyang* (Mah Meri) and can only be cured by expelling the evil spirits from the body into an effigy (*spili*) or wooden sculpture, which is later discarded. These rituals are known variously as *beni soy* (Jah Hut), *jo'oh* (Mah Meri), *halaa* (Temiar), and *piyey* (Semaq Beri).

Among the Temiar and Semai, healing rituals are usually conducted at night in a specially erected structure. The sick person is laid on the floor and a bunch of flowers and leaves (*calon*) is rubbed against the skin to drive out evil spirits. These rituals involve trance dancing, singing and music (see 'Traditional Orang Asli arts').

Right: A Semai shaman drawing out malevolent spirits from a sick person.

Far right: A Jah Hut healing ritual.

performing the rituals. Those who refuse to be involved in community activities or to help others are liable for both supernatural punishment (*tenghaak*), in the form of hardship or bad luck, and social punishment, such as ostracization by the community.

To the Orang Asli, a harmonious way of life is underscored by respect for one another's privacy and property. Respect for elders is also important, and is inculcated through a rule of *tulah*—a supernatural curse that falls upon a person who is disrespectful towards elders. *Tulah* punishment causes a person to experience physical weakness, loss of energy and the ability to think clearly. Disrespect for an individual's privacy and property, meanwhile, would result in *lawac*, *tenghaak*, *tulah* or other forms of punishment prescribed by *adat*.

A Batek midwife, 1980s.

Among the Semai, keeping a promise is ruled by *srengloog*, which causes injury or the likeness of death to a person who betrays his friends or other members of the community. In such a situation, the soul of the person becomes weak. A person in this condition would be easy prey for wild animals, or be susceptible to accidents.

Some Orang Asli groups, such as the Batek and Semai, observe food taboos that prohibit the mixing of different types of food. Adhering to this *adat* means the Orang Asli collect or hunt large amounts of one type of food at a time—which necessarily involves working together in food gathering activities—and share their resources with the community. In addition, the Semai believe that mixing different types of food, such as animal meat with fish; pork with egg; and fish with mushrooms, causes two types of disasters—*terlaij* and *penalik*. *Terlaij* is similar to *lawac*, and incurs anger from the thunder god (*ngkuu'*). *Penalik* results from a clash between spirits or guardians of the foods, and translates into health problems such as food poisoning. Food sharing among the Semai is ruled by *punan*, which normally affects a person who is unable to fulfil his or her wish to eat certain foods, and who, as a result, becomes vulnerable to accidents or other forms of bad luck.

Harmony with nature

Underscoring the Orang Asli's relationship with the natural environment is the view that all life forms are equal. Rituals are performed to maintain a harmonious relationship with supernatural forces.

An Orang Asli elder blessing a newly installed *tok batin* (headman). While the ceremony featured traditional rites, the people opted for modern batik shirts and trousers.

Rites of passage

Birth

Many Orang Asli groups, including the Jah Hut, believe that the soul bird has to be caught and eaten during pregnancy to avoid sickness or death. A midwife (male or female) assists in the delivery of the baby and, among some groups, names the child. In the event of complications a shaman is called upon to invoke the help of the spirit in a healing ritual.

Some groups, such as the Temiar of Ulu Kelantan, perform a ritual of shaving the head of an infant aged between six and eight months. A patch of hair is left on the forehead if the baby is a male, and at the back of the head if female. The hair is stored in an intricately woven pouch (*apok soi aleh*), which is woven by someone close to the baby. The Temiar believe that the pouch would keep the *semangat* (soul) intact.

Marriage

A couple being ritually bathed in a traditional Semai wedding. A *halaq* (shaman) presides at the ceremony.

Marriage ceremonies among Orang Asli communities are generally similar, albeit with some variations. However, among the various groups the ritual bathing of the bridal couple is considered the most significant wedding rite. A traditional Mah Meri wedding is more complex than that of other groups, involving seven rituals—the engagement; henna colouring; tooth filing; finding the bride; presentation of the bridal couple; dining ceremony, and cleansing ritual—that can take up to four days. The ceremony is presided by community elders such as the headman (*tok batin*), shaman (*tok jenang*) and master of ceremonies (*tok jokra*). These days young couples prefer simpler weddings for practical and economic reasons, often combining their traditions with Malay customs and those of other cultures.

Death

Ceremonies associated with death and burial vary from group to group. Most groups bury their dead together with food, tobacco as well as the valuables and personal belongings of the deceased. The Temuan also mark the palms and soles of the deceased with turmeric powder to signify the passing to the spirit world. Some groups, such as the Mah Meri and the Proto-Malays, provide the spirits of the deceased with a hut to live in.

A Mah Meri ancestor spirit hut (*rumah pangga*).

Orang Asli social organization and leadership

The Orang Asli, comprising the Negritos, Senoi and Proto-Malays, are no longer nomadic. Although the majority still hunt, fish and forage occasionally, all practise some form of agriculture and live in settlements. Many are well educated and work in the public and private sectors. Their traditional forms of social organization have also undergone a process of change. As a result of increasing relations with the wider Malaysian society, they have developed new leadership and representative systems.

Most of the Orang Asli now lead a sedentary lifestyle.

Many Orang Asli groups, especially those in the deep of the forest, rely on a traditional means of transport, the bamboo raft.

Traditional structures

Orang Asli society was traditionally structured around the nuclear family unit, with larger units or bands formed for certain economic activities. The nature of the family unit itself was governed by each group's marriage customs, in which some variety can still be observed. Leadership of these larger groups was generally by the informal appointment of the dominant male. With increasing sedentarization, patterns of leadership and social organization are beginning to more closely resemble those of the dominant Peninsula ethnic groups.

Contemporary change and leadership

The traditional relationship between the Orang Asli and the Malays has, since time immemorial, been one of mutual dependence and respect. Until the late 1940s, there was no specific administration for the Orang Asli. The post of 'Protector of Aborigines' was created in 1949. The Emergency (1948–60) also saw the passing of the first important legislation to protect the Orang Asli, the Aboriginal Peoples Ordinance, 1954. A Department of Aborigines was established and 'jungle forts' were set up in Orang Asli areas to introduce them to basic health facilities, education and consumer items. In recent decades, government initiatives have, to an extent, helped the Orang Asli to adapt and integrate with the other population groups in Malaysia. They are represented by a senator in Parliament, and several associations represent their interests and aspirations.

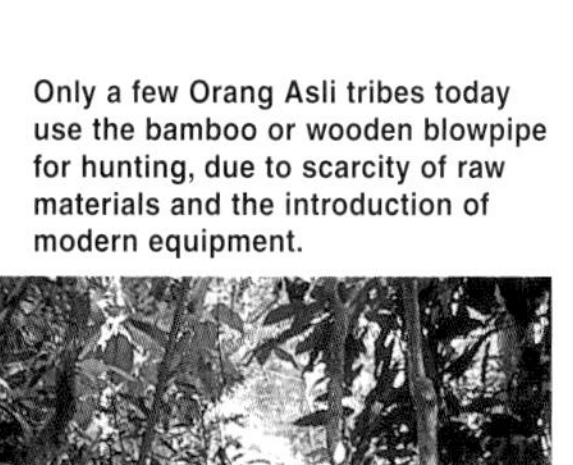

Only a few Orang Asli tribes today use the bamboo or wooden blowpipe for hunting, due to scarcity of raw materials and the introduction of modern equipment.

Mah Meri bridal party. Marriage traditions and attire among the Mah Meri (a sub-group of the Senoi) are little changed from the 1950s.

Marriage

In Negrito society, marriage is not marked by any special ceremony. Courtship and pre-marital relations are common and tolerated. When a young couple want to be married, the man will present a number of gifts, such as jungle knives, cloth and tobacco, to the girl's father in the presence of members of the band. By accepting these presents the father signifies that both he and the community accept and consent to the proposed marriage.

Incest is a very serious crime among the Negritos. They believe that those who commit incest will suffer immediate and violent death, being either struck by lightning or killed by a tiger. Adultery, too, is taboo. Offenders are believed to be stricken with serious disease leading to death. A man is not allowed to talk to his mother-in-law or have any kind of social interaction with her, and likewise for a woman with her father-in-law. Supernatural punishments are also believed to ensue from violating these taboos.

Among the Senoi, there is a lack of formality in marriage. Pre-marital relations are tolerated and common. A couple who decide to live together as man and wife will first obtain the agreement of both their parents, and the young man will give a bride price to the girl's parents. Senoi marriages are less stable than those of the Negritos. The Temiar, in particular, allow married men and women to have sexual relations with their spouse's siblings and cousins.

Marriage among the Proto-Malays is more formal than the other Orang Asli groups. Incest, traditionally punished by death, is unheard of. While marriage between members of one village is preferred, many marry outsiders. Married couples usually live with the wife's parents for at least a year, after which residence is flexible. In the case of divorce, a fine is imposed by the headman on the guilty party.

Mah Meri wedding nuptials in the 1960s.

The Negritos

The majority of Negritos, also known as Semang, live in the interior to the north of the Peninsula. They were originally nomads. Each tribe (the largest being the Jahai and the Batek) hunts, fishes and forages in the forest, and is identified with a definite territory.

The Negritos, comprising the Jahai, Batek, Mendriq, Lanoh and Kintak sub-groups, are no longer nomads and live in permanent settlements.

Traditional leadership

While elders are generally respected by the younger members of the band, the Negritos are very egalitarian. The nomadic band is led by the oldest able-bodied man who is usually chosen informally during a meeting of the adult males. The leader so appointed makes economic decisions and maintains harmony among the members. He is respected because he is the most knowledgeable and experienced, is a wise counsellor and able spokesman when dealing with others. When he dies he is usually succeeded by his eldest son, although in exceptional circumstances a son-in-law may be chosen.

A Negrito medicine man in ceremonial garb.

The family and the band

The basic unit among the Negritos is the nuclear family living in lean-to shelters made of forest materials. This forms the basic working group for daily activities. Often, five to ten nuclear families form a band. The band constitutes a larger socio-economic unit and often includes visitors and elderly relatives. Able-bodied members of the band fish, hunt and forage for several days in a particular location and move to another location after they have exhausted the available resources.

The band is the most common and largest social unit among the Negritos. Among the Jahai and the Lanoh, although not among the smaller groups, there are larger social units than the nomadic band. Commonly termed the 'horde', these usually consist of two to three related bands. Traditionally, a horde does not have an overall leader but is identified with a certain territory. The horde is the biggest and socially most significant grouping among the Negritos. It is only after government efforts to sedentarize the Negritos that a number of bands grouping together have a 'village leader'.

Members of a band of five to ten families are usually related by kinship or marriage.

The Senoi

The majority of the Senoi (especially the Temiar and the Semai) live deep in the forest of central Peninsular Malaysia. Traditionally they practised shifting cultivation, a practice common among highlanders throughout Southeast Asia. Although they still fish, hunt and forage, unlike the Negritos, the Senoi now live in relatively permanent settlements.

The longhouse community and its headman

While traditionally the majority of the Senoi lived in raised longhouses, some now live in individual family houses. A typical longhouse, usually situated close to a river, is made up of six to ten separated individual compartments and a communal living corridor in the middle. Each compartment, with its own fireplace, is occupied by a nuclear family, the basic Senoi unit.

The next largest socio-economic unit among the Senoi is the grouping of all the nuclear families living in a longhouse, and—on occasion—those families living in individual houses close by, forming a village. All these families are related by kinship or marriage to the founder of the longhouse community, who is regarded as the headman. The village may vary in size from 50 to over 100 individuals. The headman is also responsible for peace and harmony within the community. As among the Negritos, a Senoi headman chairs a council of adult males of the community. Upon his death one of his male siblings will usually take his place.

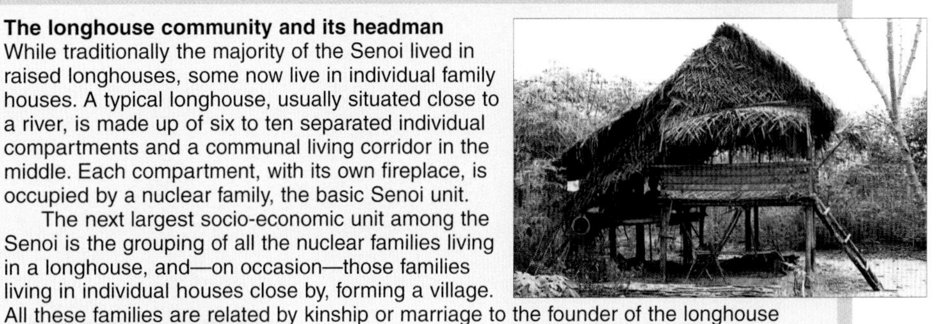

ABOVE RIGHT: A Semai dwelling in the 1950s.

LEFT: The Temiar traditionally build their houses from bamboo and rattan.

The river valley group

Population increase among the Senoi and the shortage of suitable land usually leads to the break-up of an original settlement. By mutual agreement a new settlement will be established further up-river by a younger brother or son of the headman. Over time, a few more settlements will similarly be established, resulting in the formation of the largest unit within the social organization of the Senoi, the river valley group. While the settlements are economically independent, the headmen, if not all the members of the communities, are related by kinship and marriage to those of the original village. The river valley group is headed by a chief, being the headman of the founding settlement, who enjoys considerable prestige, and is given government recognition. However, he has no political authority within the group. Nevertheless, regular visits help maintain unity among members of the community.

Senoi groups cultivate hill rice and other crops, as well as hunt, fish and forage within defined and recognized areas of the forest.

The Proto-Malays

Compared with the Negritos and the Senoi, the Proto-Malays (Melayu Asli) are economically and culturally diverse. The majority of the Proto-Malays live in areas more accessible by road, with some of them close to non-Orang Asli areas in the central and southern regions of the Peninsula. The largest groups—Jakun, Temuan and Semelai—are mainly settled cultivators. Shifting cultivation, previously common in hilly areas, has declined. Of the smaller groups, the Orang Kuala live in coastal areas while the Orang Seletar traditionally lived a nomadic sea life in individual family boats in the Johor Strait.

Kinship and social organization

The basic unit among the Proto-Malays is the nuclear family living in individual houses. A village comprises five to 20 individual raised houses on the bank of a river or a lake, headed by a headman (*batin*). Village members are usually related by kinship and marriage. The village community cultivates a defined area which it considers as its land. While each family is responsible for an individual plot, there is usually co-operation among the families, especially in the overall clearing and preparation of community land for cultivation. The headman also oversees the adherence to *adat* (customary practices) relating to marriage within the community.

The social organization and leadership systems of the Semelai and Temuan are more complex than the other Proto-Malay groups. Within both groups, the largest organization comprises five to six villages under the leadership of an overall chief (*batin*), who is the authority in all disputes and is responsible for the administration of the villages.

Among most Proto-Malays, inheritance of leadership and family property is patrilineal; among others it is bilateral. However, among the Temuan in Negeri Sembilan and some neighbouring Semelai, descent and inheritance are traditionally matrilineal.

The Proto-Malays live in individual family dwellings.

Traditional Orang Asli arts

The traditional arts of the Orang Asli are derived from their animistic beliefs and rituals. The objects they produce from wood, pandanus, rattan and bamboo, as well as their music and dance, are created for ceremonial or practical purposes, but constitute works of art, in that they are often beautifully decorated, painstakingly carved, and highly polished. The destruction of the Orang Asli's natural rainforest habitat and the relocation of some groups have affected the availability of raw materials used for these crafts, with a resultant decline in some art forms.

Temuan children entertaining guests at a traditional *sewang* performance.

Woodcarving

Woodcarving among the Orang Asli originates from a healing ritual (*sakat buang* to the Mah Meri and *beni soy* to the Jah Hut). During the ritual, the shaman transfers the evil spirit causing the sickness from the patient's body into wooden sculptures of ancestral spirits (*moyang*), which are later left in the jungle or thrown in the sea.

The Mah Meri also carve wooden masks to be worn during ceremonies and dances. These masks are used as a means of communication with the *moyang*, and have movable jaws so that the spirits may speak through them. The Mah Meri believe that whoever wears such a mask will be imbued with the particular spirit. There are believed to be more than 450 varieties of sculptures and masks used by the Mah Meri, while the Jah Hut are said to make use of some 700 varieties.

These exquisite sculptures and masks have become one of the most sought-after crafts of the Orang Asli, and are promoted as collectables.

A red hardwood, *nyireh batu* (xylocarpus), is used by Mah Meri carvers for sculptures, and a softwood, *pulai* (*Alstonia spathulata*), for masks.

Mah Meri masks representing: (1) *Moyang siamang ganti*, one of the more important spirits in the Mah Meri belief system; (2) *moyang tok naning*, guardian of the neighbourhood and protector against sickness and evil spirits; and (3) *moyang melor*, which is sent to earth when there is disunity amongst family members and the community.

Sculptures and masks

To the Jah Hut and the Mah Meri, their carvings tell stories of their tribe and beliefs. Craftsmen guard their images and pass them on to the next generation.

The legend of the *moyang lanjut* is a love story of a woman whose husband has drowned, and who waits on the riverbank, hoping for his return. The sculpture depicts a bare-breasted woman with tears from her eyes and long tresses that indicate the duration of her wait.

In the story of the *moyang harimau berantai* a tiger was caught in a trap, and died because nobody dared to release it. The sculpture, carved from a single piece of wood, features seven inter-connecting rings to represent chains and a ball in the tiger's mouth. It is considered the most difficult to carve.

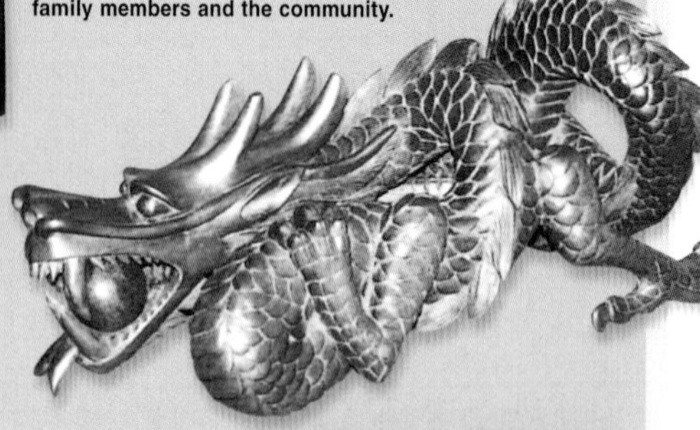
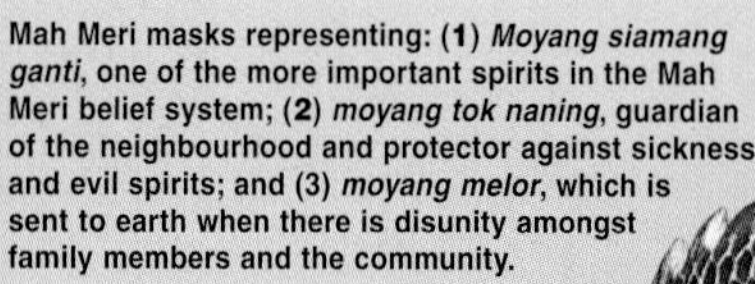
ABOVE RIGHT: The *moyang naga* (dragon spirit) is based on Mah Meri mythology, which includes creatures such as dragons, serpents and sea snakes.

RIGHT: The *moyang harimau berantai* (tiger in chains spirit) sculpture was awarded the Seal of Excellence in 2004 by UNESCO–AHPADA (ASEAN Handicraft Promotion and Development Association).

Sculpture of the *moyang lanjut*.

Bamboo blowpipe

The blowpipe is probably the most sophisticated tool devised by the Orang Asli. Indeed, it is synonymous with this indigenous group. It is used for hunting as well as for protection against animals. Made from a special bamboo about 1.8 to 2.4 metres in length and free of nodes, a blowpipe comprises two hollow tubes, one for the barrel and the other, the casing. At one end is the mouthpiece where the dart, its tip dipped into the sap of the Ipoh tree (*Antiaris toxicaria*), is inserted. Engravings on the casing and quiver are believed to enhance the performance of the blowpipe.

Stories related to the blowpipe often told of the Orang Asli's glorious past. The Temiar, for instance, marked the surface of their blowpipes after every successful hit. Such blowpipes, known as *belau jasa*, are extremely rare. The use of the blowpipe is confined to only a few tribes nowadays, due to a scarcity of raw materials as well as the advent of the shotgun. However, there is a good demand for blowpipes as souvenirs.

LEFT: Quivers and blowpipe casings (far right) with designs of mountains, plants, trees and water incised into their surface.

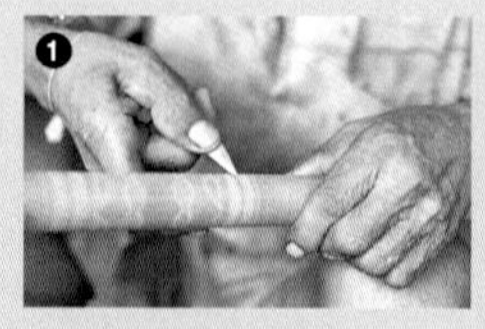

Making a blowpipe

1. Patterns are incised into the selected length of bamboo.
2. The bamboo is straightened over a fire.
3. The ends of the blowpipe are reinforced with string.
4. The mouthpiece is made and fitted to the blowpipe.

FAR RIGHT: The last of the Temuan blowpipe makers, Saia Anak Tippit, who died in 2003 at the age of 100. The Temuan blowpipe was awarded the UNESCO–AHPADA (ASEAN Handicraft Promotion and Development Association) Seal of Excellence in 2003.

Sewang

Sewang are Orang Asli ceremonies or rituals, ranging from weddings, births and welcoming ceremonies to rituals for healing, burial and warding off evil spirits. Most *sewang* involve trance-dancing and singing, to the accompaniment of musical instruments such as stamping tubes (*chat-tong*), bamboo guitars (*kreb*), mouth or nose flutes, wooden drums, gongs and jaw's harps (*genggong*).

Sewang are usually performed in a specially erected structure called *rumah sewang* which has a floor made of eight-centimetre wide bamboo strips attached with rattan strips to beams made of thick logs. The bamboo floor bounces with the rhythm of the music, enhancing the movement of the dancers. Leaves suspended from the ceiling of the *rumah sewang* brush against the dancers' heads; this is believed to have a positive effect on the ritual. The lyrics of the songs relate to the environment, their culture and the spirits that appear in their dreams. The *sewang* usually goes on all night. Dancers, with their faces and bodies painted, are attired in costumes made from tree bark, leaves and flowers.

Above: Perak Temiar men dance to the accompaniment of stamping tubes during a *sewang*.

Left: Orang Asli musical instruments such as the bamboo stringed keranting are made from forest materials.

Face painting

The Negrito and Senoi groups usually paint their faces as a form of adornment at *sewang* and other festivities. The markings are also believed to ward off evil spirits. The colours are obtained from lime, betel leaves, turmeric, soot, white clay and polygonum leaves.

Weaving

One of the most important activities of Orang Asli women is the weaving of mats, bags and baskets from wild pandanus. Pouches and exotic mats woven from pandanus strips for ceremonies and daily use are sold to supplement incomes. These intricate handicrafts are derived from their rituals and involve special techniques unique to every Orang Asli group.

The Temiar in the north of Peninsular Malaysia, for instance, weave small utilitarian pouches (*apok*) from pandanus. *Apok* are woven using a distinct weaving technique whereby the surface of the pouch is braided or decorated with curled pandanus strips in patterns that denote specific significance. Due to its laborious nature, this weaving technique is referred to as 'mad weaving' (*anyaman gila*).

The Temiar believe the technique was passed to their ancestors by a legendary creature called Woi, that lived on mountains tops. According to folklore, those who encountered the Woi mysteriously disappeared, except for one girl, who lived to teach members of her band the elaborate three-dimensional weaving technique. The *apok* comes in various sizes and has a multitude of uses. It is used to store valuables and small items such as betel nut and cigarettes, and is given as gifts. Among the Temuan of Selangor, *apok* are called *bujam* and are only used by the elders, who hang them around the neck. Courtship *apok* are woven in pairs connected by string, and do not have covers. A girl would leave buscuits in the *apok* in a place for her prospective partner to retrieve. The *apok soi aleh*, with distinct colour patterns and elaborate string designs, is used for storing baby hair to protect the infant's soul (*semangat*).

A Mah Meri woman weaving ceremonial mats.

Left: Utility and storage baskets.

Below: ntricately woven apok pouches. The apok was awarded the Seal of Excellence by Unesco–Ahpada (ASEAN Handicraft Promotion and Development Association) in 2002, and in 2004 (for the apok soi aleh, used for storing baby hair).

Dress, headdresses and ornamentation

Orang Asli men traditionally wore loincloths (*cawat*) made from the bark of the *terap* (*Artocarpus*) or Ipoh tree (*Antiaris toxicaria*), and the women wore skirts made either from leaves, pandanus or black root (black fungus rhizomorph). Contact with the outside world has led to the Orang Asli adopting Malay dress for both men and women; the use of traditional dress is restricted to cultural performances.

Simpai (rattan bracelets).

Headdresses (*tempok*) are crown-like, and made from either plaited pandanus, tree bark, rhizomorph roots, leaves, flowers, palm fronds or rattan. They are still used by the Semai, Temiar, Mah Meri and Temuan tribes during festivities.

In days gone by, necklaces—made from animal teeth, beads, rattan, vines or shells, or a combination of these materials—were used more for magical than ornamental purposes. Rattan bracelets (*simpai*) are common among the Temiar, Semai and Temuan, and are worn by women around the wrists and the men, around the biceps. Armlets made of roots and vines are also worn around the arm or below the knee. Today the *simpai* is a popular handicraft product. Bamboo hairpins and combs are widely used by the Negritos, and although their fine curly hair does not render them useful, most women wear them as adornment and good luck charms. Intricate designs engraved on them are believed to ward off evil spirits or attract good ones.

Bamboo combs.

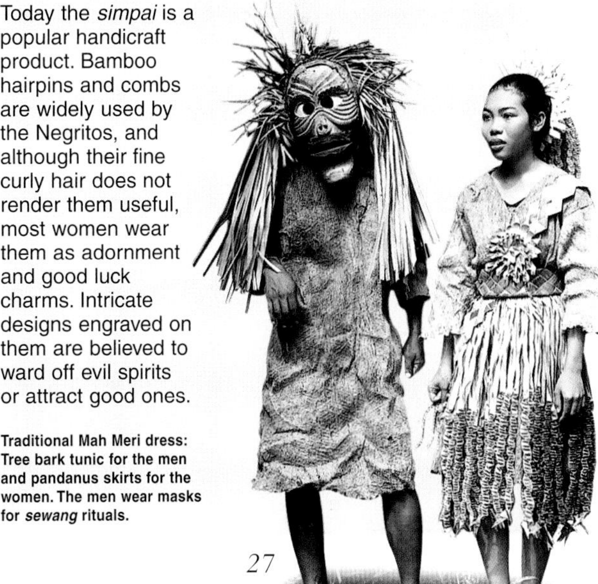

Traditional Mah Meri dress: Tree bark tunic for the men and pandanus skirts for the women. The men wear masks for *sewang* rituals.

The Malays: Identity and definitions

The identity of the Malays and the definition of the term 'Malay' has evolved over many centuries. Prior to the Portuguese conquest of Melaka in 1511, the use of term 'Malay' within the Malay World—the home of the Malays since the last Ice Age (circa 15,000–10,000 BCE)—was subject to various ethnic, linguistic and cultural variations. The beginning of European rule in 1511 marked a watershed in the Malay World, and shaped Malay polities and their thought system. The term 'Malay' is now defined in the Federal Constitution.

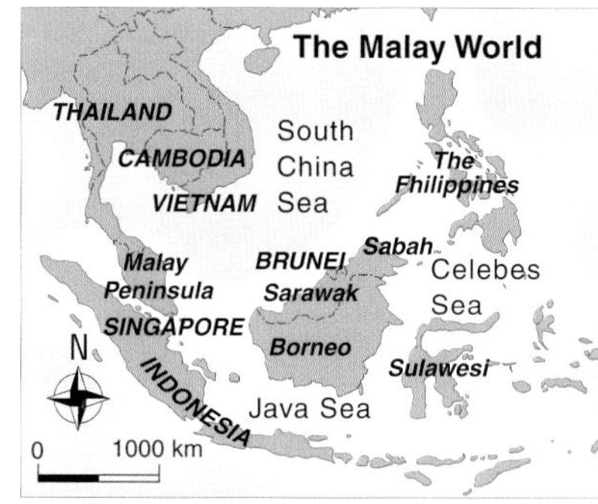

ABOVE: The precise extent of the Malay World remains the matter of debate. However, that depicted is generally accepted to be correct.

BELOW: The court of a Malay Ruler c. 1500. Kingship and Islam were the criteria of the term 'Malay' during the era of plurality, prior to European colonial rule.

Malays in the pre-European era

The term 'Malay' was initially a self-referent used by the peoples inhabiting the Malay Archipelago. Subsequently, traders from South Asia and China used it as a social label. Eventually, it became a social label used by European travellers, proselytizers, merchants and traders.

By the 16th and 17th centuries, 'Malay' and 'being Malay' were associated with two major elements: a line of kingship acknowledging descent from Srivijaya and Melaka; and, second, a commercial diaspora retaining the customs, language and trade practices of Melaka.

Plurality

Before the arrival of Europeans in the 16th century, the Malay World was characterized by the dominance of plurality as a principle of social organization. The term 'plurality' signifies a free-flowing, natural process not only through migration but also through cultural borrowing and adaptations. The dominant political order was a flexible non-bureaucratic style of management focused on a demonstrative ruler. States, governments and nation-states, with systems of bureaucratic institutions, did not exist until European colonial rule was established in the early 16th century and the traditional polities of the Malay World dismantled.

Plural society

European colonial administrators installed systems of governance which gave rise to a plural society. 'Plural society' signifies the introduction of knowledge, social concepts, vocabulary, idioms and institutions hitherto unknown to the indigenous population—examples include censuses, museums and ethnic categories. The term also signifies the introduction of a market-orientated economy and systematized hegemonic politics. The modern states of the Malay World emerged from this plural society context, and it is against this background that the ethnic groups of the Malay World came to be identified and defined, from within as well as by outsiders.

Constitutional definition

The Federal Constitution defines a Malay as a person who:

- professes the religion of Islam
- habitually speaks the Malay language, and
- conforms to Malay customs.

This is the 'constitutional Malay'. The definition has economic, political and cultural ramifications on the lives of all Malaysians—uniting the Malays and dividing them from the non-Malays.

The Bumiputera

The formation of Malaysia in 1963 introduced a new dimension to the understanding and definition of the term Malay, arising from the addition of Muslims native to Sarawak and Sabah, including many Bajau and Iranun in Sabah and the Melanau in Sarawak, to the country's diverse population. Unlike the Peninsular Malays, these groups did not constitute a majority in the states, as more than 60 per cent of the population consisted of non-Muslim

Kingship, together with its polity (*kerajaan*), was the first 'pillar' of being Malay in the area surrounding the Strait of Melaka. Islam, the second 'pillar', provided kingship with some of its core values.

The commercial diaspora comprised groups from beyond the Strait of Melaka area—Borneo, Makassar and Java. These groups defined their being Malay primarily in terms of language and customs, which were the third and fourth accepted 'pillars' of being Malay, respectively.

While Islam was an objective criterion for defining kingship and its subjects (Muslim and non-Muslims), anyone who claimed to embrace Islam could be classed as Malay. Furthermore, non-Muslims and non-Malays too could be labelled 'Malays' so long as they spoke and wrote Malay and followed a Malay way of life—that is, donned certain clothes, followed certain culinary practices, and became an integral part of the Malay-speaking trading network—known in Malay as *masuk Melayu*.

The Portuguese, Spanish and Dutch used the labels 'Malay' and 'being Malay' in this way. This subjective element allowed a distinct plurality in the composition of the category 'Malay', since it was open to new recruits from any background.

Malaysia's plural society

A plural society emerged in the Malay Peninsula at the beginning of the 20th century under the British colonial administration. It is in this context that the modern definition of the term 'Malay' and the identity of the Malays were defined. It was also in this context that the various ethnic groups occupied separate cultural, social and economic spheres.

LEFT: Malay chiefs with their subjects, late 19th century.

ABOVE: British officials with Malay royalty, early 20th century.

ABOVE RIGHT: Indian rubber estate workers, c. 1900.

RIGHT: Chinese vendors at a market, c. 1900.

natives (such as the Iban, Bidayuh and Kadazan) and Chinese. The Federal Government used the term 'Bumiputera' ('sons of the soil') to accommodate the Malays and the native Muslims and non-Muslims of Sarawak and Sabah in a single category.

The decision, in the late 1980s, by UMNO (United Malays National Organisation)—the leading Malay-based political party—to open its doors to non-Muslim Bumiputera so as to enable the Barisan Nasional (National Front) to regain control of Sabah from the opposition, illustrates that the definition of a concept can have far-reaching effects. The term 'Malay'—as defined by the Malay nationalist movement in the 1920s and 1930s, and by UMNO at the time of its formation shortly after World War II—had to be reformulated in the case of Sabah, illustrating the flexibility of the term 'Malay'.

The reformulation of the term 'Malay' also demonstrates that the concept of what is Malay is situational: it can easily shift meaning and adapt to new situations.

The advent of a plural society

The principle of a 'plural society' underscored the social order of the modern colonial and post-colonial periods. During the 17th–19th centuries, the colonial administrators—first the Dutch, then the British—redefined the meaning of 'Malay' and 'being Malay', setting boundaries legitimized by rules of law and policies.

After the establishment of the Straits Settlements in 1824, Raffles's concept of a 'Malay nation' gradually became a 'Malay race', an identity that was accepted by both the British and the Malays themselves, primarily as the result of the growing presence of Europeans and Chinese. As early as the 1840s, the writer Munshi Abdullah used the term *bangsa Melayu* (Malay race or Malay people), and that term gradually entered the public sphere.

The 1891 census recognized three racial categories: Malay, Chinese and Tamil. With increased immigration from China and India in the early 1900s, a plural society was established, in which the concept of Malay as a race became fixed. The choice of the title *Utusan Melayu* for the first Malay language newspaper in the Straits Settlements in 1907 confirmed the colonial racial classifications.

English- and Chinese-medium schools established at the turn of the 20th century were followed by Malay vernacular schools. In textbooks for Malay schools, the British constructed a distinctly Malay historiography and Malay literature in which *hikayat* (stories) were used to create and implant a sense of historical identity and literary taste. The Malay Reservation Enactment of 1913 provided a legal definition of the term 'Malay', and helped fix the idea of being Malay in the public mind. These developments gave life to the concept of Malay, which was accepted by both Malays and non-Malays alike.

Malay nationalism

Malay nationalism, which developed alongside Chinese and Indian nationalism in the early 20th century, had a cultural rather than a political character. The discussions that turned the concept of a 'Malay race' once more into that of a 'Malay nation' focused on questions of identity and distinction in terms of customs, religion and language, rather than politics. The debate surrounding this transition centred on the question of who could be called the real Malay (*Melayu asli* or *Melayu jati*). The resulting friction led to the emergence of various factions amongst Malay nationalists.

Protests from Malay nationalists against the Malayan Union, a unitary state project, forced the British to accept an alternative federalist order known as the Federation of Malaya (Persekutuan Tanah Melayu in Malay).

Malay World studies

An enormous quantity of indigenous research materials still remain in the Malay World, despite the fact that in the past much was taken to libraries and museums in Europe. In order to be accessible, these materials require prudent management.

Located at the heart of the Malay World, Malaysian institutions shoulder part of the responsibility for documenting and preserving. One such institution is the Institute of the Malay World and Civilization (Institut Alam dan Tamadun Melayu or ATMA), based at Universiti Kebangsaan Malaysia in Bangi.

ATMA developed a database, PADAT (Pangkalan Data ATMA), which has become the core project documenting research materials on the Malay World. It comprises over 51,000 articles on all aspects of Malay culture and civilization. Other related databases consist of more than 20,000 Malay proverbs, 17,000 slides on Malay architecture, 15,000 verses of Baba *pantun* (poetry) and some 240 books in Jawi script.

These important databases are accessible through ATMA's free access web portal located at **www.malaycivilization.com.**

A group of Malays in Penang, 1870s.

The Malays: Origins, beliefs and value systems

The Malays have occupied the Malay Archipelago—and the coastal region of continental Southeast Asia—since the prehistoric era. They are speakers of the Austronesian group of languages which is distributed all over insular Southeast Asia, part of the Pacific, the Americas and a small part of east Africa. In Malaysia, the Malays comprise the largest group of indigenous people, whose traditional belief system was animistic prior to the arrival of Islam in the 14th century.

Values
Malay values are based on the teachings of the Qur'an and the practices of the Prophet. Their foundation is that Allah is supreme and that man was created as the vicegerent on earth. Man is to do good and earn *pahala* (merit) by constantly practising the *rukun Islam* (pillars of Islam).

In order to accumulate merit man has to do good for himself, his parents, his family, his community and his country, all for the sake of Allah, and not out of personal egoism. He has to practise all the virtues and ethics known to man and respect all human beings, especially fellow Muslims, as well as animals and all of Allah's creatures. Virtues include truthfulness, trustworthiness, the fulfilling of all promises, sincerity, non-vengeance,

Origin theories

The peoples of the Malay Archipelago appear to have come from two probable strains of the human gene pool: the Mongoloid *Homo erectus* or *Sinanthropus* recovered at the cave of Chou-kou-tien near Beijing ('Peking Man') and the Austroloid *Homo erectus soloensis* ('Java Man'). Within Southeast Asia the two strains are believed to have evolved and hybridized, although there is a lack of evidence linking the modern Mongoloids and Austroloids to the ancient fossils recovered in both areas.

While the Mongoloids are generally well represented in the peoples of modern East Asia, Southeast Asia presents a picture of mixed population of Mongoloids and Austroloids (see 'A history of migration'). A debate exists among scholars as to whether the small remnants of the Austroloid population in Peninsular Malaysia (where they are represented by the Negritos), the Philippines, Indonesia and Papua New Guinea were replaced by successive migrations of Mongoloids from the north into Southeast Asia. It may be argued that the Mongoloids were not new migrants into the area, even though current opinion appears to indicate their immigration largely during the Neolithic period or much earlier.

The Niah Caves in Sarawak indicate the presence of the Austroloids between 60,000 and 100,000 years ago; East Asian Mongoloids were present between 200,000 and 300,000 years ago. Their movement southwards could have coincided with the widespread presence of the Austroloids in the Sunda Shelf around 10,000 years ago.

Boat-shaped coffins were found in Gua Kain Hitam, also known as the Painted cave, in the Niah Caves complex of Sarawak.

Linguistic classification

The languages of Southeast Asia are predominantly Austronesian (previously known as Malayo-Polynesian). Austronesian languages are spoken over a huge area ranging from Madagascar in the west to Easter Island in the east, and from Taiwan in the north to New Zealand in the south. There are more than 1000 Austronesian languages, about a quarter of all the languages spoken worldwide.

Malay and its cognate languages are spoken by around 300 million speakers in Taiwan, Indonesia, The Philippines, southern Vietnam, Cambodia, southern Thailand, Malaysia, Singapore, Brunei and Madagascar. While these western Austronesian languages are not mutually intelligible, they contain key root words that display almost identical forms and semantics. Although the historical distribution seems to indicate an insular origin, with no record of Austronesian speakers in mainland Asia—especially South China as traditionally postulated by early language scholars in the form of successive migration theories—there has been a great deal of theorizing as to origin or homeland. Nevertheless, since many of the speakers are of the Mongoloid racial type and they generally occupy the islands of Southeast Asia, it seems likely that the origin is located in or near this sweep of islands.

Original belief systems

The indigenous belief system of the Malays is essentially animistic: major features are the power of the natural order, the existence of spirit, *semangat* (spirit or vital energy) and *penunggu* (a natural vital force residing in designated physical locations such as trees, landscape, jungle and even human dwellings).

Semangat is a common concept among the Austronesian people and is commonly known as 'mana'. It is believed to be in all living things, including human bodies, and is described as the vital force behind strength and vitality of life. A rice plant is said to be full of *semangat* if it grows to a good height, with fully developed grains. The rice-farming

patience, forgiveness, generosity, consideration, cleanliness, neighbourliness, unity within the community, compassion, love and rationality. Malays must also avoid all the vices, especially those harmful to the individual and to others. Children are instructed in these morals (*akhlak*) at a very early age.

Within Malay culture, another revered value is *budi* (goodness), manifested through good behaviour and etiquette. A Malay child is always reminded to practise *budi* to his family, teachers, elders, leaders and God. In addition, a person should always be considerate and 'measure his cloth against his own body' (*ukur baju di badan sendiri*), an allusion to the saying 'Do not do unto others that you do not want others to do unto you'.

FAR LEFT: *Budi* (goodness) is manifested in etiquette, such as bending when walking in front of older people.

LEFT: Reverence and obeisance towards elders is demonstrated by kissing their hands.

Malay communities traditionally gave thanks for a bountiful harvest in the form of a *kenduri beras baru* (feast of new harvest); this practice has been largely discontinued. Some Malay villagers in the interior who practise traditional rice planting methods still conduct a series of rituals to invoke the protection of guardian spirits for their crop, and to keep away malevolent spirits.

Shamans, ritual specialists (*pawang*) and medicine men (*bomoh*) mediate with the spirit world, and are engaged to perform rituals for various purposes, such as village cleansing, rice planting and harvest, and sickness curing. Animistic beliefs and practices have declined, but such practitioners remain a feature of contemporary Malay society.

External influences

Religious and cultural influences from the Indian sub-continent during the first millennium introduced demi-gods (*dewa*) and goddesses (*dewi*) into the cosmology, as well as elements of devotion (*bhakti*) and magical powers (*sakti*) into the belief system. With the infusion of Hindu elements, Malay culture developed into a more universal belief system with the idea of a supreme God at its centre.

This was further developed with the coming of Islam in the 14th century with the idea of a supreme God—Allah—at the apex of the cosmology, with various angels (*malaikat*), satan (*syaitan*), genies (*jin*) and spirits, human beings, animals and plants, and the entire universe submitting to His supreme power and sovereignty. The Muslim world-view is founded on the six *rukun imam* (pillars of faith), the cardinal beliefs of Islam. Malays as Muslims also practise the *rukun Islam* (pillars of Islam): pronouncing the *kalimah syahadah* (confession of faith), performing the five daily prayers including the weekly congregational prayer that takes place on Fridays, annual fasting and payment of *zakat* (tithes), and undertaking the hajj (the once-in-a-lifetime pilgrimage to Mecca). These beliefs and practices form the identity of the Malays and the basis of their value system.

Malay residents cleaning the riverbank at Taman Sembilang, Seberang Jaya. *Gotong-royong* (mutual cooperation) such as this reflect the importance placed by the Malays on neighbourliness and doing good for the community.

ABOVE: Malay women performing prayers at a mosque during Ramadhan.

ABOVE LEFT: Muslims reciting verses from the Qur'an.

The Malay corpus

Malay literature, both oral and written, includes a repertoire of phraseologies known as *bahasa kiasan* (general metaphors) which reflect the traditional Malay world-view and provide insights into Malay folk philosophy. The term *kiasan* is derived from the Islamic logical system of analogical reasoning (*qias*). The examples below indicate the richness and profundity of thought and observation contained within the corpus.

On the universe as a source of knowledge:
Air setitik dijadikan laut,
Tanah sekepal dijadikan gunung,
Alam terkembang dijadikan guru.

A drop of water constitutes an ocean,
A fistful of earth constitutes a mountain,
An unfolding universe serves as a teacher.

On the social order:
Adat bersendi syarak,
Syarak bersendi kitaballah.

Customary laws are based on religious laws,
Religious laws are embodied in the divine book.

On the supremacy of justice:
Biar mati anak,
Jangan mati adat (undang-undang).

Do not spare the children from the death sentence,
The law must not be violated.

On the laws of nature:
Adat sebenar adat, tak lapuk dek hujan,
taklekang dek panas.

The true law is natural law, undecayed by rain,
uncracked by heat.

On being economical:
Ingat sebelum kena, jimat sebelum habis.

Reflect before anything happens, save before
everything has gone.

On courage and truth:
Berani kerana benar, takut kerana salah

Courage from truth, fear of being wrong.

On trustworthiness:
Kerbau dipegang orang talinya,
Manusia dipegang orang cakapnya.

The buffalo is held by the cord,
Humans are held by their promises.

On kinship and social solidarity:
Picit peha kiri, terasa sakit peha kanan.

Pinch the left thigh, feel the pain in the right.

On social equality:
Duduk sama rendah,
berdiri sama tinggi

Sitting, we're equally low,
Standing, we're equally tall.

On the value of kindness:
Hutang emas boleh dibayar,
Hutang budi dibawa mati.

A debt of gold is payable,
A debt of kindness is for life.

On patriotism:
Hujan emas di negeri orang,
Hujan batu di negeri sendiri,
Baik juga, negeri sendiri.

A hail of gold in foreign country,
A hail of stone in one's country,
Better still is one's country.

On determination and being thorough:
Hendak seribu daya, tak hendak seribu dalih.

Where there is will, there is a way.

Malay traditions

Drawing on their heritage, history, Islamic teachings and values, the Malays in the various states in Peninsular Malaysia have developed a rich variety of cultural traditions in the form of customs, ceremonies, dwellings, handicraft, music and dance forms. These traditions exhibit variations from one region to another, reflecting the influence of immigrants from other parts of the Malay World as well as that of exogenous cultures.

1 Traditional house types

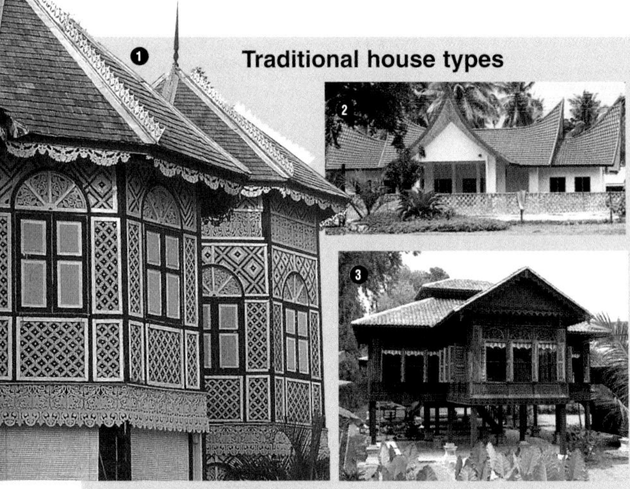

1. The Istana Kenangan in Kuala Kangsar, Perak, has walls made of woven plaited bamboo and wood.
2. Minangkabau-influenced roof in Negeri Sembilan.
3. Kedah timber house, featuring large windows with carved fanlights.
4. Bugis-style long ridge house found in Johor.
5. Pahang house, birthplace of former Prime Minister Tun Razak.
6. Melaka house with tiled steps.
7. Perak *rumah kutai* with bamboo walls and *atap* roof.
8. Traditional Selangor house.
9. Housewith Thai features, Kelantan.

The styles of the traditional Malay house, particularly the design of the roof, vary from state to state, but the basic form is similar. The design of the Malay house reflects the community's lifestyle, culture and social mores, while the materials used suit the local climatic and environmental conditions. Open, airy verandahs (*serambi*), large windows and open spaces beneath allow for ventilation and foster neighbourliness. The design also provides it flexibility so that extensions can be made when necessary.

Regional variations of the Malay house occur mainly as a result of various foreign architectural influences. The upturned long roof of houses in Negeri Sembilan represents the legacy of the 17th- and 18th-century Minangkabau diaspora from Sumatra. The Melaka house, too, is of the long-roofed type, but has a two-level roof, with the gabled ends of the roof (*tebar layar*) tilted and slightly open to allow air circulation. This house type is found along the west coast as far north as Langkawi island and in the coastal areas of Kedah and Perlis. The Melaka house is also distinguished by concrete stairs that are decorated with colourful ceramic tiles.

In some parts of Perak, the *kutai* long-roofed house stands as evidence of Bugis immigration from the Celebes (Sulawesi) in the 17th and 18th centuries. In upper Perak, where the Malay population is mainly of Patani origin, the pyramidal house, often termed the Perak design (*potong* Perak), is dominant. It is also found in Kedah, Perlis, Selangor and Pahang.

Houses in Kelantan and Terengganu feature both the long roof and the pyramidal roof. Most of the houses use the *singgora* tiles imported from southern Thailand. The old palaces in Terengganu have long roofs, while those in Kelantan have pyramidal roofs.

Cultural traditions and regional variations

The artistic and cultural traditions of the Malay communities in the various states of Peninsular Malaysia reflect their heterogeneity, including the acculturation of immigrant communities such as the Bugis, Acehnese, Banjarese, Javanese and Minangkabau, who have settled in the Peninsula and have integrated with the Malay community. Apart from differences in their ways of life, and the various regional dialects, each state's Malay community also demonstrates differences and variations in architecture, textiles and the decorative arts as well as the performing arts. It is thus inappropriate, except in very general terms, to speak of overall Malay artistic manifestations or cultural expressions.

Kris have been produced in the Malay Peninsula for centuries.

Textiles

Batik and *songket* are the most prominent of the Malay textiles, although in the past other silk textiles were also produced by the Malays.

The traditional method of making batik materials has been practised in various parts of the country for centuries, particularly in the east coast states of Kelantan and Terengganu. These methods have begun to give way to more modern methods, and the art has spread to several other parts of Peninsular Malaysia as well. Traditional designs based upon floral motifs predominate. A new phenomenon is the use of silk for batik printing.

Tekat embroidery uses gold thread in designs on velvet coverings for decorative items.

Songket (literally meaning 'digging under') is hand-woven silk decorated with gold or silver thread woven into a variety of geometric or floral patterns. *Songket* is used for formal attire, particularly by royalty, and is also popular as material for wedding costumes. On less formal occasions, *songket* may be used by men in the form of *kain sampin* (a short sarong) over the *baju* Melayu, while women traditionally wear a whole suit—*kain sarung, baju* and *selendang* (shawl)—of *songket* material. *Songket* has also found a place in Malay decorative art. Calligraphy is often woven in *songket*, while older *songket* pieces may be framed to serve as wall decorations.

Another form of textile embroidery is *tekat*, which is a form of embossed embroidery. Believed to have developed in northern India during the Mughal period, in Malaysia the art of *tekat* is mainly associated with Kuala Kangsar in Perak, although it is also found on a lesser scale in Pahang, Johor and Selangor. *Tekat* is used on decorative items and to cover material of wooden gift boxes to serve betel leaves and areca nut (*sirih pinang*).

Weaving songket on a loom.

Printing batik motifs.

Woodcarving is among the oldest craft traditions of the east coast states, and is featured in furniture, door panels and bird cages, as well as in various household and gift items such as betelnut boxes.

Woodcarving

Woodcarving is an integral part of Malay decorative culture, featured in palaces as well as in ordinary dwellings. Malay literary and historical writings such as the *Sejarah Melayu* and *Misa Melayu* indicate that this art form goes back at least to the Melaka Sultanate.

Exquisite examples are remnants of this art form survive in palaces and houses principally in Kelantan and Terengganu, some of them about 200 years old. Many of the master woodcarvers from the east coast states trace their ancestry to woodcarvers from the Patani region. Woodcarving is also used to decorate mosques and prayer houses, often incorporating Islamic calligraphy. Elaborate woodcarving representing figures from mythology or from the Indian epic *Ramayana* serve to decorate boats. Traditionally designs are drawn from nature, in particular flora and fauna; a feature shared with batik art as well as Wayang Kulit designs.

Male headgear styles and regional variations

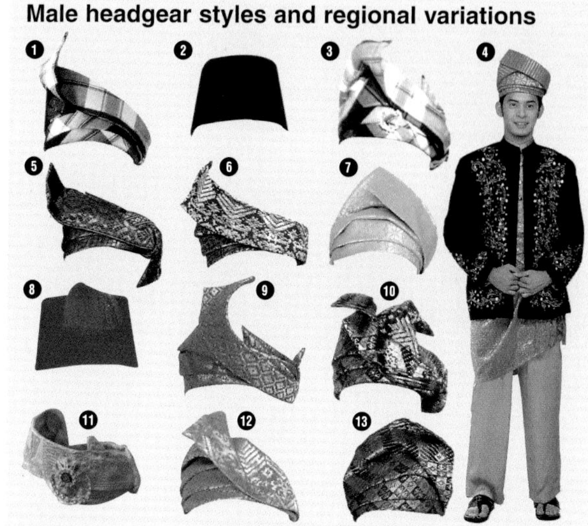

1. Federal Territory
2. Johor
3. Kelantan
4. Kedah
5. Melaka
6. Negeri Sembilan
7. Pahang
8. Penang
9. Perak
10. Perlis
11. Royal *tengkolok* (headdress) of the Yang di-Peruan Agong
12. Selangor
13. Terengganu

Traditional performing arts

Above: Bangsawan was Malaysia's first urban Malay theatre.

Left: A Wayang Kulit puppeteer manipulates his puppets behind a screen.

Right: A Tarik Selampit performer.

Of the wide of Malay performing arts, many of are localized in particular regions, while others, regional to begin with, have spread beyond their original locales. There are simple forms used for the telling of traditional stories, involving single performers, such as Tarik Selampit, Selampit and Awang Batil. Selampit, active in Perlis, is performed without the use of any musical instrument as accompaniment, while the Awang Batil performer uses a brass bowl (*batil*). Tarik Selampit, performed in Kelantan, makes use of a three-stringed *rebab*.

Early forms of ritual theatre amongst the Malays include Main Puteri and Bagih, both of which involve trance and serve as agents of healing through communication between a *bomoh* (shaman) in trance and invisible beings who are believed to be one of the principal causes of diseases.

Dance theatre includes Mak Yong, Mek Mulung and Menora, as well as several forms that have entered the country through Islamic, Thai and Javanese influences. Mak Yong, which is performed in Kelantan and Terengganu, is based on mythology. Performances involve about a dozen artists, accompanied by an ensemble of musicians playing the *rebab*, gongs and drums (*gendang*). Mek Mulung, in Kedah, is also based on mythology but, unlike Mak Yong, musical accompaniment comprises a variety of drums and wooden clappers as instruments. A third form of dance theatre, Menora, is active in the northern states of the Peninsula. This is originally Thai and essentially remains so, even though some local adaptation has taken place, allowing Malay participation principally as dancers and musicians.

The repertoire of Wayang Kulit (shadow play) is derived largely from the Indian epics the *Mahabharata* and the *Ramayana*. The most important shadow play form, Wayang Kulit Kelantan, also known as Wayang Kulit Siam, is performed in Kelantan and Terengganu. A Wayang Kulit Siam troupe consists of a single puppeteer (*dalang*) and eight or nine musicians. The Kedah-Perlis form, Wayang Kulit Gedek, uses a smaller ensemble, while in Johor, Wayang Kulit Purwa, which originally came from Java, uses a full gamelan orchestra.

Of the other performing arts, several imported dance forms such as Joget and Zapin have acquired national popularity, while others are performed in pockets in the country. These include the Middle East derived forms of Dikir Barat, Hamdolok and Dabus, and Javanese forms such as Kuda Kepang and Barongan.

Bangsawan, a form of musical theatre, developed in Penang towards the end of the 19th century as a result of influences from India. Gaining instant popularity in the country as well as in Singapore and Indonesia, it remained active until after World War II. Bangsawan was a multiracial theatre form, with troupe owners as well as performers coming from the Malay, Jawi-Peranakan (mixed Indian-Malay), Chinese, Baba, Eurasian and other communities.

Left: Dikir Barat, a modified and secularized form of *zikir* (religious chanting), is performed in Kelantan.

Below left: The hobbyhorse dance of Kuda Kepang, active in Johor, originated from Java, Indonesia.

Right and below: Mak Yong artists. It is usually women who enact the principal male roles.

Malay economy and society

Historical and social factors have shaped the economic conditions of Malay society. The traditional Malay social structure consisted of a hierarchy of authority, which located much of the wealth and power within the aristocratic group. For many centuries the Malays were mainly agriculturalists, engaged in subsistence farming and fishing. After Independence in 1957 the structure of the rural Malay economy changed with the opening up of land schemes and government intervention to correct the Malaysian social structure and to reduce poverty.

Fishermen on the east coast of the Peninsula repairing nets by their boat.

Rubber smallholder mangling rubber sheets, 1951.

The traditional economy: Subsistence and trading

The traditional economy among the Malay population consisted mainly of subsistence farming and coastal fishing. They planted rice and other crops, gathered jungle produce, and in some places also mined for tin or gold. Some were engaged as artisans for their craft skills, others did construction work. Farmers relocated at frequent intervals, after the fertility of the land they cultivated diminished. A network of limited exchange developed between the coastal and interior communities. Such product exchanges dominated the early economy. Jungle products, such as rattan, resins, sandalwood and timber, as well as rice, were traded for cloth, salted and dried fish, iron goods and ceramics, bought from coastal dwellers. In addition, a variety of valuable objects, including precious metals such as gold and tin, ceramics and cowrie shells were used as currency in exchange for goods. Gold coinage was introduced in the 15th century in the port cities.

Only a small number of commoners were involved in trading activities, and of these many were employed by the ruling aristocracy to carry out trading on their behalf. Some of the more prominent commoners were taken in by the aristocracy as officials with administrative functions and bestowed with titles (see 'Stratification in Malay society'). Others were involved in the defence of the state as warriors (*pahlawan*) and commanders (*panglima*).

Sharecropping and leasing

Within the subsistence farming system the Malays developed a pattern of sharecropping. Many villagers were involved in sharecropping through the *bagi-dua* (equal-portion) or *bagi-tiga* (third-portion) systems. The *bagi-dua* is a simple division of work and equal product distribution between an owner and a tenant. The *bagi-tiga* apportions the work and the harvest into three portions—two for the owner and the third for the tenant. If the tenant supplies most of the labour he may take two portions of the harvest. Other leasing systems between landowners and capital suppliers included *padi kunca*, *pajak* and *gadai*. Many villagers lost their land through these systems when they failed to repay the amounts borrowed.

A similar situation existed among fishermen. Fishing was not lucrative until the introduction of the drag net around the mid-20th century and, later, modern trawler fishing, which involved large capital outlay. Only those with the economic capacity were able to take advantage of these opportinuties. In the 1980s, fishermen were able to utilize special banking facilities created by the government as sources of capital. Even so, many ended up indebted as they were at the mercy of middlemen wholesalers.

From rural to market economy

The shift from rural to market economy among the Malays coincided with the boom in the rubber industry in the early 20th century, although this initially applied only to the middle class, such as the *penghulu* and traders. As the 20th century progressed, Malay farmers intensified their cultivation of rice with government assistance and irrigation, enabling them to develop rice farming and fishing into sources of cash. Some ventured into retail trade and the import of goods from inter-island trading. Further, government sponsorship and the deliberate planning of economic development gave the Malays opportunities in the modern corporate economy.

Women in the economy

Women traditionally shared work with men, both on the farm and in the coastal fishing areas. While the men were largely occupied with the more laborious tasks of ploughing the rice fields and harvesting, the women were engaged in domestic work as well as the tasks of rice transplanting and the sorting, cleaning and curing of fish for preservation or sale. The sharing of work allowed limited family labour resources to be utilized fully.

In the east coast states of Kelantan and Trengganu there has been a greater degree of work specialization, with women involved in specific economic activities. The retail of produce from the farm, fishing grounds and textile industry has been the work of women from as early as the 19th century. The printing of batik was traditionally done by men, but the weaving of the more complex and elaborate *songket* (gold thread cloth) was almost exclusively undertaken by women. Nowadays much of the batik printing and *songket* weaving is automated, and both male and female entrepreneurs engage in the business. Yet, the retailers in the principal markets of Kota Bharu, Kuala Terengganu and Kuantan are mainly women.

Women market traders, Kelantan, c. 1920.

Coastal women drying fish, 2005.

Malay economic activities through the years

The role of traders was fused with political functions. Some traders accumulated wealth to become influential men and were taken in by the Malay courts as lower officials of the state and bestowed the title of Orang Kaya (literally, men of wealth). Wealth and political power were intertwined such that state officials controlled economic activities either directly as investors or indirectly as recipients of commissions from other businessmen and traders. The officials extracted personal income from villagers or made use of *kerah* (forced labour). Provincial chiefs conducted their enterprises, such as tin mining, by using such labour. Traders from the Malay sultanates dominated the Malay waters in spite of Portuguese and Dutch attempts to impose monopolistic trade practices. However, Malay trading patterns were eventually undermined with the coming of Western open market competition and shipping technologies.

Malay houseboats on the Pahang River, c. 1906.

The British employed Malay state officials by paying them monthly salaries, thus making them, to an extent, professionals in their administrative jobs. At the same time, Malay society was depleted of potentially rich entrepreneurs from among the officials who traditionally operated mines and financed inter-island or international trades. As a result, other, more active traders, especially the Chinese and eventually Europeans, filled the vacuum left by the Malay officials.

After the establishment of the Straits Settlements in 1826, the immigration of Chinese and Indian workers was encouraged to enhance the colonial economy. The Malay population generally remained as farmers and fishermen in rural areas. Their role as farmers was enhanced by immigrants from the Malay Archipelago, in particular the Javanese, Bugis and Banjarese.

Lesser members of the Malay elite found employment in government posts such as

Irrigated rice farming formed the basis of Malay rural economy in the 19th century.

Malay fishing boats, early 1900s.

Native or Malay magistrates. Others worked as forest rangers, village school teachers, peons. Some even worked as road labourers.

The Malay College Kuala Kangsar was established in 1905 to provide English-medium education for the sons of the Malay aristocracy, to train them for employment in the Malay Administrative Service, created in 1910. Graduates of the college were posted as lower-ranking officials under British officers.

A few students, especially bright sons of sultans and future rulers, were selected to further their studies in the United Kingdom.

However, the lack of widely available English education deprived the Malays of opportunities in the medical, engineering, financial and most other professions in the early 20th century. These positions were filled by non-Malays with English education. It was only in agriculture that some Malays were trained, at the Serdang Agricultural College (which was later upgraded to a university). They went on to fill the supporting posts of agricultural assistants.

The colonial economy was centred upon large scale agricultural, mining and trading operations. However, the Malays were generally confined to the traditional small-scale rural economy, and their link with the modern sector was largely as workers in the rubber estates or as small-scale rubber planters working a few acres. They had to depend mainly on Chinese rubber dealers to sell their rubber, just as Malay rice planters and fishermen had to depend on Chinese *towkay* or patrons for cash or food supplies during fallow periods of rice cultivation and during the north-east monsoon when the seas were too rough for fishing.

In other areas of economic activity, especially in trade and business, Malay involvement was limited. They continued to trade and undertake small businesses only in the bazaar centres of the predominantly Malay

Latex-collecting station in Selangor, 1959.

A family on a Federal Land Development Authority (FELDA) settlement, 1960.

populated States. Chinese traders undertook larger scale businesses, even in remote Malay villages, aided by their system of networking in *kongsi* and trade guilds.

In later years, after Independence, attempts were made to modify the patron–client system through the setting up of government-sponsored marketing institutions for Malay rice farmers, fishermen and retail traders. In an effort to promote rural development and to improve the economic position of the rural Malays, the government initiated the integrated Federal Land Development Authority (FELDA) scheme in 1956.

Malay Armed Forces personnel, 1950s.

Significant changes in the Malay economy and Malay society occurred as a result of economic policies introduced in the 1970s. Direct government intervention aimed to correct what was perceived as an imbalanced economic system. Government ministries and institutions were created specifically to encourage Malays to be involved in businesses at various levels and in the professional arena too. Institutions and corporations such as MARA, PERNAS, the SEDCs, PETRONAS, HICOM and PNB were established to open opportunities for Malays in employment, business, capital accumulation and corporate participation.

Under the New Economic Policy, Malays were provided with greater educational opportunities in institutions of higher learning. Since the mid-1980s, a number of government departments and agencies have been privatized with a significant Malay share in their operations. At the same time, capitalization, new venture capital and training were intensified to create a Malay business community. These policy interventions have had some success, with greater participation by private Malay corporate groups in the sectors such as banking, finance, trading, construction and manufacturing as well as in the agriculture, automotive and petroleum industries.

Malay family and kinship patterns

Family and kinship linkages are significant in the life of the Malays, and reinforce their values, norms and cultural identity. This is evident at various levels despite urbanization. As Muslims, the Malays practise a high degree of affinal and consanguinal relationships, and are receptive to incoming members, regardless of their ethnic origin. Such linkages also play a vital role in binding communities.

A young boy kisses the hand of an elder in a gesture of respect.

Portrait of a Malay family, early 20th century.

Kinship patterns

Malay kinship in Malaysia generally follows a bilateral system. However, there are matrilineally organized groups residing in Negeri Sembilan and Melaka, which are historically related to the Minangkabau of Western Sumatra, and who have retained their distinctiveness.

Under the bilateral system, the family (*keluarga*) or household (*rumahtangga*) is an autonomous unit in which the husband-father is the head, and constitutes the core of the kinship universe. Outside the family unit is the larger *saudara-mara* circle of kinsmen, which is composed of families related bilaterally through blood and marriage. Closeness or remoteness is measured by the degree of cousinship. Unlike the matrilineal or patrilineal systems where membership is only recognized through either the father's or mother's side, the bilateral system categorizes kin members into several circles of kinsmen of increasing distance. The development of the family through marriage and the begetting of children systematically enlarges the circle into various family focal points at different generational levels.

Thus, the bilateral system produces a large number of members, and most of them would not recognise each other, especially if geographical mobility has occurred. Only occasional gatherings, such as ceremonies of birth, marriage and death, allow the members to gather and enquire after each other's situation. This ritual of *tanya khabar* (welfare enquiry) among elder relatives reveals the linkages and existence of relatives who reside in faraway places, and make them known to the younger members. Nevertheless, most members regard each other as relatives (*saudara-mara*), and beyond that is the circle of *suku-sakat* (remote relatives) with probable kinship relation (*bau bacang*) among them.

The principles of generation are significant features of the bilateral system whereby members of the senior generation are always accorded respect by the younger generation. This behaviour is extended to other members of the community of the same generational levels. The senior members would reciprocate by displaying moral concern for the younger members.

Adat perpatih: The matrilineal system

The Malays of Negeri Sembilan and northern Melaka maintain a matrilineal kinship system known as *adat perpatih* which arose following the migration of the Minangkabau of Sumatra from as early as the 15th century. The community is arranged in a series of kinship groups of increasing inclusiveness of which the family is the smallest. Descendants of the mother, and her sisters and daughters, count as members of a *suku* (clan), which is the most important kinship group in the *adat perpatih* system. Each local community consists of several *suku* groupings.

A bridal couple arriving for the *bersanding* (sitting in state) ceremony.

Under the *adat perpatih* system the *tua* or *kemulah* gives away the bride during the solemnization of a marriage.

Structure of the matrilineal system

1. The family: the basic unit of social organization, and is headed by a *tua* or *kemulah* (a senior male member related to the mother, most probably her elder brother).
2. The *perut* or *carak* (minor lineage): is made up of family units. Smaller groupings of *perut* are based on traceable matrilineal kinship relations from a common ancestress, and are headed by a *buapak*, an elderly male from the female line who is recognized as the most conversant in *adat* (customary) law.
3. The *suku* (clan): consists of kinship relations on the mother's side as well as members not traceable to a common ancestress, and is headed by a *lembaga*, a male member from among the heads of a specific line of descent or minor lineage within the *suku*.
4. The *luak*: a territorial grouping formed by *suku* living within a particular area. Headed by an elected *undang* or *penghulu*.

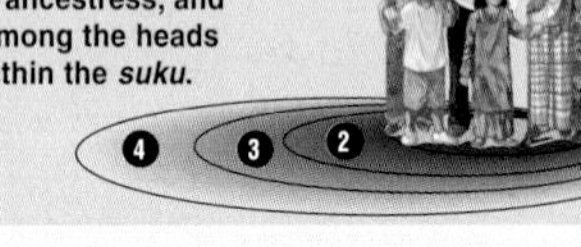

The basic difference between the matrilineal and the bilateral system is found at the level of the family or household unit. A husband who is from another suku and married into his wife's family in accordance with the principle of exogamy, would in certain circumstances—especially under Islamic law—be the lawful family guardian. However, under the matrilineal system he is an in-marrying person (*orang semenda*), and his parental power is only exercised during a bride-giving ceremony as a *wali* or legal guardian to the groom. Otherwise, he is an outsider. It is the *tua* or *kemulah*—a senior relative of the mother (and the father as *wali*)—who is responsible for the organization and conduct of affairs in the family. The father will help by providing financial, property, or manpower assistance for social events as they arise.

The matrilineal system therefore juxtaposes the mother's brother and the husband in apparent opposition. However, social decorum and etiquette do not allow such conflict to surface, and instead provide leeway for both parties to cooperate and complement each other.

Under the *adat perpatih* system, much of the pattern of life revolves around the women of the family. The mother normally owns the house, and newly-wed couples always live with the bride's natal family.

The family and the community

Traditionally, a village community consisted of various families linked by blood, marriage and, possibly, adoption. Thus, the village, as a larger and more encompassing grouping, would have the kinship network as the basis of its foundation. This was reflected by the pattern of organization in various domains of life, such as political, economic, social and religious.

Prominent families, especially the descendants of the original founder, were traditionally elected as village heads. In modern times, however, village heads are usually persons with a certain level of formal qualification, and traditional kinship affiliation does not play a role. Economic activities in the village are traditionally agriculture such as rice cultivation, and small boat fishing for domestic consumption. Land owned by villagers was divided into small plots, which in most cases only provided housing sites for family members. The local consolidation of families within related households allowed the exercise of family and social obligations among the group. This familial reciprocity and the support among family members have led to the maintenance of networks among the Malays. Those who leave the village eventually return to pay respect to the elders. It is not the nostalgia of rural life that drives a family to return to the village but filial obligation to elder members that calls them back home (*balik kampung*).

Marriage in the *kampung* is far from a private family affair; it is a gathering of relatives as well as villagers. Such occasions create solidarity and reaffirm common values among the community. Members of the village work together to prepare for the accompanying feast (*kenduri*), and help with other aspects of the wedding.

1. **The men usually undertake the cooking of the food for the *kenduri*.**
2. **The womenfolk prepare the ingredients required for the dishes.**
3. **Guests are served traditional Malay dishes such as *nasi minyak* (buttered rice).**
4. **Silat (a Malay martial art) performances may be held to welcome the groom's party.**
5. **The bride's parents welcome guests to the reception.**

A rural wedding procession in Terengganu in the 1960s, led by *kompang* drummers and followed by bearers of gifts.

Inheritance and division of property

The customary transmission of property between generations follows the dictate of equal division among children irrespective of sex. However, the intervention of the Islamic *faraid* system has given greater emphasis to the male children, who receive three-quarters of the property value; the rest goes to the female children. The rationale behind this is that while male members would have to take care of all the family members, the female members would receive the protection of their husbands and male relatives. Another factor affecting the allocation of property is the emotional attachment between parents and children. It is customary that a child who lives with and looks after the parents through their old age would inherit the parental personal property. This would be normally the last female child in the family.

Continuity and change

While the basic bilateral and matrilineal principles of the Malay system of kinship and families remain intact, much of family group formation and interpersonal interactions have changed under the pressure of changing social, religious and economic circumstances. Urban migration has affected customary practices, and while the network of familial relations and kinship remains significant in gathering members for any occasion, economic circumstance has made friendship and other networks as significant as that of familial and kin members. Intermarriage between members of the bilateral and matrilineal systems is common, causing both systems to accommodate each other in accordance with *adat* law or Islamic syariah law.

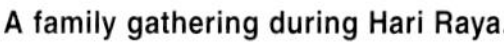

A family gathering during Hari Raya.

The nuclear family

Most Malay families are of the nuclear type, comprising the parents and their unmarried children, and sometimes a grandparent. The children usually move out into their own household units while maintaining close links with their parents. The common practice is for married children to live for a short period within the parental household until they are economically able to build another dwelling, either within the compound of the parental land or elsewhere within the village. Sometimes elderly parents take in their divorced children. Familial and kinship obligations support such family arrangements, which remain a significant feature within Malay society. Relations within a family are stable and caring. Parents normally do not disown children for their misdeeds or misfortunes. Unmarried children very often remain with their parents and look after them in their old age. Family assistance and welfare continue to be an obligation, reinforced by filial piety.

Stratification in Malay society

From the 15th-century Melaka sultanate until the late 19th century there were two distinct groups in traditional Malay society: an upper stratum of males descended from a member of the ruling group who exercised authority at the central and district levels of the state, including some aspects of religion; and the subjects (rakyat). *In modern times, social mobility and bureaucratic government have brought significant changes.*

Yang di-Pertuan Agong Tuanku Syed Sirajuddin Syed Putra Jamalullail and Raja Permaisuri Agong Tuanku Fauziah Tengku Abdul Rashid arriving at Parliament House for the opening session of Parliament, 2005.

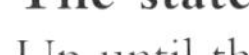

The state

Up until the late 19th century the Peninsular states each had a distinctive structure of authority, but all purported to be heirs to the pattern of monarchy (*kerajaan*) derived from the 15th-century sultanate of Melaka. Each Malay Ruler, vested with supernatural majesty (*daulat*), embodied the unity of the state (*negeri*), but delegated or shared his government with selected officers of state and district chiefs. Aristocrat and peasant alike owed loyalty to the ruler.

A female member of the ruling group with her attendants, late 19th century.

The ruling group

There were three main elements of the ruling group. The first were the *anak raja*, members of the royal dynasty descended, however remotely, from a ruler. Leading aristocratic families by custom provided the holders of high offices of state and district chieftainships. Other individuals, often of mixed Arab-Malay descent, were treated as quasi-royal by reason of putative descent from Prophet Muhammad. Members of the ruling group had an honorific prefix to their names—Raja or Tengku for royals, Dato' or Wan for the non-royal element, and Syed for the third. A privileged minority actually held royal or other office (*pangkat*) with an appropriate title (*gelaran*)—Bendahara, Laksamana, Menteri Laut and so on, conferred by the ruler in an elaborate court ceremony.

Thus in Perak, succession to the throne was indicated by holding the office of Raja Muda, with the Raja Bendahara moving up to the former's office when it fell vacant. Below the ruler, the four major chiefs of Perak, who stood at the top of the non-royal aristocracy, had eight, 16 and even 32 chiefs below them.

In states such as Selangor and Negeri Sembilan, Bugis and Minangkabau cultural traditions created a different pattern of graded status. All men of aristocratic birth, if they had the means, demonstrated their status by appearing in public attended by 40 or more followers. However, intrigue and power struggles for the limited number of traditional offices destabilized the entire political system.

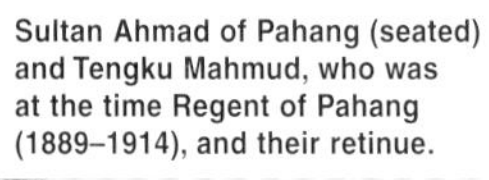

Sultan Ahmad of Pahang (seated) and Tengku Mahmud, who was at the time Regent of Pahang (1889–1914), and their retinue.

The rakyat

All Malays not of the upper stratum, including immigrants from other states and from Sumatra, were subjects (*rakyat*). Malays in debt-bondage (*orang berhutang*) were nonetheless free in contrast to slaves (*hamba*), who were typically aborigines, imported Africans, and non-Muslim Sumatrans, (Europeans, however, regarded both as slavery). There was a gradation of status within each local community, by which the village headmen, often drawn from a long-settled family, elders and mosque officials were the leaders, and prosperous families had higher standing than the poor and the landless. Foreign Malays (*orang dagang*) often lived apart under their own headman and were only gradually assimilated into the settled population, still cherishing their distinctive traditions.

Social relationships

Every 'subject' was expected to show respect to the upper stratum of society, particularly in the type of language employed. If, for example, a peasant addressed a non-royal aristocrat he referred to himself as *hamba dato'* (*hamba* meaning 'slave') and prayed for pardon for thus troubling his superior.

Status was demonstrated by a right to command the services of others and was institutionalized in two ways. A man in authority, typically a district chief or a kinsman acting on his behalf, might call on villagers for unpaid work, i.e. corvée (*kerah*), as fighting men, labourers for road construction or river clearance, or for personal service as attendants, domestic servants, field workers or boatmen. While *kerah* derived from authority, debt-bondage was nominally an economic relationship of creditor and debtor It existed within the village community, as well as between higher and lower social grades. It was hereditary on both sides, and the debtor (*orang berhutang*) might give services to a superior on the basis of an ancient and half-forgotten debt of an earlier generation. Debt-bondage was often of little economic benefit to the recipient, but it gave him command of a following. Most of the complaints came from young women conscripted into domestic service and even prostitution, and from the coterie of

Village headmen (*penghulu*) and their followers, late 19th century.

young men (*budak raja*) who followed men of power to make a career in their service.

In return for his right to command others, the superior had obligations, not always observed, to protect his people and to provide a bondsman with food and lodging.

Islam

Conversion to Islam brought a more egalitarian model of society than the indigenous system. Nonetheless, the indigenous hierarchy was preserved by absorbing religious functions. The Malay Rulers were accepted as Allah's deputy on earth. Advised by learned men (*ulama*), they decided matters of doctrine and appointed *syariah* judges. At district level, the chiefs, or someone authorized by them, collected and distributed religious alms (*zakat* and *fitrah*).

Pilgrimage to Mecca enhanced the status of a member of both upper and lower social groups and entitled a male to the title of Haji and a female to the title of Hajjah. A man who acquired expertise in Islamic matters, either by study in the course of an extended pilgrimage, or by attendance at a renowned school (*madrasah*) in the Peninsula earned respect for his learning; the mosque officials often had this qualification.

Modern developments

After the 1874 Pangkor Treaty, traditional institutions such as *kerah* and debt-bondage were abolished and the courts treated all persons alike regardless of class. Education opened the way to the rise of a Malay bourgeoisie that treated hereditary aristocrats with respect but, as civil servants, came to exercise most of the aristocrats' former powers. The basis of Malay social structure is now socioeconomic rather than hereditary. Bureaucracy has replaced traditional authority, not least vis-à-vis religion, and the Malay rulers have with some reluctance become constitutional monarchs.

Social mobility

Everyone in Malay society was born with an ascribed status, were he royalty or debt-bondsman or simply a peasant. It was very unusual, but possible nonetheless, for a subject to rise to the upper level. The turbulent mid-19th century situation in some states created such opportunities. Thus, during the Pahang civil war (1857–63), the fighting captain (*imam perang*) known as Tok Gajah earned royal favour and was rewarded with authority on a level with the four major chiefs of the state, and given charge of the important Pulau Tawar district of central Pahang. Yet his father had been a Sumatran immigrant who had married a Pahang woman.

In Perak, Che Karim was a Sumatran immigrant who began his career as clerk to the Menteri Laut. During the power struggle in Perak in the early 1870s, Karim persuaded Sultan Abdullah to give him charge of the remote Ulu Selama district. Here for a time he prospered from tin mining and the new colonial regime appointed him to its state council in 1877. However, he was uncomfortable with the greatness conferred upon him and usually absented himself from council meetings. These examples show that patronage by an established figure was often key to upward mobility. The parvenus were not popular among the established upper rank. On the other hand, an aristocrat who fell into poverty did not lose his status. There were, for example, recognized *anak raja* working in road construction gangs in Selangor in the 1890s.

An aristocrat might also enhance his position by marrying a wife whose family had higher standing than his own, especially if he made himself useful to them. Sultan Idris of Perak (r. 1887–1916) was surrounded by ambitious sons-in-law as well as sons. However, a family of superior status would not permit any of its women to bring discredit on them by marrying a husband of the subject group.

Traditional and modern titles

The present modern democratic state bestows honours and recognition to reward loyal, meritorious and gallant conduct by its subjects. The Yang di-Pertuan Agong and the State Rulers annually, on their birthdays, bestow honours and decorations on every social stratum and group in Malaysia to commemorate their contributions to society.

While the modern social orders are recent creations adapted by the Federal and State Rulers and are based on British practices, they are, in fact, a continuation of traditional Malay practices in place since the Melaka Sultanate. Many of the titles for the decorations created after Independence were based on titles that had existed during the ascendancy of the Malay sultanates.

The highest title, 'Tun', was in use among the four very senior viziers (*Menteri Empat*) in Melaka during the 15th century and in most other Malay sultanates in the region. The Bendahara, being Prime Minister of old, always carried the title 'Tun', as did other senior viziers such as the Temenggung, Bendahari and Laksamana or Shahbandar. Designated officials within the senior ranks would carry honorific titles such as Tun Seri Lanang, who later became Bendahara of Johor.

Resplendent in ceremonial dress (from left): Dato' Kamalul Ariffin Hj. Abdul Rahim, Dato' Shah Bodin, Major General (retired) Dato' Seri Abdul Manap Ibrahim, Tan Sri Ahmad Sarji Abdul Hamid, Lieutenant General Dato' Seri Mohd Yunus Mohd Tasi and Commodor Dato' Seri Ahmad Ramli Hj. Mohd Nor.

Modern needs have created numerous decorations of various grades as well for gallantry and bravery among the personnel of the armed forces and police. Among classes of decorations, distinction is made between royal recipients, the most senior officials and the ordinary rank. Royal recipients are decorated with the *Darjah Kerabat* (family order), senior recipients are decorated with a *Bintang* (star) and designated as Tun, Tan Sri, Dato' Sri—and in some cases, Dato' Sri Panglima (Sabah), Dato' Sri DiRaja (Perak) and Dato' Sri Utama (Negeri Sembilan)—and Dato', and ordinary members are decorated with a *Pingat* (medallion) and designated as *Kesateria* or *Pahlawan* (warrior), *Johan* (champion) and *Ahli* (member) for meritorious conduct and services. Recipients of the gallantry medallion are designated as *Pahlawan Gagah Perkasa* and *Pingat Gagah Berani*.

Since the 1980s, decorations bestowed in the name of each State Ruler have added to the number and complexity of decorations available. Nevertheless, these developments represent the growing recognition that the Rulers are the supreme heads of the states, symbolizing the unity and inclusion of a diverse population.

Malay festivals and celebrations

Islamic festivals predominate in the Malay calendar; the most important are Hari Raya Aidilfitri and Hari Raya Haji. A number of celebrations and observances related to traditional Malay activities pre-date the arrival of Islam, but these have declined as a result of increasing religious disapproval. Rites of passage that mark important stages in a person's life are celebrated according to Islamic tradition and are often accompanied by elaborate ceremonies.

The betel leaf tree (*pokok sirih*) is a traditional offering used in Malay weddings, and forms part of the wedding gifts (*hantaran*).

Celebrations of pre-Islamic times

The singular influence on Malay festivals is Islam. Prior to the Islamization of the Malays, festivals and ceremonies were influenced by Hinduism and animism. Islam has increasingly predominated over the years, and, as a result, cultural facets of the pre-Islamic past are disappearing.

Before the arrival of the Europeans, Malay society was feudal and largely agrarian, including large sea-faring communities. Its festivals were synchronized with the cycles of agriculture and the seasons, with celebrations marking harvests and fishing expeditions. These rituals were later eclipsed by Islam, although some aspects continue as *adat* (custom).

A family gathers to celebrate Hari Raya. It is customary to ask for forgiveness from elders and other family members with the salutation *maaf zahir batin*.

Islamic festivals

As in the rest of the Muslim world, the celebration of the two main festivals in the Islamic calendar, Hari Raya Aidilfitri (which marks the end of the fasting month of Ramadhan) and Hari Raya Haji (literally 'Haji Day', also known as Aidiladha), are integral parts of Malay life.

Maulud Nabi, the birthday of the Prophet Muhammad, is also celebrated. This is an exclusively religious occasion, with the emphasis being on the chanting of *marhaban* (songs in praise of the Prophet) and *berzanji* (compositions relating the Prophet's life story). The devout take part in a solemn, incantatory march through villages, towns and cities which end at mosques where sermons are held. Other significant dates in the Prophet's life, such as Israq Mikraj, the day of his ascension to heaven, and Maal Hijrah, marking the Hijrah (Prophet's emigration) from Mecca to Madina, are also commemorated.

Muharram, the first month of the Muslim calendar, is considered sacred and perhaps second only to Ramadhan in the conduct of obeisance.

Hari Raya Haji

Hari Raya Haji (Aidiladha, or the Festival of Sacrifice) closes the season of the hajj, the performance of which is the fifth pillar of Islam. On the tenth day of Zulhijjah, the last month of the Muslim calendar, Muslims worldwide join with the pilgrims congregated in the field of Arafah near Mecca to rejoice in this feast of commitment, obedience and self-sacrifice to God.

Malays celebrate Hari Raya Haji in the same way as they do Hari Raya Aidilfitri. Most attend morning prayers at the mosque, and then socialize, visiting each other's homes and partaking in festive meals (*kenduri*). In addition, those who can afford to do so offer livestock, usually sheep or cattle, for ritual slaughter as a symbol of Ibrahim's (Abraham's) willingness to sacrifice his son Ismail (Ishmael). The meat derived from this is distributed for consumption to family and friends, as well as to the poor and needy.

Hari Raya Aidilfitri

Hari Raya Aidilfitri marks the completion of *bulan puasa* (the holy fasting month of Ramadhan), the observance of which is the third of the five pillars of Islam. *Bulan puasa* is a time of piety and abnegation, with the breaking of the dawn-to-dusk fast each day culminating in the consumption of special foods, such as dates, sweets and other delicacies, often in family, parish and community gatherings. Ramadhan is also a month of charity and the fulfilment of dues, which are effected by the giving of alms and payment of the two obligatory tithes in Islam, *zakat* and *fitrah*.

On the last seven nights of Ramadhan, Malay households light oil lamps to glorify the mystery of the Lailatulkadar, the visitation of the archangel Jibril (Gabriel) who revealed the Qur'an to Prophet Muhammad. For the devout, these nights mark a period of concentrated prayer and asceticism. The young, meanwhile, traditionally set off fireworks from a carbide cannon called *meriam buluh*, although this practice has been curbed.

ABOVE RIGHT: Shopping for the festive season.

FAR RIGHT: Children in a kampong receiving *duit raya* (festive money).

RIGHT: Preparing *bubur lambak* (a porridge of rice and vegetables with fish, prawns and, sometimes, beef) during Ramadhan.

ABOVE: Porridge cooked with foodstuffs donated by the community is served in a communal feast during Asyura.

LEFT: *Khatam Qur'an* (conclusion ceremony) at Masjid Negara, Kuala Lumpur, to celebrate a child having finished learning to read the whole of the Qur'an.

The 10th day of Muharram (Hari Asyura) is a blessed day for voluntary fasting. It is celebrated with assemblies, *ceramah* (lectures) and prayer. In many parts of the country, Asyura is centred around the convivial cooking of *bubur* Asyura, a broth said to hark back to the Battle of Karbala in the 6th century CE, in which the starving troops of the Prophet's grandson, Imam Hussein, put all they could find into a pot to sustain themselves before making their last, doomed stand. Shia Muslims focus on the mourning of this martyrdom, but in Malaysia—where the form of Islam practised is Sunni—the cooking of the broth is the focus of a happier affair. In Penang, Asyura festivities include all-male choric performances (Borea).

In addition to the festivals in the Muslim calendar, two states in the Peninsula, Johor and Pahang, observe Hari Hol in remembrance of departed members of their respective royal families. Designated as a public holiday in both states (around August in Johor and May in Pahang), the occasion is one of solemn celebration marked by prayers (*tahlil*) held in mosques.

Celebrating Hari Raya

Hari Raya Aidilfitri begins with the official sighting of the new moon of Syawal (the tenth month in the Muslim calendar). Before dawn the following day, families perform their ablutions, dress in their finest clothes and gather at the mosque for thanksgiving prayers. They ask for forgiveness, first from their elders, and then from other family members and friends. During the day, the departed too, are honoured with visits to the cemetery. People call on one another and open their doors to all visitors in the 'open house' tradition. Here, family and community ties are reaffirmed amid offerings of *ketupat*, *rendang*, *kuih* and other festive delicacies.

These practices are packed into the first three days of Syawal, although festivities continue for the whole month. However, Malays in the north and east coast of the Peninsula celebrate only the first and second days, and many resume fasting from the third day for six days. According to Islamic teachings, fasting for six days in

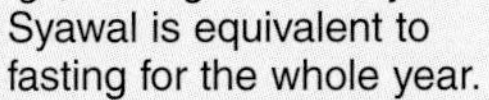

Children lighting oil lamps in the week before to Hari Raya.

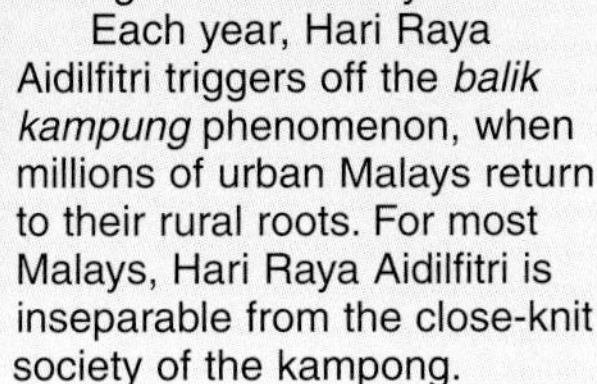

Syawal is equivalent to fasting for the whole year.

Each year, Hari Raya Aidilfitri triggers off the *balik kampung* phenomenon, when millions of urban Malays return to their rural roots. For most Malays, Hari Raya Aidilfitri is inseparable from the close-knit society of the kampong.

Rites of passage

Birth

The Malays observe prenatal and birth rituals. During the seventh month of pregnancy, a woman carrying her first child goes through the *melenggang perut* (rolling of the abdomen) ceremony. A midwife examines the woman and the foetal position by rolling a coconut on her abdomen in a simple, ceremony attended by women relatives. With greater accessibility to modern medical facilities, this ritual has become less common.

Seven days after birth, the *bercukur jambul* (head shaving) rite is performed, in which a lock of the baby's hair is cut by a midwife or imam, to the accompaniment of prayers and a feast. A comparable ceremony for girls is the *bertindik telinga* (ear-piercing).

FAR LEFT: A midwife cuts a lock of hair from an infant's head.

LEFT: Gifts of *bunga telur* (boiled eggs attached to golden-leafed stems) are presented during a child's head-shaving ceremony.

Adolescence

Of the rites of passage to adulthood, none is more significant for the Malay male than the circumcision (*berkhatan*) ceremony, traditionally performed when he reaches puberty between the ages of eight and 12. Although in most cases circumcision has been reduced to a simple medical procedure, group circumcisions are still conducted.

If a boy has completed instruction in the 30 chapters of the Qur'an, the *khatam Qur'an* ceremony is first carried out, in which he reads from the holy book and pays obeisance to his teacher and elders. The actual circumcision is performed, after the boy takes a thorough bath, by a *mudin* (village medicine man). Circumcision of girls is rare.

Marriage

Malay marriages are traditionally initiated by the parents of a groom-to-be, although today it is usually the son who makes the choice of bride. A formal proposal (*meminang*) is delivered by a deputation of older women family members to the bride-to-be's parents, who customarily make their acceptance through a delegation which negotiates and settles the terms of the marriage, such as the dowry (*mas kahwin*) and expenses. As a gesture of good faith, the groom-to-be sends a token of betrothal (*hantaran*), usually a ring, sweets, clothes and, now, a copy of the Qur'an. The more important *menghantar belanja dan akad* (sending of dowry and solemnization of marriage) follows, in which money and other gifts are presented to sanctifying the marriage according to the requirements of Islam.

Bridal couple seated upon a lavishly decorated dais (*pelamin*) in the *bersanding*, the culmination of the wedding.

The wedding celebrations, marked by Hindu and Middle Eastern influences, take place mostly at the home of the bride and begin with the *berhinai* or henna-staining ceremony. This involves elaborate cosmetic preparations for the bride (*berandam*), which culminate in the staining of her fingers, palms and the soles of her feet with henna. At the *berinai besar* (public henna-staining), first the groom and then the bride are seated on a lavishly decorated bridal dais (*pelamin*), whereupon invited guests take turns to sprinkle yellow rice and scented water on each of them, followed by a daub of henna on their palms.

Blessing (*merenjis*) the newly-weds with a sprinkling of rose water (*air mawar*).

The grandest of the wedding ceremonies is the *bersanding*, in which the bride and groom in full wedding attire are regally displayed upon a dais (*pelamin*), in line with the dictum *raja sehari* (king and queen for a day). The groom arrives in a procession of groomsmen, family members and guests. A troupe playing *rebana* or *kompang* drums leads, singing praises and religious incantations (*salawat*). A *silat* (martial arts) performance is sometimes given to mark the arrival of the groom's party. On the bride's first visit to the groom's family home, the *bersanding* ceremony is repeated, and music and dance are performed in her honour. The newly-weds customarily stay at the bride's home, for a few months. Feasts (*kenduri*) accompany each stage of the marriage, to which the entire village is invited. Many wedding feasts are now held in hotels.

Malay culinary traditions

An abundance of local ingredients gave rise to a distinctive traditional Malay cuisine, with rice as the staple food. These ingredients were subsequently augmented with the arrival of foreign influences, and a wide range of local variants developed. Although elements of Indian, Chinese, Indonesian, Thai and Arab cuisine have been incorporated into Malay food, it still retains its distinct identity, and plays an important role in Malay culture.

An array of traditional Malay dishes and ingredients.

Traditional Malay food

The Malay kampong way of life is traditionally one of agricultural subsistence; kampong compounds readily accommodate chickens and other small livestock, while fish is sourced from the sea and rivers nearby, rice is obtained from surrounding *padi* fields, and vegetables are cultivated in well-drained places. The traditional Malay diet reflects such a lifestyle. Rice is the staple food of the Malays, and everyday meals are essentially built around it. Fish is very popular in Malay cooking, as are other types of seafood such as prawns, shellfish and squid, followed by beef, mutton and chicken. Pork is never present in Malay cuisine as Muslim religious convictions prohibit the eating of pork.

Satay consists of chunks of marinated beef or chicken on skewers, grilled over an open fire. It is served with *ketupat* (rice cooked in coconut leaves), slices of cucumber and onion, and a spicy peanut sauce.

Traditionally experts at gleaning edible plants from the jungle, the Malays have always included *ulam* (wild roots, herbs and tree leaves) in their diet. Green leafy varieties are collectively known as *daun kayu*, ferns as *pucuk paku* and fungi as *kulat*. *Ulam* are eaten raw, therefore retaining their wealth of minerals and vitamins.

Apart from being a good source of fibre, leafy variants such as the *daun kaduk* (*Piper sarmentosum*) are high in calcium, while *pegaga* (*Centella asiatica*) is recognized by the World Health Organization as a herb that can stimulate brain activity in children, promote blood circulation and refine skin texture. *Jering* (*Pithecellobium jiringa*) seeds are extolled by diabetics and those with hypertension: they serve as a diuretic due to their high alkaloid content. Perhaps the most famous root is *tongkat ali* (*Eurycoma longifolia*) which some believe to increase sexual libido and vitality. *Tongkat ali* extract is available in powdered form and is added to a plethora of food and drinks including coffee. It is also packaged in tablet form. The consumption of *ulam*, until recently exclusive to the Malays, has become popular with other ethnic groups due to its nutritional value.

A variety of local vegetables feature in Malay meals, including *kangkong* (water spinach), *pucuk ubi kayu* (tapioca leaves) and *petai* (stink beans). Stir-fried *kangkong belacan* is a popular favourite while *ubi kayu* leaves are usually blanched and served with *sambal*

Dry spices
1. Star anise
2. Cardamom
3. Clove
4. Cumin
5. Dried shrimp paste
6. Cashewnuts
7. Nutmeg
8. Coriander seeds
9. Fennel
10. Cinnamon sticks
11. Black peppercorns
12. Candlenuts
13. Dried chillies

Wet seasoning
14. Shallots
15. Coconut
16. Bird chillies
17. Small sour starfruit
18. Red chillies
19. Wild ginger flower
20. Lemongrass
21. Polygonum leaves
22. Turmeric leaves
23. Mint leaves
24. Galingale
25. Limes
26. Onions
27. Curry leaves
28. Turmeric root
29. Ginger

Seasoning and spices

Seasoning used in Malay cooking can be divided into 'wet' and 'dry' spices. Fresh seasoning and dried spices are normally pounded in a *batu lesong* (mortar and pestle) to produce a fine paste (*rempah*) and cooked in oil. To boost flavours in cooking (as well as to increase shelf life), spices are often toasted and ground. Sautéing a spice in a little oil also brings out its flavour by intensifying it; the oil then becomes infused with the flavour and permeates the finished dish.

Cooking methods

Dishes can be cooked in numerous ways, be it *gulai* (a curry-like dish), *masak assam pedas* (spicy hot and sour), *goreng bercili* (fried with chillies), and of course the mandatory *sambal belacan*. Other piquant condiments that regularly feature in Malay food include *sambal tempoyak* (sambal with fermented durian and vegetables), and *budu* (fermented fish sauce) and *cencaluk* (fermented shrimp sauce). These accompaniments are also used as dips for *ulam*. Fried dishes are cooked in a *kuali* (a thicker variation of the wok). The bamboo steamer (*kukusan*) is used for steaming, while curries are customarily simmered for hours in clay pots (*belanga*).

belacan. Petai, which grow in large pods, produce an unpleasant odour. *Petai* are often added to dishes of prawns or anchovies cooked with sambal, or are eaten raw with *sambal belacan*. Any resultant bad breath can be reduced by eating cucumber.

Distinctive features

Bland is not a word that is associated with Malay cuisine. It is distinguished by signature ingredients including coconut milk, chillies and *belacan* (a paste of fermented and salted shrimps pressed into cakes). The combination of these lends the hot and spicy flavour that the Malay palate demands.

Belacan is a key ingredient of Malay food.

The pungent *belacan* is used to make *sambal belacan*, a potent concoction of *belacan*, chillies and lime juice that is a favourite accompaniment to meals or as flavouring for dishes. *Belacan* is the flavour enhancer that gives many of the Malay dishes that extra oomph.

Coconut milk is the basis of Malay *lemak* (creamy richness) dishes, whilst chillies are present in nearly all Malay dishes for added spiciness, especially in the form of *sambal* (traditional thick and hot chilli paste or sauce). *Assam jawa* (tamarind paste) is another crucial addition to many Malay dishes, especially to fish and seafood, adding a sour or tangy taste.

Traditional Malay cakes and desserts

Malay *kuih* (cakes or pastries) differ from their Western counterparts in that they may be savoury as well as sweet, and may be fried or steamed. *Kuih* can be eaten at breakfast or in-between meals. Flour from starchy grains and roots such as glutinous rice, sweet potato, *ubi kayu* (tapioca) or sago palm is usually used instead of wheat flour. The pandanus (screwpine) leaf is used as a flavouring similar to the way vanilla is used in the West, and additionally gives food an appetizing green colour. *Gula melaka* (palm sugar) is used as a sweetener, with coconut milk providing the fat for pastry dough or as a creamy sauce.

Favourite desserts include various types of sweet *bubur* (a pudding of thin, porridge-like consistency), *pengat pisang* (banana stewed in coconut milk with palm sugar and sago), *cucur badak* (fried sweet potato cakes with a spicy shrimp and coconut filling), *bengkang ubi* (steamed tapioca cakes), colourful red and white *kuih lapis* (layered cake), *seri muka* (sweet green pandan custard on a layer of glutinous rice) and *sago gula melaka* (sago pudding served with chilled coconut milk and palm sugar syrup).

ABOVE: A selection of traditional Malay cakes and sweetmeats.

RIGHT: Deep-fried salted crisps (*kerepek*) made from rice, tapioca and banana.

Many *kuih* are wrapped in banana leaves to complete the cooking process, lending an extra fragrance. Great skill is used in wrapping the *kuih* into cone-shaped or rectangular packages. Skewers made from the central rib of the coconut palm hold the parcels in shape and prevent them from opening during steaming or grilling. *Kuih koci* is a cone-shaped cake made from glutinous rice flour with a coconut and palm sugar filling wrapped in banana leaf. *Pulut panggang* (grilled glutinous rice) is a rectangular savoury pastry made of glutinous rice with spicy shrimp and grated coconut filling, wrapped in banana leaf and grilled over an open fire, similar to the manner in which *satay* is cooked.

Kuih bahulu are small baked cupcakes with a distinctive flower shape. They are sponge cake made from a mixture of flour, eggs, sugar and vanilla extract which is poured into brass moulds and baked in a Dutch oven, with the heat of glowing charcoal above and under the pot.

Malays are also fond of deep-fried and slightly salted local chips in the form of *kerepek* (crisps) made from rice (*rempeyek* or rice flour with peanuts), banana (*kerepek pisang*), onions (*kerepek bawang*) and tapioca (*kerepek ubi*, and *kuih cakar ayam* or literally 'chicken scratches' made of deep fried grated tapioca and palm sugar).

Dodol is a very sticky pudding made from rice, palm sugar, coconut and flavoured with pandanus leaves. It is cooked in a deep skillet and requires constant stirring for over nine hours until a brown shiny taffeta-like mass is formed. *Dodol* is also traditionally used as one of the many gifts (*hantaran*) exchanged between the bride and groom at Malay weddings. *Badak berendam* (literally translated to 'soaking hippos') are balls of glutinous flour with a palm sugar and grated coconut filling covered with coconut milk sauce.

LEFT: Preparing *dodol* for Hari Raya the *gotong-royong* (mutual cooperation) way. After hours of stirring, the light brown slurry turns into a thick, dark sticky sweetmeat.

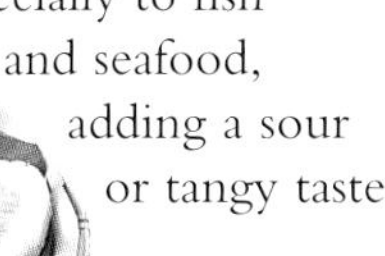

Nasi lemak, is popular among Malaysians of all ethnic groups.

Favourite Malay dishes

A typical Malay meal is exemplified by *nasi padang* or *nasi campur*, consisting of white rice with a selection of meat or fish curries and vegetables. Another Malaysian favourite, often referred to as the national food, is *nasi lemak*—rice cooked with coconut milk and pandanus (screwpine) leaves that give it a fragrant smell, served with fried anchovies, toasted peanuts, *sambal* and *sambal* prawns or fish. Normally eaten for breakfast in economically packed servings wrapped in banana leaf and newspaper, its popularity among Malaysians has made it available at anytime of the day. In addition, larger servings of *nasi lemak* come with dishes such as *sambal* squid, fried egg, fried fish, vegetables, and fried or curried chicken.

Nasi tomato (tomato flavoured rice) is another Malay favourite with regional variations. It is served with *ayam masak merah* (chicken cooked in a spicy tomato sauce) and pickled vegetables. It is also served at *kenduri* (thanksgiving feasts) held in conjunction with special occasions such as weddings or the birth of a child. Satay (pieces of beef, mutton or chicken meat pre-marinated in spices and grilled over charcoal on wooden skewers, not unlike kebabs) is another Malay local favourite. Satay is served with *ketupat* (compressed rice boiled in cases made of woven strips of coconut leaves), cucumber, raw onion, and a spicy peanut sauce.

Nasi tomato (tomato flavoured rice) with *ayam masak merah* (chicken in spicy tomato sauce) and pickled vegetables.

Regional Malay cuisine and festive specialities

Regional Malay cooking styles are traditionally distinctive, and although contemporary cooking reflects a fusion of elements from other sources, many of the traditional dishes have retained their original characteristics and flavours. Each state has its culinary specialities although the more popular dishes are usually found in other parts of the country as well. Food for special occasions, such as Hari Raya Aidilfitri and weddings, conforms to traditional norms.

Ketupat and *dodol*—traditional Hari Raya Aidilfitri delicacies—being prepared the *gotong-royong* (mutual cooperation) way.

Variations on a theme: Penang *laksa* (foreground) and Johor *laksa*.

Almost all of the 13 states in Malaysia have distinctive dishes. For instance, *laksa* in general is a rice noodle dish in fish gravy that varies from state to state. In Johor, *laksa* uses spaghetti instead of rice noodles and has curry paste added to the thick fish gravy. Whereas *laksa* Penang or the Chinese-influenced *asam laksa*, uses so-called 'glass' noodles and its fish gravy is thinner and has a spicy sour flavour that is obtained from the use of tamarind juice. The Pahang variant of *laksa* is grey in colour and coconut milk is added to the fish gravy, accompanied by lots of *belacan* (shrimp paste). The culinary styles of the northern states of Kelantan and Terengganu are influenced by neighbouring Thailand, as are those of Kedah and Perlis. The cuisine of Selangor, meanwhile, reflects Acehnese, Javanese and Bugis influences.

While each state has distinct culinary specialities, many popular dishes are found all over the country, and especially in Kuala Lumpur, Putrajaya and Labuan where the demographic structure reflects people from all parts of the country.

Making ketupat

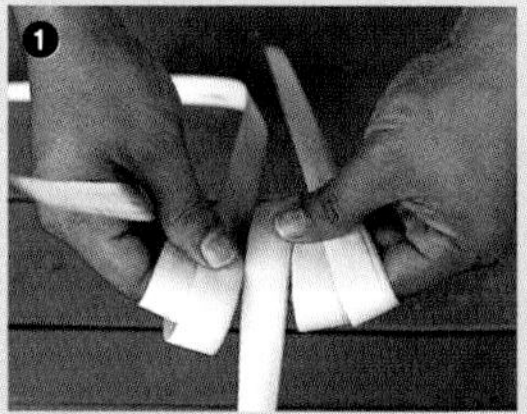

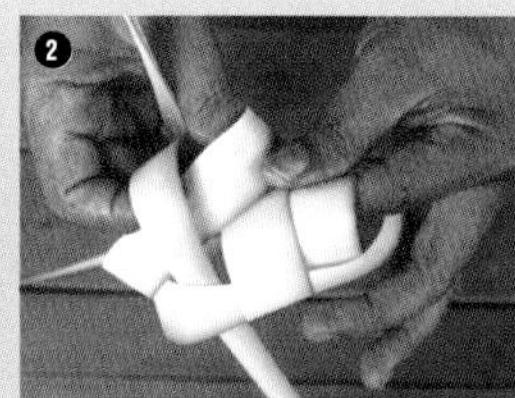

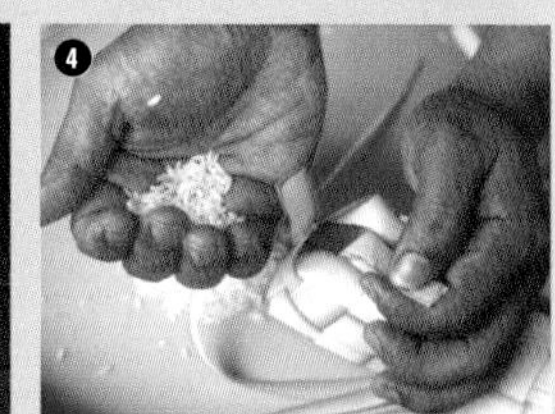

1. Two strips of from a young *daun palas* are woven together into a case. Each strip is twisted three times. Once loops have been formed in this manner, the strips are woven so that the ends pass over one strand and under the next.
2. When the weaving has been completed, the *ketupat* case is turned over, and further cross-weaving is done until the four ends meet in two pairs.
3. The weave is tightened by gently tugging at the ends.
4. The *ketupat* cases are half-filled with uncooked rice and boiled until the rice is cooked. The *ketupat* is cut open before serving.

Food for festivals and special occasions

Major festivals celebrated by the Malays are tied to the Islamic religious calendrical cycle and include Hari Raya Aidilfitri, which marks the end of the Muslim fasting month of Ramadhan (see 'Malay festivals and celebrations'). Muslims abstain from drinking and eating from sunrise to sunset during Ramadhan. *Sahur* is a meal that is taken anytime between 10.00 p.m. and sunrise. The next meal is consumed during the breaking of fast at sunset. Dates, usually imported from the Middle East, are popular at this time as the Prophet Muhammad's teachings advocate the breaking of fast with this fruit.

Food prepared for the Hari Raya festivities and the Malaysian custom of 'open house' invariably includes *rendang* (a rich, fragrant dish of chicken or beef cooked to tenderness in coconut gravy) usually accompanied by the traditional *lemang* (glutinous rice cooked in bamboo lined with banana leaf). *Ketupat* is also served with *kuah kacang* (a spicy peanut sauce). Another dish often served during Hari Raya is *roti jala* ('net' or lacy crepes), made from a mixture of flour, egg and coconut milk with a pinch of turmeric and salt, and usually accompanied by chicken curry.

Weddings are celebrated with feasts (*kenduri*) held by the families involved. Foods associated with such special occasions include *nasi minyak* (rice sautéed in ghee) served with chicken *gulai*, and *nasi tomato*. *Wajik* (a sweet candy made from glutinous rice, coconut milk and palm sugar) or attractively wrapped eggs are usually given to guests as a token of appreciation of their attendance.

Above left: A vendor cooking *roti jala* (lacy crepes) on a griddle.

Left: Rows of *lemang* (glutinous rice cooked in bamboo over charcoal) are a common sight during festive seasons.

Above: A family enjoying Hari Raya delicacies.

Left: *Pulut kuning berlauk* (yellow glutinous rice with various meats and vegetables arranged on it) is usually prepared for the *menempah bidan* ceremony, which is held in the seventh month of pregnancy to book the midwife. The dish is presented to her together with an arrangement of betel leaves (*sirih junjung*).

Culinary styles and dishes of the Peninsular states

Perlis

Dishes from Perlis incorporate elements of Thai cooking, such as the use of tamarind, an example being *ikan bakar air asam* (barbequed fish in tamarind sauce) (right). *Laksa Perlis* is distinctively spicy, with belacan added to the fish gravy.

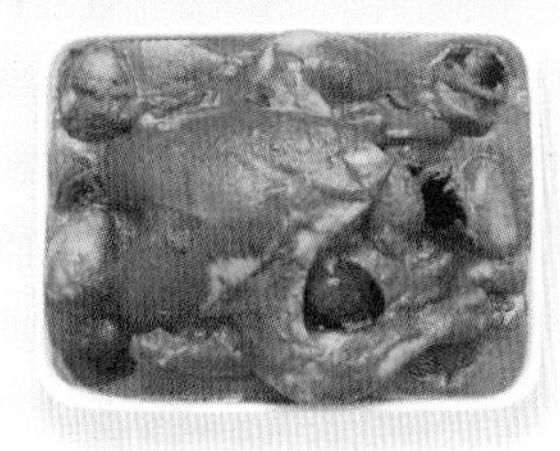

Kedah

Dishes found in this state make use of fresh ingredients. Specialities include *ayam golek* (spicy roasted chicken) (left), *daging bakar* (grilled beef tenderloin marinated in coconut milk and ground turmeric) and *bihun utara* (rice noodles in spicy beef stock).

Penang

The best known food from the island of Penang is *nasi kandar*, a rice-based buffet with no fewer than 10 meat and seafood curries and vegetables to choose from, including *kari kepala ikan* (fish head curry). Another Penang speciality is *pesembur* (vegetable salad in peanut sauce) (left), which is often served as a side dish at lunch and dinner, or consumed as a snack.

Perak

The state of Perak has its own version of *rendang* (a fragrant meat dish cooked with spices and coconut milk): *rendang tok* (right), which tends to be drier than the standard beef or chicken *rendang* prepared elsewhere in the Peninsula. The traditional delicacy of Perak is *kelamai*, made from glutinous rice mixed with brown sugar and *tahi minyak* (coconut milk residue), which is left to ferment over three days before being baked in bamboo sticks over burning charcoal.

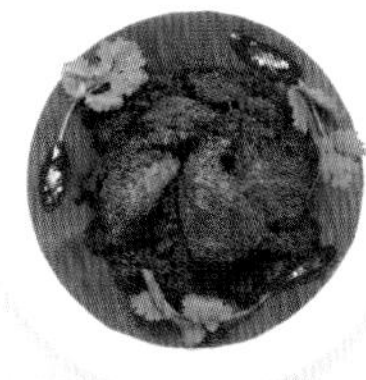

Selangor

Sambal tahun (cockles or beef tripe cooked in coconut gravy with chillies) (right) is often served with *ketupat daun palas* (glutinous rice wrapped in palas leaves). Alternatives are spicy beef *rendang*, and *ayam masak kicap* (fried chicken in soy sauce served with glass noodles).

Negeri Sembilan

Negeri Sembilan is known for its especially hot dishes that do not use chillies sparingly. *Lemak cili api* (left) is the state's signature dish, featuring fish (or chicken or prawns) simmered in coconut milk with turmeric, lemongrass and chillies. Another dish, *sambal tempoyak daun kayu*, contains no fewer than 44 types of *ulam* (wild roots, ferns and leaves) such as *pucuk lidah kerbau, pucuk pelanduk, pucuk sekentut* and *pucuk jering*, all thinly sliced and mixed with pungent *tempoyak* (fermented durian).

Melaka

Famous for its nyonya cuisine, Melaka specializes in food that reflects a blend of culinary elements. Favourites include *asam pedas* (left), a spicy and sour dish cooked with fish, coriander, lots of chillies, *daun kesum*, tamarind and *belacan*. *Bubur caca* is a sweet dessert made from steamed sweet potato, coloured balls of flour, and tapioca jelly in coconut milk.

Fruits

The king of fruits, the durian (right), is known for its strong, penetrating and lingering odour. Its soft and creamy flesh is used in Malay desserts such as *lempuk* (a sticky compact pudding made from durian, cane and coarse sugar) and as flavouring in cakes, biscuits and ice creams.

Other fruits that play a role in Malay food include the coconut, banana, mango, papaya and pineapple. Not only the fruit of coconut and banana trees but also their leaves are utilized during cooking for wrapping and aroma. Mashed boiled banana (*pisang rebus*) has traditionally been used as breakfast for babies. Preserved fruits known as *jeruk* are a much-loved snack.

Johor

Johor is home to *otak-otak* (fish mousse). *Otak-otak* (left) is wrapped in strips of coconut leaves and grilled over charcoal until the leaves are slightly burnt, or wrapped in banana leaves and steamed. *Ketupat* (compressed rice wrapped in coconut leaves and boiled) is eaten with *lontong*, a dish of vegetables, *tempe* (pressed fermented soybean cakes, fried and salted) and tofu cooked in a rich coconut sauce with turmeric. Another Johor speciality is *soto* (*ketupat* served with chicken broth) accompanied by soy sauce, *limau kasturi* juice and chillies.

Pahang

South of Terengganu is the state of Pahang, where the specialities include *lempeng nyior* (right), which are fluffy, savoury coconut pancakes accompanied by sardine or anchovy sambal and spicy egg, usually enjoyed during breakfast; and *jantung pisang masak lemak* (banana flowers cooked in turmeric-laced coconut milk, lemongrass and chillies); *tembosa* (fish curry puffs); and *satak*, a local delicacy similar to *otak-otak* but cooked with lemongrass and onion. A favourite among village folk here is *ikan singgang*, a simple stew prepared with either freshwater fish (such as *jelawat*) or marine fish (such as *ikan kembung*). Thinly sliced *lengkuas* (galingale), turmeric and fresh bird chillies are used to spice up the *ikan singgang* which is usually served with steamed white rice and *sambal belacan*.

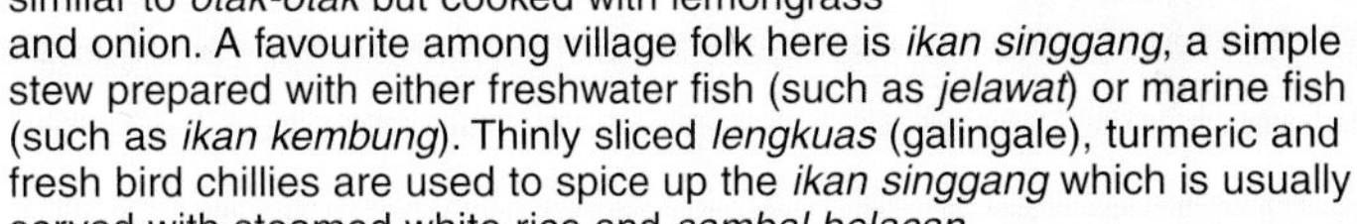

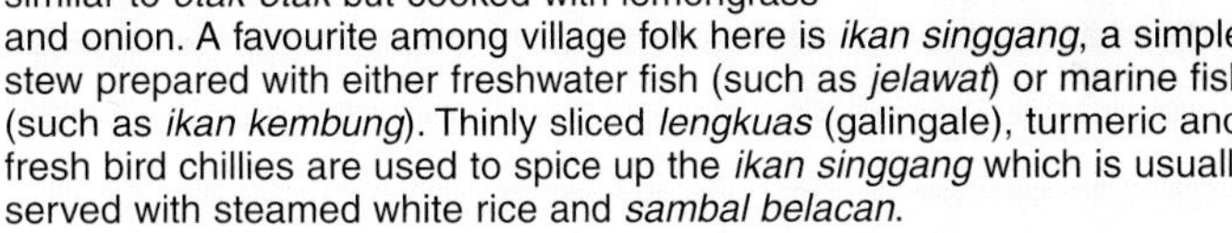

Terengganu

A favourite national snack originating from Terengganu is *keropok lekor* (left), cylindrical shaped fritters made of pounded fish and flour, fried and served with chilli sauce. Terengganu has its own version of *nasi dagang* (aromatic glutinous rice steamed with coconut milk) served with fish curry and *acar* (pickled cucumber and carrot). *Kuih akok* is a half-egg-shaped cake made from rice flour with a centre filled with sweet syrup, or minced beef and chilli.

Kelantan

Nasi kerabu (rice with salad) (right) is a speciality of this state. Traditionally, the rice is tinted bright blue with petals of the *bunga telang* (pea flower). Local herbs—*daun kentut, daun kudu, cekur*, seven types of *daun larak* and *kucing seduduk*—are used to tint the rice different shades of red, black or blue. Rice tinted in this way is served with generous amounts of *ulam*, chicken and salted eggs or fish. Another food native to Kelantan is *nasi dagang*, similar to that served in Terengganu, but served with chicken curry as an alternative to fish curry.

Chinese migration and early organization

Chinese migration to the Malay Peninsula spanned six centuries, from the time of the Melaka Sultanate around 1400 to the formation of an independent Malayan state in 1957. The geographic, economic and social patterns of Chinese immigration and settlement have been shaped by common geographic and linguistic origins in China. Since the integration of a domiciled Chinese community in the country in the 1930s–50s, the Chinese have participated fully and actively in building the political, economic and social institutions of their new homeland.

Above: Chinese market in the 1920s.
Right: Physician, late 1880s.

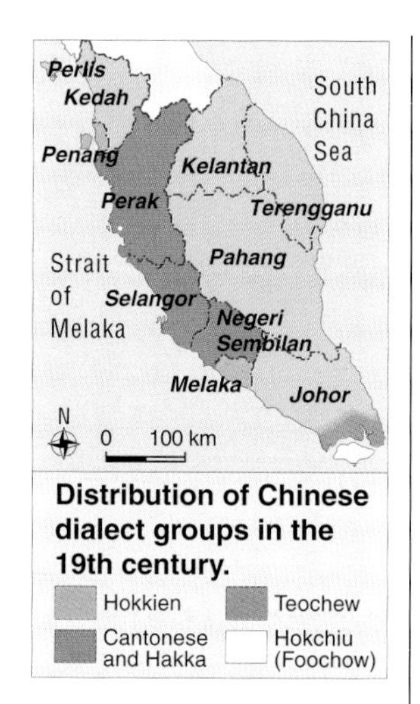

Distribution of Chinese dialect groups in the 19th century.

Chinese dialect groups (2000)

Dialect	Population	%
Hokkien	2,020,868	37.7
Hakka (Khek)	1,092,854	20.4
Cantonese	1,067,994	19.9
Teochew	497,280	9.3
Hokchiu (Foochow)	251,554	4.7
Hainanese	141,045	2.6
Kwongsai	51,674	1.0
Henghua	24,654	0.4
Hokchia	14,935	0.2
Others	202,989	3.8
Total	5,365,847	100.0

Source: Census 2000, Department of Statistics

History of Chinese migration

Hokkien traders from Fujian were the first known Chinese to establish themselves in the Malay Peninsula. They maintained a small presence in the Melaka Sultanate to engage in the thriving China–Southeast Asia maritime trade. The majority of these traders did not establish permanent homes in Melaka but returned to China upon completion of business transactions. Some of those who stayed took local wives. The Chinese Peranakan (also known as Baba or Straits Chinese) are the progeny of this wave of Hokkien traders and their local spouses (see 'Chinese Peranakan society').

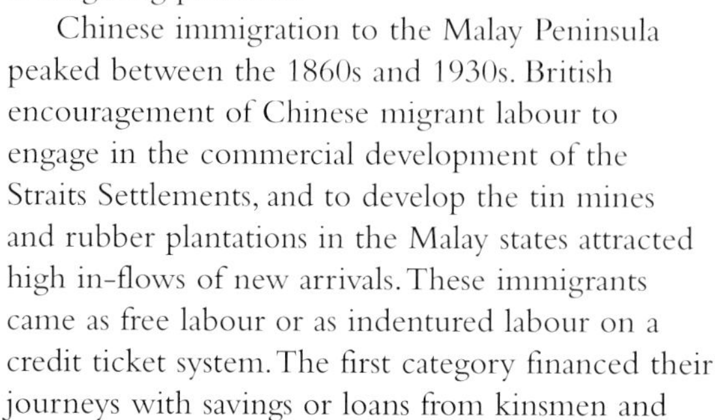

Mining for tin using the dulang washing method, 1959.

With the formation of the British Straits Settlements in 1826, waves of immigrants fanned out into the Malay states, lured by lucrative tin-mining concessions granted by Malay rulers. Up until the mid-19th century, immigrants arrived from various dialect backgrounds in Fujian and Guangdong provinces.

Chinese immigration to the Malay Peninsula peaked between the 1860s and 1930s. British encouragement of Chinese migrant labour to engage in the commercial development of the Straits Settlements, and to develop the tin mines and rubber plantations in the Malay states attracted high in-flows of new arrivals. These immigrants came as free labour or as indentured labour on a credit ticket system. The first category financed their journeys with savings or loans from kinsmen and friends, while the second came on credit advanced by Chinese entrepreneurs and employers in Malaya and China who financed the recruitment, transportation and deployment of contract labour in tin mines and other enterprises. Coolies in Malaya were routinely exploited by employers who enforced long workdays and charged excessively high interest rates for credit. Trapped in the cycle of indebtedness, many labourers did not realize their dreams of returning to better lives in China.

The transformation of the Chinese population from transient sojourners to permanent settlers began after World War I when a quota on male immigrants in 1933 resulted in large-scale Chinese female immigration to Malaya. This laid the foundations of the present-day domiciled Malaysian Chinese community. By 1947, the proportion of local-born Chinese comprised 63 per cent of the total Chinese population in the country.

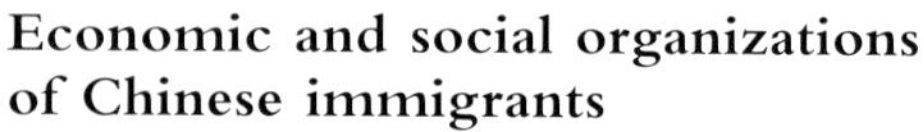

Economic and social organizations of Chinese immigrants

Chinese constitute the second largest ethnic group in the country, making up over 24 per cent of the population (approximately six million in 2004). Almost all Malaysian Chinese originated from the two southeastern Chinese provinces of Fujian and Guangdong. The organizations that recruited labour in China for pioneering work in the Malay states, and that promoted their social welfare, were based on regional and dialect affiliations.

The most important organizations were the *kongsi* (publicly managed economic undertakings) and secret societies that recruited and controlled pioneering coolie labour, clan and surname associations, trade guilds and dialect group associations (*huiguan*).

Early street vendors with their hair in a queue, 1880s.

A metalware shop in Kuala Lumpur's Chinatown, c. 1960.

For most of the 19th century and the first few decades of colonial rule, the affairs of the Chinese immigrant population were administered largely by the leadership of a widespread network of organizations under the Kapitan Cina (Chinese captain) and *kangchu* (headman of riverine agricultural settlement) system. These organizations—from the early *kongsi* and secret societies to the clan and surname associations, temple and religious organizations, mutual aid and funerary societies, trade guilds and dialect group associations—drew their members primarily from the same dialect groups. Functioning as self-governing bodies, these organizations dispensed mutual aid, met the spiritual, social and welfare needs of members, settled trade disputes and facilitated wage negotiations between workers and employer, and maintained law and order in the society at large.

The dialect-based segmentation of the immigrant community was exemplified by the membership of one of the most influential secret societies, the Ghee Hin. Although it was a multi-dialect organization, its operational functions were carried out by branches dominated by members from one dialect group, as in the Hokkien Ghee Hin, the Cantonese Ghee Hin, the Hakka Ghee Hin and the Teochew Ghee Hin. When secret societies were banned in 1889, clans and dialect group associations rose to prominence, serving to fulfil the socio-economic and welfare needs of their members, and establishing and financing Chinese schools. The language of instruction was carried out in the members' dialect until after the 1920s when Mandarin began to be adopted as the common language of instruction.

LEFT: A one-cent tin coin. In the 1860s, certain Chinese tin mine owners were authorized by the Bendahara of Pahang (from 1882, the Sultan) to cast their own *tampang* up to a limited value. On to these the name of the relevant company or *kongsi* in Chinese characters was impressed.

Talisman carried by members of the Ghee Hin society.

Occupational distribution of dialect groups

As early as the 19th century virtually all the dialect groups could be found engaging in the full range of trades, crafts and professions. Nonetheless, certain dialect groups tended to be concentrated in certain occupational categories.

Dialect group	Economic specialization	Occupations
Hokkien	Trade and commerce	Financiers of coolie labour recruitment; venture capitalists in tin and rubber industries; entrepreneurs and merchants.
Cantonese and Hakka	Artisans and craftsmen	Pioneering labour in tin industry; tailors, shoemakers, carpenters, brick makers and goldsmiths. Cantonese also excelled as chefs.
Teochew	Agriculturalists	Production of crops such as gambier and pepper, food processing and distributive trades.
Hainanese	Service-oriented	Hotel and coffee shop proprietors; housekeepers and domestic servants of European households and establishments.
Hokchiu (Foochow), Hokchia and Henghua	Transportation-related	Bus drivers, bicycle shop owners and rickshaw pullers.

Typical Chinese occupations in the late 19th and early 20th centuries: **(1)** Trader, **(2)** Five-foot way cobbler, and **(3)** Rickshaw puller.

Thus, from the 19th century until Independence, Chinese associations perpetuated dialect group identity, while at the same time preserving Chinese culture and traditions in the new homeland.

Modern context

Due to greater mobility and use of merit-based, rather than dialect-based, recruitment for employment, cross-dialect marriages and cross-dialect residential neighbourhoods, geographical and occupational dialect group concentrations in modern-day Malaysia are increasingly features of a bygone era. At the same time, the dialect-based organizations that played pivotal roles in the history of Chinese immigration and settlement have diminished in relevance, as state institutions emerged to provide the economic, social and regulatory services previously dispensed by the associations. The most significant Chinese organizations since Independence have been cross-dialect Chinese-based political parties, and the cross-dialect Chinese Chambers of Commerce and Industry of Malaysia. While most Malaysian Chinese continue to speak their respective dialects, Mandarin has become the preferred language of cross-dialect communication, along with English and Malay.

Chinese medical stores are still found in 21st-century Malaysia.

Chinese society

Chinese communities have flourished in Malaysia since at least the 15th century, but it was not until the 19th century that large numbers migrated from mainland China. Local Chinese society has evolved from that predominantly comprising agricultural and mining labourers to one made up of more mixed, sophisticated and industrialized urban communities throughout the country. Since the late 20th century, the traditional values, everyday practices and communities of the Chinese have adapted in line with development of the country.

Flag-bearers from various Chinese associations and temples in Penang participate in a street procession during a religious festival, 2004.

The committee of the Penang Chinese Chamber of Commerce in the early 1900s.

The evolving Chinese society

As the Chinese became a more settled population, they became conscious of themselves as a community within a larger society. Schools, social clubs and cultural organizations, as socialization agencies, de-emphasized dialect and ethnic differentiation. Social interaction, business collaboration and inter-marriage across dialect lines within the Chinese community became more common. Recognizing the need for community cohesion, the various associations formed themselves into federations known as Chinese assembly halls or Chinese town halls at state level, and eventually at national level. External developments such as political events taking place in China also inspired this larger consciousness.

Indeed, developments in China captured the imagination of the local Chinese for most of the early 20th century. Many Chinese saw themselves as sojourners, and the contending politics of the mainland had relevance and meaning. The events in China also drew their sympathy and support. But there was the awareness among the local Chinese, particularly the Chinese Peranakan (Straits Chinese), of the need to work out a political future for themselves in the Malay Peninsula. These thoughts were most vocally expressed by trade unions, school alumni and literary organizations—new types of organizations for the Chinese.

Leadership positions continued to be held by those from the merchant class. As with many immigrant societies, wealth determined status and influence. Freed from the bureaucratic constraints of traditional China, many of the migrant Chinese flourished as intermediaries in the colonial economy, while others successfully entered large modern enterprises in fields such as banking, shipping and insurance. They contributed generously to social and educational causes benefiting the Chinese community and broader Malaysian society. For this they were elected to various associations, school boards and philanthropic organizations. For their contribution, they were conferred recognition and awards by state rulers, the colonial government and the government in China.

Loke Yew (1847–1917), who settled in Selangor, was a successful entrepreneur and a generous philanthropist.

Clans

Clans were formed in Malaysia with Chinese immigration to help bridge the gap between hometowns in China and new settlements in a foreign land. They also provided welfare and medical services, schooling and help with funeral rites. Some Chinese guilds and associations were also formed according to dialect or hometown boundaries, rather than family clan links. Ancestral halls were built in which members, who may not have had any blood links, were worshipped. This phenomenon occurred in Malaysia, but was rarely found in China.

Kongsi were also formed to strengthen clan ties. The famous Khoo, Yeoh, Lim, Cheah and Tan clans originated from Zhangzhou in Fujian (all Hokkien speakers). Their strong alliance was enhanced by intermarriage and the formation of the Hokkien *kongsi* which was not open to other Hokkien groups and which controlled many temples—focal points for the society—in Penang.

By the early 20th century, *kongsi* were no longer the ruling power in Chinese settlements, but Chinese from each group still share a common identity and regard all people bearing the same surname as blood relatives.

The Khoo Kongsi in Penang, formed in 1835, was among the earliest clan associations to be established in Malaysia.

However, World War II and immediate post-war events seriously weakened the standing of Chinese leaders. The position of the merchant class was damaged by their collaboration with the Japanese, while the younger and more radical Chinese were marginalized during the Emergency (1948–60). At this crucial juncture of constitutional and political transition, credible Chinese leadership was required, and in February 1949 the Malayan Chinese Association (MCA) was formed. It consisted of the traditional *huiguan* (dialect group associations), the Peranakan Chinese and Chinese educationalists. In 1952, through the English-educated and Straits Chinese who had worked with Malay leaders, the MCA formed a political alliance with the United Malays National Organisation (UMNO).

Modern developments

The Chinese community is a significant minority within the larger population. They are represented in almost all levels of economic life. Nearly half the Chinese in Malaysia live in rural or semi-rural areas where they are by occupation farmers, fishermen, miners and labourers. They are also represented in the public service, the armed forces and police, and many are engaged in businesses in urban areas.

The Chinese-based political parties play a significant role in maintaining a multi-racial image of Malaysia necessary for stability. They represent mainly the Chinese, and are sufficiently effective within the Malaysian political system to have the community's concerns seriously noted.

In the business sector, the Chinese have evolved new relations with major Malay political and economic centres. The Chinese offer entrepreneurial skills and international business networking. Government policies introduced in the early 1970s to restructure the economy led to more Chinese business collaborations with the Malays, ranging from token partnerships to genuine relationships. These Sino-Malay business alliances have opened up prospects for real and productive cooperation.

Malaysian Chinese graduates. To young Malaysian Chinese, China merely serves as a reminder of the source of their identity.

Since the end of World War II, new generations of Chinese in Southeast Asia have grown up with few emotional ties to the homeland of their immigrant parents or grandparents. Most young Malaysian Chinese these days have little knowledge of their ancestral background beyond the dialect group they belong to. Even this matters little because many marry across dialect lines. Young Chinese, especially the Western-educated, are more inclined to join social clubs or professional organizations such as medical practitioners' or engineers' associations. Otherwise, they are drawn to broad-based multi-ethnic organizations such as the Rotary and Lions Clubs as well as to groups seeking advancement of human rights and justice or environmental protection.

Business ties

The opening of an Oversea Chinese Banking Corporation (OCBC) branch, 2000.

Occupational distribution and trade functions continued along dialect lines even after Independence. Clan and dialect identification were used to help open up a network for trade and business. Hence, as the Chinese adapted their economic role to modern times at the beginning of the 20th century, there was some reliance on dialect recognition. The opening of new banks, insurance companies, shipping lines and industrial enterprises was supported by the various dialect groups. The founders of Kwong Yik Bank were Cantonese while the Ban Lee Bank and Oversea Chinese Banking Corporation (OCBC) were Hokkien, and these institutions served their dialect groups.

The emphasis on family structure brought out by the practice of filial piety and ancestor worship also continues to influence the economic structure of Chinese Malaysian society. Many Chinese Malaysian businesses are family-run small and medium businesses. In modern times, some of these units have grown into large businesses and public-listed institutions although still family-dominated, where the head is the father or eldest brother. The history of many Malaysian Chinese businesses reveals that business partners, suppliers, retailers and staff were traditionally picked from amongst relatives. There is strength in this type of business structure based on solidarity, loyalty, sincerity and shared culture. However, the negative force of internal family argument is also acknowledged in the Chinese saying, 'wealth never lasts for more than three generations'.

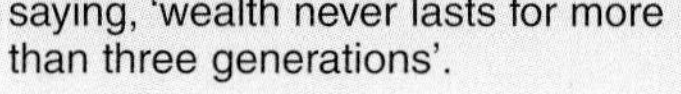

The Khoo Kongsi owns more than 100 shophouses and a land bank in northern Peninsular Malaysia.

The welfare role once undertaken by traditional trade guilds and *huiguan* has since been taken over by government and non-government bodies. And where Chinese associations once represented the community, that responsibility today falls on political parties. Clan associations, nevertheless, still see a continuing role for themselves. Beyond organizing annual dinners for members, management of cemetery matters and making small study grants to members' children, the clan associations regard themselves as custodians of the community's cultural and educational heritage.

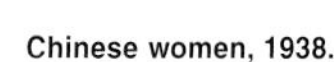

Chinese women, 1938.

Chinese values and beliefs

Chinese values and beliefs are syncretistic, blending together Confucianism, Taoism and Buddhism. These complex belief systems complement and supplement one another, integrating dynamically to shape the character of the community. Within this broad spectrum of beliefs, filial piety, ancestor worship and clan association remain important elements in Chinese culture.

Altar of Tian Guan (Duke of Heaven), who examines the conduct of individuals. It serves as a reminder to root the value of *ren* in daily life.

Confucianism

Traditional Chinese values are based substantially on the teachings of Confucius, a sage who lived from 551–479 BCE. Central to Confucianism is the value of humaneness (*ren*), along with its corollaries: righteousness (*yi*), ritual (*li*), wisdom (*zhi*) and trustworthiness (*xin*), all of which are essential to building a caring and just society. These form the five ethical codes (*wuchang*) that cement the five relationships (*wulun*): between ruler and ruled, husband and wife, parent and child, elder sibling and younger sibling, and between friends. A man who adheres to the five codes does not kill, steal, cheat, slander, commit adultery, gamble or hold others in contempt. Confucius exhorts children to love and respect their parents irrespective of whether they are dead or alive. The concept of filial piety is seen in the practice of ancestor worship. In essence, Confucian ethics, expressed through *rendao* (the Way of Humanity), seek to promote harmony and stability in human relationships.

仁

The Chinese character *ren* (humaneness) also means 'seed'—which is hidden in the human heart and needs to be nurtured.

Confucianists believe that human nature is a gift from heaven and that to think and act with ren and yi are a reflection of *Tian Ming* (Heavenly Will). Although Confucianism is more of a philosophy than a religion, it contains aspects of religiosity—all other major religions share these values of kindness and righteousness. Based on the principles of *ren* and *yi*, many local Chinese believe, 'All religions are but teachings for human beings to become good'.

Ancestor worship constitutes an act of filial piety, the ultimate and most natural expression of *ren*. Ancestral tablets are usually enshrined in clan houses on Ancestors Remembrance Day (Dong Zhi or Winter Solstice) in a ritual where a member of the family carries the tablet which is 'spiritually' dotted with red mercury before being placed at the altar.

Taoism

Taoism refers, variously, to a philosophy of nature based on the scripture known as the *Tao Te Ching* and to the Chinese religious movements that emerged, at least in part, from the teachings of the

Filial piety and family values

The Chinese believe that 'among hundreds of types of good deeds, filial piety is the first'. Traditional agricultural life in China was hard—the family was the all-important unit which kept life and society going. Knowledge was passed from generation to generation, and elderly and weak members were protected.

Historically, families were a part of communal settlements steeped in the values of kinship. Filial piety, within large extended families, encouraged everyone to understand their own role and position within the family and society, along with their respective rights and obligations. Collective oaths in front of altars and ancestral tablets reinforced familial bonds.

Chinese family values also emphasize the obligation to marry and to educate subsequent generations in order to perpetuate the name of the family, clan and the nation. The family is viewed as a refuge in times of trouble and a place for the sharing of joy. In the past, if an individual could not love his own parents, children and siblings, others would not feel confident in their dealings with him or her.

Newlyweds offer tea to their parents and other elders as a gesture of respect and filial piety.

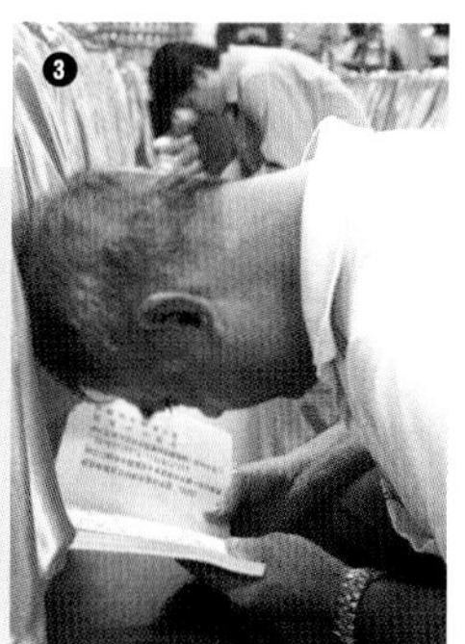

1. Taoist devotees carrying a boat-shaped float bearing the deities of the Nine Emperor Gods.
2. Procession on Wesak day in honour of Gautama Buddha.
3. Praying for the souls of the departed during the Hungry Ghost Festival.
4. Buddhist devotees in prayer at a temple.
5. Taoist monks leading the faithful in prayer during the Hungry Ghost festival.

early Taoist philosophers. Because the authorship of the *Tao Te Ching* is traditionally ascribed to Lao Tzu, who is thought to have lived in the sixth century BCE, it is he who is also regarded as the founder of Taoism. However, many of the fundamental precepts of Taoism are believed to predate Lao Tzu.

The character *tao* is often translated as 'the way' or 'the way of nature' although its ineffable quality is best captured in the opening lines of the *Tao Te Ching*: 'the *tao* that can be uttered is not the eternal *tao*'. Among the central tenets of Taoism is the belief that all things are united in the *tao*, understood as the mysterious force that is the origin of all things in the universe. Likened to a moving body of water, the flow of the *tao* is unalterable, sweeping away all human contrivances. Human life, according to Taoist belief, should therefore be lived in simplicity, through the principle of *wuwei*, the notion of not resisting the *tao*.

The dialectical relationship between the opposing yet complementary forces of *yin* and *yang* also feature prominently in Taoist belief. This and other Taoist ideas form the basis of *taiji*, *qigong*, *feng shui* and various martial arts.

Taoist values

In daily practice, Taoism suggests ten areas of virtuous conduct (similar to those of Confucius):

- Filial piety
- Loyalty to the nation and teachers
- Mercy to all things
- Tolerance
- Giving good and virtuous advice to others
- Self-sacrificing to help the poor and the weak
- Respect and caring for nature
- Digging, planting trees and building bridges
- Eliminating the wicked and guiding the ignorant and the uneducated
- Learning and respecting the Triple Treasures (kindness, a simple life and humility)

As a popular religion with its own deities, rituals, temples and priests, incorporating many Chinese folk beliefs, Taoism is practised widely by the Chinese in Malaysia. Taoist organizations such as the Federation of Taoist Associations Malaysia represent the interests of the local Taoist community.

Buddhism

The majority of Chinese Buddhists in Malaysia subscribe to Mahayana Buddhism. One of the two major divisions of Buddhism, Mahayana—literally the 'great vehicle'—developed in India in the third century BCE and was introduced to China two centuries later.

Mahayana Buddhism maintains that Gautama Buddha was an eternal and almost divine being, one of many similar beings located around the cosmos, all of whom aid people in their path toward enlightenment and are thus to be worshipped. Also central to Mahayana are the Bodhisattva, enlightened beings who voluntarily postpone their attainment of nirvana out of compassion for the suffering of human beings.

One of the branches of Mahayana Buddhism, popular among Chinese Buddhists, is the Pure Land Sect, which holds that adherents will be reborn into the 'Pure Land' if they live virtuously and repeatedly chant the name of Amitabha, the Buddha presiding over that realm. Another sect, Ch'an (or Zen) Buddhism emphasizes that the path to enlightenment lies in meditation and internal realization, not in reason and language. By contrast, T'ien-t'ai Buddhists believe that meditation must be accompanied by rational thought and study of the scriptures.

World-view

The importance of the extended family and clan in Chinese culture is expressed in Confucian maxims such as 'People under the sky are one big family', and 'Within the seas from the four directions all humans are brothers'. The Chinese also refer to other races from the same nation as being of the 'same womb'. The relationship between teacher and pupil also holds an important place: 'Once a person becomes your teacher for one day, you need to treat him as your father for your whole life'. According to scholars, Confucius's dream was that adherence to his ethical code would promote a just world—the 'Great Commonwealth'.

Chinese mediums are sometimes consulted for guidance and help in communicating with divine powers.

Chinese arts

Chinese artistic and cultural traditions found in Malaysia were brought by migrants in the late 19th and 20th centuries. Some of these, such as Chinese puppet theatre and opera, are declining arts, largely due to lack of popularity. Others, such as folk dance and music, dress styles and the martial arts, have been maintained, and in some instances have developed beyond their original forms as they absorb elements of other local and foreign cultures.

Calligrapher writing couplets representing good fortune, prosperity, health, happiness and long life. These are put up during Chinese New Year and can be left up all year round.

An itinerant musician playing the *erhu* (two-stringed fiddle) on the pavement in Kuala Lumpur.

Cultural heritage

Chinese immigrants brought to Malaysia their arts and material culture along with their social structure, religions, architecture, skills, food, values and social customs. This ancient cultural heritage has been preserved and promoted by Chinese cultural organizations across the country.

Calligraphy and brush painting

In China, the Chinese literati were traditionally expected to master the art of calligraphy and brush painting. Both visual art forms are said to reflect the breeding and character of a cultured person (*junzi*). The writing of calligraphy is described by practitioners as philosophical, and is comparable to the practice of *qigong* (a form of breathing exercise) and martial arts. It is also art for appreciation and, like Chinese brush painting, is considered valuable. Decorative calligraphy is found on pillars and at entrances of Chinese temples and associations, and adorns the walls of the buildings. Chinese cultural organizations often hold calligraphy competitions during the Chinese New Year, and these attract contestants from other ethnic groups as well.

The tools of calligraphy—brush and ink—are also used in brush painting. The themes include landscapes, birds, fish, insects, people, fauna and flora. Brush paintings displayed during the Chinese New Year usually depict auspicious symbols and wishes for the season, for example, a painting with many fish conveys abundance and prosperity; bamboo stands for peace; a bat represents blessings; an old man suggests longevity; and galloping horses symbolize good health and spirit. Brush painting

Lion dancers are required to have elegance and perfect co-ordination, especially during daring manoeuvres.

Lion and dragon dances

The lion and dragon dances that are usually performed during Chinese festivals, in particular Chinese New Year, are vigorous performances that combine martial arts and acrobatics. The dancers mimic the movements of the lion and the dragon, to the accompaniment of drums, cymbals and gongs. Two dancers are usually needed to give life to a 'lion'—one to control the movements of the head, eyes and mouth; the other to act as the body. The lion's head, which is adorned with feathers, fur and glitter, weighs about 10 kilograms or more and is held aloft by the dancer while moving vigorously. The head is usually made of papier mache and bamboo, complete with eyes that blink and a mouth that snaps open and shut.

The vigour, beauty and rhythms of these dances have attracted participation by members of other ethnic groups. In Malaysia, techniques have developed to be more sophisticated than those in China, and often involve multiple jumps and somersaults. The success of Malaysian lion dancers in the international arena has resulted in Malaysia becoming a resource for China and other countries.

Masked dancers act as jokers and provoke the 'lion'.

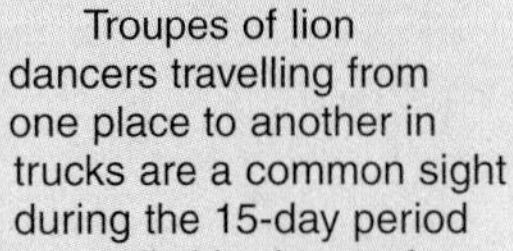

Troupes of lion dancers travelling from one place to another in trucks are a common sight during the 15-day period of Chinese New Year. They are usually hired to perform at homes and at business premises including hotels and shopping malls. They also perform at the launch of new business premises and to welcome dignitaries.

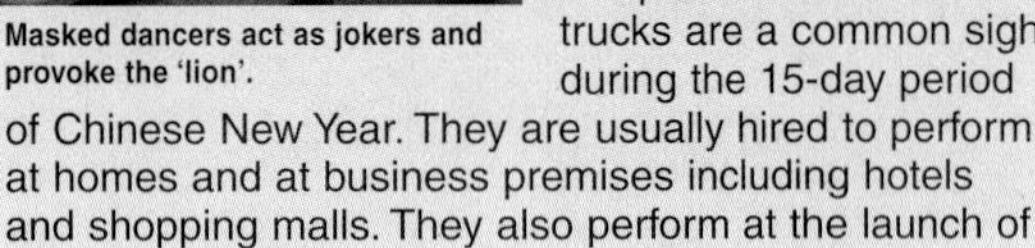

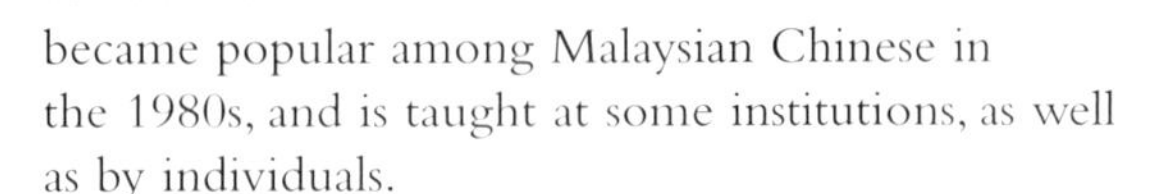

became popular among Malaysian Chinese in the 1980s, and is taught at some institutions, as well as by individuals.

Performing arts

Chinese orchestras have gained popularity among the Chinese community in Malaysia since the 1970s and are promoted by cultural organizations and Chinese-medium schools as a means to develop Chinese music and culture. Traditional Chinese instruments are mainly used, but Western instruments such as the cello are often added, and Chinese orchestras and ensembles play not only Chinese classical and folk music, but arrangements of Malay folk songs and new compositions that incorporate rhythms from other Malaysian and Western musical genres as well.

Chinese folk dance is promoted by Chinese associations and vernacular schools. While the original forms of Chinese dance are preserved, local choreographers have also created interesting

Above: The SMJK Jit Sin orchestra was the first Malaysian Chinese school orchestra to be invited to the All-China School competition in Beijing in 2005.

Right: Chinese opera. Performances typically last over three hours.

variations of folk dances by incorporating elements from other cultures. Since the 1990s, elements of Chinese folk dance have been included in official cultural performances in a blend of Malaysian dance and music.

Chinese opera, which enjoyed popularity in the early and mid-20th century, is staged primarily during religious festivals. It is performed in the Teochew, Hainanese, Hokkien and Cantonese dialects. Since the 1980s, the opera has been increasingly replaced by the *getai* (literally, 'stage for songs'), performed by pop singers. However, some Chinese associations are making efforts to revive the opera. Like the opera, Chinese puppet theatre has lost its popularity and is only occasionally seen during temple festivals.

These days, 'Canto pop' dominates the Malaysian Chinese entertainment market. The influence of 'Canto pop' on the younger generation of Chinese is pervasive. Cantonese as spoken in Hong Kong has become the lingua franca besides *putunghua* (Mandarin) among the Chinese of various dialect groups. 'Canto pop' has also influenced fashion trends, from clothes to hair styles.

Chinese drama theatre is usually based on Chinese scripts and literature; at the same time, there are efforts in experimental theatre by Malaysian Chinese playwrights and directors, employing at times scripts written by other local writers, as well as efforts at producing dance dramas based on Malaysian history.

Traditional dress

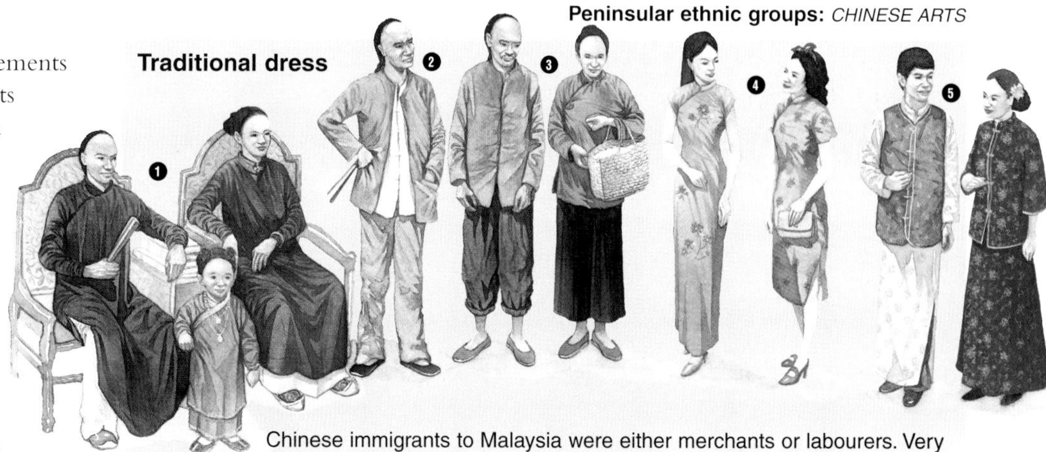

Chinese immigrants to Malaysia were either merchants or labourers. Very few were of Mandarin rank upon arrival. Later, the Qing Dynasty (1644–1911) awarded the Mandarin rank to the leaders of Chinese communities in Malaysia, particularly those achieving 'Kapitan Cina' status.

1. Portraits of early community leaders depict them in full-length, embroidered silk Mandarin robes. The women wore shorter robes over loose black silk trousers. Such elaborate robes were donned during ceremonies
2. Merchants wore similar but shorter robes than those of community leaders, of plainer cotton fabric.
3. Male labourers wore loose cotton jackets and knee-length trousers of hardy coarse cotton or hemp fabric. The samfoo, a trouser-blouse suit worn by working women, was also designed for easy movement in the fields and at home. Working-class clothes were nearly always dyed blue with indigo.
4. The modern version of the long Chinese robe buttoned at the side is the *qipao*, more popularly known as *cheongsam* (long dress). Today, women wear ankle- or knee-length versions of the *qipao* in various fabrics, including batik.
5. A Chinese bride would traditionally wear the *guaqun* (blouse with fabric buttons down the front and ankle length skirt, usually in red) made from Chinese silk. On special occasions, the men wear the *gua* (shirt with collar and long sleeves, with fabric buttons), or the *pao* (loose long gown with collar and long sleeves) with long trousers.

Chinese folk dance is promoted in Malaysia by Chinese associations.

The art of Chinese tea drinking

The tea ritual is an important part of Chinese customary practice and way of life. Serving tea to elders demonstrates respect for them. Newlyweds customarily offer tea to their parents; by drinking the tea the elders show their acceptance of the bride or groom into the family. Drinking tea with friends is an expression of friendship; and drinking tea alone is considered ideal for meditation. The preparation of Chinese tea is considered an art; however, it has become simplified by the use of teabags, and the fact that not many know the traditional way to prepare Chinese tea.

How tea is traditionally prepared:

1. The tea set is warmed with hot water. Boiling water is then poured over tea leaves in the teapot to loosen them, and the water is poured away.
2. More water is added, the pot is covered and hot water poured over it.
3. After about 30 seconds, the tea is poured into a pitcher, from which it is poured into tea cups, filling them to three-quarters level, never full (right). A batch of tea leaves may be infused five times. The temperature of the water and the time for steeping tea varies with the kind of tea leaves used.

Martial arts

Several forms of Chinese martial arts (known as *kungfu* in Cantonese and *wushu* in Mandarin) are practised in Malaysia. The main aim of martial arts training is to instil a keen sense of alertness and agility, to develop a strong body and to activate the flow of *qi* (energy). *Wushu* is considered both a sport and a form of self-defence. Original forms and styles from China are still maintained and practised, while there are also Malaysian variations which are simplified for easier learning. *Taiji* is the most popular form, and is practised for health. The essence of *taiji* is centred on balance, control, internal strength and peace of mind. *Qigong* is a combination of breathing exercises, body movements and mindfulness. There are many variations of *qigong*. It is common to see groups of Chinese and Malaysians of other ethnic groups practising *taiji* and *qigong* in parks in the urban areas.

Various *wushu* events and competitions are organized on a regular basis to advance the standard of the sport. There are also efforts by *wushu* organizations to get it accepted as an event in the Olympic Games.

Taiji is based on the activation of *qi* (energy) in the body through slow and gentle movements as well as the concentration of the mind.

TOP: Students demonstrate the art of *wushu*.

Chinese festivals and celebrations

The festivals and traditions upheld by the Chinese in Malaysia are part of an ancient cultural heritage. Festivities reflect the values and beliefs of the Chinese, and the rituals and customs associated with these occasions reinforce their cultural identity. Festivals are also vital in maintaining communal ties.

Dragon and lion dances are usually held to herald the lunar new year.

The celebrations

The Chinese calendar, which combines elements of the lunar and solar calendars, is marked by *da je zhi*, literally meaning big days. These include religious occasions, birthdays and other anniversaries of gods, goddesses and ancestors, all of which form an integral part of Chinese culture. Of similar importance are the festivals that mark changes in agricultural seasons, which, in China's agrarian society, served as important seasonal markers for farmers. In Malaysia, these festivals continue to be celebrated for their symbolic significance, as they represent the quest to attain harmonious relationships—in time and space, between the past and the present, between the living and the dead, between Heaven and Earth, and etween the Chinese and non-Chinese communities. Chinese New Year, which is the first day of the Chinese lunar calendar, is the most important of all Chinese festivals.

Chinese festivals are underscored by ancestral worship, which reflects the importance placed on family, filial piety, and one's lineage. Festivals also serve to remind the Chinese of their culture, traditions and values. As clan houses function to consolidate lineage identity, they tend to emphasize the festivals of Qing Ming, Zhong Yuan and Dong Zhi, during which they organize gatherings for ancestral worship and give educational scholarships to the children of members. Malaysian clan associations also arrange similar activities to commemorate important figures in the clan's local history.

Chinese New Year's Eve

New Year's Eve (Chu Xi or the last day of the lunar calendar) is a time for all members of the family to come together to share a meal, and to usher in the new year. The reunion dinner is usually a veritable feast of foods bearing names that have auspicious significance. For instance, *yu* (fish) means abundance and *fatt choy* (seaweed) is a call for prosperity. The reunion dinner and the wait for the new year are intended to strengthen family ties. Bad words are prohibited at the family gathering to ensure positive and respectful interaction. At night, the family burns incense and candles, and makes offerings of meat and fruit to deities at home or in temples to invoke their blessings for the year ahead.

A month-old baby's head is completely shaved.

Birth rites

Of the special events in the life journey of the Chinese, the birth of a child is cause for celebration and age-old customs are religiously observed.

Traditionally, when a child is born, the date of birth is written on a strip of red paper and kept for the purpose of predicting the future of the child. The birth of the male child in a family is marked by lighting two candles at the ancestral altar. On the third day after the birth, the baby is given his or her first bath and then carried by the paternal grandmother to worship at the altar of deities and ancestors. Chinese of Fujian origin traditionally sent lanterns to the clan house to mark the arrival of a new member of the family.

Giving thanks to the gods on the occasion of a baby's first month.

Chinese women observe a one-month confinement period after giving birth. During this time the new mother rests and has to take special care of herself by consuming salt-free food and tonics to revitalize her health.

The head-shaving ritual is performed on an infant when he or she is one month old (among some Chinese communities in West Malaysia, an additional ritual is observed, whereby the hair is placed in a coconut shell and later disposed of in the sea). Female relatives in attendance give gifts of bangles, brooches or anklets for the baby. The baby's immediate family then distributes red hard-boiled eggs and yellow rice to relatives and friends to celebrate the occasion.

A child's first birthday is celebrated with prayers and offerings to deities and ancestors. In addition, a variety of items, usually a book, pen, abacus and hammer, are placed on the altar for a male child to choose. This custom is said to help the family predict the future career of the child.

Chinese New Year

The first day of the Chinese lunar year begins with the family gathering to pay ritual homage to their ancestors, and to heaven and earth. The gathering serves to acknowledge that life is centred around one's parents, heaven and earth, and that gratitude, respect and love are vital in the continuity of life and traditions. Elders and married couples give children and unmarried adults *ang pow* (red packets containing 'lucky money'), an act that is supposed to bestow good luck on both the giver and the recipient. There are also many prohibitions to be observed on this day in the belief that it represents a new beginning. Hence, unkind words, vulgar language and quarrels are avoided; sweeping of the house is prohibited as it would mean the outflow of luck; and knives and scissors are not to be used as that would imply cutting off luck. A week before the new lunar year, offerings of candy, honey and sticky rice cakes (*nien gao*) are made to the Kitchen God so that he will say sweet things about the family in heaven.

According to tradition, the God of Wealth is welcomed into the household after midnight on New Year's Day. The seventh day, said to be the day mankind was created, is deemed 'Everyone's Birthday'. Various deities, including the God of Heaven, the Jade Emperor and Kuan Yin (Goddess of Mercy), are also offered prayers during the 15 days of the new year. Celebrations culminate on the 15th day, called Chap Goh Meh, when unmarried women, particularly among the Hokkien community in northern Peninsular Malaysia, notably Penang, throw oranges into the sea to wish for good husbands, while men who want to find partners use the occasion to identify prospective soulmates.

LEFT: Lion dances are performed at private residences and business premises during the new year season.

ABOVE RIGHT: Joss paper is arranged and burnt as offerings for ancestors.

Dragon Boat Festival (Duan Wu)

This festival honours the Chinese statesman-scholar Qu Yuan, who in 278 BCE drowned himself to protest against corruption in the government. He wrote two famous odes before jumping into the water. According to legend, the fishermen tried but failed to save him and, to prevent fishes from devouring his corpse, rice was thrown in to feed them. The occasion is observed with dragon boat races (right) and by serving glutinous rice dumplings (*chung*).

Mooncake Festival (Zhong Qui)

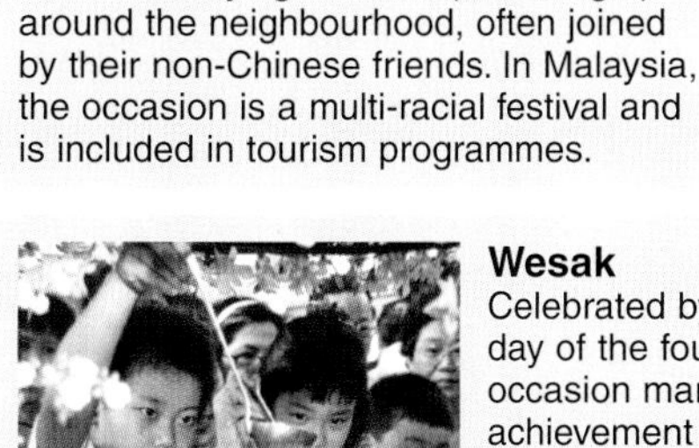

The Mid-Autumn or Mooncake Festival is a day for family reunions, as the brightness of the full moon that appears on this day represents harmony and perfection. Offerings of mooncakes, delicacies, watermelon seeds and Chinese tea are made to deities and ancestors. After prayers, there is feasting and merry-making with children carrying lanterns (above right) around the neighbourhood, often joined by their non-Chinese friends. In Malaysia, the occasion is a multi-racial festival and is included in tourism programmes.

Tomb Sweeping Day (Qing Ming)

Qing Ming literally means clear and bright, in reference to the day at the beginning of spring in China that is designated as the time during which people are to remember and honour their ancestors and departed relatives. Tombs (below) are swept and prayers, food and libations are offered to ancestors, deceased relatives, friends and even prominent historical figures.

Hungry Ghost Festival (Zhong Yuan)

It is believed that the souls of the dead ascend from the underworld during the seventh month of the lunar calendar. Family and public worship is organized for the salvation and enlightenment of these souls. On the part of the living, charity towards all creatures—including the spirits—represents repentance for past sins. Joss sticks are burnt, prayers are offered and food is prepared and placed at street corners and roadsides for hungry souls. Offerings (right) are made to the King of the Hungry Ghosts in accordance with the commandment inscribed on a plate in his right hand, bidding believers to share their surplus clothes and food. During this month, too, temple and community organizations as well as clan houses and various associations collect donations from public worship for the poor and the underprivileged.

Winter Solstice (Dong Zhi)

In ancient times, the Chinese regarded this as the New Year. In Malaysia, Fujian Chinese make *tang yuan* (marble-sized glutinous rice balls in syrup), a symbol of unity in the family. The Cantonese and Hakka regard the ancestral worship on this day as a 'family feast' and many still maintain that a year should be added to one's age after Dong Zhi. On this day, too, new tablets for the worship of the departed are enshrined at the altar.

Wesak

Celebrated by Buddhists (left), on the eighth day of the fourth moon, usually in May, the occasion marks the birth, enlightenment and achievement of Nirvana by Gautama Buddha. Celebrations begin at dawn when devotees gather at temples to meditate on the Noble Eightfold Path. Donations and food are given to the needy, incense and joss sticks are burned, and prayers are offered. Monks chant the sutras, and candle processions are usually held on temple grounds.

Nine Emperor Gods Festival

The festival is based on a belief that deifies the stars of the Big Dipper constellation, representing them as the Nine Emperor Gods, or Jieu Hwang Yeh. These nine deities are believed to control the climate and the movement of the stars, under the reign of Dou Mu, Mother of the Cosmos. They are believed to preside over blessings, life and death as well as peace and harmony on Earth. Thus, for the salvation and protection of mankind, rituals during the nine-day festival are intended to serve as channels between celestial and terrestrial beings. The gods are entertained in the temple grounds with Chinese opera performances, fire-walking ceremonies and other acts of penance. A procession to send the gods home completes the rites.

Festivals in the Chinese calendar

Chinese New Year
The first day of the first lunar month. Falls in January or February.

Tomb Sweeping Day
Based on the solar calendar. Usually falls on 5 April.

Wesak
Eighth day of the fourth lunar month. Usually falls in May.

Dragon Boat Festival
Fifth day of the fifth lunar month. Usually falls in June.

Hungry Ghost Festival
15th day of the seventh lunar month. Falls in July or August.

Mooncake Festival
15th day of the eighth lunar month. Usually falls in September or October.

Nine Emperor Gods Festival
First nine days of the ninth lunar month. Usually in October.

Winter Solstice
Based on the solar calendar. Usually falls on 22 or 23 December.

Chinese culinary traditions

The Chinese immigrants who arrived in Malaysia between the 15th and 20th centuries brought with them a tradition of food from their homeland, particularly the southern Chinese provinces of Guangdong and Fujian. While the cooking styles of these traditions have retained their original characteristics, clever adaptations of indigenous cooking reflect a rich and varied Malaysian palate. Chinese cuisine, when prepared according to halal *traditions, is enjoyed by Malaysians of other ethnic groups as well.*

ABOVE: Celebrants *low sang*, tossing the customary *yee sang* with their chopsticks, a practice said to bring renewed luck in the coming year.

LEFT: *Yee sang*, a mixed salad topped with slices of raw fish, is served during the Chinese lunar new year.

Varieties of Chinese food

Cuisine from the southern Chinese province of Guangdong mainly consists of Hainanese, Teochew (Caozhou), Hakka (Kejian) and Cantonese (Guangzhou) dishes. Chinese cuisine is generally milder than Malay or Indian fare, but adaptations and the influences of the cooking styles of other ethnic groups in Malaysia have resulted in spicy versions of traditional Chinese food and, in some cases, reinventions of classic dishes.

Hainanese cuisine

The Hainanese in Malaysia are known for their chicken rice, the one-dish meal of boiled or roast chicken and rice cooked in chicken stock, and served with a mixture of pounded chillies and ginger. The Hainanese took to being cooks for the British in the late 19th and early 20th centuries and invented dishes—not quite English, nor yet Chinese—of chicken and pork chops, which have become features of Malaysian-Chinese cuisine. They also operated restaurants and coffeeshops offering, alongside traditional cuisine, *kopi-o*, strained from local coffee beans fried with butter.

One of the oldest coffee shops in Kuala Lumpur, Yut Kee, where *kaya* (egg yolk jam) toast and *kopi-o* are served.

Hakka cuisine

The Hakka created *yong tau foo*, a delicacy of fish meat spiced with salted fish, and stuffed into beancurd and vegetables such as bitter gourd, ladies fingers and aubergine (brinjal), as well as baked salted chicken. The Hakka were traditionally farming folk, and thus all their dishes are meaty, cooked with garlic and ginger, with additions of black fungi and yam.

Cantonese food

Cantonese cooking in Malaysia has retained many of its original characteristics. Dishes are subtle in flavour, and usually lightly cooked. Roasting and barbequing are also characteristic of Cantonese and other Guangdong styles of cooking. Succulent strips of marinated pork fillets, known as *char siu* (meaning skewer burnt), are slightly burnt on the outside, and tender on the inside. Pork is also roasted to produce a very crispy skin. Dried sausages (*lap cheong*) and preserved duck may have their origins in northern Chinese traditions, but these foods usually make an appearance at the Chinese new lunar year, and are popular among the Cantonese, Hakka and Teochew. It is at this season, too, that a purely Malaysian-Cantonese creation of great popularity, *yee sang*—a salad of vegetables, pomelo, crispy dough skins, sesame seeds, oil and sweet plum dressing topped with fine slices of raw fish—is served.

Teahouse snacks (*dim sum*) are a popular Cantonese specialty, and are served in restaurants from breakfast to lunch. There are countless varieties of *dim sum*, some deep-fried, others steamed, yet others baked. Some classics are *siew mai*—thimble-shaped pastries stuffed with minced pork topped with crab roe; *har kow*—prawns wrapped in a white flour case; and glutinous rice steamed with pork and dried shrimps. Other popular Cantonese dishes are *sar hor fan* (wide rice noodles, cooked over high heat) and *wan tan mee* (egg noodles either cooked in a soup, or tossed in soy sauce gravy and served with a bowl of soup). *Wan tan* (literally meaning 'the cloud swallowed the pork') are balls of minced pork or shrimp wrapped in dough.

Teochew cuisine

The Teochew make fish balls served in a soup and fish paste noodles, as well as braised duck, fashioning it into a gourmet dish. They are also known for the popular Teochew porridge—soupy rice cooked plain or with pieces of potato, and served with an array of side dishes, mostly pickles.

ABOVE: The local crepe, popiah (inset), being made.

LEFT: Wantan mee is a popular Cantonese dish.

1. Hainanese chicken rice. **2.** Dim sum. **3.** Steamboat (thin slices of raw seafood, meat and vegetables cooked at the table in a pot of boiling soup). **4.** Dried sausages (*lap cheong*) and preserved duck.

Fujian cuisine

Fujian cooking consist of Zhangzhou, Quanzhou and Foochow (or Hokchiu) styles. Among the best known of Fujian dishes in Malaysia are *oh chien*—oyster omelettes made from small oysters fried with spring onions in egg; Hokkien *char* (fried noodles served with dark gravy), *lor bak* (pork or fish rolls wrapped in bean curd skin and deep fried). The Foochow brought with them the extremely popular *popiah* (spring rolls), of shredded turnip, beans, prawns and soybean curd rolled in a rice paper wrapper. They also brought the traditional red rice wine sediment chicken soup accompanied by *mee sua* or rice threads, which is made for the celebration of an infant's first 'full moon'. At one time families made their own red wine sediment and stored them in black jars. Today it can be bought commercially.

Malaysian-Chinese flavours

Bak kut teh

Bak kut teh (literally meaning 'tea of pork bone') is a herbal soup prepared with pork bones, ribs and meat (pictured right), served with *eu char koay* (fried puff bread stick) or rice, and optional accompaniments of *tau pok* (deep fried tofu), mushrooms and green vegetables. It is believed that *bak kut teh* was first concocted in 19th century Malaya by Chinese harbour coolies who, in an attempt to boost their health, collected herbs spilled on the floor of the harbour stockrooms, scrounged free pork bones from the market, and boiled everything together with garlic, thinking that the brew might prevent rheumatism, the deterioration of organs, as well as remedy minor illnesses.

Bak kut teh is a popular breakfast or supper meal. Although it is found in many parts of the Peninsula, the best *bak kut teh* is said to be in the port district of Klang, in the central state of Selangor. A chicken version, *chi kut teh*, is also popular. Readymade *bak kut teh* sachets, containing the herbal ingredients usually found only in Chinese medicinal shops, are now widely available and even exported.

Char koay teow

Char (literally meaning 'to fry') *koay teow* (flat rice noodles in the Fujian dialect, left) is as ubiquitous as *nasi lemak* in the wide array of hawker food found in Malaysia. The noodles, fried with prawns, clams or cockles, egg and chives, are likely to have originated from Fujian, but the Fujian would hardly recognize the local version, particularly with the addition of spicy chillies, and the use of banana leaves to line the serving plate, which gives the noodles a special fragrance.

Penang laksa

Penang *laksa* (a Malay word meaning vermicelli in thick gravy) is another example of Chinese influence, being an ingenious concoction of local flavours (right). It consists of blanched rice vermicelli in a spicy and sour fish-based gravy to which a black shrimp paste (*heiko*, produced in southern China) is added for a sweetish flavour. The gravy is prepared from mackerel cooked with ginger flower, basil leaves, and a seasoning of ground ingredients such as lemongrass, galingale, shallots, chillies, turmeric and shrimp paste. The noodles are garnished with shredded cucumber, lettuce, pineapple, mint leaves, finely sliced onions and fresh chillies.

Hokkien mee

So named due to its popularity among the Hokkien in Malaysia—although it is unlikely to have originated from their native Fujian province—this speciality is a preparation of spicy gravy ladled over blanched rice noodles, water convolvulus and beansprouts, and garnished with prawns and boiled egg, and sometimes duck meat strips or pork ribs.

Lok lok

Best described as the Malaysian hawker version of steamboat, *lok lok* (literally meaning 'dip dip', above) is a selection of bite-sized food, mainly fresh meat and seafood, skewered on bamboo sticks. Diners help themselves, by dipping the skewers in boiling water to blanch the food, and then dipping into a peanut-based or sweet brown sauce.

Kaya

A curd-like jam of cooked coconut milk and eggs yolks, flavoured with screwpine leaves, *kaya* is traditionally prepared by Hainanese coffeeshops and served spread on steamed or toasted bread.

Curry mee

Made of blanched rice vermicelli in a thin coconut curry, garnished with prawns, cuttlefish, beansprouts, clams and mint leaves, this dish originated from northern Malaya and is thought to be the creation of local Fujian.

Food for festivals

Special foods are prepared for Chinese festivals and other auspicious occasions, such as birthdays, weddings, and a baby's first 'full moon' celebrations. Certain food items are associated only with certain festivals, for instance, mooncakes (above) are made for the Mid-Autumn or Mooncake Festival (see 'Chinese festivals and celebrations'). Rich, sweet pastries traditionally made with fillings of red bean paste, lotus seed paste and whole duck egg yolks, mooncakes these days come in a variety of new flavours as well, ranging from nuts and jelly to durian and chocolate.

Nien gao (*kuih bakul*) is a sticky cake made of glutinous rice flour and sugar (above), and is prepared during the lunar new year, as an offering to the Kitchen God who is believed to watch over the household.

Dumplings (*chung*, below) made of glutinous rice with meat fillings wrapped in bamboo leaves, are prepared for the Dragon Boat Festival which falls on the fifth day of the fifth moon in the lunar calendar. Variations of the *chung* include additional fillings of chestnut, salted egg yolk and mushroom.

The *ang ku*—small cakes made of glutinous rice flour with green bean paste filling—are part of offerings of food, flowers and fruits made to the deities during special prayers held at temples and in homes on certain days of each month. This cake is also an essential part of a baby's 'full moon' celebrations. Longevity buns (*mi ku*, above), which are shaped like a turtle and pink in colour, are popular during birthday celebrations.

Food values and flavours

To the Chinese, the harmonization of food relates the five flavours of food—sweet, sour, bitter, piquant and salty—to the nutritional needs of the human body's five functioning systems—the heart; liver; spleen and pancreas; lungs; and kidneys. Traditionally, all foods are said to be either *yin* (cooling), such as vegetables, most fruits and clear soup; or *yang* (warming), such as starchy foods and meat. Cooling food should be balanced with warming food.

The correct proportions of ingredients are important in the preparation of food to ensure that the colour, aroma and flavour are brought out, and the nutritional purposes of the food are achieved. Cooking methods include stir frying, stewing, steaming, deep frying, pan frying, or a combination of two or more methods. Supporting ingredients are often used to neutralize the flavour of the main ingredients or balance their effects. For instance, meat-based dishes would include vegetable and plant ingredients such as scallions, ginger, garlic, chilli peppers, dried lily buds and mushrooms.

Claypot rice, a one-pot rice meal with a variety of meat or seafood, has a smoky aroma.

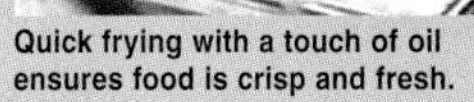

Quick frying with a touch of oil ensures food is crisp and fresh.

The Indians: Classification, origins and social organization

Indian merchants traded in the Malay Archipelago as early as the first century CE, and established a settlement in Melaka in the 15th century. However, it was only in the 19th and 20th centuries that large numbers of Indian migrants, mainly from South India, arrived in the Peninsula, brought as indentured labour primarily to work on the rubber plantations. Since Independence, the Indian community, consisting of various ethnic sub-groups, has integrated with other ethnic groups in Malaysia and contributed to national development.

ABOVE: Indian labourers at an estate in Klang, Selangor, c. 1910.

RIGHT: A Chettiar money-lender.

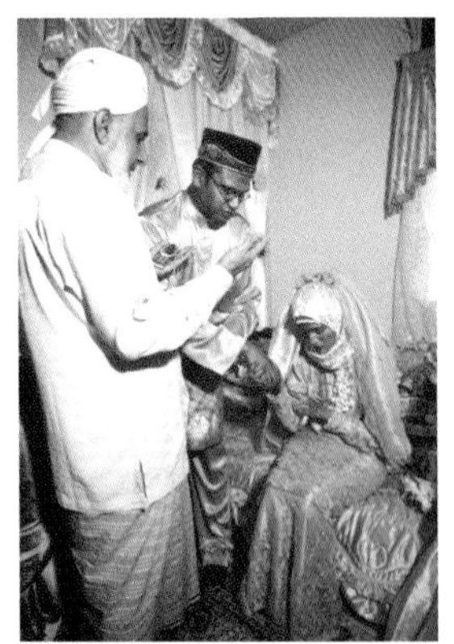

A Chitty wedding. The Chitties are a distinctive community based in Melaka and descended from early Indian traders.

Early Indian migration

Indians have been present in the Malay Peninsula since the beginning of the Common Era when trading activities between Indian kingdoms and their counterparts in the Malay Archipelago resulted in the establishment of settlements in the Peninsula. Archaeological and historical evidence indicate the kingdom of Langkasuka in the northern region of the Peninsula as one such example, and suggest that Kedah (referred to as Kadaram in early Tamil texts and called Kataha in Sanskrit) was the main focus of Indian commercial interests in Malaysia.

The presence of Indians in the Melaka Sultanate in the 15th and early 16th centuries is reflected in historical references to Indian participation in the political, economic, religious and social life at that time. Evidence of Indian influence in the Sultanate can be found in the introduction of the *devaraja* concept of kingship, and the *Sejarah Melayu* (Malay Annals). The large number of Sanskrit and Tamil loan words in the Malay language further points to the presence of Indians both during the Sultanate and thereafter. The Melaka Chitties, descendants of Indian settlers in Melaka, still retain Indian culture and the religion of their forefathers but have adopted Malay clothing, language and food (see 'Other ethnic communities').

Migration in the 19th century and beyond

The arrival of the British in the 19th century set the pace for large-scale and permanent Indian settlements in the Peninsula. Indian prisoners were put to work in the construction of roads, buildings and other civil works in the Straits Settlements of Penang, Melaka and Singapore in the early 1800s. Some settled in these places, while others returned to India.

Further migration of large numbers of Indians occurred in the late 19th century when the British transported hundreds of thousands of labourers to the Malay Peninsula to clear the virgin jungles for plantation agriculture, such as tea, coffee, rubber and coconut, and to lay the roads and railways needed to link the states. They were drawn largely from south India, due to its proximity to the Peninsula as well as the socio-economic conditions on the subcontinent at the time.

To man the government departments created by the colonial system of administration and the railways, English-educated staff were needed: South Indians and Sri Lankan Tamils emigrated to meet this need. North Indians, especially Sindhis and Gujeratis, came as commercial immigrants to capitalize on the growing Malayan economy and focused on the textile industry, while Chettiars from South India monopolized the money-lending business, and the Indian Muslims engaged in import and export between the two countries. The links established by the commercial classes between India and Malaysia have prospered ever since. The process of emigration continued until 1957.

Chronology of Indian migration

1st–14th centuries
An Indian colony reportedly existed in he early port kingdom in Kedah's Bujang Valley, where some architectural remains are believed to be Hindu-Buddhist temples.

15th–18th centuries
Indian merchants and traders established a settlement in cosmopolitan Melaka.

Early 19th century
Indians were brought in for early civil works in the Straits Settlements of Melaka, Penang and Singapore.

Late 19th century–1957
Mass migration of indentured Indian labour for plantation agriculture and infrastructure work. By 1957 more than four million Indians had come to Malaya.

A Sikh squadron in a British settlement, c. 1900.

Social organization

Indian migrants brought with them their traditional social arrangements in addition to their respective religious affiliations. Migration had a significant bearing on the caste system that eventually emerged. Neither the four-tier *varna*

(caste) system prevalent in North India nor the three-tier division of society into Brahmin, non-Brahmin and Adi-Dravida (Harijans or scheduled castes) existing in south India occurred.

What eventually evolved was a two-tier system that divided the community into higher and lower castes, irrespective of sub-ethnic origins. The small number of Brahmins scattered across the country were unable to have any lasting impact on the evolution of caste prejudices. The two-tier system was reflected in social interaction, commensal and connubial relations, and even resulted in the formation of caste-based associations with social and economic agendas for their members. However, since the late 20th century, caste-based prejudice in Malaysia has become less common and has been largely confined to marriage arrangements.

Political structure among the early immigrants was closely identified and associated with caste and caste-occupation categories. The only 'political' movement among the early population was to ensure their continued livelihood and to maintain order in the community. Initially, leadership emerged within the *kangany* (indenture) system. However, at the beginning of the 20th century, organizational activity was initiated by the urban middle class consisting of a group of mixed origins. Clerical and other sub-managerial workers in the government and private sectors formed the backbone of this group. Wealthier businessmen bore the financial burden of the early Indian associations and provided them with facilities.

The first Indian association was inaugurated in 1906, supported by Indian Muslim merchant families and led by professionals from the community. Soon after, the Selangor Indian Association was formed in 1909. This was supported by professionals and businessmen in Kuala Lumpur. These associations served primarily as social and recreational clubs. However, the direction of Indian organizations invariably took on a political orientation.

Classification of Indian ethnic sub-groups

The migration of Indians to Malaya has resulted in the emergence of a heterogeneous community differentiated not only by language and ancestral origins but also on the basis of religion, caste and class. The lack of homogeneity is also evident in their religious affiliation, i.e. among the Tamils there are Hindus, Christians and Muslims; the Punjabis are followers of either Sikhism, Hinduism or Islam; the Malayalis practise Hinduism, Christianity or Islam; and the Telugus are largely Hindus. The majority of Indian Malaysians are Hindus.

In Malaysia, ethnic sub-groups that are broadly classified as North Indian include the Punjabis, Sindhis, Gujeratis and Pathans. South Indians comprise the Tamils, Telugus, Malayalis and Kannarese. Sri Lankans comprise Tamils and Singhalese, although many Sri Lankan Tamils identify themselves as Indians. The Tamils constitute the largest ethnic sub-group, forming more than 85 per cent of the Indian population in Malaysia (a total of approximately 1.8 million in 2004).

Gujerati wedding.

Indian migrants in the late 19th century, comprising Tamils, Bengalis, Sindhis and Gujeratis.

Indian ethnic sub-groups in Malaysia (2000)

Group	Population	%
Indian Tamil	1,396,480	87.6
Malayali	35,809	2.3
Telugu	38,993	2.4
Sikh	33,231	2.1
Punjabi (except Sikh)	23,147	1.5
Other Indian	41,477	2.6
Pakistani	11,313	0.7
Bangladeshi	2,951	0.2
Sri Lankan Tamil	8,735	0.5
Singhalese	1,641	0.1
Total	1,593,777	100.0

Source: Census 2000, Department of Statistics

Distribution of Indian settlements

The economic development of the country defined the distribution of Indians in Malaysia in the 19th and 20th centuries. States where plantation agriculture was introduced, such as Selangor, Perak, Negeri Sembilan and Johor and smaller areas in Kedah and Pahang, saw a greater influx and settlement of Indians.

The rural–urban distribution of Indians has altered dramatically since the 1980s. A predominantly rural population that had worked in the plantations began to migrate to urban centres, due to retrenchment caused by a shift in plantation agriculture from rubber to less labour-intensive oil palm, improved education and industrialization which lead to greater employment opportunities in the urban areas. The percentage of Indians in rural areas decreased from about 65 per cent in 1970 to less than 30 per cent in 2000.

Workers hanging out rubber sheets to dry, 1967.

Indian office workers. Indian professionals, managers and clerical staff work in all sectors of the modern economy.

Indian news vendor, Kuala Lumpur.

Indian mobile bread vendor.

Indian kinship, beliefs and value systems

The family is the basic unit of society among the Indians. Despite the erosion of the traditional extended family system due to migration and a growing pattern of nuclear families among Indian urbanites, the family provides the fundamental social organization for many of an individual's principal needs. It is through this unit that values, culture and religion are adhered to and imparted to the younger generation, and through which matrimonial alliances are contracted. While Indians in Malaysia follow various faiths, the majority practise Hinduism.

Indian family, early 20th century.

Parents and elders are honoured in Indian society, as demonstrated by the custom of kneeling at their feet to seek their blessings.

BELOW: Hindus believe that various aspects of human life are governed by the position of planets at the time of birth as noted in horoscopes, which are consulted on important occasions such as weddings, and are read either by priests in temples or by professional astrologers.

Kinship

The most common kinship system among the Indians is the patrilineal system. In the traditional extended family, parents, their children and their spouses lived under one roof in a mutual support system that emphasized the male line of descent. While this living arrangement has been replaced in many instances by the nuclear family, it is still common for the elderly parents to live with one of their children and his or her family.

All family members accept the authority of the elders in the hierarchy. Elders are ranked above the juniors and, among those of similar age, males outrank females. The father commands the family, but the position of the mother is respected. Though females have to accept their position as subservient to males, they are the ones who care for the needs of the family and kin group. A woman is not expected to call her husband by name nor openly object to his decisions or opinions. Although this has been affected by modernization, educational opportunities and equal rights for women, devotion is still regarded as a virtue in an Indian wife.

Children are expected to show deference to parents in keeping with the Tamil adage *matha, pitha, guru, deivam* (mother, father, teacher and God). Thus, children do not openly contradict their parents' views even if they disagree with them, in a display of respect for them. A son is expected to take care of his parents, especially if he is the eldest child.

Traditionally, the relationship between father and son is formal and restrained. Mothers, on the other

The social significance of marriage

Marriage forges alliances between families. Endogamous marriages are common, with consideration given to caste, ethnolinguistic origins and religious affiliation, although exogamous marriages within specified boundaries are accepted. Other factors that influence marriages, especially arranged marriages, are the matching of horoscopes, age, occupation, material status, caste and, sometimes, dowry.

Dowry is a status symbol and is paid either in cash or kind by the bride's family to the groom's family with the giving away of the bride (*kanya dana*, *kanya* meaning daughter, and *dana* meaning gift). The ritual of *kanya dana* is an essential aspect of Hindu marriages. The desire and responsibility to get daughters married is overwhelming among Indian families. Parents feel guilty if their sons are unmarried, but the guilt is greater in the case of a daughter.

Marriage requires the participation of all kinsmen through gift giving, performing services or attendance at the wedding. A wedding is the culmination of complex negotiations involving social and financial considerations. It is a demonstration of one's wealth and status, and an occasion to affirm traditional values and customs. For the newlyweds, it marks the beginning of a new life; for the parents of the bride and groom, it is the end of a responsibility and the fulfilment of a desire.

Once an agreement between the families of the prospective groom and bride has been reached with regard to the items to be exchanged, the paternal guardians exchange trays containing a coconut, fruits, flowers, betel leaves and areca nut in a ceremony attended by relatives.

Religious beliefs

Indians in Malaysia practise numerous religions, including Hinduism, Christianity, Sikhism, Islam and Buddhism. However, the majority of Indians, especially those from south India, are Hindus.

Hinduism

Hinduism subscribes to the existence of a pantheon of gods, in which Shiva, Vishnu and Brahma form the Trinity at the highest level. Other gods include Murugan, Ganesha, Parvathi, Lakshmi and Sarasvathi. The pantheon of gods in effect reflects the various potencies of the Supreme God, which are regarded as manifestations of God. The source of the Hindu pantheon is the Veda (scriptural texts dating back to 1500BCE–500 BCE). The worship of these deities constitutes an important element of both temple and domestic worship, which consist of rituals and ceremonies, and offerings of fruits, sweetened rice and flowers. There are large urban temples dedicated to specific deities, and smaller temples located on estates all over Malaysia. In addition, there are deities who are regarded as non-Sanskritic and placed lower in the Hindu pantheon, such as Muniandy, Pechaayee, Angalama and Katteri. Worship of these gods, regarded as guardian deities, does not involve recitation of religious hymns, and offerings are normally non-vegetarian items including, up till recent times, animal sacrifice. Worshippers of these deities are mainly from the lower socioeconomic strata, and who have little or no religious education.

Most Hindus in Malaysia are Shaivites who worship Shiva as the Supreme God. Some are Vaishnavites (worshippers of Vishnu) who regard Vishnu as the pre-eminent god.

The image of the goddess Sri Muthu Mariamman is borne on a ox-drawn cart during the Mariamman Thirunal festival.

Beliefs and values

The basic beliefs of Hinduism are: God; prayers; law of karma; reincarnation; and compassion. Hinduism is a way of life based upon two key concepts: *dharma* and *moksha* (salvation). *Dharma* emphasizes a person's duty to behave according to religious and social codes, and *moksha* refers to the ultimate release from the world that can only be obtained by transcending physical and social limitations. Karma is the moral law of cause and effect. Every thought and deed has an effect on one's destiny. Karma is tied to the journey of the soul through successive life forms (*samsara*), before *moksha*—eternal bliss and union with the Almighty—is realized.

Hindu world-view

The Hindu world-view is underscored by six basic themes: diversity, time, tension, tolerance, monism and religious integration. It does not recognize any dichotomy between the sacred and the secular, and can be best summarized as 'individuals get what they deserve'.

Above: Children donating to charity at a temple.

Right: A family praying at the home altar.

Other beliefs

Sikh women in prayer at a gurdwara (Sikh temple).

Indians and other Malaysians of Christian faith celebrate St Anne's feast in Bukit Mertajam.

hand, usually have a close relationship with their sons, and often act as an intermediary between father and son in times of strained relationships. In contrast, a daughter enjoys a close relationship with both parents.

Beyond the immediate family a man or woman is related to several classes of kinsmen. The most frequent interchanges are usually with those members of the family closest to him or her in patrilineal and matrilineal descent, namely, brothers or patrilineal cousins, and sisters and their children. These kinsmen are involved in all customary occasions and ceremonies conducted by the family, especially marriages and funerals. A second class of kinsmen is related through a man's wife, his sisters, his married daughters, and his brothers' wives. Of these kinsmen the closest would usually be his wife's brothers.

Hindu movements and organizations

Developments in religious education in recent decades have resulted in a revival of Hinduism among Indians in Malaysia, and the establishment of organizations such as the Malaysia Hindu Sangam, the Hindu Darma Mamandram and the Arulneri Thirukkoottam, which conduct religious classes and teachings, mainly to improve the knowledge of Hinduism among people and to bring unity.

The neo-Hindu movements based on the teachings of religious saints, philosophers and spiritual leaders which have emerged in the last two decades continue to attract followers from among the educated, middle-class urban Indians. The Satya Sai Baba Society, Hare Krishna Movement, Divine Life Society, Church of the Shaiva Siddhanta, Brahma Kumaris and Ananda Marga are among the popular movements in Malaysia that offer alternative or complementary Hindu beliefs and ideas, based on the teachings of the founders. Some of these organizations, such as the Divine Life Society and the Satya Sai Baba Society, have their headquarters in India. Despite some differences between these organizations, their common denominator lies in the teaching and practice of Hinduism, and the emphasis on social welfare activities.

Hindus distributing food to the public after the consecration of the Sri Karumariamah temple, Seberang Jaya.

Indian festivals and celebrations

The Indian community in Malaysia celebrate a variety of festivals and celebrations, including life cycle rites. For Hindus, who comprise the mjority of Malaysian Indians, Deepavali and Thaipusam are the major festivals, celebrated with much pomp and rejoicing. Hindus and Sikhs celebrate their respective new years in April.

Oil lamps are lit and colourful floor designs made out of coloured rice flour called *kolam* adorn homes and temples at Deepavali.

Deepavali (Diwali)

Also referred to as the Festival of Lights, Deepavali is celebrated by Hindus on the 14th day following the new moon in the month of Aippasi (October–November) to symbolize the destruction of evil forces as depicted by the slaying of the evil demon Narakasura by Lord Krishna. Homes are lit with oil lamps. On the eve of Deepavali, prayers are offered to deceased family members. People exchange greetings and visit each other, welcome friends, including non-Hindus, into their homes, offering traditional festive specialities including ghee rice, curries, and sweetmeats such as *pal khova* (sugar balls) and *kesari* (pudding).

Major festivals and holy days

The Hindu calendar identifies several holy days which are observed by Hindus either as temple or domestic festivals, and are marked by prayers and offerings to the gods, and the consumption of vegetarian food. Deepavali and Thaipusam are the major festivals celebrated by Malaysian Hindus. Other religious festivals are celebrated on a smaller scale but are regarded as significant.

The Hindu New Year, variously referred to as Varusa Pirappu (among the Tamils), Ugadi (by the Telugus) and Vishu (by the Malayalis), falls around mid-April, and is marked by prayers offered in temples and in homes. The Sikh New Year (Vaisakhi) also falls in April and is celebrated with prayers and, on occasion, Bhangra (traditional Punjabi music and dance) performances.

TOP: Bhangra performance during Sikh New Year (Vaisakhi).

ABOVE: A family watches as milk boils over an earthen pot during the Thai-ponggal harvest festival.

Navaratthiri, literally meaning 'nine nights', is celebrated for nine days in the month of Puraddasi (September–October), beginning with the new moon. The festival is devoted to the goddess Shakti in her manifestations as Durga (Goddess of Bravery), Lakshmi (Goddess of Wealth) and Sarasvathi (Goddess of Knowledge and Art).

Thai-ponggal, traditionally a harvest festival celebrated by agricultural communities in India at the beginning of the month of Thai (January–February), is usually observed by Tamils over three days, beginning with the *bhogi pandikai* (disposal of old items), *mattuponggal* (honouring of cows) and *kanniponggal* (prayers for unmarried women). As part of the celebrations, rice is cooked in milk and sugar in a new pot outside the home, and as the milk boils over, the members of the family shout '*pongalo pongal*'.

Thaipusam is also observed in the month of Thai (January–February) as an occasion to give thanks to Lord Murugan for prayers answered and to fulfil vows. Devotees usually fast for up to seven days before the festival and fulfil vows by carrying *kavadi*, shaving their heads, breaking coconuts as the chariot bearing the statue of Lord Murugan passes by, or by serving devotees with free meals (*annathanam*).

In recent years Thaipusam has gained prominence as a major Hindu festival observed in major cities and towns such as Kuala Lumpur, Penang, and Ipoh. The Batu Caves Temple in Kuala Lumpur and the Waterfall Temple in Penang attract hundreds of thousands of devotees annually. The festival has also become a major tourist attraction.

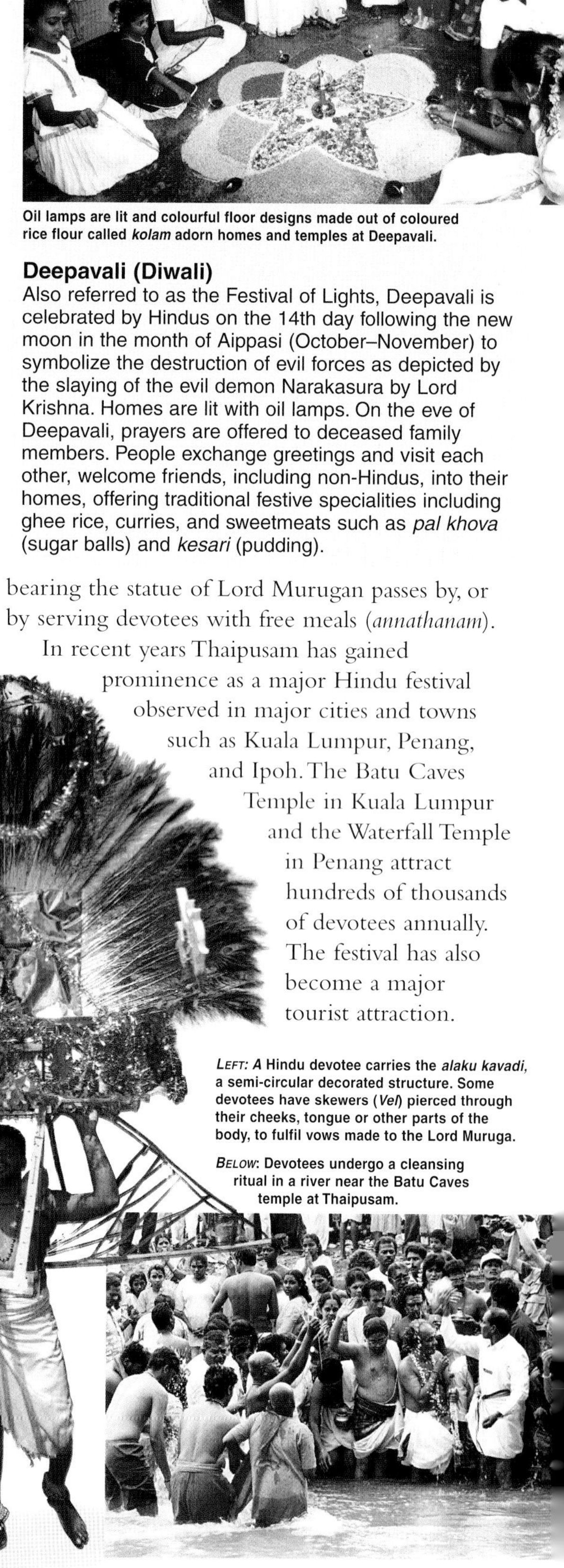

LEFT: A Hindu devotee carries the *alaku kavadi*, a semi-circular decorated structure. Some devotees have skewers (*Vel*) pierced through their cheeks, tongue or other parts of the body, to fulfil vows made to the Lord Muruga.

BELOW: Devotees undergo a cleansing ritual in a river near the Batu Caves temple at Thaipusam.

Temple festivals

Festivals dedicated to particular deities are celebrated more elaborately in temples than in homes. One such festival is Vaikasi Visakam, which falls in May–June, and is considered the birth star of Lord Subramaniam. Vinayagar Cathurthi, which falls on the fourth day of the month of Avani (August–September) in the Hindu calendar, is dedicated to Lord Vinayagar—popularly called Lord Ganesha—who is believed to help worshippers overcome obstacles in their life. Kartikkai Deepam is dedicated to Lord Shiva and falls in the month of Kartikkai (November–December), and Skanda Shasti, which is dedicated to Lord Subramaniam or Lord Murugan, falls on the fifth day of the new moon in the month of Aippasi (October–November).

In addition, certain holy days are observed as temple festivals, such as Sivarathiri which falls in the month of Masi (February–March). It is believed that Lord Shiva manifests himself in all the Sivalingams (image of Lord Shiva) on the day. Temple prayers are held at regular intervals with four ritual ablutions (*abhishekam*), and devotees keep awake throughout the night. Devotees also offer special prayers to Lord Shiva on the occasion of Panguni Utthiram, which falls on the full moon day in the month of Panguni (March–April).

A devotee performs fire walking (*thimathi*) to fulfil vows during the Chittirai Paruvam festival, which falls in April-May.

Priests give thanks to the Goddess Sri Muthu Mariamman in a ritual bathing of the deity with milk, honey, lime and sandalwood paste.

Hindu life cycle rites

The Hindu texts prescribe 18 *samskara* (rites of passage) for an individual from birth until death. With increased urbanization, education and a growing number of nuclear families, many of these rites have lost their importance. However, orthodox Hindus continue to observe most of them.

Birth

The birth of the first child has great significance for a family, and various precautions are observed to ensure no harm befalls the mother and her unborn child. It is believed that women in an advanced stage of pregnancy are vulnerable to evil spirits, and ceremonies are conducted during the seventh and ninth months of pregnancy (known as *valaikappu* and *cimantham* respectively) to ward off any negative influences (above). Both mother and her newborn undergo a purification rite on the 31st day after birth (left).

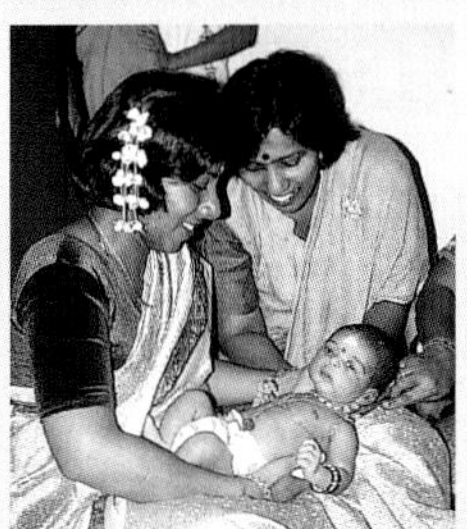

Hair ritual

A ceremony is held to shave a child's 'first' hair after his or her first month. A priest usually presides, and performs a prayer (*pooja*) to Lord Ganesha and to the nine planets (*navagragam*) before the head is shaved (right), after which sandalwood paste is applied to the head, and the child is ornamented. A feast follows.

Ear piercing

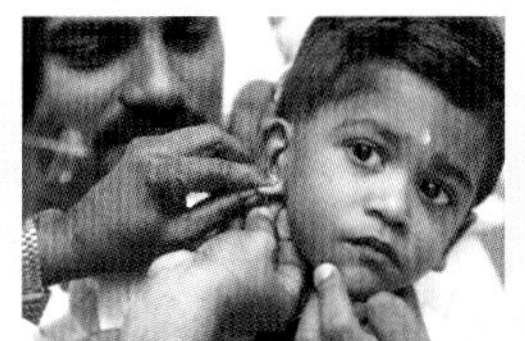

Among orthodox Hindus, a ceremony is held to pierce a child's ears. Kinsmen attend the ceremony, especially a maternal uncle on whose lap the child sits while a goldsmith pierces the ears (above). Earrings are then inserted. Since the late 20th century, ear piercing has been done only for girls.

Puberty

A girl's first menstruation is marked by a purification ceremony on the ninth day of menses. From the first day of menses until the ceremony, the girl is confined to a room. The isolation is deemed necessary by orthodox Hindus who believe that she is in a state of ritual pollution (*thittu*). In the past, a shed was erected outside the house in which the girl would spend the nine days until the purification ceremony, which was sometimes conducted with great pomp and publicity. This served as an announcement that the daughter had reached marriageable age. While Hindus write a child's horoscope (*jatakam*) after birth, it is believed that a second *jatakam* based on the date and time of her first menstruation has much significance and bearing on her future.

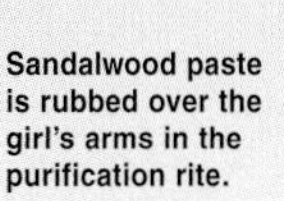

Sandalwood paste is rubbed over the girl's arms in the purification rite.

Marriage

The bride and her entourage arrive at the venue of the wedding accompanied by members of the groom's family as well as musicians.

Marriage is viewed among Hindus as a religious sacrament and occupies a significant place in the life on an individual. The importance accorded to the ceremonies associated with marriage is also extended to the preliminaries prior to the wedding. Beginning with the procedure to ensure compatibility of the prospective bride and groom by comparing horoscopes, to viewing the girl, confirmation of the wedding (*nitchiathartham*), and the engagement (*parisam*), most Hindus adhere to traditional practices that include determining auspicious times, type of exchanges and the number of persons attending the wedding.

Pre-wedding rituals include melting of gold (*ponnu urukku*) to make the sacred pendant (*thali*), and ritual purification baths and anointing ceremonies at dawn for the bride and groom in their respective homes. Before the bath they are anointed with oil.

The marriage ceremony usually takes place at a temple or a public hall. The bride's brother usually acts as the best man, while the groom's sister would be the bridesmaid. The couple is seated on a marriage dais (*manavarai*) before a fire and a priest recites Sanskrit prayers. Wedding rituals vary according to the customs of the sub-groups; however, an important part of the South Indian wedding is where the bride and groom wash their parents' feet. The tying of the *thali* around the bride's neck follows. This forms the climax of the wedding and is accompanied by loud drumming and oboe (*nagasvaram*) music. The groom then leads the bride around the sacred fire seven times. She places her feet on a grinding stone one at a time and he slips a ring on each of her second toes in a symbolic gesture of his family honouring her. The ceremony ends with blessings for the couple from kinsmen and well-wishers, and is followed by a feast.

The groom ties the *thali* around the bride's neck with three knots, to signify union of the spirit, mind and body.

Indian artistic and cultural traditions

The artistic and cultural expressions of Malaysian Indians are part of a rich, ancient heritage brought by their forebears in the 19th and 20th centuries. These traditions are mainly associated with Hinduism and Hindu mythology, and reflect the life, ethics and beliefs of the Indian people. The traditions active in Malaysia have retained many of their original styles and characteristics; at the same time, some have incorporated elements from other cultures.

A Bharata Natyam performance accompanied by an ensemble of musicians on traditional South Indian instruments including the *vina*, *mridangam* drum and violin.

Indian music

Musicians playing the *tavil* drum and the *nagasvaram* (oboe) at a wedding.

A primary example of the South Indian music tradition found in Malaysia is that of the *nagasvaram* (a double-reed aerophone also known as *nagas-varam*), a 95-centimetre long wooded instrument with a flared wooden, sometimes metal, bell. It is accompanied by a drone instrument (*ottu*), which is a slightly longer version of the *nagasvaram*, and a double-headed drum (*tavil* or *melam*). The left side of the *tavil* is played with a stick, while the right side is played with fingers wearing metal thimbles to give a sharp sound. The *nagasvaram* and *tavil* are usually played during temple ceremonies and festivals, processions, weddings and other occasions requiring a ceremonial ensemble.

The South Indian Carnatic music tradition is predominant in Malaysia, and has its roots in ancient Hindu culture. Most of the songs belonging to the Carnatic tradition are of a devotional nature, and they refer to various beneficent aspects of divinity, and are aesthetically expressed in melodious form. The languages in which the songs are composed include most of the South Indian languages such as Tamil, Telugu, Kannadam, and Malayalam, in addition to the classical language of Sanskrit. In ancient times, Carnatic music performances were held in temples, and this tradition has been followed in modern times in south India as well as in Malaysia. In addition, Carnatic music performances are organized by private associations such as the Sangeetha Abhivirdhi Sabha (Association for the Propagation of Music) in Kuala Lumpur. Organizations such as the Temple of Fine Arts also offer classes in Carnatic music.

Classical and folk dances

The South Indian classical dance form of Bharata Natyam is popular in Malaysia, not only due to its intrinsic merits, but also as a result of efforts taken by its Malaysian exponents such as Shivadas and Vatsala, Gopal Shetty, Chandrabhanu and Ramli Ibrahim, as well as private associations and organizations such as the Sangeetha Abhivirghi Sabha and the Temple of Fine Arts in Kuala Lumpur, to teach the art. In addition, local choreographers have made efforts to modify the traditional repertoire of the Bharata Natyam by adding new compositions and blending them with various other classical elements to create a contemporary form.

There are three main characteristic elements of Bharata Natyam: *nritta*, which is pure dance consisting of only rhythmic body movements; *nritya*, which consists of both body movements and expression; and *naatya*, which is the dramatic element, where the dancer plays the role of a character in a dance drama. The dance is accompanied by songs expressed in mime (*padam*). The music is based on Carnatic music, and the main musical instruments used to accompany Bharata Natyam include the cymbals, which provide the timing, and the *mridangam* drum. Sometimes the ensemble includes the *vina* (plucked lute), violin, *ghatam* (clay pot) and flute.

Popular folk dances include the Kolattam and the Karagattam and are associated with Hindu festivals. Karagaattam (pot dance) is of Tamil origin. *Karagam* refers to a clay pot, adorned with mango leaves and flowers, though nowadays vessels made of bronze and stainless steel are also used instead of the traditional clay pot. Karagaattam is performed by male and female dancers who balance the pots on their heads as they perform intricate steps and movements. The dance is traditionally performed in praise of the Hindu Goddess of Rain, Mariamman.

Above: A dance drama incorporating both classical and folk dance movements.

Top: Dancers striking sticks with their partners at cross rhythms in the Kolattam folk dance.

Pottery

Clay pots and pans, mostly unglazed, are used by people of Tamil descent in Malaysia for various purposes in their daily life. Large pots are used as containers for rice, water, milk, butter, ghee (clarified butter) and spices. Smaller pots and pans are used for cooking rice and curries, which are believed to taste better than when cooked in aluminium or stainless steel vessels, apparently because the clay pots absorb and release heat gradually while the food is being cooked. Smaller clay vessels are used as oil lamps (*akal vilakku*), which are an important feature of popular festivals such as Deepavali and Kaarttikai-Deepam; as censer stands (*duupakkaal*); and as *kendi* (water goblets). Clay pots are also used in religious festivals such as Ponggal, and in ceremonies such as weddings. A clay pan (*kollic catti*) is used in funerals to carry the fire brand for cremation. Clay pots (*ghatam*) are also used as musical instruments.

The art of making mostly unglazed pottery is practised by three main enterprises in Malaysia, located in Teluk Intan and Parit Buntar in the state of Perak, and in Kuala Selangor in Selangor.

Devotees lighting small oil lamps.

Above: Clay pots for various purposes: **1.** Cooking, **2.** Containers for rice, milk and spices, among others, **3.** Censer stands, and **4.** Oil lamps.

Left: Pots used in wedding ceremonies are known as ***muhuurttak kudam*** (auspicious pitcher), or ***puurana-kumbham*** (wholesome pot), for the water in them symbolizes the fullness of life.

Traditional costumes

The traditional attire of Indian women is the sari, worn with a tight-fitting blouse (*choli*). A sari is a rectangular piece of cloth about 5.5 metres in length, traditionally made from cotton or silk, but available since the late 20th century in a variety of synthetic fabrics as well. The sari fits any size and, if worn skilfully, can either accentuate or conceal. It can be worn in several different ways, but the most common style is to wind the cloth around the waist, with pleats in front, and drape the ornamental end (*pallu* in Tamil) over the left shoulder.

Women also wear the *salwaar khamez*, which is a long tunic (*khamez*) over trousers (*salwaar*, known as *seluar* in Malay). The *churidaar* is a slim-fitting version of the *salwaar*, and is worn with the *khamez* or *kurtaa*.

Men traditionally wear the *dhoti* (known as *veshti* or *vetti* in Tamil), an ankle-length rectangular white cotton cloth tied around the waist. Sometimes the end of the longer piece of the *dhoti* is pulled up between the legs and tucked into the back of the waist. A *dhoti* of silk with borders is used on ceremonious occasions. An informal outfit, similar to the *dhoti*, is the *lungi* (known as sarong in Malay). A piece of cotton or silk (*angavastiram*, also known as *thundu*) is traditionally draped around the shoulder like a stole. Nowadays, it is also used as a scarf around the neck and over the *jibbaa* (a collarless loose shirt of cotton or silk), or over a modern Western shirt. Contemporary Indian men sometimes wear a formal long-sleeved jacket with a Nehru collar.

Some men use the 'preformed' turban, similar to the turban worn by men of the Sikh faith, as a headdress, or simply wrap the *thundu* over their heads (known as *mundacu* in Tamil), especially when they carry out certain work, or when they play an important role in religious ceremonies.

Young Indian girls dress in a long skirt (*paavaaadai*) with a short bodice, and sometimes drape a separate piece of cloth (*thaamani* or *thaavani*) over the left shoulder. Young boys wear a *jibbaa* over trousers.

1. *Dhoti* worn with *jibbaa*.
2. Sari.
3. Modern *khamez* and *churidaar*.
4. *Jibbaa* over slim trousers with a *angavastiram* (long scarf) draped around the neck.

Ornamentation and adornments

Ornamentation among Indian women is quite elaborate; this is in accordance with the traditional Indian view that only things that are covered with ornaments or adornments are considered beautiful.

Traditional Indian jewellery includes necklaces, bangles, earrings and anklets, which are made of copper, gold and silver, and precious stones as well as pearls. Married women wear a special ornament, the *thali* or *mangala-sutra* (wedding string) as a symbol of their marital status. Traditional Indian jewellery is popular among Malaysian Indians as well as those of other ethnic groups, and is made by goldsmiths of Indian and other descent in major urban centres in the Peninsula.

Indian girls and women generally use the mark of *tilakam* or *pottu*, made of vermillion (*kunkumam*) on their foreheads as an adornment of cultural and aesthetic significance. Hindu men use the mark of *tiruniiru* or *vibhuuthi* (sacred ash), and a perpendicular mark of *naamam* on their foreheads as symbols of spiritual purity, associated with the Hindu Shaivite and the Vaishnavite faiths, respectively.

Women use flowers such as jasmine to adorn their hair, and garlands of flowers are used to adorn bridal couples. Garlands are also used to honour special guests and community leaders at social and cultural functions. The demand for garlands has contributed to the flourishing flower production industry in the country.

Indian goldsmiths use traditional methods to make jewellery.

ABOVE: Floral hair decorations:
1. A thick braid of jasmine (*malligai*) flowers as part of bridal headgear,
2. *Kanakambaram* strung together, and
3. Jasmine clusters.

LEFT: Flower garlands are used to adorn deities in temples as well as during religious rituals and festivals.

Kolam

Kolam are drawn by applying white or coloured coarsely ground rice with the thumb and forefinger on predetermined designs.

Kolam (meaning beauty or beautiful pattern in Tamil) is one of the most common and popular Indian cultural and artistic expressions. A similar art is known as *rangavalli* or *rangoli*, and as *aalpoonaa* in Bengali.

Kolam are usually drawn by women or girls, who learn the art as young as the age of five. They are traditionally drawn daily before sunrise and sunset at the main entrance of the artist's house as a symbol of good luck and welcome. They are also drawn in the prayer room, especially on festive occasions such as the Navarathri and Ponggal festivals, or on auspicious occasions such as weddings. Among the Malayalis, there is a custom of making *kolam*-like patterns with flowers on festive occasions such as the Tiruvonam festival.

Kolam may be drawn in various designs, such as dots (*pullikkolam*), straight lines (*kottukkolam*), inter-twining lines, intersecting lines, and in squares or circles. Intricate geometrical patterns may be pentagonal, hexagonal or octagonal.

The Tamil month of Maarkali (mid-December to mid-January) is a special month for drawing large *kolam* in front of the house. On certain festive occasions such as Ponggal or harvest festival, a large *kolam* is drawn to resemble a chariot with the figure of the sun inside. On Fridays, *kolam* are drawn in the shape of a lotus flower.

The drawing of beautiful patterns on the ground, floor or wall is said to have aesthetic, spiritual and psychological significance. It is also believed that the patterns help a person partake of the spirit of the occasion, be it festive, religious or social.

Indian culinary traditions

Indian food reflects the culinary traditions of southern and northern India as well as Sri Lanka, and those of the Indian Muslims, which were brought by migrants in the 19th and 20th centuries. In the years since, Indian cooking styles and tastes in Malaysia, whilst retaining their original flavours and characteristics, have evolved in the local cultural milieu to adapt to an environment that is multiracial and diverse.

Banana leaf cuisine is popular with non-Indian Malaysians too.

After a meal it is customary, especially among older Indians, to chew betel quid, which is areca nut and betel leaf coated with lime (*verrilai paaku* in Tamil or *pan* in Hindi or Hindustani).

South Indian food

South Indian (mainly Tamil) food includes *thosai* (rice and lentil pancakes), *idli* (steamed rice patties) and *vadai* (deep fried lentil or rice cakes), served with dhal curry and chutneys made of grated coconut, mint or coriander leaves, or mango. The popular and widely available banana leaf cuisine (so called because the food is served on banana leaves instead of plates) originates from south India, and is an elaborate meal of rice, vegetables, dhal curry or *vendayakari* (curry containing fenugreek seeds), meat and fish curries, *rasam* (a soup made with spices), *tayiru* (yogurt) or *mor* (buttermilk), *appalam* (lentil crackers) and lime or mango pickles (*acar*).

South Indian curries are usually hot, and typically use such spices as turmeric, coriander, ginger, garlic, mustard seeds and chillies. They are also wet, with the addition of coconut milk or tamarind juice, although there are also dry curried preparations.

North Indian food

North Indian food tends to be milder, and curries feature aromatic spices such as cinnamon, cloves, cardamom, aniseed and saffron, as well as cashewnuts, almonds and raisins, and dairy products such as milk, cream, yoghurt, cheese and cottage cheese (*paneer*).

Meat kebabs and tandoori *murgha* (chicken), grilled in a clay oven, are served alongside chicken or mutton *korma* (mild curries cooked with spices and milk) as accompaniments to a variety of breads made from wheat, including *parata*, *chapatti* (unleavened bread cooked on a griddle), *puri*, *naan* and *murtabak*.

North Indian traditions also include *briyani* (made of the long grain, aromatic Basmati or Patna rice which is flavoured with saffron), and pastries such as *samosa* (pastry stuffed with peas and potatoes) and *pakora* (savoury fritters).

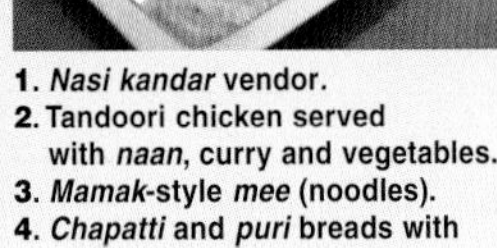

1. *Nasi kandar* vendor.
2. Tandoori chicken served with *naan*, curry and vegetables.
3. *Mamak*-style *mee* (noodles).
4. *Chapatti* and *puri* breads with vegetables and curries.
5. *Thosai* (rice and lentil pancakes) with accompaniments of chutney and dhal.
6. Spicy roasts of lamb and chicken served with curries and *korma*.
7. *Briyani* (flavoured rice).

Preparing roti canai

1. The popular *roti canai* is made by kneading wheat flour into a dough. **2.** The dough is twirled repeatedly through the air to spread it thin. **3.** It is then folded into layers. **4.** It is cooked on a griddle and served with dhal or curry. **5** and **6.** The bread has undergone much innovation in Malaysia, and is also made with a variety of fillings—banana (*roti pisang*), egg (*roti telur*), sardine (*roti sardine*), or meat, potato and onions (*murtabak*).

ABOVE: Twenty-four-hour Indian and *mamak* (Indo-Muslim) eateries, some of them furnished café style, are ubiquitous in Malaysian towns and cities.

LEFT: Indian-style tea (*teh tarik*, *teh* is 'tea' in Malay and *tarik* means 'to pull') is prepared by pouring the hot tea from one container into another several times. The higher the pull, the thicker the froth.

Indo-Muslim or *mamak* cuisine consists of mutton or chicken soup, and *nasi kandar*, a rice based buffet featuring a variety of meat curries which are thicker and have a distinctive flavour, and vegetables. Sri Lankan cuisine is found in a variety of spicy curries of mutton, chicken, fish or vegetables, served with *idiyappam* (steamed rice noodles called stringhoppers and known as *putu mayam* in Malay).

Influences and innovations

Indian cuisine in Malaysia has developed unique flavours due to the influence of Malay, Chinese, Nyonya and other culinary styles. The Malay style of cooking *nasi lemak*, and of the use of tapioca, yam and lemongrass (*serai*); and the Chinese style of cooking rice or wheat-based noodles as well as the use of beansprouts (*taugeh*), soybean cake (tofu), spring onions and bamboo shoots in the preparation of vegetable dishes and the use of soya sauce, have had some impact on Indian styles of cooking, so as to make the food palatable to a wider segment of the Malaysian population.

A recent innovation in Indian cooking is the use of soybean-based vegetarian food that is flavoured to taste like meat and seafood, which is perhaps derived from a similar practice associated with Chinese cuisine. Indeed, the Indian culinary tradition itself boasts of a fish-tasting curry that is made of unripe bananas. Elements of Malay cuisine have similarly been adopted, such as the use of *ikan bilis* (anchovies) *sambal*, and Indian cooks produce their own versions of *nasi lemak, nasi goreng* (fried rice) and *goreng pisang* (banana fritters).

Local Indo-Muslim hawkers have created unique dishes that are not found in India. One such dish Indian *mee goreng* (fried noodles), made of Chinese yellow egg noodles (*chow mein*) stir fried with mutton or lamb, tofu, beansprouts and tomato ketchup.

Spices in Indian cooking

A significant characteristic of Indian cuisine is the use of a variety of spices including asafoetida, cardamom, cloves, cinnamon, coriander seeds, cumin (*jiirakam*), fennel (*perum jiirakam*), fenugreek seeds, mustard seeds, nutmeg, pepper, saffron powder, sesame seeds and turmeric powder.

One reason for the use of several kinds of spices is that they are believed to preserve cooked food, especially in humid climates. In addition, spices stimulate the appetite. An Indian meal will certainly lack its characteristic verve without the presence of spices.

Some spices such as turmeric and coriander are also known for their antiseptic and curative qualities and have long been part of Ayurveda, the ancient Indian system of herbal medicine.

In the past, the spices used in the preparation of curries were laboriously ground on a grinding stone or pounded in a mortar with a pestle. These days curry powders are readily available, both separately and mixed (for meat or seafood dishes), and are produced by a number of commercial manufacturers in Malaysia.

Spices are freshly ground and added to dishes in many different combinations.

Preparation techniques

Naan is baked on the wall of the *tandoor*, an earthenware pot traditionally fired by charcoal. Marinated chicken or kebabs are skewered and grilled in the centre of the pot.

Rice dough is pressed into circular formations on rattan trays and steamed to form *idiyappam* (stringhoppers).

Vadai, a deep-fried savoury snack, is made from ground dhal and rice.

Food for festivals

Traditional festive fare includes special food items such as *pongal* (rice boiled with milk and brown sugar) which is a significant aspect of the Thai-ponggal (harvest) festival that falls in January or February (see 'Indian festivals and celebrations'), and *puliyodarai* (cooked rice mixed with saffron or turmeric powder and tamarind juice). Various sweetmeats such as *adirasam, laddu, halwa* and *kesari*, and savoury tidbits including *murukku, omapodi* and *vadai* are prepared for most Indian celebrations, including Deepavali and important occasions such as weddings.

An array of traditional Indian sweetmeats (left) and savoury tidbits *murukku* (below).

Another Malaysian Indo-Muslim creation is *mee rebus*, a dish of yellow noodles and bean sprouts in a gravy made with sweet potatoes, and garnished with squid, prawn fritters, boiled egg and fried shallots.

Chinese Peranakan society

The Chinese Peranakan (Peranakan Cina) *were localized Chinese in the Straits Settlements of Penang, Melaka and Singapore who wielded great influence over local affairs until Independence. Also referred to as Baba-Nyonya and Straits Chinese, today they exist as a distinct community and take pride in a rich heritage derived from the Chinese with Malay influences and other local innovations.*

Porcelain plate featuring the phoenix, a popular Peranakan motif.

Identity and community

Certain groups of Chinese in the former Straits Settlements identify themselves as Baba. Those in Melaka and Singapore also call themselves *Peranakan*, that is, *Peranakan Cina* (Chinese Peranakan), *peranakan* being Malay for 'local-born person or a person of mixed local and foreign parentage'. The Baba in Melaka speak a Hokkien-influenced Malay creole, while those in Penang speak a localized version of Hokkien. Most Chinese Peranakan are of Hokkien origin, but some are from other speech groups such as the Cantonese, Teochew and Hainanese. The men are known as Baba and the women, Nyonya, hence the term Baba-Nyonya.

There are a few thousand Chinese Peranakan in Melaka, although their exact number is not clear as they are classified in the census as Chinese. In Penang, there is no longer a distinct community of Chinese Peranakan, although the terms 'Baba' and 'Nyonya' are popularly used in the historical sense, and with reference to the localized Penang Chinese food and well-known Chinese Peranakan families.

Historical background

The Chinese Peranakan history in Malaysia can be traced to the Chinese settlement in Melaka in the 15th century. Due to a lack of Chinese women, the early settlers married local women. Their female offspring usually married Chinese immigrants whose numbers kept increasing in the 19th and early 20th centuries, although some intermarriages continued.

While such early intermarriages help to explain the ease of acculturation, with the offspring of such a union speaking Malay, the formation of a separate Chinese Peranakan community was due to their cultural uniqueness, the distinction of local-born versus foreign-born Chinese, their economic dominance in the 19th century and the political bond between the Chinese Peranakan elite and the colonial power. After World War II, they lost their economic dominance, and with Independence they lost their political influence as well. Nevertheless, the Chinese Peranakan survived as a community albeit they were looked down upon by the mainstream Chinese.

Religious beliefs

Most of the Chinese Peranakan in Malaysia follow Chinese popular religion, which involves worshipping deities and ancestors as well as placating ghosts. The deities and rites are Chinese, generally Taoist and Buddhist in origin, but the Chinese

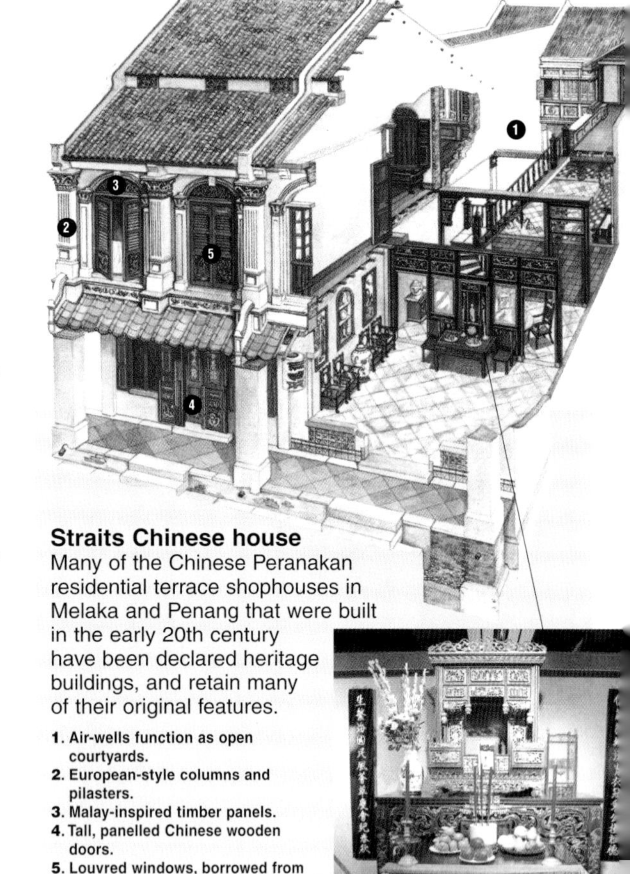

Straits Chinese house

Many of the Chinese Peranakan residential terrace shophouses in Melaka and Penang that were built in the early 20th century have been declared heritage buildings, and retain many of their original features.

1. Air-wells function as open courtyards.
2. European-style columns and pilasters.
3. Malay-inspired timber panels.
4. Tall, panelled Chinese wooden doors.
5. Louvred windows, borrowed from Portuguese colonial architecture.

RIGHT: An altar in a Peranakan home.

Peranakan dress through the ages

1880s: Peranakan men wore traditional Chinese garments and wore their hair in a queue.

1900s: A Peranakan family. The women dressed in traditional Malay-style baju kebaya, embroldered Chinese shoes and wore their hair in chignons, while men wore Chinese jackets, loose trousers,and, often, Western hats.

2000s: The *kebaya* is short and close-fitting—or long and loose—with intricately embroidered motifs. It is worn over a sarong, and adorned with a *kerongsang*.

Cultural traditions

The Chinese Peranakan are known for their localized cultural features such as spicy food, the women's adoption of the Malay sarong and *kebaya* (blouse), Malay folk songs, *pantun* (four-line poetry), Dondang Sayang (exchange of *pantun* accompanied by music) and *joget* dance. While older Nyonya women still wear the sarong and *kebaya*, the younger ones tend to prefer the 'modern' style dress like other Chinese women. Nevertheless, the Chinese Peranakan are proud of their heritage. This includes the famed Straits Chinese ceramics, silverware and antique Chinese furniture, mostly imported from China. These are part of the general Chinese material culture, but many of them have characteristics preferred by the Chinese Peranakan. For example, the colourful vases (*paso Shanghai*), incense pots (*nyolo*) and teapots (*tekoan*) commonly use phoenix and peony motifs. Various aspects of Chinese material culture are so associated with the Peranakan that they have been described as Straits Chinese.

Nyonya performers clad in sarong and *kebaya*.

ABOVE: An intricately carved wooden washstand with basin and chamber pot.

LEFT: Straits Chinese pot and teapot (*tekoan*).

Peranakan cuisine

Nyonya *angkoo* (literally 'red tortoise') *kuih*.

Peranakan Chinese food contains both Chinese and indigenous (mainly Malay and Indonesian) elements as well as the Nyonya's own innovations. The food is generally spicy, characterized by the use of *sambal* (chilli paste) and curry. The Peranakan Chinese are also well known for their *kuih* (sweets and pastries). Some dishes like *ponteh* (meat and vegetables cooked in a sweet sauce) and *kuih koci* (a *kuih* made of glutinous rice stuffed with coconut filling and coconut sugar and wrapped in banana leaves) are ritually significant in that they are used for offering to ancestors. Penang Nyonya food differs from the Melaka Nyonya style as it has Thai influences.

Leading Baba

Tun Tan Cheng Lock (1883–1960) was a Melaka-born Peranakan Chinese. A prominent nationalist who campaigned for Independence in the 1950s, he was also the founder of the Malayan Chinese Association (MCA), the leading Chinese political party in the ruling coalition (Barisan Nasional).

Tan Cheng Lock in 1949. He was conferred the title Tun in 1958.

Other Peranakan-type communities

The localized Chinese in Kelantan who speak a creole of Hokkien and the local Malay dialect, are similar to the Baba-Nyonya. They are mostly rural dwellers in northeast Kelantan, and in Terengganu they are found mainly in Tirok and Pulau Bahagia. Although they are often referred to by the other Chinese as Baba, they do not call themselves such, identifying themselves as Teng-lang ('Chinese' in Hokkien) as do the Malaysian Hokkien. Some of those in Kelantan also speak a local Thai dialect. Their cultural practices reflect Kelantan and Malay influences. For example, they often carry a long piece of cloth called *kain batik lepas*, which the women use as a head scarf, while the men tie it around their waist or use it as a *semutar* (head-cloth). It is also common for the men to wear sarongs.

Straits Chinese publications

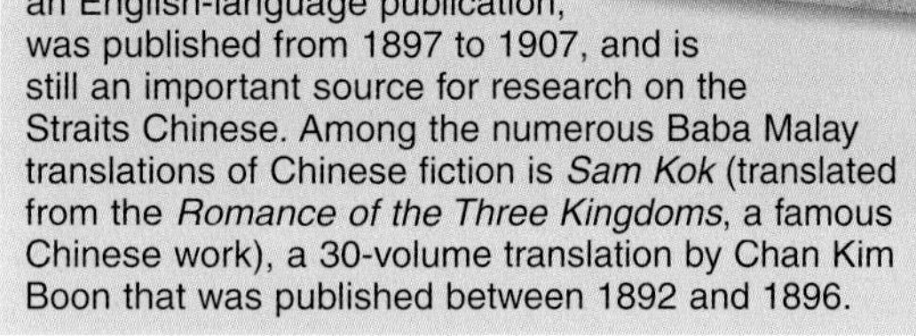

Between the late 19th century and the 1940s, the Baba-Nyonya, mainly those in Singapore, published newspapers, writings, and Baba Malay translations of Chinese fiction. They pioneered the publication of newspapers in romanized Malay, with the titles *Surat Khabar Peranakan* and *Bintang Timor*, both in 1894. The *Straits Chinese Magazine*, an English-language publication, was published from 1897 to 1907, and is still an important source for research on the Straits Chinese. Among the numerous Baba Malay translations of Chinese fiction is *Sam Kok* (translated from the *Romance of the Three Kingdoms*, a famous Chinese work), a 30-volume translation by Chan Kim Boon that was published between 1892 and 1896.

Peranakan have also incorporated the Malay beliefs in *keramat* and guardian spirits of sacred sites. The Peranakan observe all major Chinese festivals (see 'Chinese festivals and celebrations'). Ancestor worship is observed in two ways: the *piara abu* (installing ancestral altars) system and the *chhia abu* (invitation system). In the latter, there is no regular ancestral altar at home, and a temporary one is installed on the day of worship, mainly on a festival or the death anniversaries of ancestors. Funerals are largely conducted according to Hokkien rites.

Modern-day Chinese Peranakan

The Chinese Peranakan had to adjust to their declined status in a predominantly Hokkien-speaking mainstream Chinese community. Their children attend national schools, where Malay is the medium of instruction, although some attend Chinese-medium schools. Unlike in the 19th and early 20th centuries, marriages between Chinese Peranakan and non-Peranakan Chinese now often involve the Peranakan partners being absorbed into the mainstream Chinese community.

Peranakan weddings

The Peranakan still observe many traditional Chinese wedding rites, mostly simplified or shortened, and more elaborate if the old-fashioned wedding (*kahwin dolu-kala*) is observed. The hairdo rite (*chhi-thau*) is still practised in an old-fashioned wedding. This rite, performed in the early hours of the day of wedding, involves sitting on a *gantang* (wooden rice measure) and a specialist performing ritual combing. It marks the new marriage status of a groom or bride.

While the Nyonya have adopted the Western style wedding dress, as have other Chinese, some weddings still involve costumes that can be traced to the late Qing period. Unlike the old-fashioned marriage ceremony which in the past lasted 12 days, nowadays it is conducted in a single day, ending with a feast in the evening.

Bridal couple in traditional wedding costumes.

Eurasians and their traditions

Most Malaysian Eurasians trace their origins to the original Portuguese-Malay community of Portuguese Melaka in the 16th and 17th centuries, although some are descendants of unions between other colonial powers—the Dutch and the British—and local women. Through further intermarriage in pluralistic Malaysia, the community today comprises members of different religious beliefs, but the majority are Christian. They have a rich and diverse cultural heritage, reflecting a syncretism of cultural elements, both of Asian and European origin.

A cultural dance at one of Melaka's landmarks, the A Famosa, part of the fort built by the Portuguese.

The early Melaka community

The initial community that was established in Melaka during its occupation by the Portuguese (1511–1641) was almost entirely of Portuguese-Eurasian descent, a people known as the 'Luso-Malays'. The community enjoyed many privileges and became actively involved in the administration of the town and the running of the hospital, schools, convents and churches that were built by the Portuguese. The community also included some people of Castilian origin , reflecting the close collaboration between Portugal and the Kingdom of Castile (former kingdom comprising most of modern Spain).

The Dutch, who seized Melaka from the Portuguese in 1641, further developed the town with additional buildings and facilities to protect their interests and control the lucrative spice trade. The Stadthuys, Christ Church and other buildings in the complex now known as Red Square are examples of Dutch architecture of the time. The Dutch, too, intermarried with local women and further expanded the Eurasian community.

Thousands of Christians bearing candles gather at Saint Peter's Church in Melaka on Good Friday. The church, built in 1710, during Dutch rule, is the oldest Catholic church in Malaysia.

Migration

Due to oppression under Dutch rule, many Luso-Malays moved to the island of Phuket in Siam (now Thailand), then Kedah (referred to by Europeans at the time as Port Queda) and eventually to Penang, where the British arrived in 1786. The Church of the Assumption in Penang was named to coincide with the Feast of the Assumption on 15 August, the day the Catholic Eurasians arrived in Penang. The majority of the early Eurasians settled along the island's coastline in the vicinity of Pulau Tikus. To meet the demand for staff in its administration, the British encouraged the immigration of Ceylonese Dutch Burghers (members of a mercantile class) in the late 19th century. From thence and with intermarriage, the Eurasian community in Penang grew and moved to other parts of the Peninsula, taking up a wide variety of employment, although many served as public servants of the Straits Settlements and the Federated Malay States.

Eurasian girls perform a lively folk dance.

Following Independence in 1957, some members of the community emigrated to Britain, Australia and Canada. The majority, however, identified themselves with Malaya and remained in the land of their birth. The community is small (some 12,640 in 2004), and dispersed throughout the country, with the majority to be found in the states of Melaka, Penang and Selangor.

Occupations

Eurasians were the founding students and teachers of modern education in Malaysia through the early church schools and the De La Salle and Holy Infant Jesus missions. They were also the founding parishioners of the Roman Catholic Church. Many Eurasians have served—and continue to serve—the Malaysian government in the education, legal, civil and administrative services of the nation, including the armed forces and police. They have particularly excelled in education, law, public administration, engineering, the military and security services (some have been decorated with the highest awards for courage and bravery), music and the arts. In sports, several Eurasians have represented the nation in hockey, cricket and soccer.

Cultural traditions

The culture of the Eurasians is strongly Portuguese and Malay influenced. The Portuguese Settlement in Melaka remains the bastion of the community's

Festivals

The traditions of the Eurasians are essentially Melaka Portuguese and are closely tied to Roman Catholicism. They are passed down the generations and mostly practised in the privacy of homes or localized social settings, except for the practice of curry lunches and tea dances on selected Sundays and 'Open House' during the season of Christmas.

Some traditions, however, are more publicly celebrated with the more popular ones included in the tourism calendar, such as Festa Intrudo (Water Festival for the cleansing of spirit before the season of Lent), Festa San Juan (Festival of Lights in recognition of Saint John the Baptist as the bearer of the torch), and Festa San Pedro (Feast of Saint Peter to ensure safe passage and bountiful harvests for fishermen), which is the best known Melaka Portuguese festival.

The Festa San Pedro, held each year in June, attracts visitors to join the residents in songs, dances, fun fairs, game stalls, the decorated boat festival and the solemn procession of the statue of Saint Peter. The special position of the festival among the Melaka Portuguese community dates back to the days when fishing was the main livelihood.

Festa Intrudo (Water Festival) marks the last day of merriment before Lent, the Christian fasting period. In Melaka, people celebrate the festival by donning fancy dress and splashing water on each other.

ABOVE: Young girls sporting painted faces during the Festa San Pedro.

LEFT: The highlight of Festa San Pedro in Melaka is the procession bearing the statue of Saint Peter to the shore where the fishing boats are anchored.

RIGHT: A priest blesses the boats and prays for a bountiful harvest throughout the year. This ritual is symbolic of the Festa San Pedro.

LEFT: A parade of floats adds to the carnival atmosphere in Melaka during the Festa San Pedro.

preservation, growth and development. It was in Melaka that the *branyo*, a dance form similar to *ronggeng* and *joget*, and the music of *keroncong*, Mata Kantiga (singing of verses by men and women resembling the Malay *pantun*) and the popular Kristang tune *Jingli Nona* (meaning Singhalese girl) first found expression.

The Portuguese Settlement and Medan Portugis (Portuguese Square, built in 1983 to resemble a typical coastal town in Portugal) are the main conservatories of original dance forms, music and traditions. The settlement is administered by an officially appointed headman (*regedor*).

Some 1000 members of the Melaka Portuguese community, particularly its older members, speak the creole known as *Kristang* or *Papia Cristaõ* ('the language of the Christians'), which is a hybrid language of Portuguese, Malay and English.

The piquant flavours and variety of cuisine of the Melaka Portuguese reflect the syncretism evident in their culture, with creative variations to cater for more cosmopolitan palates. Popular Portuguese dishes include devil curry, *pacey singgang* (baked fish), *sambal belacan* vegetable, curry 'kapitan' and *feng* (a spicy dish of pork, pig's tongue and intestines).

Thai communities

During the 18th and 19th centuries, Thai settlers migrated south into the northern states of the Peninsula, which were then under Siamese suzerainty. The Thais of northern Peninsular Malaysia are mainly rural, engaged in rice farming and other agricultural activities. Most of them are Buddhist, and the temple and the institution of monkhood are central to their social and religious life. They have adopted to some extent the culture of the Malays, and are recognized as Bumiputera.

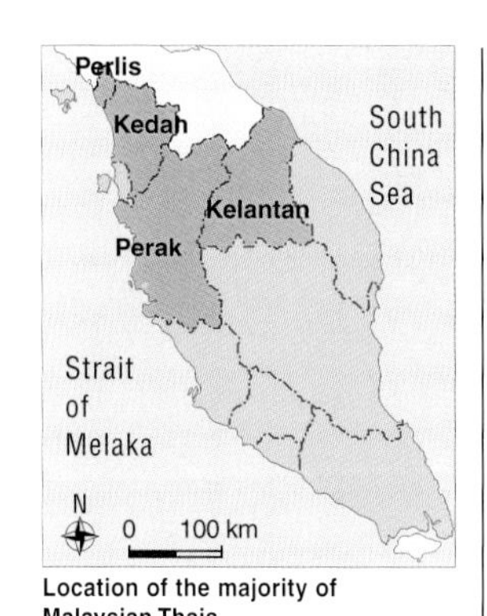

Location of the majority of Malaysian Thais.

History and demography

The migration of Thais into the Malay Peninsula between the 18th and 20th centuries occurred in response to political and economic circumstances in southern Thailand. Historical records indicate the presence of Thais in Kedah as early as 1782. Kedah, Perlis, and Kelantan were under the direct political sovereignty of Siam in the 18th and 19th centuries. In Kelantan, oral traditions confirm that some of the Thai settlements there are more than 100 years old.

The 1909 boundary demarcation between Kelantan and Thailand resulted in the Thai communities on the southern bank of the Golok River being made 'natives' of Kelantan overnight. The flow of Thai immigrants ceased after the four northern states of Kedah, Perlis, Kelantan and Terengganu were ceded to the British in the early 20th century.

Thai villages are mostly found in the border districts, or along traditional routes to Thailand. Most of the pioneer settlements were located within river flood plains, as in Kelantan, Perlis and Kedah. According to official statistics, the Thai population in Malaysia was approximately 38,400 in 2004. The majority are settled in Kedah, Perlis, Kelantan and Perak, with Kedah having the largest community.

The Thais are mainly rural dwellers and mostly engaged in rice farming and the cultivation of rubber, oil palm and tobacco. An increasing number are in the various professions and are engaged in urban-based employment.

Thai girls floating *krathong* (small lotus-shaped vessels made of banana leaves) containing candles, incense, flowers and coins on the waters off Penang during the Loy Krathong Festival, which is of Thai origin and falls around mid-November.

Assimilation

The Thais occupy a special position within Malay society with regard to land ownership and other privileges accorded to the Bumiputera. In Kedah and Kelantan, they are allowed to open up land in Malay reservation areas and are given legal titles to the land. Unlike the Malays, however, they are not allowed to buy an already developed piece of land in Malay reservation areas and can only sell their land in these areas to a Malay or a Malaysian Thai. They are also allowed membership of the political party originally reserved for the Malays, the United Malays National Organisation (UMNO). In addition, they are eligible for Bumiputera equity acquisition schemes such as the Amanah Saham Nasional and the Amanah Saham Bumiputera, as well as government education loans and scholarships provided for Bumiputera. This has helped improve the socioeconomic status of young Malaysian Thais, resulting in a small number of them becoming government officials, teachers and professionals, while the community remains agrarian in outlook.

The Thais have adapted to the local culture, assimilating Malay cultural habits, dress and speaking local Malay dialects. At the same time, they have exerted considerable influence on local Malay culture, for instance, on dance theatre forms such as Menora.

LEFT: Malaysian Thais represented at the annual Colours of Malaysia parade.

RIGHT: Menora is a Thai-influenced dance drama performed in Kelantan, Kedah and Penang, which has integrated elements of other local theatre forms.

Social and religious life in Thai villages

Most Thai villages are made up of between 15 and 25 households. The headman (*phuyaiban*), the village elders and the monks (*phra*) play a dominant role as community leaders. The headman normally mediates with government agencies, while the monks look after the religious affairs of the community.

In terms of social leadership, the influence of the monks is quite extensive because many of them are consulted beyond the call of their ritual duties. Some monks are experts in traditional methods of healing, while others are involved in community work, teaching youths to read and write the Thai language, and instructing them in the teachings of the Buddha. Thai monks from Kelantan and Kedah also serve in temples in other parts of Peninsular Malaysia. A religious and communal network links Thai villages and rural temples with Buddhist religious establishments in urban centres in other states, where the devotees are mainly Chinese.

Central to the culture and lifestyle of the Thai villagers are Theravada Buddhism, the Thai language and practices of Thai culture based on Buddhist teachings. Most of the monks who control the state ecclesiastical organizations (*sangha* or the institution of the monks) in Kelantan and Kedah are ethnic Thai. Although Buddhism is a minority religion, the *sangha* enjoys royal patronage of the Muslim ruler in both states. Senior monks in the Malaysia Thai *sangha* are required to obtain recognition from the Thai *sangha*, through examinations and appointments by the head of the Thai *sangha*.

The Songkraan water festival is celebrated with processions in Thai villages.

FAR LEFT: Postcard of Siamese Padoga, Penang. The King Edward VII stamp dates the card to between 1899 and 1911.

LEFT: The Giant Buddha Temple, Kelantan.

BELOW: The oldest functioning Thai temple in Kelantan is Wat Uttamaran, at Repek.

The wat (temple)

Most Thai villages have a temple (*wat*) of their own which is the centre of social and religious life. In smaller villages, a pavilion (*samnaksong*) is built to accommodate visiting monks who make regular rounds to conduct rituals. Material and financial support for the temple and its clergy comes from village residents as well as from other devotees who live outside the village. Households take turns to deliver cooked food to the monks at the temple on a daily basis. The Chinese, especially those who live in nearby rural areas, also provide financial material to the temple and regularly attend temple events.

Temple celebrations (*ngaan*) are held annually on certain dates according to the lunar and Buddhist calendar to commemorate various events in the life of the Buddha, including his birth, enlightenment and death (Wesak, around May); the Buddha's first sermon (Makhapuja, around February); the Buddhist new year (around second week of April); the Songkraan Festival (water festival, lunar New Year for Thai Buddhists); the beginning and the end of Khao Phansa (Buddhist retreat, from around July to October), and Loy Krathong in November. These celebrations often incorporate authentic Thai food fairs, and performances of Thai traditional dance theatre, shadow puppet shows and music. Such occasions also provide an opportunity for socialization between the villagers and Malaysian Thais from other villages.

BELOW: Monks giving holy strings to Buddhist devotees at a wat in Pasir Panjang, Kelantan.

Novice monks and nuns reciting text at their ordination.

Ordination ceremony

An ordination ceremony, like other major ritual undertakings of the temple, forms an integral part of the ritual cycle of the village. It brings together not only people of the same village, but also Thais and other Buddhists from around the district, as well as relatives and monks from across the border in southern Thailand. For a man, to be ordained as a monk (*phra*) is an important part of his being a Buddhist Thai; it symbolizes renunciation, uplifts his status and brings merit to both himself and his family. Ideally, a Thai is ordained as a monk upon reaching the age of 20. He may be ordained as a novice (*nen*) at an earlier age to get familiarized with the monastic routine. There are two kinds of ordination: one is for long-term service in monkhood, the other, for a short period lasting between seven days and three months. Most Thais who opt for the first kind remain in the *sangha* and serve as career monks.

Other ethnic communities

Adding to the ethnic diversity of Peninsular Malaysia are minority groups that settled in the country at various times over the centuries. Among the longest established are the Chitties, who are descended from Indian merchants in the Melaka Sultanate. The Nepalese, some of whom were Gurkha soldiers brought in by the British during the Emergency (1948–60), also came to Malaya to work in the gold mines and plantations. More recent migrants from various parts of Asia have established small communities in the country.

Top: A Chitty family outside their home in Melaka.

Above: Chitty youngsters playing a game of *congkak*.

A Chitty with a portrait of his mother. The Chitties are a distinctive community descended from Straits-born Indians.

The Chitties of Melaka

Indian tin and spice traders from the Coromandel coast of eastern India came to Melaka in the 15th century and found a niche in the vibrant commercial life of the city as merchants and goldsmiths. Members of that community and their descendants intermarried with local Malay women, and adopted the Malay language, customs and culture, and are known as Chitties. In religious matters, however, they maintained their strict practice of Shaivaite Hinduism.

The Portuguese and Dutch occupation of Melaka did not affect the Chitties adversely and during these two periods of colonial rule the community acquired land on which to build temples, the oldest surviving one being the Sri Poyatha Vinayagar Temple, built in 1781. Under the British, however, the community was edged out of the tin trade and other occupations, and by the end of the 19th century was dependent upon rice farming. Many Chitties left for Singapore before World War II, and today the Melaka community comprises only a few hundred people living at Kampung Tujung in Gajah Berang, which name local tradition claims is a corruption of Kanchipuram, the ancient Indian port on the Coromandel coast.

Chitty culture and religion

The Chitties maintain a vibrant cultural and religious life. In terms of language, dress and food, the community is Malay. Women traditionally wear a sarong with the *kebaya panjang* (long blouse) or *kebaya pendek* (short blouse), depending on their marital status, with the *binpoh* (handkerchief) worn as a shawl. Men wear the *dhoti* (rectangular piece of unstitched cloth wrapped about the waist and legs) for religious occasions whilst for traditional events they wear *kain pelekat* with a Nehru jacket. Daily dress follows modern Indian and Western trends.

While the Chitties do not speak Tamil but speak Malay as their daily language, many Tamil words have been retained, particularly those relating to socio-cultural religious matters such as *sami* (god or holy man), *ubayam* (auspice), *poosari* (priest), *abishegam* (bathing the deity), *maalai* (garland) and *poojai* (ceremonial offerings).

Chitty food is entirely Malay with dishes such as *nasi lemak* (or *pulut tekan*) prepared on special religious occasions and regarded as a delicacy.

The focal point of Chitty cultural life is their Hindu religion. The community has a number of temples and shrines, the most important being the Sri Muthu Mariamman and Anglamman, both in Kampung Tujung, and the Sri Poyyatha Vinayagar Moorthi Temple in Melaka. Several religious festivals are celebrated annually, including Bhogi Parachu (Thai-ponggal) in January, Mariamman Thirunal (Pesta Datuk Charchar) in May, and Deepavali in November. Religious observances are strictly maintained during these festivals, particularly with respect to food and dietary rules. Hindu days of fasting are observed and the consumption of beef is prohibited.

Mariamman Thirunal is the most important Chitty festival. Several thousand people (including

Sri Poyyatha Vinayagar Moorthi Temple, Melaka, is over 200 years old.

ABOVE: Malaysian Gurkhas Association founding member Bhakta Bahadur Rana (second from left) offers prayers for Gurkhas slain during the Emergency.

TOP: Gurkha security guards at an exclusive apartment complex in Kuala Lumpur.

The Nepalese

The Nepalese in Malaysia, popularly known as Gurkhas, are a minority group that settled in Peninsular Malaysia in the 1950s. Although some were Gurkha military personnel recruited by the British to fight communism in the country and who remained upon completion of their service, many of the early Nepalese migrants worked in the gold mines of Raub and in the plantations, as well as in the auxiliaries under the British. Many became naturalized citizens after Malaya became an independent nation in 1957. Today the Nepalese, numbering some 1000, are mainly found in Kuala Lumpur and the state of Selangor.

The Gurkha Society of Selangor and Federal Territory maintains and promotes Nepalese cultural and social practices within the community. It also encourages interaction amongst the Nepalese as well as with other ethnic groups. Although the community has its share of doctors, engineers, bank officers, businessmen and teachers, the majority of the Nepalese work as bodyguards and security guards, a throwback to the reputation of the Gurkhas.

An elder blesses a young relative during Dashera, which is the main celebration observed by the Nepalese community in Malaysia.

Culture and traditions

Although the Gurkhas were mainly Buddhists, the majority of Nepalese in Malaysia are Hindus. The main Nepalese celebration, Dashera, which falls in the month of October, is a celebration of victory over evil, and is marked by nine days of prayer, followed by six days of visiting amongst family members. It is customary for the younger generation to visit their elders at this time, and for older people to bless their younger kin by putting a *tika* (mark) made of rice mixed with yoghurt on their foreheads. The occasion also gives families the opportunity to reaffirm ties and mend any rifts that may have occurred during the previous year.

Most Nepalese speak five languages (English, Malay, Nepalese, Hindi and Tamil), but few are literate in Nepalese. Their children attend government schools.

The Gurkha tradition of bravery and skill

The Gurkhas became legendary soldiers during the Anglo-Nepali conflict (1812–15) when Britain was preventing the kingdom of Nepal from expanding. Though they were defeated in the end, the bravery of the Nepalese made such a great impression on the British that Britain started recruiting them into its own army the following year, setting up in the process, the Brigade of Gurkhas.

Labelled 'Gurkha' after the Gorkha region of Nepal, from which the first group of these soldiers came, the term has become synonymous with bravery, loyalty and warring skills. Legend has it that the sharp curved Gurkha sword (*kukri*), cannot be sheathed until it has drawn blood, and in peacetime, a Gurkha must nick himself first before sheathing the knife. For almost two centuries the Gurkhas have participated in almost every armed conflict involving Britain and British colonies, including World Wars I and II. Gurkhas in the British army were involved in the Emergency (1948–60) as well as the Confrontation between Malaysia and Indonesia (1962–66). More recently, they were with the first peacekeeping troops sent to Kosovo and East Timor in the 1990s.

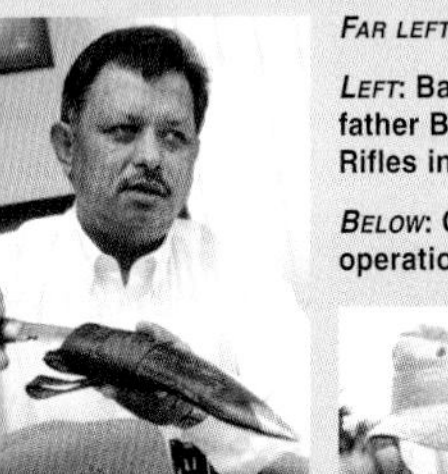

FAR LEFT: Bhakta Bahadur (left) with another Gurkha, 1942.

LEFT: Bal Bahadur Rana with a *kukri*, the Gurkha weapon. His father Bhakta Bahadur came to Malaysia with the 2nd Gurkha Rifles in 1942.

BELOW: Gurkha soldiers and the company commander during operations in the Labis area in Johor in 1964.

large numbers of Chinese Peranakan or Baba) escort the image of the goddess from the Sri Muthu Mariamman Temple to the Sri Poyyatha Vinayagar Moorthis Temple. Many of the devotees perform *alboo* (piercing of the cheek and tongue by long skewers), others carry pots of milk on their heads or *vel kavadi* (large semi-circular steel frames decorated with flowers and colourful motifs). On the return journey, the chariot bearing the image is drawn by priests and devotees and is accompanied by musicians playing the *melam* (drum) and *natheswaras* (flute).

Given the small size of the community and their lack of knowledge of Tamil, Tamil-speaking priests from other Hindu communities are called upon to conduct rites and prayers during religious festivals, and other Tamil Hindu communities cooperate to support their temples.

Social organization

Although they do not observe strict caste rules, the Chitties are divided into a number of castes: the Pillay (the most numerous), Naiker, Chitty, Pandaran, Rajah, Kallan, Pathar, Padaichi, Konner and Mudaliar. The origins of some castes are in ancestral occupations; for instance, the Pathar are said to have been goldsmiths in the past.

The community has organized itself to collectively administer temple lands and the cultural and religious traditions central to their life. Apart from religious links with other Tamil Hindu communities, such as the Nattukottai Chettiars and the Jaffna Tamils, the Chitties maintain close links with the Chinese Peranakan of Melaka.

The mother of a Chitty bride offers her blessing with a sprinkling of *air mawar* (rose water).

5. Iban men in warrior costumes carry a carved hornbill effigy that will be hoisted on a tall pole during the Gawai Kenyalang (Hornbill Festival), in honour of the God of War, Singalang Burung. These effigies now commemorate Iban heroes in the armed forces. In the past, they were used to invoke blessings upon warriors.

6. Penan elders.

7. Sarawak Malays (with headgear) and Chinese (without headgear), 1900.

1. Dayak war dance, 1846.
2. Kelabit headman Dita Bala with his son, early 1950s.
3. Bidayuh Jagoi priestesses presiding over a ceremony at which they present spirit offerings on behalf of their womenfolk who stand behind them.
4. Dayak men quench their thirst with water from hanging jungle vines, early 20th century.

ETHNIC GROUPS OF SARAWAK

Sarawak's rich cultural diversity reflects its heterogeneous, multi-ethnic population. More than 72 per cent of its population of approximately two million are indigenous peoples, with migrant communities making up the rest. As Malaysia's largest state, it is home to more than 20 indigenous groups who are collectively known as Dayak, who, in addition to the Malays, are recognized as Bumiputera and enjoy special rights. The non-indigenous population comprises mainly Chinese, many of whom are descendants of early settlers and who have been dominant in the economic sector since the 19th century. The Chinese are largely concentrated in the urban centres.

The indigenous communities—comprising the Malays, Iban, Bidayuh, Melanau and the Orang Ulu groups—are traditionally rural based. However, since the 1960s migration has resulted in many indigenous people leaving their traditional habitat for the urban centres and other parts of the state. Increasingly, too, they have abandoned the old ways and cultural practices of their forebears as they have modernized. The majority of the Dayaks have also turned from traditional beliefs to Christianity.

The Sarawak government takes pride in the state's diversity of people and traditions, as well as the tolerance and understanding that exists among the various communities towards each other's way of life, including religious practices. The state government actively promotes the culture and customs of the various ethnic groups. Major festivals are organized at state level, including Dayak Gawai, the Melanau Kaul festival, Chinese New Year and Malay Hari Raya Aidilfitri. The essence and spirit of these occasions have been carefully preserved, although some of the rituals associated with them have been abbreviated for tourism purposes. Gawai, for instance, was originally a three-day affair. While rural Dayak longhouse communities continue to observe their age-old thanksgiving customs, the official celebrations are a shortened form of the original, to cater better for tourism and the state's urban communities. The rich heritage of the indigenous groups has spurred the growth of cultural tourism in Sarawak. For instance, longhouse living has been successfully introduced in holiday resorts, and ethnic festivities are promoted as tourism attractions. Organized cultural tourism allows tourists to gain an insight into, and experience, local culture without intruding into the lives of the indigenous people.

The task of preserving local customs and traditions is entrusted to the Council of Local Customs and Traditions (Majlis Adat Istiadat). Its functions include recording and preserving the oral traditions of the indigenous communities so that their descendants will have access to such information. In addition, the council has codified the *adat* (customary law) of the native groups.

The last Kayan wedding held at Long Liko in Balui in 1998, before the community resettled due to the Bakun dam project.

Classification and identity of Sarawak ethnic groups

There are more than 20 indigenous groups in Sarawak, accounting for approximately 72 per cent of its population, while the remainder comprise mainly Chinese, descended from immigrant labourers brought in during Brooke rule in the mid-19th and early 20th centuries, and other migrant communities such as the Indians, Javanese and Eurasians. Traditionally, the indigenous groups lived within their own geographical and cultural confines, separated by the natural terrain of river systems, jungles and mountains.

LIMBANG RIVER
BARAM RIVER
KEMENA RIVER
Miri
Bintulu
South China Sea

Bidayuh girls performing a traditional dance, 2005.

Population (2004)

Ethnic groups	Population ('000)	%
Iban	657.7	29.0
Chinese	578.7	25.6
Malay	505.8	23.4
Bidayuh	181.5	8.0
Other Indigenous*	128.8	5.7
Melanau	124.3	5.4
Others	4.6	0.2
Indian	4.3	0.2
Non-Malaysian citizens	77.0	3.4
TOTAL	2,262.7	100

* Includes the Orang Ulu communities.

Source: Department of Statistics, 2004

Kelabit schoolchildren in Bario.

Ethnicity and classification

Sarawak's diverse ethnic population of over two million people comprises over 20 indigenous groups. The main native peoples consist of the Iban (or Sea Dayak), Malays, Bidayuh (or Land Dayak), Melanau and Orang Ulu (literally meaning 'people of the interior'), a grouping minority communities. Since 1963, when Malaysia was formed, these indigenous groups have been classified as Bumiputera, and enjoy special rights and privileges similar to Peninsular Malays (under theConstitution).

There have been instances of the various ethnic groups being classified and reclassified, mainly for political reasons, into categories such as Muslim Bumiputera, non-Muslim Bumiputera and Chinese; Dayak, Malay-Melanau, and Chinese; or Iban, Bidayuh, Kayan, Kenyah and Kelabit (Orang Ulu), Malay-Melanau, and Chinese.

In the early 1970s, the use of the terms of Dayak, Malay-Melanau and Chinese was probably related to the emerging political cleavage between the Dayak, who rallied around the Sarawak National Party (SNAP), the Malay-Melanau, who were behind the Parti Pesaka Bumiputera Bersatu (PBB), and the Chinese who supported the Sarawak United People's Party (SUPP). This ethno-political trichotomy gained momentum when, in 1983, the Parti Bansa Dayak Sarawak (PBDS) emerged to promote the Dayak political cause.

Where once the term Dayak was regarded as derogative, a change in perceptions occurred in the early 1980s, when the Iban, Bidayuh and Orang Ulu began to take pride in identifying themselves as Dayak. Although the government no longer uses the term Dayak for classification purposes, identification with the term among the Iban, Bidayuh and Orang Ulu is still strong. This identification is enhanced by common characteristics, such as rural lifestyles, socio-economic displacement and customary practices.

Administrative officers during a visit to an Iban longhouse, early 1960s.

Traditional Kayan and Kenyah longhouse settlement.

The Malay-Melanau proximity, on the other hand, is fostered by the close political association between the two communities due to the merger between the Malay-based political party, Parti Negara Sarawak (PANAS) and the Barisan Rakyat Jati Sarawak (BARJASA) to form PBB in the late 1960s. Melanau domination of the Malay-Melanau political bloc in the Parti Pesaka Bumiputera Bersatu served to cement close working political relations. The relationship is not underscored by adherence to the Islamic faith, however, as only some of the Melanau are Muslim.

A heavily tattooed Punan Busang man.

Thus, within the scenario of political developments in the state, changes in the use of the various ethnic categories appear to be driven by political correctness at any given time based on prevailing sentiments.

Iban longhouse at Nanga Sumpa.

Distribution and settlements

Modern Iban longhouse at the Baleh River.

The indigenous peoples of Sarawak continue to occupy traditional areas of habitation, although development and modernization have resulted in increasing migration to urban areas, and have affected traditional rural agricultural practices.

The Iban, the largest native group, live primarily along major river systems such as the Saribas-Skrang and Rajang. The first area to be settled by the Iban, who migrated from central Kalimantan in the 17th century and 18th centuries, was the Saribas-Skrang area, now known as the Sri Aman Division. The Rajang river basin was the second area where large groups of Iban settled.

The Bidayuh are an inland group, and are found mainly in the Kuching, Bau and Serian areas of the Kuching and Samarahan divisions.

The Kayan, Kenyah, Kelabit and other Orang Ulu communities inhabit the highlands of northeastern Sarawak.

The Malays are traditionally a coastal community, living along river banks in villages made up of individual family dwellings.

The Melanau, too, are coastal dwellers and are said to be among the earliest inhabitants of Sarawak. They are mainly settled in the Mukah area. Traditionally fishermen, they are reputed to be among the finest boat makers and craftsmen in the region. Many have embraced Islam, and some, Christianity, while the rest continue to observe animist beliefs.

Melanau village at Mukah.

A modern Bidayuh village near Kuching.

Heritage and cultural identity

The non-Muslim indigenous communities, namely, the Iban, Bidayuh and Orang Ulu, share a similar heritage and identity as they are longhouse dwellers and their socioeconomic lives revolve around the cultivation of rice.

Traditionally animists, most Iban, Bidayuh and Orang Ulu have embraced Christianity and, although they no longer subscribe to pagan beliefs, they continue to observe age-old customs and practices, such as harvest thanksgiving rituals, which reflects the importance of these rituals in maintaining community identity and cultural heritage.

Sarawak Malays, 1890s.

Chinese and other non-indigenous communities

Teochew Association Band in fancy dress in front of the Chinese temple in Kuching in 1930.

RIGHT: Chinese shop signs demonstrate the strong Chinese presence in Sibu in the 1970s.

The Chinese form the largest group among the non-indigenous peoples in Sarawak. They are mainly descendants of immigrant Chinese labourers who were brought to the state during Brooke rule (1841–1941) to work the economy. They have since become an integral part of the state political process as well as the state economy and society. They are found in large numbers in major towns and urban areas, and dominate the commercial sector of the economy.

Adat and the longhouse community

The various non-Muslim native groups of Sarawak—collectively known as Dayak—each have their own customary laws or adat. Adat *is the foundation for their community solidarity, survival and continuity.* Adat *refers to a wide range of native customs and also comprises accepted codes of conduct, manners and conventions by which Dayak society is ordered. It is enforceable in courts of law, and is administered by the Office of the Chief Registrar of the Native Courts of Sarawak.*

Artist's impression of a traditional headman's court in the early 20th century.

Dayak hierarchy
The Dayak traditionally lived in longhouses comprising between ten and 40 or more family apartments. The longhouse is a community and has a headman who presides over its activities. He is the guardian of the *adat* and acts as an arbitrator in conflicts between members of the longhouse. Above the headman are the regional chiefs, or *ketua masyarakat*, the lowest level of which is the *penghulu*, rising to the *pemanca* and then the *temenggong*. Besides administrative functions, these regional chiefs are given power to hear native cases, including appeal cases from the headman's court.

Adat as the basis of longhouse society

Adat comprises a vast range of customs and practices, including way of life, basic values, beliefs and indigenous religious systems, together with their associated rituals. It also extends to resource tenure and management, agriculture and other forms of forest use by which the Dayak traditionally gain their livelihood. Above all, it governs life in the longhouse, including social relationships, marriage and sexual matters, death and burial, and the distribution of property. Each ethnic group employs different terminology in its own language for the *adat* that it practises. Although *adat* differs from group to group, the basic concept remains the same.

Central to the concept of *adat* is the idea of 'balance'—between individuals as well as between the longhouse community and its physical and spiritual environment. When life in the longhouse is in 'balance', it is considered healthy and tranquil. *Adat* safeguards this state of affairs. When *adat* is breached, the 'balance' is disturbed. Depending on the seriousness of the breach, the family, the community and the environment may become 'heated up' (*angat*). To restore the 'balance', the person who has breached *adat* must provide *tunggu* (restitution) to the aggrieved party.

The future of adat

Adat performed effectively when society changed at a relatively slow pace. In modern times, it has proved less resilient as Dayak societies have experienced rapid change. This change, often termed 'development', is a powerful force against equilibrium, giving rise to a state of imbalance. The future role of *adat* largely depends on the ability of Dayak societies to adapt their *adat* to manage this imbalance such that their communities and basic values can continue to survive while still enjoying the benefits of development.

Native Courts
There are four native courts of jurisdiction and two courts of appeal.

Native Court of Appeal
Final court of appeal. Presided over by a judge and two people knowledgeable in adat law, e.g. *pemanca* or *temenggong*.

Resident's Native Court
First court of appeal. Presided over by the Resident or an officer with rank equivalent to Resident.

District Native Court
Presided over by the District Officer or a magistrate with the rank of a District Officer, assisted by two assessors from the district office.

Chief's Superior Court
Presided over by the regional chiefs (*pemanca* or *temenggong*), with assistance from two assessors from the district office.

Chief's Court
Presided over by the village headman (*penghulu*), who is assisted by two assessors from the district office.

Headman's Court
Presided over by the longhouse headman, who is assisted by two assessors from the district office.

Head of the Majlis Adat Istiadat, Datu Nellie Tangai.

Published codes of adat

During the rule of the Brooke family known as the White Rajahs of Sarawak, from 1841 to 1941, *adat* was jealously guarded as unwritten law. In 1915, one of the Brooke officers, A. B. Ward, secretly recorded in writing some aspects of the Iban *adat*. This work was only published in the *Sarawak Museum Journal* in 1960.

The first *adat* to be officially codified was the Iban *adat*, initially as the Sea Dayak (Iban) Fines, 1952. This was revised in 1955 under the Native Customary Laws Ordinance 1955. This marked an important watershed in the development of *adat* law in Sarawak as it provided that all customary laws gazetted under it become legal documents. This ordinance was replaced by the Native Customs (Declaration) Ordinance 1996. Other *adat* codified by the colonial administration resulted in the Orang Ulu Customary Code of Fines 1957.

Two important works on *adat* law, both compiled by A. J. N. Richards, are the Dayak (Iban) Adat Law 1963 and the Dayak (Bidayuh) Adat Law 1964. Although not gazetted under the Native Customary Laws Ordinance 1955, they have nevertheless been used by the Iban and Bidayuh as a guide to settle disputes and grievances.

Another important piece of legislation, the Native Courts Ordinance 1992, which replaced the Native Courts Ordinance 1955, prescribes the jurisdiction of the Native Courts and specifies the maximum penalties each native court can impose. The 1992 ordinance extended Native Courts jurisdiction to cover criminal cases and also increased the quantum of both restitution and secular fines.

In 1974, the Majlis Adat Istiadat (Council of Local Customs and Traditions) was established as a centre for the collection, codification, interpretation and dissemination of *adat* laws for the various Dayak peoples. The Majlis is custodian of the *adat*; the Office of the Chief Registrar of the Native Courts is responsible for its administration and implementation.

The codification of *adat* (customary) law provides a guide for the settlement of conflicts among Sarawak's indigenous communities.

Eight gongs and eight swords were given to the affected community for spiritual protection.

Dayung reciting a chant during the animal sacrifice.

Propitiation rite at dam site

A ritual cleansing of the land (*pelah daleh*) was conducted by the Orang Ulu at the site of the Bakun hydroelectric dam project in the mid-1990s. The ceremony was held to appease the spirits and to invoke their blessings for the community affected by the development.

Four senior ritual specialists (*dayung*) presided at the ceremony, and made offerings of food and 16 eggs (*tapo'*) placed atop splayed sticks, and eight sacrificial pigs. A ritual pole (*kayu belawing*) was raised at the site.

Restitution (Tunggu)

Tunggu comprises two essential aspects: restoration to the aggrieved party, made in *mungkul* (one *mungkul* has the value of RM1.00) by the person in breach of *adat*, thereby restoring the 'balance' between the two individuals; and appeasement in terms of *genselan* (ritual propitiation) or *pelasi menua* to 'cool' the environment and appease all concerned, namely the aggrieved party, the community and individuals, as well as the spirits.

If the breach of *adat* disturbs the state of the environment, the person responsible is required to provide further *tunggu* by *genselan*, that is the ritual slaughter of a chicken or a pig. A piece of iron for *kering semangat* (strengthening of the soul) and a small jar for *kurung semangat* (soul protection) are also provided as *genselan*.

Large jars are a part of restitution (*tunggu*) in certain breaches of *adat*.

For the most serious *adat* transgressions such as incest or causing death, the transgressor must provide *pelasi menua* (ritual cleansing of the land and people) by slaughtering a pig. A ceremonial sword for *kering semangat* (soul strengthening) and a large jar for *kurung semangat* (soul protection) are also provided as components of *pelasi menua*.

Adat was adopted by James Brooke, the first White Rajah, as a guide to administer justice when he established a Sarawak government in 1841. However, in addition to the *tunggu* paid to the aggrieved party, he introduced the secular fine, known in Iban as *ukum*, paid to the government, where a breach of *adat* was considered an offence against individual rights. Both *tunggu* and *ukum* are used and enforced by the native courts.

The harvest festival in Sarawak

Among the rice-farming communities of Sarawak, the harvest is an important occasion as the economic and social life of these groups revolves around the cultivation of rice. It is marked by elaborate rituals to give thanks to the gods for a bountiful harvest, and to invoke their blessings for the next crop. Traditionally, the Dayak communities celebrated their respective harvests at various times of the year, depending on the rice growing cycle. However, since 1965, the official Gawai Dayak (harvest festival) has been held on 1 and 2 June, which are state holidays.

Winners of the 2002 Kumang Gawai beauty pageant. In Iban mythology Kumang is the heavenly goddess and consort of Keling, a celestial cultural hero and prince charming. She is the model of beauty, love, fidelity, resourcefulness and talent, and he represents the ideal of manhood.

The Gawai Dayak is officially opened by dignitaries performing a symbolic pounding of rice.

Gawai Dayak

Prior to the formation of Malaysia, the Dayak communities in Sarawak traditionally held thanksgiving celebrations (known variously as *gawai* among the Iban, *gawia* among the Bidayuh and *ledoh* among the Kayan) at the end of the rice harvesting season. The harvest also marked the beginning of the next farming cycle and rituals were performed to seek the blessings of the gods and spirits for the coming year. Hence, the harvest festival is also celebrated as the New Year among these communities, namely the Iban, Bidayuh, Kayan and Kenyah and other Orang Ulu groups.

After 1963, however, these communities felt it was necessary to set a date for a joint harvest festival in order to gain recognition from the state government for the occasion and to get a public holiday declared on the day. Talks between community leaders and the government resulted in 1 June being chosen for the official harvest festival, as most Dayak groups begin their rice growing seasons around the middle of the year. The first officially sanctioned Gawai Dayak was held on 1 June 1965.

Gawai Dayak is now observed on 1 and 2 June each year. Both days are public holidays in the state.

Iban women in traditional finery at the annual Gawai Dayak parade in Kuching.

As with other major ethnic celebrations, there is an air of festivity in the cities and main towns, where markets and shops sell festive food, decorations and other items.

In the villages, harvest celebrations in the longhouse may last from three days to a week, featuring communal rituals and feasts participated by the entire longhouse community. Those who have moved to the urban centres in the state and other parts of Malaysia usually return to their village for the festivities.

In contrast, the celebrations in towns and urban centres feature fewer traditional trappings. Urban dwellers usually hold dinner celebrations on the eve of the harvest festival and usher in the new year. The followings days are 'open house' for visitors, who are entertained in similar fashion as in the longhouse.

Over the decades, new ceremonies have been introduced into the Gawai Dayak, such as beauty contests—Kumang Gawai for the women and Keling Gawai for the men. Since the mid-1990s, the state-sponsored Gawai Dayak has been celebrated on a grand scale, with an organized parade of indigenous groups in traditional costume, an abbreviated *miring* (food offerings to the spirits) ritual performed by priest-bards (*lemambang*), and cultural events to showcase various Dayak traditions. The government also actively promotes it as a tourism attraction, and in 2005 initiated a World Harvest Festival to coincide with the Gawai Dayak, inviting participants from indigenous communities in other Asian countries that observe similar harvest celebrations.

The Iban Gawai

Several weeks before the Gawai, households brew the festive drink of rice wine (*tuak*). The longhouse apartments are cleaned and decorated with *pua kumbu* (woven ritual blankets), new mats (*tikai*) and buntings, and traditional cakes are prepared. In the week before the Gawai, relatives who have moved away to work in various parts of the state return to their village to join the celebrations.

Gawai celebrations in the longhouse begin before dawn on 31 May, with the laying out of the mat (*beranchau tikai*) in the open gallery (*ruai*) to signify a *gawai*. The headman (*tuai rumah*) beats the gong to wake the residents. Final preparations are made for the *miring* ceremony (offerings to the gods) later in the afternoon.

Each family conducts two *miring* ceremonies: one in their respective portion of the *ruai*, and the other in their apartment. The *piring* (offerings) consist of glutinous rice, salt, boiled eggs, pancakes, betel nuts and *tuak*. This is followed by the family reunion dinner. In some longhouses, the families eat together on the *ruai*. Dinner is followed by merrymaking until just before midnight, when the priest-bard (*lemambang*) invokes the blessings of the gods for good fortune, good health and longevity. At midnight, the *tuai rumah* leads the longhouse community in ushering in the new year with a toast, and greetings of *gayu guru gerai nyamai* (longevity, good health, prosperity) are exchanged. This is followed by a bath to symbolically wash away any bad luck.

Entertaining guests at an Iban longhouse during the Gawai.

The next two days (1 and 2 June), are 'open house' for relatives and friends. Visitors from other longhouses or towns nearby are entertained with food, *tuak*, music and dance. On the third day, the *piring* are opened and examined, before being discarded.

The Gawai usually lasts a week, and ends with a closing ritual (*gawai ngiling tikai*, literally meaning ceremony to fold the mat).

Bidayuh thanksgiving festival

The Gawia Pinonguh (thanksgiving and appeasement festival) is a lavish three-day celebration that marks the culmination of a series of elaborate rituals observed by the Bidayuh throughout the rice-planting cycle (see 'Bidayuh society and traditions'). It takes place after the crop is harvested and the grain is stored, usually in May or June.

The festival is a time for feasting, merrymaking and spreading goodwill. People from neighbouring villages and longhouses are invited to join in the feast. While it is a social event that provides the longhouse occupants an opportunity to relax, renew friendships and meet new acquaintances, it is also a religious occasion. Various cleansing, appeasement and invocation rituals are conducted by ritual specialists and priestesses (*dayung boris*), mostly at night. Gongs are beaten throughout the period to invite the spirits to the feast.

On the first night, a *tipuo* (basket) filled with uncooked rice is placed in the longhouse apartments to welcome ancestral spirits to the festival. The following night, food offerings for the demons and spirits of the animals, insects and plants that were killed during the rice-planting season (*pingarang*) are placed on a platform outside the longhouse facing the west. On the third and last night, the chief ritual specialist and *dayung boris* recite sacred texts and perform rites to remove malignant influences from the apartments, rice bins and hearth. They then perform a ritual dance to summon the rice spirits to return. The dance marks the end of the *gawia*.

A four-day *ranung* (religious restrictions) period is observed after the *gawia*. The chief ritual specialist plants a bamboo pole in the path leading to the village as a sign to outsiders that entry into the village is prohibited during the period. It is believed that violating the taboo will bring harm and sickness to the villagers.

TOP: Priestesses place offerings outside the longhouse for the demons and spirits.

ABOVE: Gongs are beaten to invite spirits to the thanksgiving feast.

LEFT: Bidayuh priestesses (*dayung boris*) reciting sacred text during thanksgiving rituals.

FAR LEFT: The harvest festival begins with a ritual led by a shaman to thank the rice spirits.

Kayan harvest festival (Ledoh)

Among Kayan communities in the Belaga District, the *ledoh* (harvest festival) is held in April, with each longhouse celebrating it on a different date during the month so as to allow them to visit one another. The festival usually lasts three days, in contrast with week-long celebrations in the past. Rituals performed during the festival are those associated with the Bungan religion. As the majority of Kayan have embraced Christianity, only those longhouse communities that adhere to the Bungan faith conduct these rituals.

The main celebration

The festival begins with a visit to the cemetery on the first day to make offerings to the spirits of the departed and to invite them to join in the festival.

Meanwhile, at the longhouse, preparations for the celebration are underway. The *juk* (altar for the deity Bungan Malan) is erected on the headman's gallery for the main ritual. Visitors are welcomed with *borak* (rice wine) and feted at lunch.

This is followed by the *mara uting* ritual (consulting the oracle through the sacrifice of a pig), during which blood is collected in the sacrifice for two rituals that follow: the *pelah kemehing* (soul strengthening), and *pelah hingo* (soul protection). In the *pelah kemehing*, curls of shaved wood are dipped into the blood and placed on the blade of a ceremonial sword (*malat buk*). A shaman holds the sword above the heads of the longhouse members as they hold onto a parang positioned perpendicular to the floor with its sharp end downward. The *pelah hingo* ritual follows a similar procedure, with the shaman using a small flat gong (*sanang*) instead of the sword.

A Kayan shaman performs the *pelah hingo* (soul protection) ritual.

The *pelah kemehing* (soul strengthening) ritual at a Kayan longhouse.

In the evening, the longhouse members and their guests eat dinner in the gallery. Sharing food in the gallery on this occasion signifies communal solidarity. Later, everybody gathers around the *juk*, where rice wine is served, and two or three shamans sing sacred verses (*peleken dayong*) that describe the journey of the sacrificial pig to the spirit world. The audience joins in the chorus. The singing may go on till past midnight. When the singing is over, the *juk* is taken down, and one of the shamans performs a ritual dance to the accompaniment of gong music. The dance marks the end of the ritual.

Kuman Bahe'

On the second day, the longhouse community and their guests partake in the *kuman bahe'* (picnic) by the river, where they swim, fish and relax. The merrymaking continues in the evening on the longhouse gallery.

Ngayo

The *ngayo* (headhunting ritual) is performed on the third and final day. In the past, the significance of this ritual was that head trophies were believed to have inherent power over illness caused by breaking a taboo. These days, the *ngayo* has been redefined as a way of instilling discipline in a person to fight the 'enemy', which may take the form of ignorance or poverty. In the ritual, men in traditional battle dress with palm leaves tied around their right leg and right arm go into the bush and 'kill' a symbolic 'enemy'. The 'head' is taken back to the longhouse, where the men are welcomed by young women holding eggs in their hands. The *ledoh* festival ends with a communal meal on the gallery.

Shamanism in Sarawak

Shamanism forms a major component of the religious life and belief systems of most indigenous ethnic groups in Sarawak, even among some of those who have embraced Islam or Christianity. Using a variety of sometimes dramatic techniques, shamans work alongside other ritual specialists to perform a number of useful functions in their community, the most common being healing. Changing religious and secular influences, however, are now altering the shaman's traditional position.

Functions of shamans

Curing

Diagnosing and curing illnesses appears to be the most common function performed by shamans in Sarawak. Curing is often effected by recovering lost souls, or by confronting malevolent spirits. Shamans may also 'neutralize' inauspicious omens or dreams, and perform divination, often by communicating with spirits. In diagnosing affliction, shamans may use various objects, including quartz crystals, stones, eggs and plants.

An Orang Ulu shaman conducting a curing ritual in the mid-20th century. He beats a drum while seated on a length of rattan suspended from the ceiling of the longhouse. Once in a trance, he then peers into the drum to find the cause of his patient's ailment.

Shamans and other ritual specialists

Shamans typically coexist with other ritual practitioners, including priests, augurs, magicians and herbalists, as well as lay healers. In most communities, for example the Kayan and Iban, priests are distinguished from shamans. Traditional Melanau society was exceptional, having shamans, but not priests. Among the Bidayuh, shamans constitute a subcategory of priestesses known as *dayung boris* (or *baris*) who specialize in curing.

In the past, a common trait in most communities was that major calendrical rites, including those associated with agriculture, were performed by priests, priestesses, or other ritual specialists, rather than by shamans. Kayan priests, for example, had charge of all communal rituals, as well as rites of passage, while shamans performed only curing ceremonies. Iban shamans, too, were, and continue to be, concerned primarily with curing, while agricultural rituals were the domain of priest-bards, augurs, and farming specialists.

Where shamans coexisted with other ritual practitioners, their role was frequently peripheral, or subordinate to that of other specialists, as well as to secular leaders. Kayan shamans were never included in the inner circle of village leaders, whereas priests, as agents of established authority, frequently were. The Iban similarly attached greater prestige to priest-bards than to shamans, although shamans might become community leaders and sometimes doubled as priest-bards.

In addition, some groups recognized more than one kind of shamanic practitioner. Thus, the Iban distinguished between shamans (*manang*) and soul guides (*tukang sabak*), the former concerned chiefly with healing, the latter exclusively with the souls of the dead, while both were distinguished from priest-bards (*lemambang*), specialists responsible for invocatory rituals associated mainly with farming, material wealth, and community well-being.

Shamanic status

The status of the shaman varies between different ethnic groups. Among the egalitarian Iban, there is some ambiguity over the status of shamans as the role offers few economic rewards and little influence outside a purely ritual sphere. In stratified communities, shamans are

Becoming a shaman

The decision to become a shaman is usually a matter of individual inclination, as the role is rarely hereditary, although it may be associated with particular families. Shamans are sometimes recruited from those suffering physical or psychological afflictions. Bidayuh shamans, for example, are ordained by supernatural intervention in the form of an acute illness. However, apart from their religious calling, shamans are generally described as being identical to other community members.

Bidayuh *dayung boris* (priestesses) sing chants while seated on a swing. Each *dayung boris* is said to be aided by a spirit husband (*leng*) who assists her in communicating with the spirits and journeying to the unseen world.

Among some groups, such as the Bidayuh and Kayan, shamans are chiefly women, while among others such as the Iban, they are mainly men. In Kayan society, there is some association of shamanism with androgyny, while among the Iban, a small number of shamans alter their gender identity upon entering the calling and so become transvestite or 'transformed shamans' (*manang bali*). These *manang bali* were thought to be particularly effective.

An aspiring Iban shaman typically serves a period of apprenticeship with one or more established shamans, during which he learns the wording, composition and performance of complex poetic songs, followed by a public ritual of initiation (*bebangun*). First of all, however, he or she must be called by a spirit which subsequently becomes the novice's primary spirit helper. The call is experienced through dreams and is often validated by a gift from the spirit of curing charms. Later, practising shamans typically receive additional spirit helpers and undergo further *bebangun* until they attain the status of a fully 'ripe' or senior *manang mansau*. For aspiring Kayan shamans, the call is experienced not in dreams, but through dissociation, which the novice gradually learns to bring under control with the help of established shaman colleagues.

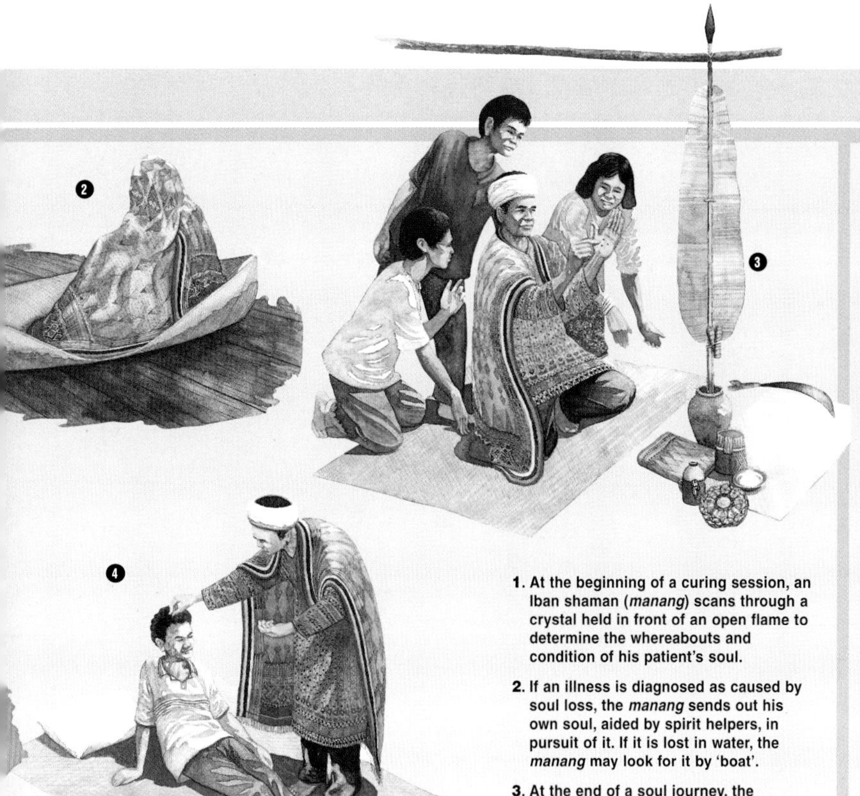

1. At the beginning of a curing session, an Iban shaman (*manang*) scans through a crystal held in front of an open flame to determine the whereabouts and condition of his patient's soul.
2. If an illness is diagnosed as caused by soul loss, the *manang* sends out his own soul, aided by spirit helpers, in pursuit of it. If it is lost in water, the *manang* may look for it by 'boat'.
3. At the end of a soul journey, the *manang* displays the recovered soul of the patient in the palm of his hand.
4. The shaman bathes the soul to ritually cool it before he reinserts it into the patient's head.

Guides for departed souls

Among some groups, shamans act as psychopomps, guiding the newly dead to the other world. Among the Iban, this role is performed, however, not by the *manang* (shaman), but by the *tukang sabak* or 'soul guide'. The latter, almost always a woman, sings a nightlong lamentation (*sabak*) immediately before burial, during which her soul is said to leave her body to escort the soul of the dead person to its place in the otherworld. The Iban shaman plays a different part in death rituals, severing the deceased's now dead plant image (*bungai* or 'flower'), a symbol of mortal life, from a living main plant stalk, symbolizing the surviving family, thereby effecting the deceased's final separation from the living.

An Iban *manang*, with a ritual *ikat* cloth draped over his shoulder, severs the deceased's plant image, whose picture is displayed at the base of the main plant stalk. This image is represented by a single branch to which a bead and shell armlet has been attached. The main stalk is left intact, symbolizing the still living rootstock of the deceased's family.

rarely, if ever, drawn from the highest strata. Among the Kayan, for instance, shamans (*dayung na'ah*) formerly constituted a lesser subcategory of ritual specialists including male priests (*dayung*). While priests were often included among the aristocratic elders who acted as village leaders, shamans never were. Among the similarly stratified Melanau, aristocrats in the past were generally suspicious of male shamans, who they feared might employ their knowledge of the spirit world to claim unwarranted authority. Hence, the role of shaman was considered incompatible with aristocratic status. On the other hand, powerful, high-ranking spirits were thought to be unable to form satisfactory relations with human beings of low status. Thus, most Melanau shamans came from the middle ranks of society. Shamanic success did, however, confer influence among the Melanau, and persons who found their ambitions blocked by birth might seek to realize them by becoming shamans, although, in doing so, they ran the risk of being accused of witchcraft.

Technique and performance

Among all groups, shamanic performances take place mainly at night and may be either private or community occasions. As public performances, they are sometimes elaborately staged. Ritual singing is central to shamanic rituals, and during the singing of ritual songs, shamans send out their soul on journeys into unseen realms. The ritual songs sung by the shaman narrate an account of the travels of his soul. These narratives are expressed in a poetic form of speech, which, although metaphoric, is nonetheless intelligible to lay audiences.

A Melanau shaman, mid-1900s, chants while seated on an elaborately carved swing or 'spirit bridge', which facilitated the summoning of spirits.

Melanau curing rituals

In the past, before their conversion to Islam and Christianity, the Melanau staged elaborate shamanic curing ceremonies within a complex sanctuary made to symbolize the cosmos. The top of the sanctuary was covered by a white cloth representing the sky, and the sanctuary contained a model house, placed in the rafters, where spirits of the upper world were received and from which a ladder descended to a model boat below, which served as the reception place of water and underworld spirits. A rattan swing or 'spirit bridge' was hung directly across the sanctuary and from it the officiating shamans swung while summoning spirits and treating patients. An orchestra signalled the arrival of different spirits by varying musical motifs. Fittingly, these ceremonies were described by the Melanau as 'entertainment'.

Spirit possession and trance

A characteristic of Malay and Melanau society in Sarawak is the practice of spirit possession with trance. As in Peninsular Malaysia, Malay shamanism involves spirit-mediumship, trance, seances and exorcism. Such practices appear to have long coexisted with Islam in Malaysia and are seen as reflecting the historical influences of Hinduism and Islamic Sufism. In traditional Melanau society, those who became shamans typically experienced a history of ailments and initiatory ceremonies, sometimes beginning in adolescence.

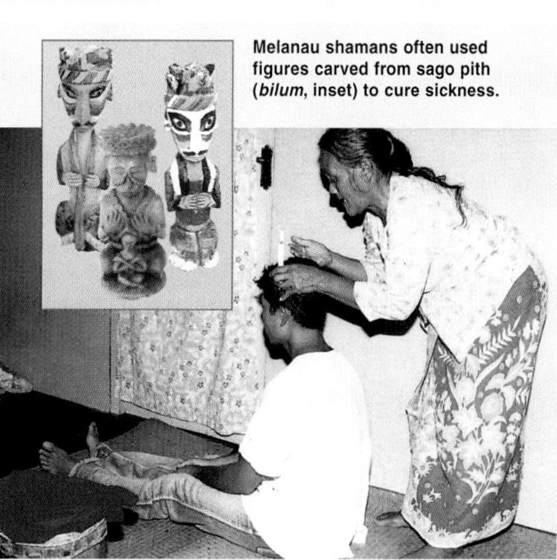

Melanau shamans often used figures carved from sago pith (*bilum*, inset) to cure sickness.

Melanau society and traditions

The Melanau are believed to be among the earliest inhabitants of Sarawak, and for at least half a millennium have settled in the coastal areas in the vicinity of the Rajang delta. Once noted for their houses built on spectacularly tall poles for defensive reasons, the Melanau constitute the fifth largest indigenous group in the state. Sago cultivation remains a vital part of their economy, and is linked to their socio-culture and heritage, which they have preserved despite religious influences.

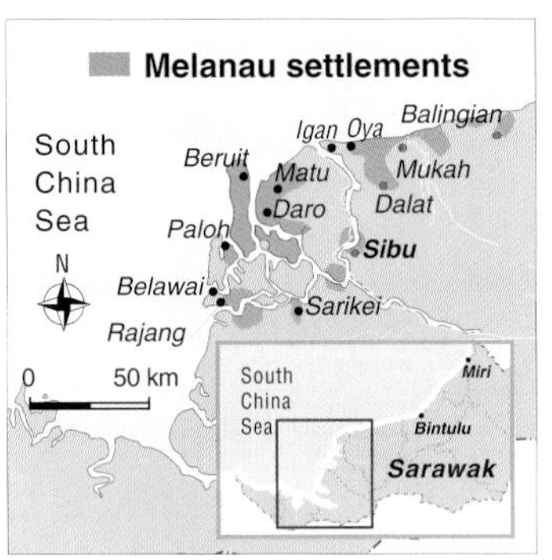

The Melanau are settled in the coastal lowlands of the Rajang estuary, and as far north as Bintulu and Miri.

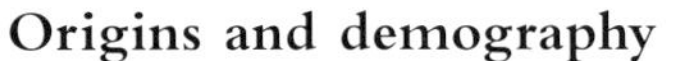

Origins and demography

The Melanau are believed to share common origins with the Orang Ulu, in particular the Kajang. Melanau oral history suggests that part of the Kajang group moved down the Rajang River, as a result of the expansion of the Iban into the Rajang basin, and settled in the coastal region of the Oya, Mukah and Balingian rivers, considered to be the Melanau heartland. In 2004, the Melanau, with an estimated population of 124,000 were concentrated in the coastal region stretching from Daro on the western edge of the Rajang delta, to Bintulu and to Miri in northeast Sarawak. About 80 per cent of them are rural dwellers, with the rest residing in the urban centres of Kuching, Sibu and Miri, where many work as civil servants and professionals. Some have become politicians and successful businessmen.

Sago pith preparation.

Kinship

Kinship among the Melanau is bilateral and cognatic, and is relevant for the purpose of identifying duties and responsibilities among kin. These include the obligation to protect, support and care for families; to maintain peace and good relationships among kin; and to help during illnesses, harvests, ceremonies and rituals. Social impropriety such as disrespect to elders is penalized under their *adat* (customary law). Traditionally, order in Melanau society and adherence to their *adat* were maintained by educating children in the ways of the community and through arranged marriages. However, this has been affected by assimilation with other ethnic groups, especially with the Malays through intermarriage.

The *cherindak*, a colourful conical sun hat woven from nipah (*Nypa fruticans*) and bamboo, is a cultural icon of the Melanau. The hat's conical shape has influenced the design of the roofs of several buildings in Sarawak, including the Mukah mosque.

A Melanau village in Mukah with houses fronted by trampling platforms, on which sago palm flour is worked. In the past, the Melanau referred to themselves as *a likou* (meaning 'people of the river').

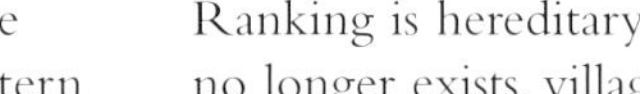

Political hierarchy

The Melanau were a stratified society with three traditional classes: aristocrats, freemen and slaves. Ranking is hereditary, and although the class system no longer exists, villagers are still able to identify their ranks; the aristocrats are wealthier, especially in terms of sago production, and are usually the custodians of *adat*.

Prior to Brooke rule, villages were controlled by the aristocratic elders, some of whom became the headmen (*ketua kampung*, *pemanca* and *temenggong*). During Brooke rule, rural councils were introduced to control land and designate development, while law and order was the responsibility of the police. This administrative system is still in place today, with the headmen appointed by the state government. Nevertheless, the elders remain prominent figures in the community, and oversee the *adat*, especially those relating to ceremonies and rituals associated with birth, marriage and death, as well as that of the Kaul (sea-appeasing and village purification ceremony).

Healing rituals

The relationship between the Melanau and the sago palm is the result of the latter's 'healing' value. The pith or trunk is carved into effigies of figures (*bilum* or *dakan*) that are used in traditional healing rituals. Complicated rituals (*payun*) may last up to a week, depending on the severity of the illness, and often involve the shaman (*a bayoh*) entering a state of trance.

1. The shaman goes into a trance to communicate with the spirit said to cause the illness afflicting the patient. He negotiates with it to leave the patient's body.

Kaul

The annual Kaul (sea-appeasing and village purification festival) is celebrated in early January by Melanau communities in Dalat, and in late March or early April by those in Mukah and other coastal areas. Late March or early April is equivalent to *bulan pengejin* in the Melanau calendar, a time when the weather is good and the sea calm. The Melanau believe that this is the period when the *ipok laut* (spirit of the sea) will listen to their prayers for good health, peace and prosperity. The highlight of the ritual is the construction of the *serahang* (baskets made from sago trunk, bamboo and nipah leaves, that contain food offerings for the spirit of the sea) hoisted on decorated poles.

Among the Muslim Melanau, Kaul is celebrated as a non-ritual festival, and is usually accompanied by traditional sports such as the giant *tibau* swing, martial arts, music, dances and feasting on traditional delicacies.

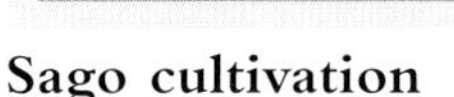

ABOVE LEFT: The *tibau* swing, which is up to six metres high, offers thrills for youth during the Kaul festival.

FAR LEFT: A martial arts display at the festival.

LEFT: Villagers place food offerings in a hut specially built during Kaul at Medong in the Dalat area of Sibu Division.

Decorated baskets of offerings (*serahang*) for the spirit of the sea are mounted on poles and planted in the banks of rivers.

Sago cultivation

The main occupation of the Melanau communities in coastal areas was traditionally that of fisherman, while those living in the mangrove swamp are traditionally sago smallholders. In the Dalat, Oya and Mukah areas smallholders plant smooth bark sago (*Metroxylon sagu*), whereas in Balingian they plant the thorny species (*Eugeissona utilis*). Sago plantations and mills were established by the state government in the 1990s to improve the Melanau's socio-economic status.

Sago cultivation is intricately linked to the culture of the Melanau. Sago is traditionally their staple food and is also believed to possess 'spirits' which are said to have healing powers.

Other economic activities include the cultivation of swamp rice, fruit and vegetable farming, collecting jungle products, hunting wild game, and working as lumberjacks for timber companies.

Belief and value systems

Since the 1940s, many Melanau have turned from traditional beliefs to Islam or Christianity. The traditional belief system subscribes to a universe of various levels—the sky, inhabited by both good and bad spirits; the middle world, inhabited by man; and the underworld of animals and vegetation—in which *adat* provides the principle of order. The spirits that are believed to inhabit the environment surrounding the villages should not be disturbed; neither should plants or animals be harmed.

2. He pierces the eyes or some other part of the effigy to symbolise the entry of the spirit. He then spits a chewed mix of betel leaf and areca nut into the pierced eyes.

3. The effigy is placed in a carved pith boat (*rabuong*) for disposal.

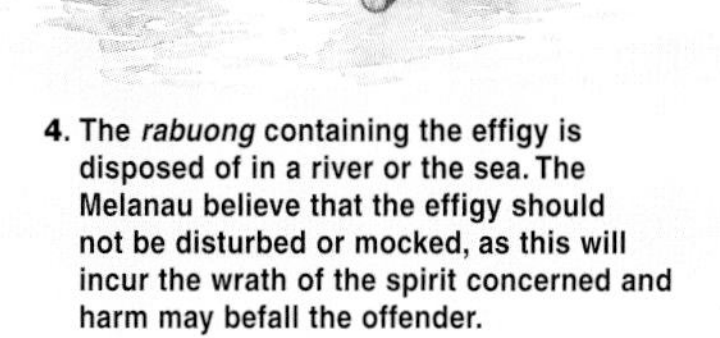

4. The *rabuong* containing the effigy is disposed of in a river or the sea. The Melanau believe that the effigy should not be disturbed or mocked, as this will incur the wrath of the spirit concerned and harm may befall the offender.

Bidayuh society and traditions

The Bidayuh, who make up over eight per cent of Sarawak's population, are believed to have been the first people to settle in the original territory of Sarawak acquired by James Brooke in the mid-19th century, and were formerly known as Land Dayak. Although they regard themselves as one community, they speak five main dialects. Traditionally swidden rice farmers, they now grow permanent crops in response to government initiatives to improve their lives. Many Bidayuh have also moved away from traditional occupations and can be found working in both the private and public sectors.

Bidayuh wedding ceremony, the *man stabi'*.

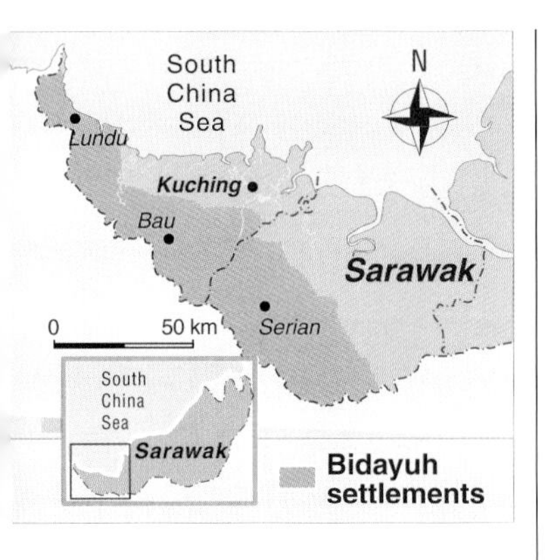

Kinship and social organization

The Bidayuh are an egalitarian people and the mainstay of their society is equality, which is central to the concept of their customary law (*adat*). The household (*rawang*) is the basic social unit, and it is economically and socially independent. Families are close-knit, sharing strong kinship ties; households usually consist of three generations living together. As children get married, they establish their own households, with the youngest child usually remaining with the parents.

Bidayuh villages (*kupuo*) are contained within their own territory, separated by natural boundaries (*baat*) such as a river or a rock. A village consists of a group of houses and other buildings, namely, a chapel and a *baruk* or *panggah* (ceremonial building and council chamber). Each village is autonomous and is under the leadership of a headman (*piayuh kupuo*), who oversees the welfare of the villagers, acts as an arbitrator and advisor, and settles minor disputes between members of the community. While in the past anyone could become the headman, today the appointment requires the approval of the district officer. Each village also has a *pinyigar* (ritual expert) who oversees matters relating to beliefs and rituals.

Adat and social customs

The social life of the Bidayuh is guided by their customs and *adat*. The main functions of customs are to maintain a harmonious

The baruk (headhouse)

The *baruk* is distinguished by its unique architecture—round in shape with an effigy of a hornbill on the apex of its conical thatch roof. It is usually built on high ground so that it overlooks the village. Although it serves as a lodging place for adolescent males and visitors, the primary purpose of the *baruk* is as a venue for discussion of *adat*, customs and practices. It is also a council chamber; a venue for ceremonies; and a place for men to make handicrafts, weapons and work tools.

The *baruk* is common property, and thus not only unites the Bidayuh, but is their cultural icon as well. Its distinct shape has become part of the architectural landscape of Sarawak, and is featured in other buildings, such as a civic centre in Bau, restaurants in Kuching, holiday chalets at Pantai Damai, and a church at Mt. Singai.

1. The floor of the *baruk* is raised about two metres above ground and is made of split bamboo, which allows cool air to enter from underneath.
2. In the centre of the *baruk* is a hearth; a fire is lit for warmth on cool nights.
3. In the past, ritualists and warriors performed dances around the hearth to celebrate a successful headhunting raid.
4. Skulls (*tikurok*) and talismen (*guna*) are hung in a *singari* from a rafter.
5. A platform (*akat*) along the sides provides seats and sleeping space for male adolescents and visitors.
6. Food offerings (*sadis*) for the spirits are placed in a special spot on the platform (*akat bating*) beneath the skulls. Only the chief ritualist may sit next to the offerings.
7. Drums three to five metres long (*tigudoh*) and gongs used for ritual ceremonies.

The headhouse (*baruk*) is usually built on higher ground and overlooks the houses in the village.

relationship between members of a community as well as with the spirits. The most important virtues instilled are obedience, respect for elders and truthfulness. In the past, *adat* was transmitted orally from generation to generation. It has now been codified (see 'Adat and the longhouse community'). Much of the code of individual and social conduct was decreed by the Bidayuh's traditional animistic beliefs. But, with the majority of Bidayuh embracing Christianity, it became necessary to secularize customary law so that the community, regardless of religion, would have a common code of conduct.

Modern farmers

Programmes introduced by the government have resulted in Bidayuh farmers moving from traditional swidden cultivation of rice to cash crop farming of pepper, cocoa, rubber, coffee and oil palm. Educational and economic opportunities have also attracted many Bidayuh into the construction, hotel, food, petroleum, gas and fishing industries, as well as the public sector.

Preserving a cultural heritage

Aware of changing social and economic influences on their lives, culture and traditions, the Bidayuh have made efforts to preserve their heritage. Through organizations such as the Dayak Bidayuh National Association, children are taught traditional songs, dances and music, and people are encouraged to use the Bidayuh language at home.

Bidayuh women in a ritual dance (above left)), their arms and legs adorned with brass coils. Ritualists (above right) perform a traditional dance, usually performed to welcome guests and during the annual harvest festival, circa 1950.

Beliefs and rituals

Two priestesses at a ritual in a rice field.

The traditionally animistic Bidayuh subscribe to the existence of a spiritual world with which man needs to maintain a harmonious relationship—through rituals—in order for peace in the human world. Thus, rituals play an important role in Bidayuh life, and are observed on the occasions of birth, marriage, sickness and death, as well as for specific purposes such as house-building and rice planting.

The purpose of rituals is to invoke the protection of ancestral spirits against misfortune and sickness said to be caused by demons and hostile forces; to placate spirits with food offerings; and to thank the gods for their blessings. Rituals form the highlight of Bidayuh *gawia* (festival).

Rice rituals

A series of rituals are conducted at various stages of the rice-planting cycle. These include rituals to determine the suitability of land for planting rice, blessing of the footpath and the rice seeds, and end with a thanksgiving and appeasement ceremony (see 'The harvest festival in Sarawak').

Gawia oran

The blessing of the footpath from the village to the padi fields is to ensure the safe conduct of padi souls, to drive away evil spirits and to invoke the protection of good spirits for the people who will use the path.

Gawia satak sopa

This serves to pacify the souls (*ieng*) of the vegetation and living things which were destroyed to make way for the rice fields, so that they will not disturb the farmers and their crops (right).

Gawia nuruk

Before planting takes place, the blessings of the gods, spirits and ancestors are invoked to ensure good growth and to protect the seeds from malignant influences. A cockerel is sacrificed, and its blood is mixed with *tuak* (rice wine), and sprinkled over the rice seeds. The *pinyigar* (ritualist) makes seven holes in the ash under the altar and drops a grain of rice into each hole (left). The growth of the seven grains will indicate if the farmers will have a bountiful harvest.

Nuboh omuh

Aimed at curing sickness of young rice plants, this ritual takes place between 3 and 4 a.m. The *pinyigar* calls upon the gods, good spirits and their ancestors to drive away evil spirits and pests from the rice fields. Carrying a shield and a fighting knife (*buku bai*), he leads the farmers as they walk around the field, making loud noises.

Gawia man kudos

The first harvested crop is offered to the creator, the ancestors and all the spirits, to avoid incurring their anger, and to ensure their support and protection in the future (left).

Iban society

Traditional Iban social structures were organized around the efficient cultivation of hill rice, which was crucial for the community's survival in the past. The large tracts of land required for this caused the Iban to establish a mobile and martial society for which longhouse living was conducive. Once known as Borneo's infamous headhunters, the Iban form Sarawak's largest indigenous group. Theirs is an egalitarian society, with cooperation and group conformity as its basic tenets.

A child performing the traditional Ngajat dance in a longhouse. Iban children are taught their native tongue at both primary and secondary school level.

Iban chiefs in ceremonial dress in the early 1900s. Their headdresses are capped with a silver crown and adorned with hornbill feathers and goat hair. Silver necklaces, belts and armlets symbolize wealth.

Traditional costumes

Iban women's costumes are elaborate, consisting of *kain pandak* (short skirt) or *kain tating* (weighted short skirt); *lampit* (girdle), *rawai* (corset) with a belt of silver coins; *marik empani* (beadwork collar), *selampai* (shawl); *sugu tinggi* (silver headdress) decorated with metal ornaments (*enguga*) on the tiara; silver necklace, bracelets and anklets.

Costumes for the men are less elaborate, consisting of *sirat* (loin cloth); headdress decorated with bird feathers or *selapok tunjang* (woven bamboo adorned with feathers); silver bracelets and ivory armlets; and a sword, its scabbard decorated with beads and hornbill ivory. Some also wear the *baju burong* (woven cotton vest with decorative designs).

Social organization

Traditional Iban society can be divided into three levels: the nuclear family, the longhouse community, and the territorial tribe. These organizational structures are based on spatial divisions and social inter-relationships among group members. An Iban is a member of a nuclear (*bilek*) family which, in turn, is one unit of a longhouse. The longhouse is part of a group of longhouses situated in a particular territory, usually a river catchment area. Members of these three levels are inter-related by kinship ties, ceremonial relationships, economic interests, political loyalty and, in the past, military alliances.

The Iban nuclear or *bilek* family—comprising an average of five individuals—constitutes a basic unit of a longhouse structure. The fundamental value of this unit is self-sufficiency and all aspects of family life are geared towards attaining self-sufficiency in the production of their staple food—rice. Each member of the family is required to play their part towards this goal and to uphold the honour of the family. It is obligatory for the young to care for the elders. The need to sustain the respect of others in the longhouse motivates the Iban family to emphasize personal values such as hard work, skills in producing household goods and willingness to venture out for the good of the family.

The Iban longhouse is an institution akin to a federated union of several *bilek* families living under one roof. Individuals have interrelated interests and are bound by kinship connections. An Iban owes loyalty to his longhouse after his allegiance to his family. From childhood, the longhouse provides a sense of belonging. An Iban develops intimate interactions with kinsmen and towards friends which result in strong feelings of loyalty to his longhouse. This upbringing in the longhouse results in the Iban subscribing to values of self-sufficiency, equality and inter-dependence in their relationship with one another. Longhouse living also inculcates values and norms of their community.

An Iban fishing with a casting net. The Iban previously practised shifting cultivation of rice. Now they also grow cash crops and undertake other economic activities such as logging, hunting wild game and river fishing. An increasing number of younger Iban people have moved to urban centres in the state and other parts of the country in search of more lucrative livelihoods.

The territorial tribe is the grouping of kindred found in a river system, constituting an association of longhouse communities who share common interests such as farm land, ceremonial functions and, in war times, military alliances. In the past, outstanding personalities emerged as leaders to mobilize tribal loyalties for war or trading expeditions. Since the late 20th century, however, such alliances are utilized for political support.

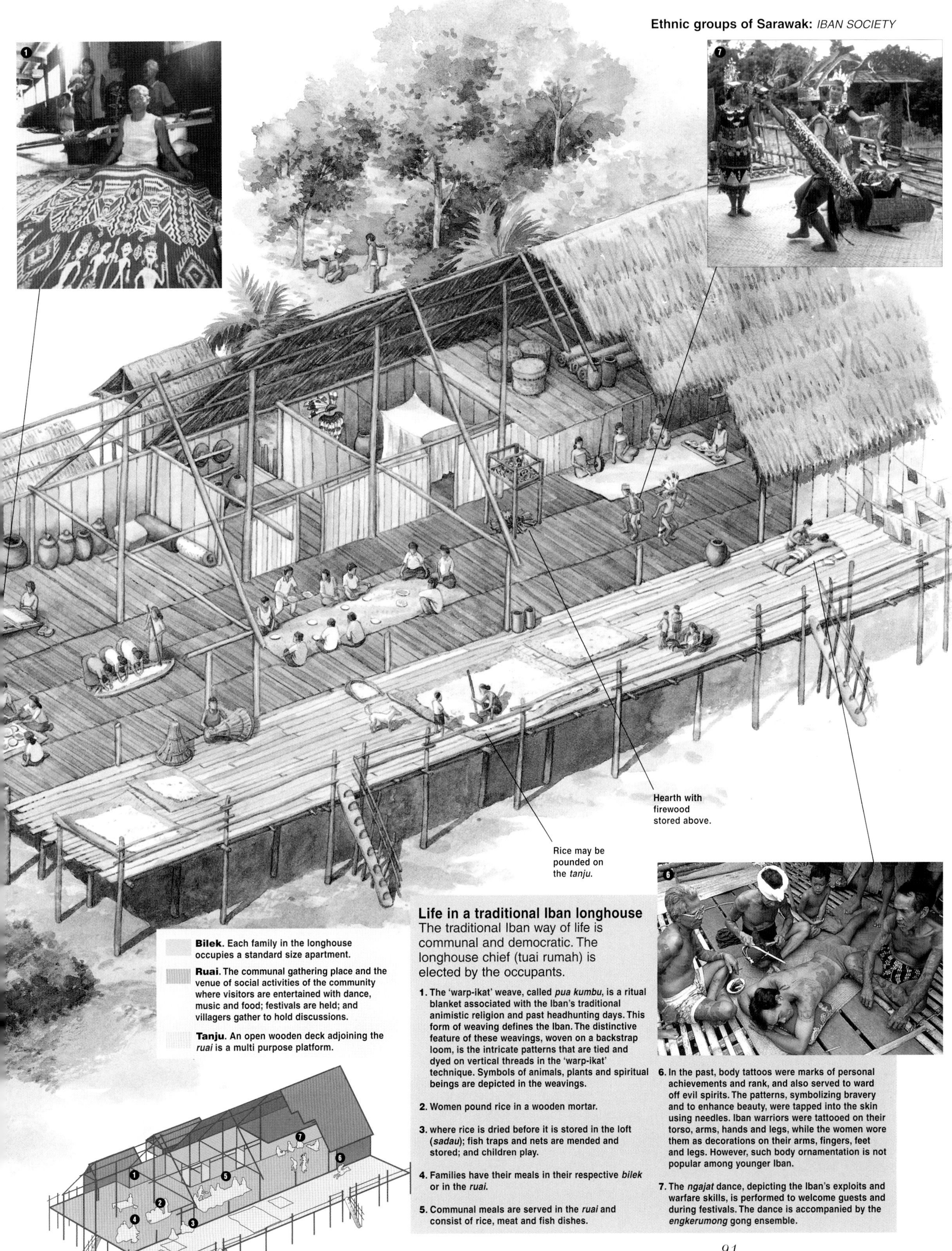

Bilek. Each family in the longhouse occupies a standard size apartment.

Ruai. The communal gathering place and the venue of social activities of the community where visitors are entertained with dance, music and food; festivals are held; and villagers gather to hold discussions.

Tanju. An open wooden deck adjoining the *ruai* is a multi purpose platform.

Life in a traditional Iban longhouse

The traditional Iban way of life is communal and democratic. The longhouse chief (tuai rumah) is elected by the occupants.

1. The 'warp-ikat' weave, called *pua kumbu*, is a ritual blanket associated with the Iban's traditional animistic religion and past headhunting days. This form of weaving defines the Iban. The distinctive feature of these weavings, woven on a backstrap loom, is the intricate patterns that are tied and dyed on vertical threads in the 'warp-ikat' technique. Symbols of animals, plants and spiritual beings are depicted in the weavings.
2. Women pound rice in a wooden mortar.
3. where rice is dried before it is stored in the loft (*sadau*); fish traps and nets are mended and stored; and children play.
4. Families have their meals in their respective *bilek* or in the *ruai*.
5. Communal meals are served in the *ruai* and consist of rice, meat and fish dishes.
6. In the past, body tattoos were marks of personal achievements and rank, and also served to ward off evil spirits. The patterns, symbolizing bravery and to enhance beauty, were tapped into the skin using needles. Iban warriors were tattooed on their torso, arms, hands and legs, while the women wore them as decorations on their arms, fingers, feet and legs. However, such body ornamentation is not popular among younger Iban.
7. The *ngajat* dance, depicting the Iban's exploits and warfare skills, is performed to welcome guests and during festivals. The dance is accompanied by the *engkerumong* gong ensemble.

Iban values, beliefs and rituals

The Iban traditionally lived in a forested world replete with beasts, myriad insects and thousands of other living organisms. By sharing this dynamic environment, the Iban have interpreted their existence as a state of continuous balance with other beings, whether natural or supernatural. This forms the basis of their philosophy: all objects have souls. However, many of the traditional beliefs and customs associated with longhouse living and rice cultivation have been affected by modernization as well as changing religious and social influences.

An Iban in warrior costume complete with feathered headdress and ceremonial sword.

Social values

Egalitarianism is one of the most important central values of the Iban and is ardently practised at all levels of their social organization, be it within a family or between families and the longhouse community. A spirit of cooperation exists in all aspects of life and in collective endeavours such as house building, rice cultivation and ritual festivals.

As the Iban expanded their territory, primarily to acquire land to cultivate rice, their spiritual beliefs provided the rationale and psychological support to subdue their adversaries. In their mythology and sacred texts, such behaviour was accepted as the right way to ensure the continuity of the group. The past practice of taking heads as trophies or as symbols of courageous achievements arose from this. Iban soldiers in the Malaysian armed forces have exhibited their legendary courage during incursions and have been awarded medals for bravery.

Through their martial values, young Iban men are instilled with the spirit of adventure to venture beyond their longhouses in search of 'fame and fortune'. The traditional custom of *bejalai* (going on a journey to seek prestige and wealth) is one of the driving forces that motivates young Iban to go out of their longhouses; in the modern context, this manifests itself as labour migration. Iban workers can be found on offshore oil platforms in Miri, Brunei and beyond, and also in factories in Singapore and Peninsular Malaysia.

The Iban are highly motivated to demonstrate their achievements; in traditional society, this was manifested in annual bountiful rice harvests. While the Iban now follow modern trends—through education, world religions and new economic opportunities—they still retain their heritage and traditional material culture. Ritual occasions help to maintain family and longhouse ties, and provide a basis for reunions amongst kin, friends and the community. Festivals, including the annual Gawai Dayak (see 'The harvest festival in Sarawak'), also serve as displays of their cultural and ethnic identity.

BELOW: Trophy skulls are a reminder of the Iban's head-taking days and of the battles they fought in the 19th century.

BOTTOM: Intertribal Dayak warfare, circa 1905.

An Iban medicine box (*lupong*) made of bark, with carved figures attached to its sides.

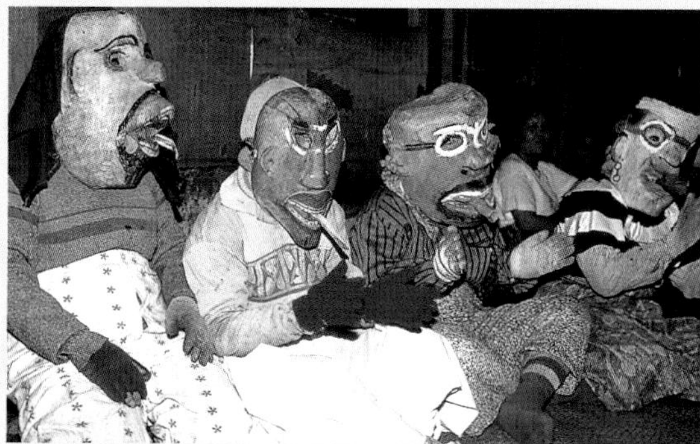

Masks are used in rituals to scare away evil spirits from the longhouse, or for clowning and merrymaking.

Festivals and augury

Festivals (*gawai*) mark important times in the life of the Iban. The main ones are related to the cultivation of rice (Gawai Batu and Gawai Memali Umai); health and longevity (Gawai Ngintu Orang Sakit); warfare and bravery (Gawai Kenyalang); and death (Gawai Antu). The *gawai* follows a general pattern of rituals, beginning with the offering of food (*miring*), followed by invocations and chanting (*biau*), and ending with ritual incantations (*timang* or *pengap*) by ritualists (*lemambang*). The *timang*, which are chanted in polyphonic prose and imageries, narrate the journey of the *lemambang*'s soul as he invites the gods to attend the celebrations. The rituals may go on all night, and include dances to welcome the spirits.

The Iban have a system of augury in which they believe that their gods communicate with them through the calls and sightings of birds—such as the banded kingfisher, rufous piculet and maroon woodpecker—and by the actions of animals, reptiles and insects. This is, in fact, a system of divine guidance for the well-being of man. For this reason, augury ritual experts (*tuai burung*) are consulted before any important activity is undertaken, such as building a house, starting the rice farming cycle, going on expeditions (*bejalai*) or to war (*ngayau*).

Wooden figures affixed to the tail of hornbill effigies.

RIGHT: The *miring* (appeasing the spirits) ceremony marks the beginning of a *gawai*.

Souls and beliefs

The traditionally animist Iban believe that all beings possess separable souls, and this belief forms the foundation of their structure of various rituals. In mortal life the Iban's soul is a medium of communication with unseen powers through dreams and other ethereal encounters when the gods appear before a select few. It is from such experiences that many Iban creative works of art originate, such as *ikat* (intricate cotton weaving), highly symbolic and rich oral traditions such as the *timang* (sacred text), *pantun* (poetry) and *ensera* (legends).

A ritualist (*lemambang*) conducting rites during the Gawai Kenyalang (hornbill festival), which is celebrated in honour of Singalang Burung, the bird-god of war.

ABOVE LEFT: A longhouse headman makes a formal offering to the spirits by waving chickens over an assortment of food, thereby invoking the goodwill of the spirits.

ABOVE RIGHT: Elaborately carved hornbill effigies are elevated on tall poles during the Gawai Kenyalang.

The Iban believe that during daily activities, the soul of man (*mensia*) and that of gods or spirits (*petara/antu*) often impinge upon one another, and it is from this perception of the world that their cultural and social values are derived. Thus, the Iban practise their beliefs through rituals concerning their economic, social and political welfare. Examples of such rituals are those related to rice, shamanism, bravery and death.

The basis of the rice rituals underscores the importance the Iban attach to the cultivation of rice. To them rice seeds (padi) possess spiritual souls and therefore, the planting of rice is essentially a ritual undertaking, with rites performed at each stage of the rice cultivation cycle, from clearing of the field to tending the growing plants and harvesting.

The healing or *manang* rituals are based on the Iban idea of the separable soul. The job of the *manang* (shaman) is to recover the missing souls of sick Iban who, in their wanderings away from the human body, may become lost and entrapped by evil spirits.

Rituals related to death reflect the Ibas belief in the afterworld (*sabayan*) to which all souls (*semangat*) go after death, and involve elaborate ceremonies observed upon the death of an Iban (See 'Shamanism in Sarawak').

The Iban pantheon is complex with many anthropomorphic deities who have specialized functions and powers. The two most important gods are Simpulang Gana (god of rice cultivation and tutelary deity of the soil), and Singalang Burung (god of war and Iban welfare). Simpulang Gana presides over the farming of rice and is invoked in every stage of cultivation. Should any disease affect the growth of the rice, the Iban conduct rites and offer *piring* (food offerings) to propitiate him, and for the restoration of healthy rice crops. Sacrifices are also made to Simpulang Gana when building a new house and before a burial to acknowledge the use of the land.

The god of war, Singalang Burung, was invoked during warfare and bravery rituals. The Iban also believe that 'superhuman' beings (*antu*), some harmful, others benevolent, exist in the forest, along rivers, on pathways and even in their own longhouses.

Customs and adat

The Iban believe that their customs and *adat* (traditional law) were given to them by their gods and, therefore, anyone who repudiates the *adat* would be duly punished supernaturally, if no immediate reparation is made. Hence, *adat* is regarded as hallowed and conceived as a body of correct behaviour essential to the well-being and continued existence of their community. These customs require that in addition to monetary reparation, ritual payments have to be made by transgressors to compensate for the damage inflicted on the victims' souls. Iban *adat* condemns vices such as laziness (*burok*), greed or selfishness (*rangka*), whilst virtues such as courage (*berani*), masculinity (*gagah*), and fame (*berita*) are praised (See 'Adat and the longhouse community').

Gong and drum ensembles are usually in attendance at Iban festivals.

Preparing a death hut (*sungkup*) for the deceased.

Gawai Antu

The Gawai Antu (spirit festival) marks the journey of the dead. The ritual ensures that the souls of the departed remain beyond the River of the Afterworld (Sungai Mandai) in the land of the dead (*sebayan*). It culminates in the erection of death huts (*sungkup*) in the communal graveyard. The entire longhouse community takes part in the ceremonies and feasting.

Jars containing rice wine for the souls of the departed at the Gawai Antu feast.

Bisaya society and traditions

The peoples known as Bisaya can be found in the Philippines, Brunei and Malaysia, where they live in Sabah and the northern part of Sarawak. Traditionally swidden agriculturalists, increasing contact with the outside world has led to an expansion into trade, as well as changes in their religious beliefs and living arrangements. The Bisaya are best known for their music and buffalo races, and efforts are being made to retain and promote these and other cultural traditions.

A Bisaya farmer and his family.

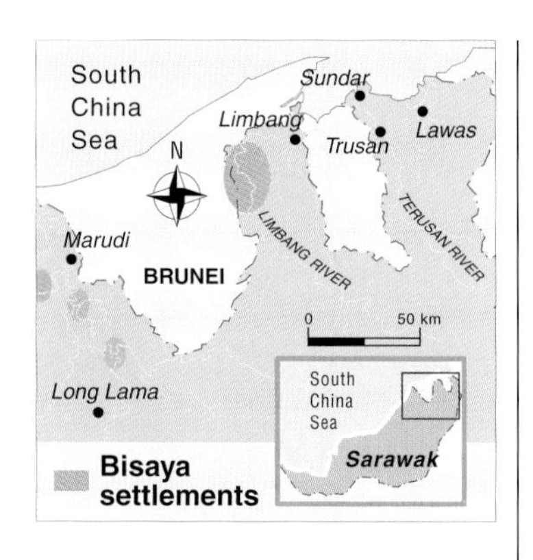

Demography

With a population estimated at over 10,000, the Bisaya are classified as Orang Ulu, together with the Kajang, Kayan, Kenyah, Kelabit and Lun Bawang and several other minority non-Muslim groups (see 'Kajang and other Orang Ulu groups'). The Bisaya, however, refer to themselves as midlanders (*jalamaq tangaq*) or people of the river (*jalamaq bawang*). They reside mainly in the north of Sarawak in the districts of Limbang and Baram. In addition, many Bisaya have settled in major towns, such as Kuching, Bintulu, Miri and Lawas, primarily to seek employment.

Traditional ceremonial attire for Bisaya women is a Malay-style sarong and jacket (*baju masuk*) with embroidery, while the men wear a jacket and headcloth (*singal*).

Kinship

The Bisaya descent system can be traced from both the paternal and maternal sides. The simplest is the single-line genealogy, termed *rayan*. This is used to validate or re-establish land rights, and to pay homage to renowned individuals, especially at funerals. Knowledge of genealogy and kinship is important in order to establish a Bisaya's position or rights in society. For example, rights to land descend from both parents.

The major kin groups are the households (*sanan lobok*) and the house family (*sanan alai*). The household or apartment family is corporate in nature, sharing expenses, pooling harvest, common hearth, rituals and prayer for crops. The house family, on the other hand, shares certain ceremonial objects, observes common taboos, cooperates in house maintenance, and shares common rituals.

Close kin are expected to aid one another in emergencies, attend and contribute to major rituals, such as at death and marriage, and support one another during disputes. Within villages, there is a tendency for close kin to build their houses near each other.

The Bisaya live in extended family units, with more than two generations living together. A house may contain two or several families; rarely one. The occupants of a house will all be close relatives, and will normally comprise an elderly couple, their children, and their children's families. This structure, however, is changing, with younger Bisaya preferring to live in nuclear family units, especially those who have settled in the urban areas.

Unlike other indigenous groups in Sarawak who traditionally lived in longhouses, the Bisaya live in detached houses that comprise several apartments (*sirang*). A typical traditional Bisaya house is up to 60 metres long, and built on piles three to five metres high.

Traditional power structures

Written culture among the Bisaya is of recent origin, having started during the so-called Bewsher Era (1931–44), during which Bewsher, a Christian missionary, started a mission school under the auspices of the Borneo Evangelical Mission. Bisaya

The Bisaya are reputed to be among the best gong musicians in Sarawak. Prior to World War II, full 19-piece Bisaya gong orchestras were taken to Kuching to play during state occasions. More recently, these gong orchestras have performed at the annual World Rainforest Music Festival held at the Sarawak Cultural Village.

Music and dance

The Bisaya have a wide variety of music, songs and dances. The music is performed by a gong orchestra, or on the *bungkau* (kazoo-like instrument) or the *babanci* (flute). Their dances include the Alai anding (anding dance), Alai ancayau (celebration dance) and Alai gandang parang (warrior dance).

Anding

Anding (Bisaya traditional song) and Alai anding are among the best known forms of Bisaya artistic culture. Indeed the Anding is synonymous with the Bisaya. It is performed on joyous occasions such as weddings, feasts (*babulang*), *makan selamat* (thanksgiving feast), *lapas niat ceremonies* (ceremonies to celebrate fulfilment of promises or goals) or to welcome visiting dignitaries.

Anding lyrics range from welcoming expressions, praise or advice, expressions of feeling, faith, gratitude, hope and happiness.

Healing rituals

When sickness is believed to be caused by bad or angry spirits, ghosts or charms (*limuq*), curing rituals (*belian*) are performed to appease the spirits and to restore the *lingu* (soul) of the sick person. It is performed by a spirit medium (*penumbui*) who negotiates with the spirits to leave or to stop disturbing the sick person. The ritual involves three stages—diagnosis (*pendauq*), negotiating and peace-making with the spirits (*najiq*) and an elaborate ceremony after the sickness is cured (*tamarok*).

The medium first communicates with the spirit world through the aid of good spirit (*duato*) to determine the cause of illness. This ritual normally takes place at night, in a dimly lit room. The negotiation stage involves an elaborate offering of bananas, eggs, alcohol, rice pancakes and coconut oil cakes. While in trance, the medium tells the 'offending' spirit that the sick person has brought offerings and wants to be relieved of his or her suffering. After negotiations, the 'offending' spirit agrees to leave the sick person, with certain conditions to be met during the *tamarok* (appreciation ritual), which usually takes place after the next harvest.

Womenfolk prepare for the *tamarok*, which marks the end of a healing ritual.

The *tamarok* is an elaborate array of offerings, such as unhusked rice (*parai*) spread in the shape of a crocodile (*buayo*), bananas, husked rice (*agas*), eggs and carved dolls (*anak andakan*).

The *tamarok* ritual is conducted over two nights. On the second night (*tamarok gayo*) an elaborate spread of offerings is laid out on the verandah. Sometimes, several cured persons would jointly host the *tamarok*. Family members, relatives, the village community and people from other villages are invited to attend the occasion. Musicians as well as a gong orchestra would be in attendance. The *tamarok* usually lasts through the night.

society is based on kinship, and does not have a class system or related political hierarchy. Status was based on wealth (in the form of buffalo and brassware), feast-giving ability and age. Slavery (*miyan*)—a form of debt-bondage—was practised, although its precise nature is unknown. It is known, however, that in 1895 a slave was required to pay 36 Strait Dollars to secure his freedom. Slavery was abolished by 1928.

Prior to Brooke rule (1841–1941), the Bisaya were subjects of the Sultan of Brunei, who introduced a number of titles such as *janang* (village or clan chief), *panglima* (a rank in the army), *penghulu* (regional chief) and *orang kaya* (equivalent to an area chief).

Items woven by the Bisaya include the *saging* (a multipurpose basket) and *tudung tarindak* (food covers).

From subsistence farmers to businessmen

The Bisaya were traditionally subsistence farmers, planting swamp and hill rice, with sago as a second staple food. Today, cash crops such as rubber, pepper, fruit trees and vegetables are also grown in their swiddens. They also rear buffalo, pigs and chickens.

Economic development, improved education and infrastructure have enabled many Bisaya to move away from traditional economic activities. The better-educated Bisaya now tend to be employed with the government as civil servants, or work with private companies in Malaysia, Brunei or elsewhere. A small number are involved in trading, operating eateries, and construction work.

Beliefs

Traditionally, the Bisaya were animists who believed in the mighty spirit, Ala Talaq, and a number of other spiritual beings, including spirits of the deceased (*lamatai*) and souls (*lingu*). *Lamatai* are considered dangerous and are believed to cause a number of illnesses or even death. They take on various forms including the *sampar* or *ko awad atis* (long-legged ghost), *pontianak* (ghost of a woman who died in childbirth), and *ogol* (headless ghost).

The Bisaya also traditionally believed that the mistreatment of plants and animals—which would cause discomfort and harm to their *lingu*—would invite accidents on the perpetrator. Another source of unexplainable malaise and discomfort was mischievous spirits (*anak duato*) who preyed on those with *lambut lingu* (literally, weak soul).

Bisaya rituals include those observed at birth, marriage and death, as well as healing (*belian*). They also place great significance on omens, particularly bird omens and dreams. Certain birds, such as the *sasat* (spiderhunter), *kanui* (red hawk eagle), *tikbadan* (piculet), *jeriot* (wren babbler), and *layod* (weaver bird); as well as the *liong* (pipe snake) and the *bondolon* (python) are regarded as messengers of God. The Bisaya believe that if a *sasat* bird chirps, it means no harm will come to the traveller. If it flies from the right side of the road towards the left, it indicates that the journey will be successful; however, it is considered a bad omen if it flies from the left to the right, and the traveller should not proceed with the journey.

Most Bisaya are now Christians and, as a result, some traditional practices are no longer observed.

Handicrafts

Bisaya handicrafts include basketry and weaving. Materials used are obtained from the forest, such as tree bark, arrow shoots (*bamban*), bamboo, sago fronds and rattan. Items produced are functional in nature, and used for either farming, fishing or hunting.

Buffalo races are among the various activities organized by the Sarawak Bisaya Association and Village Development and Security Committees to revive aspects of Bisaya culture and to popularize them. Other efforts include promoting local handicrafts, cultural performances and gong orchestra competitions.

Kayan and Kenyah communities

The Kayan and Kenyah, though ethnically and linguistically different, share a common cultural heritage as they originally came from what is now Kalimantan, Indonesia, in the latter part of the 1700s, and have lived in close proximity with each other in the northern interior of Sarawak. Many Kayan and Kenyah have embraced Christianity and discarded traditional pagan beliefs, yet they have retained their longhouse lifestyle, stratified social system, values and cultural practices.

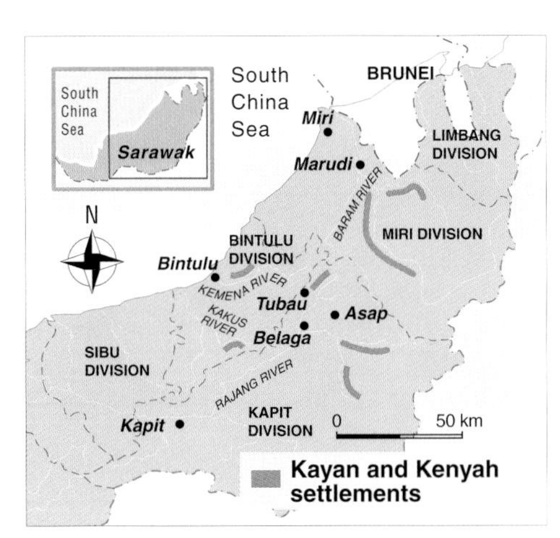

Kayan and Kenyah population (2000)

Kayan	25,542
Kenyah	24,906
Total	**50,448**

Source: Statistics Department, Sarawak.

Origins and demography

The Kayan and Kenyah traditionally live in the Miri, Kapit and Bintulu divisions in the northern interior of Sarawak. Both groups claim to have originated from the Apo Kayan in the upper reaches of the Kayan River in Kalimantan, Indonesia. From the Apo Kayan they moved into the Balui and Baram river basins, in what are now Belaga District in the Kapit Division and Baram District in the Miri Division respectively, around the end of the 18th century or the beginning of the 19th century. In the interior of the Bintulu Division they are settled along the upper Kemena River. A settlement of more than 10,000 people, originally on the Rajang River in Belaga district in Kapit Division, was relocated to Asap in the late 1990s to make way for the Bakun hydroelectric dam.

Social organization and values

Like most Sarawak ethnic groups, the Kayan and Kenyah are traditionally longhouse dwellers. A longhouse usually comprises about ten family apartments. Very long longhouses may contain about 100 family apartments. Among some Kenyah groups, a village may comprise clusters of several longhouses. Each longhouse community has a headman who looks after the general affairs of the longhouse community and acts as an arbitrator in disputes between members of the longhouse. Above the headmen are regional chiefs such as the *penghulu*, *pemanca* and *temenggong* who look after the welfare of several villages in a river system or designated area.

Right: In the past, Kayan women, including those of aristocratic rank, donned heavy earrings from elongated ear lobes. Such adornment, however, is not popular among younger women.

Far right: Kayan women traditionally tattooed their forearms from the elbow to the fingers, as well as their legs from the thigh to halfway down the calf, and their feet. These artistic tattoos were considered a mark of beauty.

The egg chant ceremony is believed to determine the sex of a couple's first child.

Religion and rituals

In the past, Kayan and Kenyah beliefs were steeped in augury and shrouded in taboos and omens. Both communities were traditionally animist, subscribing to the existence of a supernatural world and the existence of good and bad spirits. Although the majority have, since the 1950s, become Christians, they continue to observe age-old customs, rituals and practices, such as their rites of passage, and those related to the rice cultivation cycle, the most important being the harvest festival (see 'The harvest festival of Sarawak').

Bungan religion

In the 1950s, a syncretic religion known as Bungan (named after a benevolent goddess) was introduced among some Kayan and Kenyah groups. Founded in the late 1940s, it emerged in the Apo Kayan, Kalimantan as a consequence of contact between two cultures: Western Christianity and Borneo paganism. A few Kayan and Kenyah groups continue to practise it.

Shamans make offerings to the goddess Bungan, after whom the religion is named.

Child naming ceremony (pusau anak)

Among the milestones in the life of the Kayan and Kenyah, the child naming ceremony is especially significant. The Kenyah conduct this ceremony twice for a child. The first is held shortly after birth. A small feast is held when a newborn is given a name.

The second ceremony, called *pusau anak* in Kenyah, is a community affair and usually involves all the young children in the longhouse. The purpose of the ceremony is to celebrate the lives of the children and welcome them as important members of the community. The children are seated in prominent places, while infants are carried by their mothers in a carrier (*ba*). A feast is prepared for the occasion, and the children are formally introduced to the community and guests. Ginger water is served to all present as a symbol of healing for the bodies and souls of the celebrated children and to signify the role of the children in strengthening the community. An elder of the community addresses the gathering before the commencement of the feast.

This is followed by the *ngalang* (meaning 'life journey') ceremony, which signifies the future duties and responsibilities of the children in the community. The children and their parents form a procession along the length of the longhouse verandah, led by a male elder in traditional costume, who holds a ceremonial sword (*baying*) high in his hand and lightly chops at suspended logs as he walks down the verandah.

In the past the *pusau anak* was usually held to coincide with the harvest festival. Since the 1980s, some longhouses have been incorporating it into Christmas celebrations.

LEFT: The *ngalang* (life journey) ritual in the child naming ceremony involves a procession of parents and their children along the longhouse verandah. Logs suspended from the rafters represent the journey of life. The leader of the procession lightly chops the logs as he walks past, the action signifying that an individual's decisions affects the entire community.

RIGHT: A Kenyah woman with her child in a baby carrier.

The Kayan and Kenyah are stratified societies with a hierarchy of upper, middle and lower classes. The ruling or upper class of aristocrats is hereditary, but nowadays, inter-class marriages are common.

Social interaction in the longhouse adheres to *adat* (customary law). The longhouse system fosters close bonds between members, and promotes a sense of belonging and security, such that occasions such as marriage, birth and death in any of the families in the longhouse involve the entire community.

Kayan hunting party at a camp in the jungle, c. 1905.

Economic activities

The Kayan and Kenyah are farming communities, and traditionally cultivated hill rice. Those residing in areas accessible to the market also cultivate cash crops. In addition, they hunt and fish to supplement their diet, and collect jungle produce for domestic use and for sale. A large number live in urban areas where they are employed in the public and private sectors, and a few have ventured into business.

Kayan woman making a beaded hat, c. 1960.

Arts and crafts

The artistic and material culture of the Kayan and Kenyah depict their customs, beliefs and way of life. Both groups have a central art form, known as *kayo urip* in Kayan and *kayu udip* in Kenyah, meaning the tree of life. This is a mythical tree, whence, according to their beliefs, sprung all life forms on earth. The curves and tendrils of the tree denote the development of individuals. Various aspects of this art form appear in their woven mats and baskets, as well as their beadwork, carvings and wall paintings.

Both groups are also excellent musicians and dancers. Songs, music and dances feature prominently in their festivals and celebrations. They are best known for the *sapeh*, a lute with a unique mellifluous sound.

The *sapeh* lute is carved from a single bole of soft wood.

Kelabit and Lun Bawang communities

The Kelabit and Lun Bawang are minority indigenous groups inhabiting the highlands of northeastern Sarawak. These traditionally rice-farming people produce the famous Bario rice. Like most other indigenous groups, they are longhouse communities, although there is a growing tendency to prefer single dwellings. They have discarded their head-taking ways, and the majority have adopted Christianity over traditional animistic beliefs. Despite the rapid changes in their lives in recent decades, they have preserved their unique cultural traditions.

Demography and economy

With a total population of about 25,000 (in 2000), the Kelabit and Lun Bawang, who are classified as Orang Ulu, are culturally and linguistically related, and traditionally occupy the highlands in the north and northeastern parts of Sarawak. The Kelabit are settled in the Kelabit Highlands, located above the furthest reaches of the Baram and Limbang rivers, while the Lun Bawang are found in the interior parts of Limbang Division. They are related to a number of groups occupying the border areas between Sarawak, Kalimantan and Brunei, and also the Lundayeh in Sabah.

Both groups are mainly subsistence rice farmers, and use an irrigation system for wet rice cultivation which has been refined over more than a century. They cultivate the fine Bario rice, which is known for its aroma and delicious taste. They also rear buffalo, cattle and poultry, and are the only groups in the interior of Sarawak that make salt from salt springs. The cool climate in the highlands also makes it possible to grow citrus fruits. In addition, they hunt or fish to supplement their diet. The Lun Bawang who live in areas accessible to the market also cultivate cash crops. Many Kelabit and Lun Bawang have moved to urban areas for further education and better job opportunities in the public and private sectors. In fact, only about 1500 of the approximately 5000-strong Kelabit community still remain in the highlands.

A Kelabit man in loincloth trims his hair en route to a longhouse party, mid-20th century.

Social and political structures

Traditional Kelabit society was stratified into three classes and a fourth rank of slaves, with the *lun merar* (big people) occupying the uppermost rank; followed by the *lun pupa* (half people); *lun da'at* (bad people); and the *demulun* (slaves). Differentiation between ranks was based on various factors, but the most important was the possession of valuables such as antique dragon jars (*belanai ma'un*), beads and beaded caps (*peta*), and animals such as water buffaloes, cattle and pigs. However, the possession of *demulun* differentiated the uppermost rank from the others.

In the past, leadership in the longhouse was tied to the *lun merar* rank, and members of the council of elders of the village (*bawang*) were drawn from the upper ranks. Each longhouse or village was an independent unit, and the head of its council was the headman (*la'ih rayeh*), a post that was usually inherited. The council of elders was responsible for the upholding of *adat* (customary law). Under a modern system introduced by the state government, a *penghulu* oversees the Kelabit community, and a *tua kampung* (village chief) replaces the *la'ih rayeh*.

The first Kelabit paramount chief, Pemanca Ngimat Ayu with his wife Sinah Ngimet Ayu.

ABOVE: Bario, traditional homeland of the Kelabit.

RIGHT: A farmer and his wife in their rice field.

Cultural traditions

Music and beads

The Kelabit and Lun Bawang are talented musicians and are famous for their bamboo bands. Instruments such as the *sapeh*, a plucked lute, and the bamboo *pagang* (zither), are played to accompany traditional hornbill, warrior and long dances.

Lun Bawang bamboo flute band.

Beads

Beads, like ceramic jars, are greatly valued among the Kelabit, and are significant as displays of a woman's wealth and status. Different kinds of beads have different values and are used for various purposes. For example, the *ba'o alai*, a shiny yellow, long, oval Venetian glass bead, is used in necklaces (*bane*), while the *ba'o rawir*, which normally comes in lengths of 15–25 millimetres and is made of very fine, smooth, opaque, pale dusty orange glass, is commonly used in the bead cap (*peta*). The *ba'o bata' madi'* and *bata' agan* beads are used for berets or belts. The former are tiny glass beads with a light green and blue shading, whereas the latter are blue glass beads with white interior. The *alai* is the most highly valued bead, and is either in plain yellow or patterned with rose buds and golden dust (*alai barit*). The old *alai* (*alai maun*) used to cost about RM200–250 a bead. Most of these beads are family heirlooms, are very valuable and treasured.

Beaded adornments such as caps and necklaces are prized among the Kelabit.

Besides settling disputes between members of his village, the *tua kampung* also acts as an intermediary between the villagers and the government, and is responsible for the implementation of government policies. At the turn of the 21st century, a *pemanca* (paramount chief) was appointed.

Belief systems

The traditional beliefs of the Kelabit and Lun Bawang revolve around a supreme god called Derayeh, whose powers were believed to manifest themselves through omen birds, animals and plants. They had a system of bird augury, dreams and omens, which necessitated the regular performance of rituals. Since the 1970s, however, most of them have embraced Christianity, and the church is the focal point of community life. Most events in the longhouse are organized through the church, including communal farming work. Christmas and Easter are celebrated as major holidays.

A village elder performs the warrior dance in traditional attire.

Family, kinship and community

Kinship and communal relations are important to the Kelabit as their settlements are remote and thus resources are shared by all. They are a closely knit community; sharing and helping one other is obligatory. The emphasis on communal life is reflected in the way longhouses are built without partitions between family sections.

The family is not only a social unit, but an economic one as well, and all members of the family share the work in the rice field. A family may consist of three or even four generations, and sometimes includes the siblings of the husband and wife. Elderly grandparents often live with the family, and thus, a family may consist of 12 to 15 members. However, this has changed since the 1990s with many younger Kelabit migrating to the urban areas.

ABOVE: A computer class at SMK Bario. Formal education was introduced in the Kelabit Highlands in 1946.

ABOVE LEFT: Traditional costumes and beaded caps of the Lun Bawang.

Kelabit women wearing bead caps perform the long dance during a name changing ceremony.

Kelabit name changing ceremony (irau mekaa ngadan or irau naru ngadan)

The *irau mekaa ngadan* is part of an elaborate and fascinating teknonymic system which distinguishes the Kelabit from the other Orang Ulu communities. It marks a couple's attainment of parenthood upon the birth of their first child, and to affirm this transition, the couple and their parents assume new names, which are announced during the ceremony. Under this system, the couple is addressed by parenthood titles, which are determined by the sex of their first born. A father of a boy will be addressed as *Temabu'* (literally meaning 'father of a boy') or *Temamu'* if the first child is a girl, while the mother will be addressed as *Sinabu'* (meaning 'mother of a boy') or *Sinamu'* (mother of a girl). The couple carry these titles until their first grandchild is born, when they have to take new titles. If the first grandchild is a boy, the grandparents are addressed as *Tepuabu'* (meaning grandfather or grandmother of a boy), or in the case of a girl, *Tepuamu'* (grandfather/grandmother of a girl). The ceremony ends with a feast (*irau*) in the longhouse gallery (*tawa*), attended by the entire longhouse community.

Mortuary rituals

Conversion to Christianity among the Kelabit has resulted in their abandoning several traditional rituals, including those associated with death. One such ritual was the death feast (*irau ate* or *burak ate*) held on the first anniversary of a person's death. Rice wine (*burak*) would be brewed in abundance and stored in jars (*belanai*) for the week-long feast.

The main purpose of the ritual was to take the bones of the departed to the cemetery for burial. In the past the Kelabit kept their dead in a coffin or a jar, either in a small hut erected outside the longhouse, or in a corner of the family's house, for a year, after which it would be taken to the graveyard during the death feast. These days burials are conducted according to Christian rites and usually take place within 24 hours after death.

The Lun Bawang, too, conducted elaborate mortuary and head-taking rituals prior to their conversion to Christianity. Both rituals were characterized by much feasting and consumption of *burak*. The death ritual stretched over 15 days, beginning with the placing of the body in a *lungun* (wooden coffin) or a *rubih* (earthenware jar), which would be placed in a small hut (*lapo lungun*) built a distance away from the house. After 14 days the remains would be transferred to a new container together with the personal possessions of the deceased, such as sword, gun and gong for a man, and beads, blouse and cooking pots for a woman, and taken to the *lengutan* (cemetery) where it would be placed under a rock crevice or a tree, inside a cave, underneath a megalith-related structure or simply buried in the ground.

Kelabit hospitality traditionally revolved around the consumption of rice wine (*burak*) brewed in ancient Chinese jars, mid-20th century.

Penan community and traditions

Traditionally a nomadic people, the Penan live mainly in the most remote parts of northern interior Sarawak. Although the majority of Penan have now settled, with only a few hundred still nomadic, the forest remains an integral part of their lives, and is the source of food, building materials for houses and boats, as well as materials for their cultural expressions. They continue to practise resource tenure unique to their community, and are renowned for their exceptional rattan weaving and blowpipe making skills.

A group of Penan hunters at a shelter.

Right: Penan on a fishing trip in the Mulu area.

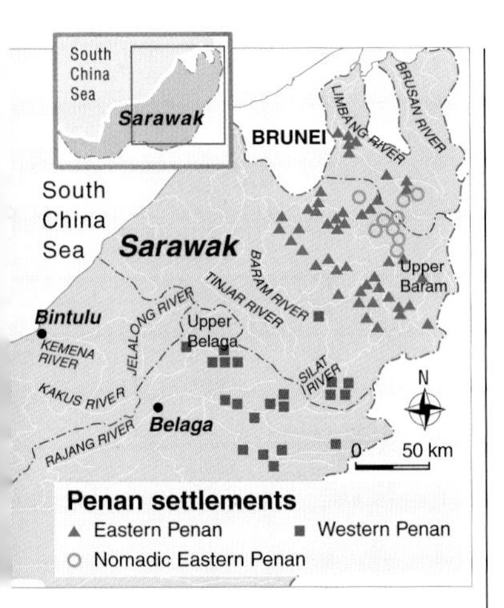

Origins and demography

The Penan are believed to have their origins in the upper Kayan River of Kalimantan in central Borneo. After moving westward towards Sarawak, they split into two groups, one settling along the Baram River (referred to as Eastern Penan) and the other along the Rajang River (Western Penan). Today, the Eastern Penan comprise those sub-groups living to the east of the Baram River, while the Western Penan are located around the watershed of the Rajang River, and along the Silat River in Baram District. There are also some settlements along the Tinjar River in Baram District, along the Jelalong River and in the coastal areas of Bintulu District, and in the Suai-Niah area of Miri District. With a total population of about 14,000 (in 2004), the Penan regard themselves as one people, speaking one language, with dialectal variations. Most of them live in settlements; only some 400 of them remain nomadic.

Bands and settlements

The small number of nomadic Penan live in bands, each made up of

Territory and resource tenure

Within the forest complex, each Penan group has its own foraging area (*tana' pengurip*) in which members hunt and gather food and other necessities of life. Each *tana' pengurip* has defined boundaries (*saang tana'*) which follow streams, ridges and other landmarks, and which are respected by other groups. When the foraging area of one group overlaps with another, the groups involved reach a mutual agreement to use the area in common.

Ecofriendly harvesting strategy

Perhaps the most important aspect of Penan resource management is the practice of *molong*, or sustainable yield, which forms the basis of their harvesting strategy. *Molong* can be done communally or individually. For example, when harvesting sago, they cut only one or two of several trunks, leaving the palm to re-sprout. They never cut down the entire plant at the root clump as this would kill it. Similarly, mature rattan is selectively harvested, allowing the young rattan plants to mature for future collection.

In their harvesting strategy, the Penan hunter-gatherers migrate, within their foraging area, from one area that has been harvested to another where resource replenishment has taken place. The settled Penan clear part of the *tana' pengurip* for cultivation, mainly swidden farming. Beyond the farms is a stretch of forest where they still exercise stewardship, and in which they rotate their harvest of forest resources from one place to another, allowing harvested areas to regenerate.

Above: The Penan's traditional hunting equipment consists of a dual-purpose blowpipe with spear, poisoned darts and a *parang*.

Left: Penan chipping pith of wild sago palm to make flour.

Differences between Eastern and Western Penan

	Eastern Penan	Western Penan
Referents	Penan Selungo, after the Selungo River, tributary of the Baram.	Penan Silat (Baram District), Penan Geng, Penan Apau and Penan Bunut (Belaga District).
Band size	20–40 members	60–200 members
Average household size	Four to five persons	Six to ten persons
Settlement system	Occupy camps for 1–3 weeks. Settlements built on ridge tops, some distance from source of water.	Large central base camps occupied for up to one year, and dispersed short-duration sago camps. Settlements built adjacent to rivers and streams.
Foraging areas	Small, overlapping areas used by different bands.	Large, little overlap of areas between groups.
Hunting styles	Rely on blowpipes, hunt wide range of game species.	Use dogs and spears, primary game wild boar.
Leadership institutions	Less developed institutions of leadership. Any individual can assume post of headman.	Strong institutions of leadership, aristocratic status for some individuals. Headmen related by kinship, some able to trace the office holders unilineally, back seven or eight generations.
Genealogical knowledge	Shallow	Extensive, extending to more than seven generations.

Young Penan girl making the *ajat*, a cylindrical back pack with shoulder straps.

Rattan weaving

The Penan, in particular the Western Penan, are the best weavers of rattan mats and baskets in Sarawak. Processing involves splitting each length of rattan into eight strips which are then shaved into appropriate widths and fineness for weaving. These strips are left to dry before being woven into closely plaited, soft and pliable mats and baskets that are decorated with hornbill, spider and floral motifs in black or dark brown. A single mat may take three weeks to a month to complete. The Penan take pride in the quality of their weaving, They are major producers of mats and baskets, and sell them to other communities as well as to merchants. However, they face a growing scarcity of rattan due to over-exploitation of the forest and development.

Blowpipe making

The Penan make excellent blowpipes. Previously made solely as weapons for hunting, blowpipes are now produced for sale, resulting in a growing cottage industry for the Penan. Wood from some 14 species of trees is used for making blowpipes.

Some Penan continue to hunt with blowpipes.

about 40 people. They live in camp huts which they abandon as they migrate from one place to another within a defined area. The settled Penan live in either longhouses or in single houses in village settlements. A band, longhouse or village is led by a headman (*pengajau uma*). Above him is a regional chief (*penghulu*) who looks after the affairs of several bands, longhouses or villages within a designated area.

Hunters and farmers

The nomadic Penan are hunters and gatherers of forest resources such as wild sago, fruits, game and non-timber resources for subsistence and for trade. Those who are settled grow hill rice, hunt, fish and rear chickens for domestic consumption. Virtually none of the Penan who settled after the 1950s are involved in the cultivation of cash crops, mainly because they live in the remote interior and access to the market is difficult. They rely on the sale of rattan mats and baskets, multi-purpose bush knives and blowpipes, as well as jungle produce, mainly *gaharu* (incense wood), for income.

Penan child with pet hornbill.

However, groups that became settled in the early or mid-20th century are involved in the cultivation of cash crops. These groups, who live in Suai-Niah and Lower Tinjar in Miri Division, and Jelalong and Labang in Bintulu Division, cultivate pepper, cocoa and, previously, rubber. In addition, some of them have ventured into oil palm planting. Modern infrastructure and access to the market have contributed to their success with cash crops.

Beliefs and values

Traditionally animists, the majority of Penan have embraced Christianity and, a small minority, Islam. Regardless of religious affiliation, they adhere to age-old values and norms, such as respect for elders and caring for them. During their nomadic days, whenever they moved camp, the young would carry the old who were not capable of walking.

Entertainment and pastimes

Although many Penan groups are discarding their traditional dance and music, opting for those of their Kenyah and Kayan neighbours, some groups have preserved them. The traditional version of the Penan *ngajat* dance is still performed by some groups. It involves vigorous shuffling of the feet, waving of the hands, hitting and rubbing the body, and hopping. The movements to some extent reflect their environment. For instance, the hit-and-rub part is an imitation of animals which populate their forest world. The stylized movements often imitate monkeys, bears or a hunter stalking game, or a man pulling rattan. The shuffling of feet suggests the trampling of sago pith to extract flour, and hopping is a sign of having successfully completed a task, whether hunting or some other activity. Like their dance, some of their traditional songs are in praise of the spirits, and of their environment.

The Penan in the 21st century

The number of Penan children attending school continues to lag far behind other groups, although there are slight increases in attendance every year. At the beginning of the 21st century, only about a dozen youth have attained university education. The number of Penan in the civil service is also very small, with a few holding positions in the state administrative service, and in government departments.

A Penan dances to the accompaniment of the *sapeh*.

Penan woman and her children, c. 1990.

Kajang and other Orang Ulu groups

The Orang Ulu are a conglomeration of minority indigenous groups that make up five per cent of the population of Sarawak. They are mainly found in the northern interior of Sarawak, in the Belaga, Baram, Limbang and Lawas Districts, and comprise the Kayan, Kenyah, and Kajang and several other related groups. The main Orang Ulu groups are featured separately in this volume. Despite their small numbers, they are represented in both the private and public sectors, and take pride in contributing to the state's development. They have also withstood the pressure of modernization and retained much of their cultural heritage.

Top: A staged Orang Ulu wedding.

Above: A Sekapan chieftain.

Left: Orang Ulu *penghulu* and his followers, 1950s.

The highlight of the Kajang people's traditional *save'* ceremony is the erection of a massive ritual pole (*kelaman*).

Ethnic variety

The Kajang and related communities form the second largest Orang Ulu group after the Kayan and various Kenyah subgroups (see 'Kayan and Kenyah communities'). The Kajang are believed to be the earliest inhabitants of the upper Rajang River, and comprise six main subgroups—Kejaman, Sekapan, Lahanan, Punan Bah, Seping and Bemali. They live in the Belaga, Tatau and Bintulu districts. More than 15 other indigenous groups in the northern interior of Sarawak associate themselves with the Kajang on the basis of cultural and linguistic similarities. The population of these groups range from fewer than 100 to about 4000 people each, with the smallest group, the Lisum, comprising just four families.

Social organization

The Orang Ulu are longhouse dwellers, with each longhouse led by a headman (*ka'ayo' lovou'* among the Kajang) who oversees the affairs of the village and acts as an arbitrator in disputes between members of the longhouse. Above the headman are the regional chiefs (*ketua masyarakat*), namely, the *penghulu*, *pemanca* and *temenggong*, who look after the general affairs of several villages within a river system or designated area. As with other longhouse groups, social interaction among the Orang Ulu communities is governed by *adat* (customary law).

Economy and livelihood

The Kajang and other Orang Ulu groups are hill rice cultivators, combining this activity with cash crop farming. They also hunt and fish, mainly for domestic consumption, and collect jungle produce such as rattan for domestic use and for sale. The Kajang are among the least mobile groups of Orang Ulu, and only a few young educated members have moved to urban areas to seek employment.

Culture and belief systems

The Kajang have adopted much of the culture of the Kayan as a result of intermarriages and of their long association with them. Their dances and music are similar and, like the Kayan, they are gifted craftsmen. In the past, they carved and raised spectacular wooden structures known as *klirieng* in which were kept the remains of dead chiefs.

Changing religious influences have affected the practice of rituals and ceremonies observed by the traditionally animist Orang Ulu. Many have embraced Christianity and a few, Islam. In the past, the Kajang conducted an elaborate ceremony called *save'* that was associated with headhunting. *Save'* is now held as part of rites of passage marking the transition from puberty to adulthood, or to celebrate a bountiful harvest.

Above: The Kajang's *save'* ceremony involves elaborate rituals, sacrificial offerings, dancing and feasting.

Left: An Orang Ulu performs the warrior dance.

Kajang sub-groups

1 Kejaman and Sekapan
These communities comprise a total of about 2000 people living in four longhouse settlements close to Belaga. Both groups were at one time politically dominant.

2 Lahanan
A community of over 600 people in two longhouse settlements: one above the Bakun Rapids, at Long Pangai, and the other below the Bakun at Long Semuang. The Long Pangai group is surrounded by Kayan, Kenyah and Penan groups and, as a result, is multilingual.

3 Punan Bah
This group claims that their original homeland is the upper Bah River, tributary of the Rajang. They live in eight settlements in Belaga, Tatau and Bintulu districts. Their language is related to that of the Kejaman and Sekapan.

4 Seping and Bemali
These communities share a common origin. A long time ago, the Seping used to live by the Seping River while the Bemali lived by the Mali River. The two rivers join to form the Belepeh, a tributary of the Murum, which in turn is a tributary of the Balui River. Oral history suggests that their names were derived from the Seping and Mali rivers. Two longhouse settlements; one at Long Bala and the other at Long Koyan.

Other Orang Ulu groups

5 Beketan
Comprising some 1800 people in 13 longhouses in the Kapit and Tatau districts, living in close proximity to the Iban. They are mainly hill rice cultivators, with some families growing cash crops such as pepper.

Orang Ulu longhouse.

6 Berawan
One of the largest groups of about 4000 people living in nine longhouse communities in Baram District. Their ancestral home is in the Usun Apau, which straddles the Belaga and Baram districts. They are shifting hill rice cultivators who also grow cash crops such as pepper and cocoa, vegetables and fruits for sale and for domestic consumption. Known for their exquisite wood-carving.

Berawan women in traditional costumes and headdresses.

7 Buket
Previously nomadic hunters and gatherers, the Buket originated from East Kalimantan. There is only one longhouse community, of about 300 members, in Asap by the Belaga River. They were headhunters feared by the Iban and other groups because they hunted by night and killed quietly with blowpipes.

8 Lisum
Perhaps the smallest ethnic group in Sarawak, comprising only four families who live together with a group of Tanjong people in a longhouse at Long Pawah, Belaga. Previously a nomadic people who roamed central Borneo, they came to Belaga from Kalimantan in the late 1960s.

9 Punan Busang
The group is named after the Busang River, a tributary of the upper Balui River, which they claim as their place of origin. Once nomadic, their harvesting strategy and management of forest resources is similar to that of the Penan. Now settled, they cultivate hill rice, vegetables and fruits, and raise poultry. They weave rattan mats and baskets, and make blowpipes for domestic use as well as for sale.

The traditional attire of the Punan Busang is similar to that of other Orang Ulu groups.

10 Sa'ben
Comprises a single village community at Long Banga by the upper Baram River, in Baram District. The group share kinship ties with the Kelabit. Their language is similar to that of the Lun Bawang and Kelabit, while culturally they have much in common with the Kenyah.

11 Sihan
There is only one village of 31 households at Sungai Menamang. The group was previously nomadic, surviving on wild sago, game and fish. Intermarriage with outsiders is common.

12 Tabun and Tring
These groups are closely related by kinship ties. Their language is similar to that of the Kelabit and Lun Bawang. The Tabun live by the middle Limbang River in Limbang District, and the Tring live at Long Terawan, in the Baram District, with the Berawan people. They are separated geographically by the Mulu National Park. The number of pure Tabun in Sarawak does not exceed a two hundred. Over the years they have been assimilated by the Iban, Lun Bawang and Kelabit. The Tring have been living with the Berawan at Long Terawan for over a century, and intermarriages between them are common.

13 Tagal
This group comprises just over 1000 people in four villages in Lawas District. They live side by side with the Lun Bawang, and as a result virtually all Tagal speak the Lun Bawang language and are familiar with Lun Bawang customs. They cultivate hill rice and cash crops for sale.

14 Tanjong and Kanowit
The Tanjong live in two settlements in the Kapit and Belaga districts; the Kanowit comprise a single settlement in Kanowit District.

15 Tatau
This group comprises a single community in Tatau District, sharing a longhouse with the Iban. They claim cultural affinity with the Punan Bah, but intermarriages with the Iban are common.

Orang Ulu catching fish. Other economic activities include hunting and rice farming.

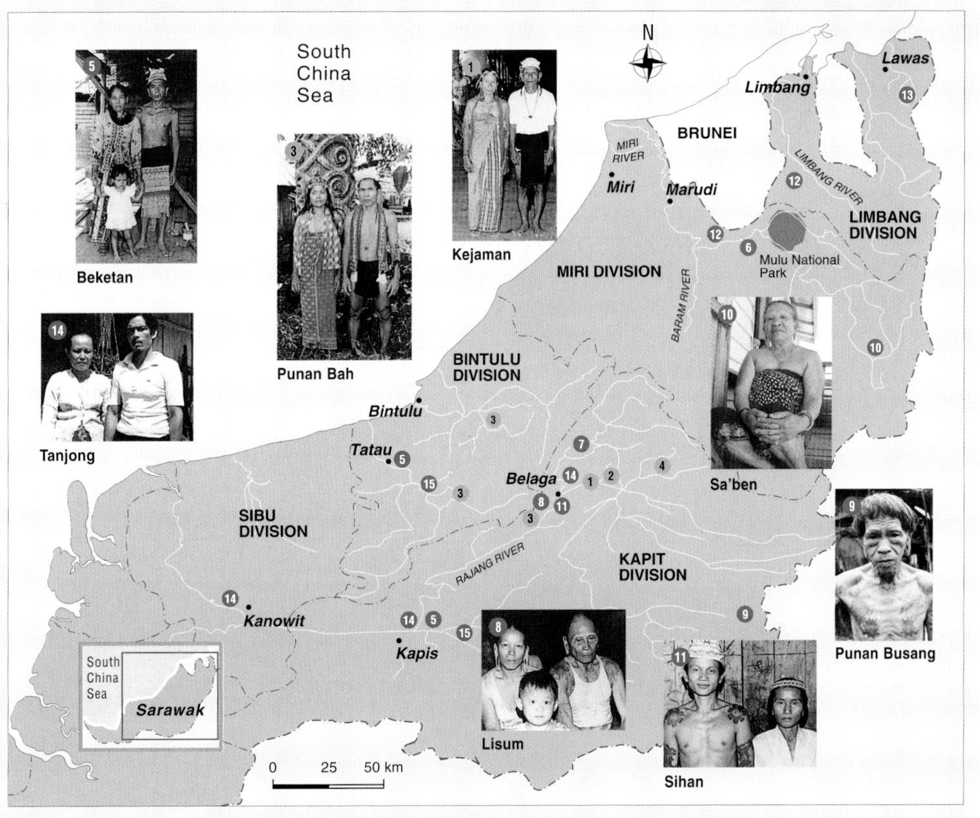

Non-indigenous peoples of Sarawak

About 30 per cent of Sarawak's estimated population of two million are non-indigenous peoples. The majority of them are Chinese with Indians, Indonesians, Eurasians, Europeans and other minorities comprising smaller numbers. They were originally migrant communities whose cultural identities and traditions can be traced to their countries of origin. Although there is a consciousness of ethnicity and cultural identity among the non-indigenous peoples, they identify themselves as part of Sarawak's multicultural society and as citizens of Malaysia.

Faces of a multi-cultural generation:
1. Eurasian.
2. Indian.
3. Javanese.

Additions to the ethnic diversity

Chinese immigrants came from China and neighbouring countries as early as the late 18th century to work in gold, antimony and mercury mines. Most of these immigrants were Hakkas. Hokkien merchants who arrived in the mid-19th century were involved in the spice trade and the import of goods from China. Other Chinese immigrants in the 19th and early 20th centuries included the Teochew who opened sundry shops in various parts of the state; the Henghua fishing community; Foochow rice farmers who later became involved in logging and the timber trade; and the Hainanese and Cantonese. By 2004, a population of about 578,700 Chinese was to be found mainly in the trading and commercial sectors, and settled in the urban areas.

The Indians are mainly descendants of contract labourers who entered Sarawak when it was under Brooke administration in the late 19th century. They are a varied group, differing in regional origin, religion and occupation. The community, with a population of 3851 (in 2000), is made up of various ethnic sub-groups, namely Tamils, Sikhs, Sri Lankans and Pakistanis. Most of them are employed in the civil service, security forces or as professionals, while some are land and property owners,or entrepreneurs. The Indian Muslims are mainly traders in textiles, books, sundry goods and spices, as well as money changers. There was an influx of Indians from the Peninsula after the formation of Malaysia in 1963, a number of whom intermarried with local Indians. This resulted in the establishment of a small number of south Indian restaurants.

A family at the Foochow agricultural settlement sharing a meal, mid-20th century.

The Indonesian community, comprising mainly Javanese and Bugis, is the third largest non-indigenous group in Sarawak, with a population of 2,382 (in 2000). They are mostly descendants of migrants who came in the early 20th century, and are mainly engaged in agriculture, cultivating coconuts and other market crops. Many of the younger Indonesians are professionals and in the civil service. Some are politicians.

Other smaller communities are the Eurasians (about 300), Europeans, Filipinos, Japanese, Thais, Koreans and Myanmar. Most of the Eurasians work in the public and private sectors, or with security forces. Some have risen to top posts in government departments as well as the police force.

Values and traditions

The Chinese, like those in other parts of Malaysia, belong to a patriarchal, hierarchical society that emphasizes the family unit as a component of the larger community and society. Social relationships are based on respect for authority and elders.

Chinese families value education for social security and mobility. Although education has been

Traditional Chinese occupations

1. Rickshaw puller in Kuching, early 20th century.
2. Chinese merchant assessing native artefacts, 1990s.
3. Businessmen at a Hokkien Association committee meeting, c. 1950s.
4. Foochow noodle maker, 1950.

ABOVE: A Sarawak Chinese family portrait, early 1900s.

LEFT: An Indian family with friends in Kuching, 2000.

responsible for raising the living standard of the Chinese in creating wider job opportunities, it has invariably brought changes to their values. Extended families with several generations—grandparents, parents and children—staying together are being replaced by nuclear families.

The changes affecting the Chinese affect the other non-indigenous groups too, with the trend towards smaller nuclear families and individualistic traits, mainly due to the impact of education.

Reinforcing the role of values in Chinese cultural life is the observance of festivals associated with the lunar calendar. The Chinese in Sarawak observe a blend of Taoism, Confucianism and Buddhism, and some are Christians. But regardless of their religious beliefs, the lunar new year is celebrated on a large scale. During Chap Goh Meh, Kuching is lit up by scores of lanterns. On the fourth day of the Chinese New Year, hundreds of thousands of pilgrims pay homage and seek fortune readings at the over 200-year-old Ching San Yen (Green Hill) temple outside Kuching. Other major days in the lunar calendar are also observed, such as Qing Ming, Dragon Boat Festival, Hungry Ghost Festival and Mooncake Festival.

Sarawak Indians belong to the Hindu, Sikh, Muslim, Buddhist and Christian faiths. The Addipuram festival in honour of the goddess Kaliamman is the biggest Hindu celebration in Sarawak. Other Hindu festivals are Navarathri, Vinayake Chargutri and Chitra Pornami, Thaipusam, Ponggal and Deepavali. Prior to the formation of Malaysia in 1963, Thaipusam was observed only on a very small scale. In 1967, the first Thaipusam procession was held in Kuching. In the years since, Thaipusam celebrations have steadily grown, although they are not as massive as those in Kuala Lumpur and Penang. The Sikhs celebrate Vaisakhi.

Most Indians speak the local Sarawak Malay dialect, but children of intermarriages speak the mother tongues of their parents as well. Younger Indians are well-versed in formal Malay and English, while Tamil and Urdu are also spoken at home.

The Indonesian community in Sarawak has integrated with the Malays and Muslim-Melanau communities. Most have joined Malay organizations, Islamic groups and societies, and celebrate Haji Raya and other Islamic festivals.

Sarawak Eurasians are mainly Christians, and celebrate Christmas and Easter. Those who are descended from the Dayaks also hold 'open houses' during Gawai Dayak and observe some of the native festivals. Some Eurasians are Muslims and observe Hari Raya and Malay-Melanau customs.

The mayor of Kuching City South, Chan Seng Khai (left) and Parliamentary Secretary in the Public Works Ministry, Datuk Yong Khoon Seng (second from left) receiving blessings from the priest at a temple in Kuching during the Hindu Navarathri festival, 2004.

Social organization

The first Sarawak Chinese Chamber of Commerce was formed in 1910 by early Chinese traders in Kuching. In 1965, the Associated Chinese Chamber of Commerce and Industry was established, and today it has 22 constituent Chambers in the main towns representing more than 4000 Chinese companies in the state. The Chinese have also set up associations, guilds, clans and temple organizations in all the major towns in the state. Temple organizations such as the Tua Pek Kong in Kuching and Sibu are managed by representatives of Chinese associations and collect donations for the needy and the poor. They also provide education loans to students from various ethnic backgrounds.

There are about a dozen Indian temple associations, organizations and sports bodies, all based in Kuching, as well as an organization which looks into the community's educational needs. The first Indian Muslim religious school in Sarawak, Al-Madrasatul Islamiah, was established in 1939. In 1959, the Persatuan Kebajikan Islam Sarawak was formed to look into the welfare of Indian Muslims.

BELOW FAR LEFT: Special prayers held at a temple in Sarawak to usher in the lunar new year.

BELOW AND BELOW LEFT: Dragon dances and stilt walking are organized in Kuching and other towns to celebrate the Chinese New Year.

BOTTOM: Built in 1903, the Ching San Yen (Green Hill) temple, about 30 kilometres from Kuching, is Sarawak's most elaborately decorated temple.

1. Murut men in warrior dress. The Murut were once feared for their headhunting raids.

2. Weaving at a Rungus longhouse.

3. Bajau horsemen, dubbed the cowboys of the East, are renowned for their equestrian skills.

4. Many of the Dusunic people of Sabah, such as the Kadazandusun, continue to observe age-old rituals and customs relating to health, marriage, death and rice cultivation. Priestesses and ritual specialists are usually called upon to perform such rituals.

5. The annual harvest festival (Pesta Kaamatan) is a state-level celebration that brings together ethnic groups from across Sabah in a display of culture, traditional sports and rituals.

ETHNIC GROUPS OF SABAH

Sabah has an ethnically complex and diverse population. Its demographic profile lists 24 indigenous or Bumiputera groups, and several other tribes as being 'other indigenous'. The latter category is made up of small groups concerning whom there is a lack of ethnographical information, although the customs and traditions of some groups among the Kadazandusun and Bajau have been extensively recorded. The Iban, who are associated with Sarawak, have formed a community in Sabah as a result of economic migration during the timber boom from 1950–70s. Malay Bumiputera in Sabah comprise not only Malay Muslim migrants from other parts of Malaysia but also Muslim indigenous people, such as the Brunei Malays on the southwest coast of Sabah, who are distinguished by their dialect and by their use of hereditary titles that reflect their historical links with the Brunei Sultanate.

Other migrants, too, have become part of the indigenous population or have assumed new ethnic identities to differentiate themselves from those in their original homeland. These include the Suluk, who have lived in Sabah for centuries and are known as Tausug in the southern Philippines, while the Kagayan are known as Jama Mapun in the Philippines. The Bugis, too, distinguish themselves from their Indonesian counterparts.

The largest non-indigenous group in Sabah is the Chinese, most of whom are descendants of late 19th- and early 20th- century settlers. The Chinese have influenced the cultural, social and economic face of Sabah, notably dominating trade and commerce. Their offspring from intermarriage with indigenous people have come to be known as Sino-natives, who in all but name have assimilated indigenous identities and customs.

The hallmark of Sabah's multicultural population is the tolerance and harmony between the ethnic groups. It is not unusual for family members of different faiths to live together harmoniously as a household. Groups from varied cultural, ethnic and religious backgrounds have lived contiguously with each other over the years leading to symbiosis and interdependence. These relationships have provided the foundation for the harmony and well-being among the groups that exist today. Kadazandusun and Bajau farmers continue to help each other to plant and harvest rice. The weekly *tamu* (market) evolved from a need to provide ethnic groups with an avenue for trade with one another, and a meeting point for interaction and exchange. Feuding tribes respected the neutrality of the *tamu* ground, and oath stones were erected as permanent reminders.

Modernization, education and improved infrastructure have begun to have an impact on Sabah's indigenous population and their cultural traditions. Practitioners and keepers of old customs are diminishing in number. Initiatives are aimed at revitalizing cultural traditions to ensure, at the very least, their documentation for future generations.

Cocos Islanders perform a traditional dance. The Islanders migrated to Sabah in the 1940s and 1950s.

Classification and identity of Sabah's indigenous groups

Sabah is home to some 50 ethnic groups, with about 30 regarded as indigenous to the state. The indigenous composition is diverse and complex, as methods to determine ethnic identity since the late 19th century have been inconsistent. Arbitrary claims account for fluid ethnic boundaries and changes in the indigenous listing since the first official census in 1891. These anomalies are due to a number of factors which have shaped the demographic character of the population.

Some Sabah indigenous groups in traditional costume

1. Dusun Tindal
2. Rungus
3. West coast Bajau
4. Lotud
5. Suluk
6. Penampang Kadazan
7. Bisaya
8. Papar Kadazan
9. Murut

The culture of the west coast Bajau is influenced by other ethnic groups living around them, in particular, the Kadazandusun and Iranun.

Population of Sabah 2004 ('000)

Kadazandusun	514.4
Other Bumiputera	421.7
Bajau	381.5
Malay	330.6
Chinese	277.3
Others	127.4
Murut	94.0
Indian	10.7
Non-Malaysian citizens	704.8
TOTAL	2862.3

Source: Department of Statistics, 2004

Location and migration

The geographical location of Sabah and its long indented coastline bordered by seas on three sides have provided entry for travellers, traders and migrants since ancient times. Early seafarers who settled along the coast were believed to have been gradually driven inland by later arrivals. The natural environment of mountains, rivers, valleys and forests created boundaries that kept these groups separate. The descendants of the inland inhabitants are broadly classified today as the Dusunic, Murutic, Paitanic, and a number of other smaller groups.

Early European travellers observed that the heterogeneous and seafaring Muslim population inhabiting the coastal inlets and river estuaries had minimal contact with the animistic peoples in the hinterland. The present-day coastal and island communities of Bajau and several related Sama-speaking tribes, the Suluk and Iranun, claim descent from these original seafaring settlers. Many of these people still rely on the sea for their livelihood and shelter, but others have abandoned their seafaring ways for mixed farming and fishing activities. The west coast Bajau, for instance, are distinguished by their successful adaptation to settled agriculture and cattle farming, as well as their equine skills.

Additions to the ethnic mosaic

Towards the late 19th century Sabah's population was already ethnically complex and mixed parentage was common. Pirates plying the shipping lanes around Borneo were responsible for much of the movement and transfers of people in the region through slave trading and intermarriage. The influx of foreigners enhanced the cosmopolitan population of the frontier town of Sandakan. Intermarriage between various ethnic groups was common, and Europeans in the area found it difficult to

A Lundayeh bride and her family at Long Pa Sia, in the interior of Sabah.

Classifications and the census

The North Borneo Government census of 1951 laid the foundation for the broad-based classification of the general ethnic character of Sabah's population. The 1951 and 1960 censuses, conducted when Sabah was still a British crown colony, reflected the major ethnic groupings at the time. These were the Dusun, Bajau, Murut, other indigenous, Chinese, Europeans and others. In the 1970 census, Malay replaced European as a differentiated category. In the 1980 census, however, the indigenous groupings were collectively labelled *pribumi*, and enumerated along with non-citizens with origins in neighbouring countries. In the 1991 census, the Dusun and the Kadazan were identified as two different indigenous groups, although they had merged the names to form Kadazandusun the same year. The Indonesian category was added due to their significant numbers in Sabah as citizens. The 2000 census reverted to the 1970 method of classification, comprising the groupings of Malay, Kadazan-dusun, Murut, Bajau, other indigenous, Chinese and others. In all censuses taken since 1911, the three largest indigenous groups—Kadazandusun, Murut and Bajau—and the Chinese have been constant ethnic entities.

Census enumerator (centre) collecting population data in a longhouse, 1960s.

Enumerators gathering census information among the Kadazan, 1960s.

identify the ethnicity of the people they met.

In 1858, Spenser St John, a British explorer, described his guide as a mix of 'Baju (Bajau), Lanun (Illanun), Malay and Chinese', and another 'claimed to be descended of four races...Baju, Sulu, Lanun and Malay.' He also met 'many Bisayas, Muruts Kalias, Padas Membakut and Patatan who could speak Chinese... and who acknowledged their mixed descent from the Chinese and the aborigines'.

Chinese men who participated in the trade in forest and maritime products between China and the local sultanates married local women. Under Chartered Company rule, arrangements were made to bring in settlers and workers from China and, later, Indonesia. These immigration policies continued until World War II, resulting in a sizeable Chinese population and a small Javanese community.

Confusions in classification

The interchangeable use of ethnic references has been a recurring phenomenon of Sabah's census-taking history. Government attempts to enumerate, identify and classify the population at various censuses held from 1891 were unable to produce a reliable indigenous ethnic profile due to erratic listings of diverse groups.

Above: Bonggi from Banggi Island call themselves Bajau after migrating to the coast and intermarrying with them.

Left: Dusun woman fishing in a pool near Penampang, 1960.

Dusun Tindal, sometimes known as Tempasuk Dusun, of Kota Belud district.

The weekly *tamu*, where traders from the indigenous groups offer their produce and handicraft for sale.

The people of Sabah use multiple references to identify themselves, for various reasons. At times, claims and declarations depend on circumstances, and may be motivated by opportunities offering social or economic advantage based on factors such as religion, social class, ethnic groupings and other criteria. For example, indigenous people have special rights and privileges through their Bumiputera and Sabah native status.

Assumption of another ethnic identity through intermarriage, and assimilation with another group, or by migration to another area, often takes place. In mixed marriages, kinship and residential ties influence declarations of ethnic identity of offspring. Children of the same parents are known to be registered under different ethnic groups. A prime example, the Sino-natives—children of intermarriages between Chinese and indigenous people—became an official ethnic category in the 1951 census.

On conversion to Islam many groups call themselves Malays, or by the name of the group they have assimilated with. The Tambanua are classified as Orang Sungai on becoming Muslim. Muslims may also call themselves Malays if they speak Malay, observe Malay customs and comply with the definition of a Malay in the Federal Constitution.

Recent changes

While Sabah's indigenous groups continue to live in their traditional areas, improved communication links and infrastructure have made many parts of the state accessible, and allowed more people to move away from their place of traditional residence. With such migration more intermarriages are likely to take place, making ethnic divisions less distinct.

Ethnic definition is a continuing process among indigenous people in Sabah. Murut groups call themselves after a river, place, tree or event. For instance, those on the banks of the Tagal River call themselves Tagal Murut.

Distribution and language of Sabah's ethnic groups

Ethnic group	Location	Language
Bajau	Coastal, islands	Sama-Bajau
Bisaya	West coast interior, Beaufort, Kuala Penyu, Sipitang	Dusunic
Cocos Islanders	East coast around Tawau and Lahad Datu	Sundic (Malay)
Dumpas	Upper Kinabatangan River	Dusunic or Paitanic
Dusun and Kadazan	Western coastal plains and interior, northern	Dusunic
Ida'an	Lahad Datu, Segama River	Other Borneon
Iranun	Kota Belud and other coastal areas	Maranao-Iranun
Kedayan	West coast, Beaufort, Sipitang	Sundic
Kwijau (Kuijau)	Keningau plains	Dusunic
Lotud	Tuaran, west coastal plains	Dusunic
Malays	Throughout Sabah	Malay
Mangkaak	Assumed to be around Labuk-Kinabatangan	Dusunic
Maragang (Kimaragang)	Kota Marudu, north	Dusunic
Minokok	Upper Kinabatangan River	Dusunic
Murut	Interior, southeastern Sabah	Murutic
Orang Sungai	Riverine areas, Kinabatangan, Segama, Labuk and Paitan rivers	Paitanic
Other Bumiputera	Scattered throughout Sabah	Various
Paitan	Paitan River	Paitanic
Rumanau	Upper Kinabatangan River	Paitanic
Rungus	Northern Sabah, mainly around Kudat and Pitas	Dusunic
Sino-native	Traditionally west coast	Dusunic
Sulu/Suluk	Coastal, mostly north, Kudat and east coast	Butuan-Tausug
Tambanuo (Tambanua)	Paitan River, northeast Sabah	Paitanic
Tidong	Tawau, Lahad Datu, inland and coastal	Murutic

Source: Department of Statistics, 2004

Native law in Sabah

Native law is derived from adat, *and is recognized by and alongside State and Federal law in Sabah. The term* adat *is commonly used to cover all aspects of customary behaviour among the indigenous people of Sabah, and denotes customs handed down through the generations. Cases are heard before courts with an official structure. Whilst modernization and changing religious beliefs have altered attitudes towards* adat, *key elements retain their vitality.*

The Native Courthouse in Sapulut in Pensiangan District in the interior of Sabah.

Adat and taboo

Adat regulates customary behaviour associated with the daily life of the indigenous people of Sabah both at home and in the workplace, with rules governing, amongst other things, traditional occupations such as hunting, fishing, planting and harvesting, relationships with others and man's relationship with the environment. A large number of customs are associated with the major events in a person's life, such as birth, marriage and death.

Much of *adat* consists of taboos based on traditional religious beliefs which are themselves founded on concepts of the supernatural. Most offences against *adat* are similar to universally recognized offences against natural justice. However, there are novel offences that would not be considered as such in the majority of other cultures. Whilst some *adat* have gone into disuse and others are gradually disappearing, the more durable have been incorporated into Native customary law.

The impact of religious beliefs

One important factor which has helped to reinforce adherence to Native law has been the belief among the indigenous people that a breach of *adat* constitutes an offence against a supernatural spirit, and that failure to atone would result in punishment in the form of sickness, disease, fire, loss of crops or animals or some similar calamity. Such punishment is believed to befall not only the offender, but the entire community. Offenders are therefore pressured to make an offering to the offended spirit on behalf of the community, failing which, they will be brought before the Native Court.

A Native Court hearing
Cases are heard by a panel of Chiefs and observed by village headmen. The parties to a dispute represent themselves.

Adat offences

1. If a person dies in the house or on the land of another person who is not a relative, compensation has to be paid by the family of the deceased.
2. If a person enters a private residential house uninvited after attending a funeral, compensation must be paid to the owner of the house.
3. If a woman gives birth in the house of another person, compensation must be paid.
4. If, during the customary bereavement period for a deceased spouse, the mourning widower or widow or a member of his or her immediate family walks under any fruit tree or enters any orchard belonging to another, this is a breach of Native customary law and compensation is payable to the owner of the fruit tree or orchard.
5. If a person marries earlier than an older brother or sister, he or she is required by customary law to pay compensation to each older unmarried brother or sister.

Native Chief beside the oath stone in Pensiangan which was relocated to the site of the new courthouse in 1992 after the old one was demolished.

Oath stones

Sometimes a stone is erected as a perpetual reminder of an oath taken by two or more parties. Oath stones (*batu sumpah*) may be erected to mark an agreement to live according to *adat* and to preserve peace among different tribal groups.

There are also oath stones associated with Native Courts. In the past, when a case in the Native Court could not be resolved due to contradictory evidence, both parties in the case would take oaths of honesty at an oath stone usually located nearby. The local people believed that a spirit living in the stone would show by a sign who was the untruthful party, and that such a sign came in the form of a severe loss.

RIGHT: The inauguration of an oath stone in Apin-Apin in Keningau District in 1990. Three ritual specialists (*bobolian*, shown here) officiated at the ceremony. The stone was erected to renew promises made in 1960 by the various groups in the area to live in harmony and to abide by local *adat*.

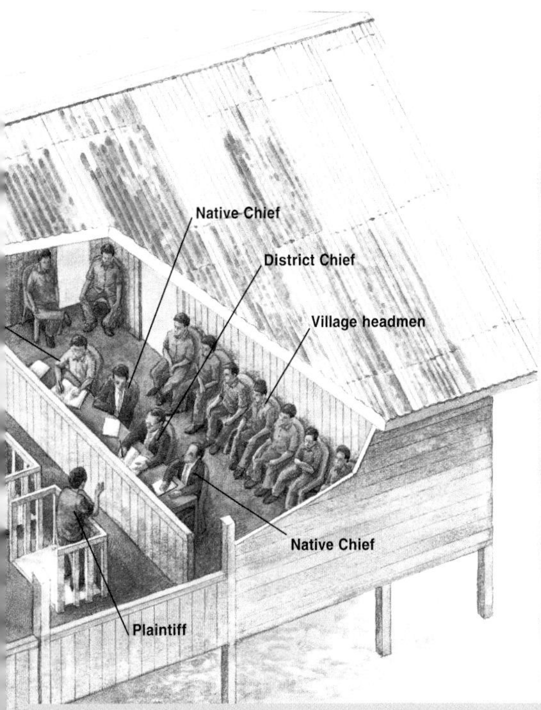

The Native Courts

Each of the 26 districts of Sabah has at least one Native Court. Cases are initially heard in a Native Court by three Native Chiefs, who are appointed by the government. There is no jury, and advocates are not permitted. If a party is not satisfied with the decision handed down by the Native Court, an appeal can be brought to the District Native Court which is presided over by a District Officer assisted by two Native Chiefs. A further and final appeal may be made to the Native Court of Appeal which is presided over by a Judge and two District Chiefs or Native Chiefs. Advocates are permitted at this final stage.

The District Chief and two Native Chiefs (seated at table) ready to hear a case in the Native Court at Nabawan. Seated behind them are village headmen, who follow cases in order to be familiar with the rules of Native law and procedure of the Native Court. Some of them may become Native Chiefs in the future.

Native Court appeals

Procedure in the hearing of a case arising from a breach of Native law or custom.

Hearing
NATIVE COURT
Three members consisting of District Chief (presiding member), and two Native Chiefs or headmen.

First Appeal
DISTRICT NATIVE COURT
Three members consisting of District Officer (presiding member) and two Native Chiefs.

Second and Final Appeal
NATIVE COURT OF APPEAL
Three members consisting of a Judge (President) and two District Chiefs or Native Chiefs.

Adat penalties

The penalty for breach of Native customary law is twofold: *sogit* (cooling compensation) and a fine. *Sogit* comprises a payment intended to bring about reconciliation between the offender and the victim; it is a type of spiritual atonement. *Sogit* may be paid to an individual, a family or a village community. It is believed that the possibility of an ill omen associated with death or bleeding has to be neutralized or removed and this is done by the payment of *sogit*. The fine serves as compensation to the injured or aggrieved party and is based on the principles of natural justice.

Notwithstanding widespread uniformity in the principles of Native law, variations do exist between different ethnic groups in the manner of carrying out penalties. Uniformity in the imposition of penalties was enhanced by the Native Courts (Native Customary Laws) Rules 1995 enacted by the Sabah State Assembly. However, the rules permit the imposition of traditional penalties so long as they are not contrary to the principles of natural justice.

Penalties in the Kadamaian District

In this district, where most of the residents are Kadazandusun, sentences for crimes traditionally consisted of two parts, namely, a punitive fine named *salak* (on account of the crime committed) and *sogit*. In cases of theft or loss, however, the penalty differed, with one commentator in the 1940s recording that a thief who stole a gong had to return the gong to the owner together with an additional gong. This payment was called *pongaiyud*. In the same district petty thieves had to return the item stolen together with a fowl as *sogit*.

There were three categories of offences, each carrying an appropriate *sogit* penalty. Thus, a fowl and an earthenware bowl was *sogit* for small offences, a pig and an earthenware jar for serious personal offences, and the payment of one or more buffaloes for serious offences against the natural order (such as incest) or the community in general. The last of these categories carried the possibility of the additional penalty of banishment. The *sogit* of an earthenware item for the first two categories of offences has special significance. A bowl or jar becomes dirty with usage, but when it is washed it becomes as clean as new. As *sogit*, it signifies the reconciliation that takes place between the parties.

The handing over of a fine supervised by a Native Chief.

Penalties in the Tambunan District

In Tambunan, when a buffalo was paid to the community it was the custom to take the animal to the bank of a river or stream on the upper side of the village, where it would be slaughtered. The buffalo's blood mixed with the running water and flowed past the village and in this way carried away the guilt of the crime. The people believed that the removal of the guilt would save them, their animals and crops from punishment by inhabitants of the spirit world, which would inevitably follow in the absence of atonement.

Penalties in the Murut Nabawan District

The vast majority of the people of Nabawan District are Murut. Among this group, offences of a sexual nature are considered particularly serious, especially incest. Apart from paying compensation, both offenders have to pay *sogit kampung* (village cooling compensation) of one buffalo to the community. This *sogit* could not be replaced with cash. The first buffalo would be slaughtered at the scene of the crime. A representative of each household in the area would come and receive a portion of the meat of the buffalo, with the amount of meat varying with the number of households. Those present would then return home and rub the meat so obtained against each of their fruit trees and then throw it away; it could not be eaten. The rubbing was to remove *kepanasan tanah* (anger in the earth) to ensure that there would be a normal fruit crop. If it was not done, it was believed the fruits might become diseased, or fail to develop properly or even fall off the trees whilst still small. The second buffalo was surrendered to the Native Court and consumed at a forthcoming public festival.

Applying the blood of a sacrificial animal to the trunks of fruit trees.

Until the early 19th century, traditional forms of punishment for murder, incest and adultery included banishment for life, and death by stoning. There were several forms of punishment for adultery, one of which was to tie the offender(s) on a raft which was then floated down a river and out to sea. If people living in villages downstream took pity on the offenders it was permissible for these villagers to untie the offenders and accept them into their own village.

The harvest festival in Sabah

The annual Kaamatan (harvest festival) is celebrated by Sabah's indigenous groups who were traditionally rice-farming communities. These groups comprise more than 30 per cent of Sabah's population of 2.8 million and include the Kadazandusun and their sub-groups as well as smaller tribes belonging to the Murutic, Paitanic and other Dusunic language groups. The festival commences on 1 May and culminates on the last two days of the month, which are state holidays.

Tamu market at Tuaran, Sabah, circa 1915.

Traditional harvest rites

Small, village-wide celebrations and thanksgiving harvest rituals were customary among the many Sabahan rice-farming communities that traditionally grew both wet lowland and dry hill rice. These rituals were observed at different times during the year, depending on the rice cultivation cycle of each village. Each part of the cycle defined time periods and governed social, cultural and economic activities, with the harvest one of the most important periods, shaping both the life and fortunes of the community.

Over time, settled rice farmers on the western coastal plains and interior of Sabah developed cultivation and harvest rituals more complex than those of the mobile groups practising shifting cultivation and swidden agriculture. This is evident from the number of shamans and ritual specialists who are called to conduct the necessary rice ceremonies for settled farmers. Each year, festival organizers invite shamans from different districts to perform ritual ceremonies. Rites vary between ethnic groups, though they serve the same function, and involve the process of recovering rice spirits, known variously as *bambaazon, bambarayon, bambarazon* or *toguruwon*, which may have been dispersed during harvesting activities such as reaping, transporting, winnowing, and milling. Rice spirits are believed to inhabit rice grains and are the source of its fertility. As part of the rituals, seven stalks of rice are cut and transferred to the barn to indicate the home-coming of the rice spirits. These stalks are stored in the barn to guard the grain.

A procession led by a male elder holding a ceremonial sword, circulating the floor with shrill cries and foot-stamping movements, as part of harvest rites in Penampang.

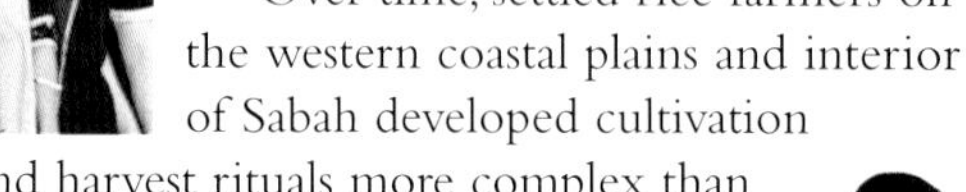

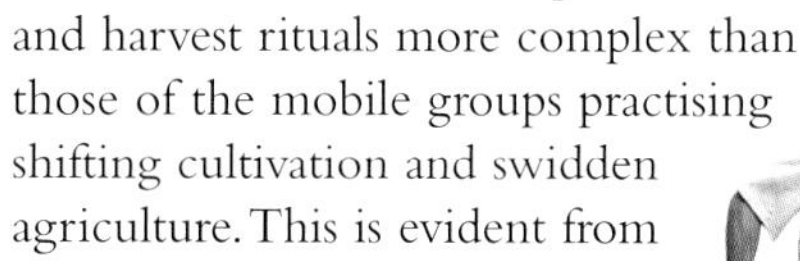

Buffalo races are held during Kaamatan.

Modern celebrations

The origins of the harvest festival in its present form can be traced to the agricultural exhibitions held during the administration of Sabah by the British North Borneo Chartered Company (1881–1946), and to the later agricultural fairs of the British North Borneo government (1946–63). Various sporting events and competitions involving crafts and agricultural produce were held during these fairs, which were usually organized to mark significant events such as the coronation of George VI in 1937, and that of Queen Elizabeth II in 1953.

Since 1989, during the celebrations on 30 and 31 May each year, indigenous peoples from across Sabah converge at a designated venue to participate in a variety of organized programmes. They compete or display their talents and skills in traditional arts, handicrafts and culture. Many attend wearing full traditional ceremonial attire, in order to exhibit their respective cultures and identities. A variety

Murut man drinking *tapai* (rice wine) during harvest celebrations.

Kaamatan

The event held to celebrate the coronation of Queen Elizabeth II in Kota Belud district in June 1953 took the form of an elaborate *tamu*, a traditional market held for different ethnic groups to meet and trade their goods and produce. It was filmed and shown worldwide as a documentary, and its success prompted the government to organize annual *tamu besar* (grand *tamu*) in various districts. From the mid-1950s these became regular features of the annual calendar, laying the ground work for future harvest festivals.

Local indigenous leaders, aware of the cultural and social importance of the harvest festival to the ethnic groups, wanted celebrations observed on fixed days to enable more than one group or village to celebrate at the same time. In 1956, a local indigenous leader Orang Kaya Kaya (OKK) Sedomon bin OKK Gunsanad proposed that the harvest thanksgiving to be celebrated at state level from 24–26 April each year. At his proposal too, these rituals were in 1957 incorporated into the annual Tamu Besar. However, the harvest festival only came into its own as a recognized official event in 1960 as a result of successful lobbying by Donald Stephens (later Tun Mohd Fuad Stephens), an influential member of the North Borneo Legislative Assembly.

In 1986, the month of May was designated for villages throughout Sabah to hold separate small-scale celebrations culminating in the main events at the end of the month. At the same time, the festival was officially named Kaamatan, a Kadazandusun term meaning 'festival after the harvest'. It is now a government-sponsored event organized by a committee headed by a Cabinet Minister.

Kaamatan features events such as stilt games and the sale of traditional crafts.

of food and beverages, goods and crafts and agricultural produce is offered for sale at these celebrations, which over the years have expanded in range and diversity.

The first day of the event is devoted to traditional sports competitions, such as arm wrestling (*mipulos*), knuckle wrestling (*mipadsa*), catapult shooting (*momolositik*), blowpipe contest (*monopuk*), tug-of-war (*migazat dukug*) and stilt racing (*rampanau*). Singing and dancing and exhibitions of crafts, skills and talents continue the next day when stage and cultural performances are held to entertain state dignitaries and the public. The second day begins with a parade of indigenous people in their traditional costumes. This is followed by a performance of traditional religious rites in abbreviated form by shamans depicting the fundamental essence of harvest thanksgiving. The shamans recite sacred texts, and perform ritual movements, and symbolically harvest rice in the same way as the priestesses (*bobohizan*) in traditional thanksgiving (*magavau*) rituals.

Harvest festivals of various groups

Each indigenous group in Sabah has its own name for the harvest festival. For instance, the Rungus call it *kokotuai*, the Kadazandusun, *kokotuan* or *kaamatan* and the Timugon Murut, *orou napangaan nanantab*.

Rice rituals of the Tuaran Lotud

These involve relatively low-key celebrations and merrymaking. The rituals comprise eight separate rites—*mansalud, monuras, tumakau, matang, mohogoi rumahi, mogimpuun, sumondot* and *monumbui*—in which the spirits are invoked to protect the rice fields. For these rites a piglet is sacrificed. The *tantagas* (priestesses) also perform the *bosilat*—a form of self-defence—to symbolically remove the influences of evil spirits on the harvest. A small celebration, with food and *bahar* (coconut toddy), follows.

Lotud priestesses making offerings to the spirits.

Thanksgiving by the Timugon Murut of Tenom

Mansisia (thanksgiving) festivities are celebrated by the Timugon after the harvesting season. Each family donates cash or kind to the village headman for the feast and celebration which take place in his house. All members of the village take part in the *tapai* (an alcoholic brew made from rice or tapioca) drinking session (*pansisiaan*). Partaking of every community member's contribution to the feast is an important function of the festivities and serves to foster communal ties.

Harvest celebrations of the Tagal Murut of Nabawan and Pensiangan

The Tagal call their festival *napangaan nongotom nalaparan*, which is celebrated over seven days. Celebrations take the form of cockerel fighting matches, drinking sessions and dancing on the *lansaran* (a springy platform).

A male priest (*bobolizan*, right) performs Rungus harvest rice rituals.

Harvest rituals of the Kudat Rungus

These comprise thanksgiving rituals involving the sacrifice of poultry and animals in honour of the *bambarazon* (spirits of the rice). Chickens are sacrificed in the rice fields during *mongigivit* rites as thanksgiving for a good harvest. Pigs are sacrificed for the *magahau* (purification ceremony), and the blood is used to ritually cleanse household tools, jars and gongs which the Rungus believe are inhabited by spirits. The meat is cooked for the feast. During the nightlong festivities following the feast, the Rungus perform the *mongigol sumundai*, a ritual dance, along the corridor of the longhouse.

The importance of rice

Harvest rituals are based upon the communities' respective religious beliefs, which are closely linked to the cultivation of rice. In addition to being a staple food, rice is an important resource for the creation of wealth and status in the traditionally agricultural communities. Indeed, rice serves as currency to pay for labour, shamans' fees, and to sponsor feasts. Other rituals are performed throughout the rice cultivation cycle, to maintain harmony between man and the environment, and to ensure a good harvest.

Rice origin theories

Beliefs and myths concerning the origin of rice vary between Sabah's ethnic groups. Generally they contain a common theme concerning the sacrifice of a beloved female relative. In Kadazandusun mythology, the daughter of the principal deities is sacrificed to provide food for her people. Her body parts became a variety of edible plants—her head produced the coconut; her flesh, rice; her blood, red rice; her fingers, ginger; her teeth, maize; her knees, yams, and so on.

Seven stalks of rice are symbolically cut at the harvest festival.

Likewise, in the Murut (Tagal) genesis myth, Olomor and Sulia are brother and sister; he sacrificed her for the same objective. According to the myth, Olomor and Sulia were clearing land to grow rice. Later that day, while resting, Olomor had a vision in which he saw Sulia being sacrificed to produce rice seedlings. Although he felt guilty, he felt obliged to sacrifice Sulia. He brought her to the clearing, and killed her. Her body rolled on the ground and her blood flowed to every corner of the cleared land. Seven days later, Olomor returned to the spot to find that a variety of plants had sprouted, and one of these was rice.

Unduk Ngadau

Tales of female sacrifice have been reinvented for the contemporary festival and provide a valid reason to hold the annual beauty pageant and selection of the Unduk Ngadau (harvest festival queen, literally meaning 'the sun at its zenith—the brightest point of the day' in Kadazandusun). The pageant has come a long way from the costume competition held during the *tamu besar*, and which was developed into a cultural beauty pageant in 1958. The parade of girls in traditional costumes is seen as a means to promote and preserve the cultural identity of the indigenous peoples.

The harvest festival queen is said to epitomize beauty, love, compassion, courage and self-sacrifice, attributes ascribed to the daughter of the traditional Kadazandusun deities.

Priestesses, shamans and ritual specialists of Sabah

Shamanism is an intrinsic part of the life of Sabah's indigenous communities which practise rituals derived from traditional belief systems that subscribe to the existence of a spirit world. Shamans, priestesses and ritual specialists act as intermediaries between the human and the supernatural worlds, and perform ceremonies to maintain harmony between the two. These ritual and spiritual experts, who are also regarded as mystics, may perform other roles in their communities—as healers, herbalists, midwives and advisers on local customs and beliefs.

Priestesses and ritual specialists in Sabah are known by various names depending on the ethnic group and their role. Among the Kadazandusun they are referred to as *bobohizan*, *babalian*, *bobolian* (above), *babalizan* or *bobolizan*, *tantagas*, *bobogo* or *ponyupi*, while among the Murut they are known as *lumahon* or *mogogondi*, and *omboh* among the east coast Bajau.

Kadazandusun ritual specialists from Ranau wearing traditional wide-brimmed hats.

Traditional belief systems

A number of indigenous communities in Sabah still observe and perform rites and rituals that are based on their traditional belief systems. These groups believe in the existence of a supernatural world that is inhabited by a pantheon of spirits which affect the well-being of humans. Modification of the environment through various social and economic actions is believed to displace or affect spirits in the unseen world, causing disharmony in the relationship between man and these spirits. Rituals or ceremonies are therefore performed from time to time to invoke, propitiate or exorcise spirits—both good and evil, to restore the peace and harmony in the relationship. These ceremonies may be elaborate public displays or privately held rituals.

Rituals are performed by a special category of people—shamans, priestesses and ritual specialists. Reputed and effective shamans command great respect, prestige and a high social status. Some groups, such as the Lotud of Tuaran District, have a complex hierarchy of priestesses (*tantagas*), whose competence and training vary according to the rituals they perform.

While ceremonies vary between different Kadazandusun groups, they all share a common creed, centred around the cultivation of rice, and a multitude of spirits presided over by two supreme deities. Rice is the staple diet of the Kadazandusun and provides the fundamental source of their wealth, good health and well-being. Great care is thus taken throughout the rice cultivation cycle to maintain a good relationship with the spirit world, and to avoid offending various spirits that are said to govern each stage of the cycle. Good spirits are invoked and appeased for abundant harvests, while evil spirits are exorcised and made to stay away. Environmental calamities such as drought and floods that cause rice and other crops to fail are said to be bad luck. Illness in the household, too, is seen as the work of evil spirits. When such incidents occur, elaborate rituals are performed to appease and cajole the spirits.

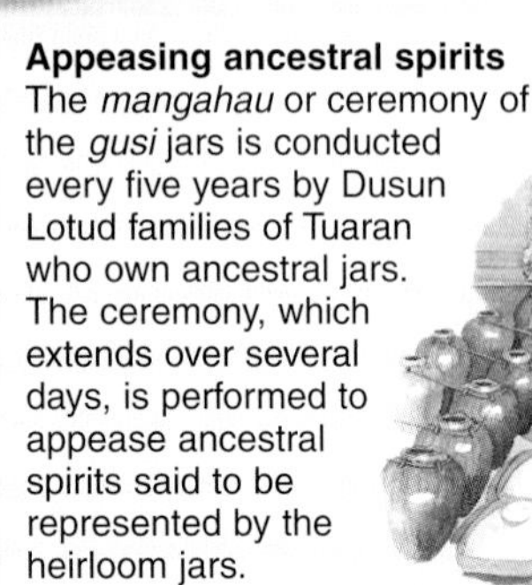

Male ritual specialist from Keningau.

Prominent rituals

The most celebrated rituals in Sabah include those related to rice cultivation, the environment and the spirit world.

The Dusun Lotud and Kadazandusun of Papar District observe a series of rituals throughout the rice growing cycle. The Dusun Lotud also perform the *mamahui pogun* rituals to cleanse the universe (see 'Kadazandusun beliefs and traditions').

The Kadazandusun of Penampang observe the *mongihozop* ceremony, in which the *bobohizan* (priestess) enters the spirit world to send the spirit of a person after death to its resting place. In addition, they hold the *magang* ceremony when hereditary skulls are transferred from one location to another.

Appeasing ancestral spirits

The *mangahau* or ceremony of the *gusi* jars is conducted every five years by Dusun Lotud families of Tuaran who own ancestral jars. The ceremony, which extends over several days, is performed to appease ancestral spirits said to be represented by the heirloom jars.

1. The *mangahau* ceremony begins with a prayer session by priestesses. Offerings of rice are made to the spirits. The *rumantas* ritual, performed by the head priestess (*moinat*) during a lull in the ceremony, involves reciting sacred text (*rinait*) while waving a piece of cloth over the *gusi* (jars).
2. A week later the *mohbok* (expiation ritual) is conducted. A ritual boat (*paradas*) is constructed in which wooden figurines representing the ancestors and food offerings are placed. The *paradas* is then carried to the river.
3. Food and sacrificial offerings are made before the *paradas* is floated downstream and drifts to the open sea. The ceremony ends with the participating families and priestesses leansing themselves in the river to wash off any bad luck.

Functions of shamans

Shamans, be they priestesses, ritual specialists or spirit mediums, perform a number of services which are in demand in traditional communities. Services include those related to rites of passage—at birth, various stages of a child's growth, marriage, and death. Shamans are also called on to perform healing and curing rituals, and ceremonies for agricultural practices. In addition, they are consulted in situations such as house-building, hunting, for the interpretation of omens, signs and the use of oracles, and in times of calamity, whether personal or communal, when rituals are deemed necessary to restore harmony between the supernatural and human worlds. They are also advisers to village heads on matters related to local customs and beliefs.

Some shamanistic practitioners have the capacity, or are imbued with, 'gifts' to be spirit mediums and enter a trance to communicate with spirits. Some ritual specialists can only perform certain rituals that do not require them going into a trance, while others can do both, functioning as ritual specialists and spirit mediums. Many senior priestesses among the Lotud are accomplished in both functions. In healing ceremonies, spirit mediums are employed to communicate with the spirit world to diagnose illness, and to advise on remedies to restore the health of the person.

Male *bobolian* (priests, with backs to the camera) blessing Datuk Joseph Pairin Kitingan, the Huguan Siou, or paramount chief of the Kadazandusun, in 2004. The ceremony was held at the Nunuk Ragang in Ranau District, said to be the place of origin of the Kadazandusun people.

Training and skills

Some ritual specialists and shamans inherit their skills as part of ancestral legacies, although all are required to undergo a long process of initiation and apprenticeship. Apprenticeship may begin as early as the age of seven. Apprentices are sometimes selected through divination in dreams, spirit possession or by having some special aptitude to receive instruction from a senior practitioner. Throughout their apprenticeship novices have to make ritual payments (*sogit*) to compensate the teacher for their instruction and to sanction their contractual obligations. The duration of learning depends on the capacity of the student to memorize and recite the sacred texts (*rinait* or *inait*), as well as the context and rituals in which they are used. At the end of training, students are tested—sometimes through divination using oracles or through dreams—to establish their new status. Not all students complete the entire process, with some graduating at lower levels of the ritual curriculum.

Ritual paraphernalia includes ancient beads, dried rhizomes, animal bones and gongs.

Kadazandusun priestesses are believed to be a replication of the supreme female deity, Suminundu or Umunsumundu who, according to folklore, was the first priestess and sacrificed her daughter to produce rice as food for mankind (see 'The harvest festival in Sabah'). Another practical reason for the predominance of priestesses lies in the traditional gender division of labour, which kept females close to the home. Women help facilitate the passing on of information and knowledge between females, and from one generation to the next.

Shamans in contemporary life

The number of shamans and ritual specialists is declining due to a lack of interest among younger people to acquire the necessary skills. The lengthy apprenticeship is said to be a major deterrent, and as an economic activity it is not as lucrative as other livelihood forms. With the declining numbers of ritual specialists, many previously important ceremonies have ceased to be performed. With the demise of each senior priestess, a wealth of ritual knowledge dies too.

Shamanistic beliefs and practices have diminished among many traditional communities due to modernization and changing religious influences. In addition, the context of performance of many of the rituals has changed. Some of the ceremonies are sponsored and staged more as cultural displays than for actual need. The incorporation of new terms in the *rinait* to reflect changes in the development of the human environment suggest that the rituals are not inflexible. In one *rinait* recited during a Lotud religious ceremony in the early 1980s, helicopters were described in the prayer invoking blessings for the people. Costumes and ritual paraphernalia have also been modified according to availability.

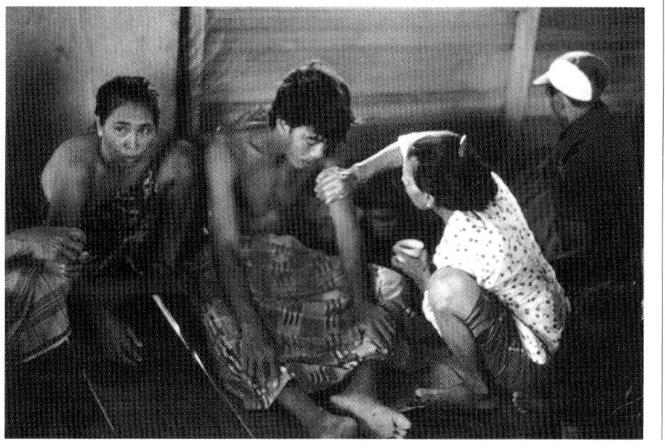

Famous shamans

The late Odun Piduru (1890–1992, above) was a high priestess (*tantagas*) among the Lotud, and led the *rumaha* ceremony held in the early 1980s in Kampung Tolibong, Tamparuli, to appease the spirits of skulls. Upon her death, a vast collection of ritual knowledge disappeared. Odun Rinduman (Uwoi bte Bialang), who was one of her assistants, took over as head of the Lotud clergy.

The *Bohungkitas Bobohizan* (high priestess) of Penampang, Inai Binjulip (1900–92), was responsible for anointing the first *Huguan Siou* (symbolic paramount chief) of the Kadazandusun people, Donald Stephens (later Tun Mohd Fuad Stephens), in 1960.

ABOVE: Lotud priestesses (*tantagas*) praying in the rain.

ABOVE LEFT: A male *bobolian* (priest), with a group of climbers, performing the ritual involving the sacrifice of seven white fowls and other offerings before an ascent of Mount Kinabalu. In the past, these rites were mandatory before every ascent. Now they are held annually. In Sabah, male shamans only perform specific rituals; ritual specialists are predominantly female.

LEFT: A Bajau *omboh* (spirit medium) treating a patient.

Kadazandusun communities and lifestyles

The Kadazandusun are the largest ethnic group in Sabah, accounting for over 25 per cent of its population, and comprise both the Kadazan and Dusun peoples as well as sub-groups. At least a dozen Dusunic languages, and many more dialects, are spoken. Traditionally subsistence padi farmers, government efforts to modernize their agricultural lifestyles and improve their socioeconomic status have enabled these people to become part of Sabah's mainstream society, and several Kadazandusun have become political leaders, entrepreneurs and professionals.

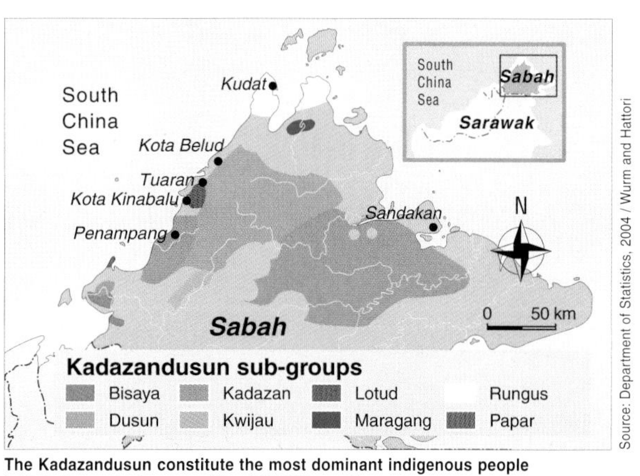

The Kadazandusun constitute the most dominant indigenous people in Sabah, numbering more than 510,000 people.

Kwijau ritual specialists from Keningau chanting during a ceremony.

Definition and demography

The Kadazandusun are a collection of tribes classified as speakers of languages of the Dusunic family, and who traditionally occupied the fertile plains of the west coast of Sabah from Kudat to the border of Sarawak, and in the interior areas of Ranau, Tambunan and Keningau. Comprising the Kadazan, Dusun, Lotud, Kwijau, Bisaya, Rungus, Dumpas, Mangkaak, Minokok, Maragang, Tangaah, Liwan, Tatanah, Sino-natives and other tribes, the Kadazandusun are a Bumiputera or indigenous group and enjoy special privileges and customary rights such as ownership of native titled land (see 'Classification and identity of Sabah's indigenous groups'). In the past, they were collectively labelled 'Dusun' (meaning 'orchard' in Malay) and described as being mainly agricultural, cultivating rice and other subsistence crops. The term 'Dusun' continues to be used by some groups to refer to themselves, e.g. Dusun Lotud of Tuaran.

They traditionally occupied the fertile plains of Sabah's west coast from Kudat in the north to the border of Sarawak in the south, and in the interior areas of Ranau, Tambunan and Keningau.

A Kadazan farmer distributes rice seedlings for planting in irrigated fields.

A small community of Kadazandusun people who migrated from Penampang on the west coast to the east coast refer to their new settlement as Penampang Baru. Inevitably, the intrinsic character of their culture has undergone changes with acculturation, diffusion and influences from a new environment and from other contiguous ethnic groups. Intermarriage between Kadazandusun and other ethnic groups frequently occurs, and has contributed to new configurations in classification of ethnic identity and cultural hybrids, such as the Sino-Kadazan.

Origins

According to folklore, many Dusunic groups trace their origins to Nunuk Ragang, a fig tree located at the confluence of the Liwagu and Kogibangan rivers in the heart of Sabah. Several theories exist as to the diaspora of the Kadazandusun from the area, including overpopulation and environmental calamities that caused the rivers to overflow.

Social organization and kinship

The Kadazandusun are an egalitarian society with a bilateral descent system. In the past, they lived in villages composed mainly of longhouses comprising several families living together under one roof. Longhouse living provided a defence against external aggression for its residents, as well as a ready pool of labour for communal village activities. With the transformation of the economy from a largely subsistence one to a wage-earning and consumer society, longhouse villages have virtually disappeared amongst most groups. Many Kadazandusun now live in clusters of single unit dwellings housing nuclear

Sino-natives

Archaeological evidence reveals the presence of Chinese people in Borneo as early as 117 BCE. Early Chinese settlers were farmers who brought with them their own farming techniques, which were later adopted by the Kadazan, such as the iron plough pulled by buffaloes. Traders, meanwhile, brought ceramics, textiles, coins, jewels, precious stones and metal artefacts for barter trade. These goods were later incorporated into the material culture of the Kadazan. The jars, for instance, were used for burial and in ritual ceremonies.

Sino-native youngsters enjoying a lion dance during Chinese New Year celebrations.

The Sino-natives are a community with Chinese-Kadazan ancestry dating as far back as the 10th century CE. These descendants of Chinese immigrants who settled and intermarried with the indigenous people—mainly Kadazan—prefer to be known as 'Sino', which is generally understood to be of native and Chinese ancestry. They are found mostly in the west coast districts. While many maintain their Chinese ancestral surnames, they do not practise Chinese customs or speak the Chinese language, having assimilated the Kadazan culture, language and lifestyle. The majority of Sino-natives are Christians, with some practising ancestor worship.

Many Sino-natives are successful professionals and agriculturalists. They have also contributed to the socio-political development of Sabah since the formation of the state's first political party, the United National Kadazan Organisation, in 1961. Nearly half of the committee members in the party were Sino-natives. They have also been elected village headmen, and have presided over Native Courts.

and extended families. The Rungus of Kudat and Pitas districts, however, continue to maintain their longhouse tradition, which is a distinctive feature of their culture and lifestyle (see 'Rungus traditions').

The nuclear family forms the fundamental social unit and basis of the household. Marriage is a community event, and not just a union and transaction between two individuals. Marriage is exogamous, extending to third cousins, and is legalized by payment of bride price (termed *nopung* by the Kadazandusun of Penampang, Tambunan and Ranau, and *berian* by the Lotud) from the groom's family to the bride's family. The bride price comprises property such as land, heirlooms such as gongs, jars, swords, blowpipes and cloth, and the mandatory buffalo. Many of these items have now been substituted with modern goods or cash, and validated with a token buffalo or its monetary equivalent.

Traditional power structures

Prior to North Borneo Chartered Company rule in the late 19th century, the indigenous people of Sabah in coastal areas were under the control of the Sulu and Brunei sultanates. The local political systems that prevailed were either tribal, being an extension of the sultanate system, or controlled by independent petty chiefs.

The Kadazandusun were traditionally organized on a tribal basis. *Adat* (traditional law or customary law) provided the legal and social framework to govern and regulate the conduct of the community (see 'Native law in Sabah'). In Penampang, four institutions of authority governed the village: a village head (Huguan Pogun or orang tua), a council of elders (Komohoingan Tangabaa), priestesses (*bobohizan*) and warriors (*pangazou*). All four worked together to safeguard the interests of the community in both secular and religious matters. A warrior with proven courage, fighting ability and leadership qualities became the paramount leader of the tribe (i.e. several villages) or *Huguan Siou*, and usually led the warriors in battle to defend their territory and other rights. The Lotud had a similar administrative system, which continues today, comprising the council of elders, village chiefs, and female ritual specialists (*tantagas*), who advise on *adat*.

Traditional administrative system among Kadazandusun in Penampang

Authority	Function
Village head (Huguan Pogun or *orang tua*)	Chief administrator of the community, chosen by the council of elders. Presided over community meetings and hearings. Ensured that traditional land boundaries, individual ownership of certain natural resources, and customary laws and rituals were followed.
Council of elders (Komohoingan Tangabaa)	Knowledgeable in Kadazandusun *adat*, and advised the village headon the conduct of village affairs.
Priestesses (*bobohizan*)	Influential figures who advised the village head on matters relating to traditional beliefs, customs and *sogit* (compensation). Involved in all aspects of community life—birth, marriage and death, and daily activities such as farming, hunting and fishing.
Warriors (*pangazou*)	Looked after the security of the village, protecting it from intruders.

Traditional skills

The Kadazandusun are skilled craftsmen, using natural materials such as rattan, bamboo and wood to produce household items and utensils, as well as farming and hunting implements. They are well-known for their basketry including back-carriers, hats, mats, traps and containers. They also make a variety of musical instruments from natural materials, such as the *sompoton* (mouth organ), *bungkau* (jew's harp), *tongkungon* (tube zither), *sundatang* or *gagayan* (a string instrument). The men are skilled house-builders, and the knowledge of these traditional skills is passed from generation to generation.

Music and dance

The musical repertoire of the Dusunic people is said to be as rich and complex as their languages, and forms an integral part of their oral tradition. Dance forms have equally complex meanings and symbolism. In ritual performances, music and dance are used to indicate various phases of the ceremony and communication with the spirit world, as well as to express joy and sorrow. In the *mangahau* and *rumaha* rites of the Dusun Lotud of Tuaran, for example, gong music and a slow, sedate dance called *mongigol-sumayau* are performed to honour the spirits of ancestral jars and skulls. The *mongigol sumundai* dance of the Rungus of Kudat and Kota Marudu region was once performed strictly for ritual purposes. These days, modified forms of ritual dance are a feature of secular entertainment, and are choreographed for presentation at weddings, festivals, concerts and cultural and tourism events. One such dance is the *sumazau* from Penampang.

Lotud elder performing the *mongigol sumayau* dance.

ABOVE: A Kadazan playing a *turali* (bamboo nose flute).

TOP: Rungus girls learn to weave at a young age.

The Village Administration Ordinance introduced by the British North Borneo Company in 1891 modified the traditional administrative system. Only the village head was retained, and was appointed in villages with at least 250 people, except in isolated villages. The village head was subject to a district chief who chaired the Native Court. A symbolic Huguan Siou (paramount chief) was ceremonially appointed in 1960.

From farmers to politicians

Traditionally agriculturalists, the Kadazandusun cultivated wet and hill padi and other subsistence crops; surpluses were bartered or sold. They also collected wild produce, trapped small animals and fished in rivers to supplement their diet. Farming activities were generally small scale, with each family tending to its own plot. Traditional farming practices, however, have yielded to modern methods, and subsistence agriculture has been replaced by market-based systems introduced by the government to increase productivity and raise their standard of living. While many in the rural areas still adhere to traditional lifestyles, several Kadazandusun have become political leaders serving in the state and federal governments, and many are professionals and businessmen.

Kadazandusun women elders of Penampang District.

Kadazandusun beliefs and traditions

A definitive characteristic of the Kadazandusun groups is the creed shared by the various communities within the group. They subscribe to the existence of a supernatural world that is presided over by two supreme deities and inhabited by a multitude of good and evil spirits, as well as agricultural beliefs centred around the cultivation of rice. Following the conversion of many Kadazandusun to Christianity, Islam and other religions, ritual practices are maintained to display cultural heritage and ethnic identity rather than for religious purposes.

Shamans (*bobolian*) of Tempasuk Dusun, Kota Belud, perform an oath stone ceremony with the assistance of female *bobolian*.

Kadazandusun priestesses from Papar.

Traditional religious system

The traditional Kadazandusun world-view holds that secular life is intimately connected to the spiritual world in a relationship which must be maintained to keep both in a state of balance and harmony. A series of prescribed rituals must be regularly performed and practices observed for this purpose.

The fundamental tenets of the Kadazandusun belief system stem from a deep respect for man's symbiotic relationship with his environment—which provides the resources for life—including the spirits that govern it. This concept of respect is also extended to elders, senior members, leaders and those with ritual authority (shamans and priestesses), who are recognized as keepers of *adat* (customary laws) and acknowledged as the experts on how to regulate both secular and spiritual life.

Disrespect for the environment, *adat* and fellow human beings through irregular actions can cause an imbalance between the secular and supernatural worlds, resulting in tragedy, suffering, death, crop failures, and other disasters.

Man is also expected to adhere to a code of social conduct and ethics prescribed in the *rinait* or *inait* (sacred texts) and believed to be sanctioned by the supernatural world. Contravening this code means upsetting the balance and defiling the universe. If this occurs, ritual specialists, priestesses or shamans are called to restore the spiritual equilibrium by performing rites (see 'Priestesses, shamans and ritual specialists of Sabah').

Rice rituals

The Lotud observe eight rituals during their rice cultivation cycle.

1. Mansalud
Rice seedlings are transferred from the nursery to the field (above) in a ceremony when they are four inches high. An effigy of a bird is placed in the field to protect the new rice plants.

2. Monuras
A fertility rite is performed by two priestesses (*tantagas*) every two or three years in the field after the seedlings are planted. A piglet is sacrificed to keep evil spirits at bay.

3. Tumakau
During the rice-growing season, the head of the household takes a few stalks of rice, recites prayers to ancestral spirits before tossing them towards Mount Kinabalu, which is the abode of the dead.

4. Matang
Just before the harvest a *tantagas* makes sacrificial offerings to the rice spirits (*toguruwon*), to ensure their presence in the field to provide a good harvest. The offerings are placed on a bamboo pole.

5. Mongoi ramahi
Before the main harvest seven stalks of rice are transferred to the barn to ensure a good harvest.

6. Mogimpun
A portion of the rice is offered to appease malevolent spirits (*pongompuan*) to keep them from disturbing the harvest.

7. Sumondot
A day after rice is offered to appease malevolent spirits, a piglet is sacrificed to feed these spirits. A feast follows with *kulintangan* (kettle gongs) entertainment.

8. Monumbui popouli sinduan parai
After the harvest, rice spirits that may have been dispersed during the harvest or captured by malevolent spirits are invited to return and reside in the rice barn. During the ceremony the *rinait* (sacred text) is recited and a polished stone is placed in the barn to symbolize the presence of the spirits.

Above and top: Offerings of rice, chicken, eggs and bananas are made to the spirits just before the harvest.

Deities, spirits and rice rituals

The Kadazandusun believe that the spiritual universe is presided over by two supreme deities, Kinohoringan (or Kinoringan or Kinoingan) and his wife, Umunsumundu (also known as Suminundu or Huminodun). At the command of these two deities is a pantheon of lesser spirits, both good and evil, who exert their influence over mankind by interfering or withholding largesse in the secular world, and require regular sacrifices and offerings of appeasement.

Rice offerings used in rituals.

The structure of the spiritual world varies between groups, likewise the folklore and myths concerning their genesis. The daughter of the supreme deities was sacrificed to create food for man during a famine. From the myths surrounding the sacrifice stem various rice beliefs. Traditionally, a Kadazandusun household with an abundant harvest would sponsor feasts, rituals and other communal activities to gain respect and prestige in the community. Kadazandusun religious practices were, therefore, largely centred around rice cultivation. The attention shown to the rice spirits forms the

Rites of passage among the Kadazandusun of Penampang

Birth

The hair-cutting (*momuga*) ceremony (pictured, right) is a traditional announcement of the arrival of a new member of the community. It usually takes place when the child is a month old. Guests invited to witness the ceremony bear gifts, usually cash, for the infant.

Marriage

There are three stages to a marriage, beginning with representatives from the boy's family making enquiries (*monohuku'*) about the suitability of the girl for marriage. Marriage is exogamous up to third cousins.

The engagement (*momuaboi*) takes place after the proposal is accepted. The bride-price (*nopung*) is negotiated, witnessed by the village head. If the couple is related, a *sogit* (fine) has to be paid before the wedding. The bride's older unmarried sisters are also entitled to receive gifts from the prospective groom, and her younger unmarried brother is given a buffalo to signify brotherhood.

The wedding ceremony (*matod*) takes place first in the bride's residence, followed by another ceremony at the groom's house, where the couple feed each other (*miohon pinisi'*) to formalize the union.

The bridal couple step on a round stone and are sprinkled with ceremonial water by a *bobohizan* (priestess) upon arrival at the groom's family home.

Death

The *momisok* ritual is conducted seven days after burial to invite the spirit of the departed, with the help of a priestess, for a last visit and a meal at home, and to send it on its way with the deceased's belongings. The lights are switched off for a short while for the spirit to enjoy the meal. In a Christian household a prayer service is held on the seventh day, followed by a feast for relatives, friends and invited guests. Seven days after the *momisok*, a *humontog* ceremony is held to ensure that the spirit of the departed has been safely conveyed to the spirit world, and is reminded not to return to haunt members of the household.

Priestesses communicating with the spirit of the a recently departed Kadazandusun.

essence of the annual harvest festival celebrations in Sabah (see 'The harvest festival in Sabah').

Continuity of traditions

Although many Kadazandusun have embraced Christianity, Islam and other religions, traditional ceremonies are still performed, albeit for different reasons. These ritual occasions help maintain and strengthen family and village ties, and provide a basis for reunions amongst kin, friends and the community.

However, as many Kadazandusun communities enter the mainstream of industrialized and consumer society, traditional agricultural practices and beliefs are being discarded. Traditional beliefs and values are also affected by education, the electronic media and organized religions.

Traditional music, dance, craft, and artistic skills are preserved though cultural displays, and some traditional skills and knowledge such as the use of herbal medicines, massage and other forms of healing are being researched and documented with support from cultural associations, so that the Kadazandusun cultural heritage is not lost.

A Papar *bobohizan* (left) and a Lotud *tantagas* (right) in ritual costume.

TOP: A distinctive feature of Kadazandusun rituals is the predominance of priestesses and ritual specialists who act as intermediaries with the spirit world and perform various ceremonies including elaborate rice rituals.

Mamahui pogun: Cleansing the universe

This is a major Lotud communal event involving several villages, and is held every five or ten years to address perceived imbalances in the universe causing calamities such as drought, flood, war and strife, that threaten the well-being of mankind. Rituals are performed to neutralize the causes of such phenomena and flush out evil forces. The ceremonies are elaborate and are conducted in three phases extending over several weeks.

Manawah do turugan

In the first phase, ritual houses (*turugan*) are constructed at various points in the participating villages. Ten or more *tantagas*, recite the *rinait* (sacred text) and make offerings of rice at each hut. Spirit mediums (*libabou*) assist in the communication with the spirit world.

Monumbui sidangon

The rituals continue at a place by the river where as many as 40 priestesses assemble in a circle to pray and make more offerings.

Monumbui mahanton

The clergy and villagers travel by boat to the mouth of the river—though increasingly road transport is preferred—for the final expulsion of the evil forces. The ceremonies end with the priestesses returning to the headman's house where they communicate with the spirits to ensure their return to the spirit world.

Rungus traditions

The Rungus are one of two indigenous communities in Sabah who live in longhouses. Although they belong to the Kadazandusun group, they take pride in their ethnic identity and distinctive lifestyle. Traditionally animists, the majority of this subsistence farming community have, since the 1950s, embraced Christianity. Despite the influence of modernization on their lifestyle and livelihood, they have maintained many traditions as part of their cultural heritage.

Traditional Rungus longhouse
A Rungus village is made up of at least one longhouse and several detached houses. Villagers are related through consanguineous or affinal ties. The village headman (*vozoon*) chooses the site of the longhouse. He builds his apartment (*sirang*) first; his relatives build adjoining apartments on either side. Each village has territorial borders marked by features such as rivers, trees, a mountain range or a hill.

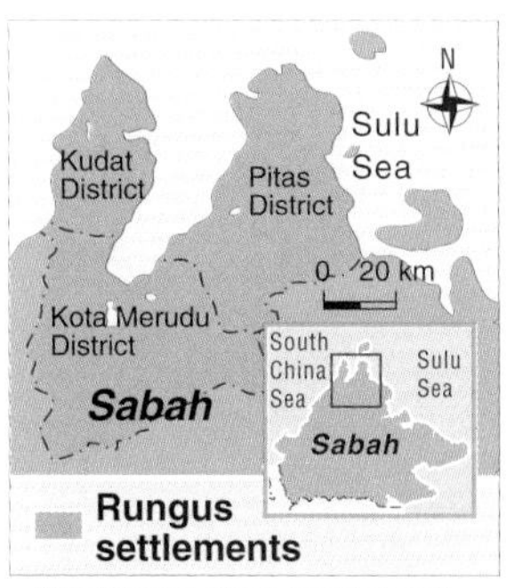

The Rungus, with a population of over 44,350 (in 2004), constitute the largest indigenous community in the Kudat Division in northern Sabah.

Identity

The Rungus, who are officially classified under the Kadazandusun grouping, prefer to identify themselves as Momogun, which means 'people of this land'. Their settlements are concentrated in the north of Sabah, in particular in the Kudat Division, which is regarded as the Rungus hinterland.

Like other Kadazandusun communities the Rungus are mainly rice farmers and live in villages made up of a cluster of dwellings (see 'Kadazandusun communities and lifestyles'). They are the only sub-group who continue to live in longhouses. However, the number of longhouses is decreasing as modern-day Rungus prefer to live in their own detached houses.

Rungus bridal couple in traditional costume—the bride in a three-piece handwoven suit (*banat ondu*) and forearm and hip brass coils; the groom in embroidered shirt (*badu*), cotton trousers and headcloth (*sigal*).

Dress styles

Daily attire for older Rungus men consists of black cotton trousers—traditionally made from homespun cotton (*gapas*)—tied at the waist with a cotton sash (*hogkos*), shirt and headcloth (*sigal*). The *sigal* is an important item and is associated with special attributes, such as political leadership, economic status and personal well-being. Younger men prefer jeans and Western-style dress.

Women usually wear a knee-length black cotton skirt (*tapi*) and blouse. Older women wear the *sukolob*, (a black shoulderless shift). The women adorn themselves with ornamental jewellery. Beaded necklaces made from coloured stones and tiny iron bells are considered priceless heirlooms. In the past, older women wore brass coils around their necks (*ganggalung*), forearms (*saring*), hips (*orot*) and ankles (*lungaki*). They are now rarely worn, except at weddings.

Rungus men wearing headcloths (*sigal*).

Longhouse tradition

A longhouse comprises several related families living in a web of social relations based on kinship ties, apartment position and need for mutual assistance. These relationships are the main feature of longhouse social organization as there is no formal longhouse leader, no corporate ownership of property and no economic enterprise associated with the longhouse.

Life in the longhouse is governed by a code of rules, customs and sanctions to regulate behaviour and maintain solidarity in the face of living in close proximity and against dangers from enemies, wildlife, forces of nature, sickness and the unseen world.

The Rungus have developed a labour exchange or mutual aid service to render assistance to one another in their farming activities. Labour exchanges may be in the form of reciprocal labour without cash payment (*mirogob*), waged labour (*gumaji*) or unconditional labour and assistance (*mokitulung*).

Harvested rice is stored in a rice hut (*sulap*) built near the longhouse. The Rungus traditionally observed rituals throughout the rice-growing cycle, culminating in harvest and thanksgiving rituals performed by priestesses (*bobolizan*).

Cottage industries

In the late 1990s, the state government introduced the 'one village, one industry' project to eradicate poverty and to reduce migration among Rungus youth. Four villages were chosen for the project, each with its own specialization, namely, traditional longhouse living, handicraft making, gong making, and bee farming.

Some Rungus have ventured into small and medium-scale businesses, such as the production of handicrafts, motor workshops and retail shops. Others work in the public and private sectors in urban centres in Sabah, Sarawak and the Peninsula.

As part of the Rungus wedding ceremony, a Rungus bride presents a brass box containing betel leaf and lime (*kinggaton*) to her in-laws to seek acceptance into the bridegroom's family.

The longhouse is built with forest materials, such as timber, thatch, bamboo and bark. The roof is made from flattened bark and palm leaves.

Bamboo, split and tied together with string made of tree bark or rattan, is used for the walls and the flooring.

Longhouse life

1. In the *ongkob* (private quarters), there are designated sections for sleeping (*tingkang*), cooking (*ropuhan*), washing (*salow*), eating and work area (*lansang*). Family heirlooms such as gongs and brassware are usually kept in a corner of the *tingkang* area.
2. The *abai* (loft) above the *ongkob* provides storage space for mats, gongs and winnowing trays.
3. Woman weaving using a backstrap loom.
4. Winnowing (right) and pounding (left) rice.
5. Guests are entertained with traditional *mongigol* dance and music.

Ongkob. Each family's apartment (*sirang*) consists of private quarters (*ongkob*) and an unwalled public area in the communal gallery (*apad*).

Apad. The communal gallery that runs the length of the longhouse. Many activities take place in the *apad*. It is also where unmarried men and male visitors sleep at night. The outer wall of the gallery slopes outward and is made of evenly spaced bamboo poles to allow air circulation.

Rungus crafts

RIGHT: Woven headcloths, jackets and sashes (*inavol*) are made by Rungus women. For their part, Rungus men weave carrier baskets and winnowing trays, and also produce long-handled, multi-purpose knives (*dangol*).

BELOW: Rungus women produce fine beaded necklaces. They also create baskets (*rinago*) made from rattan and creeper plants.

BELOW RIGHT: The *sundatang* is a two-stringed musical instrument, one of several made by Rungus men. Others include drums (*tontog*) and nose flutes (*turali*). Instruments are produced for domestic use as well as for sale.

ABOVE: Family relaxing in the *apad*.

LEFT: Woman being fitted with brass coils, still worn by Rungus women on special occasions.

Bajau society

The Bajau are the second largest indigenous group in Sabah after the Kadazandusun, numbering over 381,000 in 2004. They are Sama-Bajau speaking people who spread southward through the Sulu Archipelago of the Philippines, reaching the northern tip of Sabah by the 16th century. Here they split, some settling on the north and west coasts, others along the east coast.

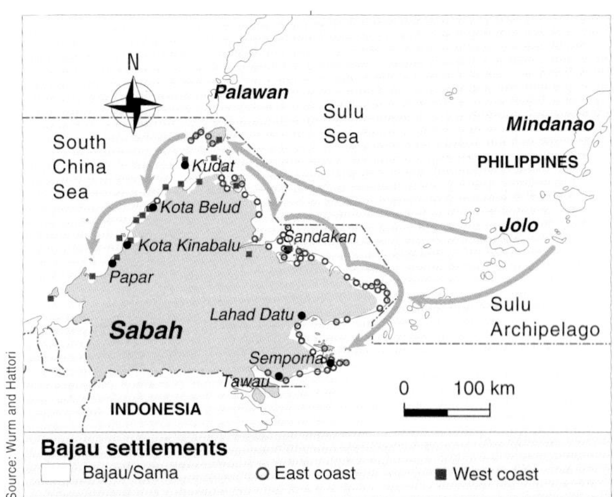

Linguistic evidence suggests that proto-Sama-Bajau speakers originated from the islands bordering the Basilan Strait that lies between southern Mindanao and the Sulu Archipelago.

Traditional settlements and economy

The Bajau are a predominantly coastal people. Most Bajau villages are concentrated along the lower rivers, coastal estuaries and plains, or built directly on the coast, around inlets and beaches, and on offshore islands. Settlements are typically aggregated, comprising densely clustered houses raised on piles. In fishing communities, settlements are sometimes sea-bound, with houses built directly over the water, sometimes connected to the shore by stilted bridges. Inland settlements tend to be more dispersed.

Fishing was traditionally a major occupation, particularly on the east coast. However, it is now common for Bajau families to combine fishing with farming. On the west coast, most rural Bajau farm, often in combination with cattle, buffalo and horse rearing. The chief food crops cultivated are rice and maize, while fruit and sugarcane are secondary crops. On the east coast, tapioca replaces rice as the main food crop, while copra was, until recently, the chief cash crop.

The Bajau have a long history of active trading. Early accounts describe them as skilled boat-builders, mariners and suppliers of commodities such as *trepang* (sea slugs), shark's fin, salted fish, pearls, turtle eggs, tortoiseshell and mother-of-pearl. European visitors in the 18th and 19th centuries noted east coast Bajau involvement in the birds' nest trade, and on the west coast, in salt- and lime-making. Since the formation of Malaysia, many Bajau have migrated to urban areas in response to educational and employment opportunities, where they work in both the public and private sectors.

Mengkabong, a Bajau water village on the coast near the town of Tuaran to the north of Kota Kinabalu.

The Bajau of Kota Belud have developed a distinctive equestrian style. Parades of horsemen and ponies, outfitted in colourful trappings, are a regular feature at major ceremonial events, including state functions and celebrations.

Regional variation

The Bajau population is diverse. The west coast Bajau are more reliant on the land than those of the east coast, and have been influenced by other coastal groups, especially the Iranun and Brunei Malays (see 'Coastal and island groups of Sabah').

The north coast of Sabah is home to a variety of Bajau groups, including Sama Ubian and Binadan communities, both largely maritime, as well as Sama Kagayan or Jama Mapun, members of a group that traces its ancestry to Cagayan de Sulu Island in the southern Philippines.

On the east coast, while the major centre of Bajau settlement is in Semporna, scattered communities are found all along the coast, and

Top right: Bajau fisherman at sea off the coast of Tuaran.

Right: Grated cassava, staple food of the east coast Bajau, sold in slabs at the market, Semporna.

Far right: A Bajau woman harvesting rice with a traditional knife (*lingaman*).

include both long-time residents and recent immigrants. For several centuries prior to colonial rule, the east coast came within the political sphere of the Sulu sultanate, and the Bajau population of the region remains closely linked to Sulu by ties of history, trade and ancestry.

Social organization and kinship

In contrast to the egalitarian east coast Bajau, some west coast Bajau have adopted elements of social ranking. Those claiming *datu* status base their claims on hereditary titles transmitted by agnatic descent.

Certain ranks are entitled to wear different colours of clothing on ceremonial occasions such as weddings and funerals. Those of *datu* and *sharif* status (the latter, putative descendants of Prophet Muhammad) are entitled to use yellow clothing; those of *sheikh* descent, yellow and green clothing; and commoners, white clothing. Status is also signified by differences in bridewealth and other marriage payments.

Islam exerts a major influence on social behaviour among the Bajau. Persons known for their religious learning and piety (*pakil*) are accorded special respect. Among both agricultural groups and settled fishermen, the basic unit of social organization is the household, consisting of a nuclear family, but often comprising a larger family group, including married couples, elderly parents, and sometimes siblings, their spouses and children. Married daughters tend to stay in their parent's house until they and their husbands have begun families of their own. Household partition occurs as married children depart with their families to found new household groups, usually leaving the youngest to inherit the property of the parents.

Related households are grouped into larger units (*tumpak* or *ba'anan*, meaning, literally, cluster). In daily life, these units represent important support groups, lending help in farm work, childcare, house-building, or in village ceremonies. Kinship ties tend to be heavily focused within these groups, and are often reinforced by intermarriage. Each cluster has a spokesman, and the spokesman of the largest cluster in a village serves as village headman.

The headman, who is now appointed by the government, administers village affairs and enforces *adat* (rules of behaviour that regulate interpersonal relations) in the community. He is also empowered to convene hearings in the event of minor village disputes. More serious disputes relating to *adat* and other breaches of moral conduct are brought before the Native Court—which is presided over by a hierarchy of district and native chiefs, and may impose fines or penalties (see 'Native law in Sabah')—or the Syariah Court, which deals with marital and family matters, including inheritance.

In rural areas, work is largely communal, carried out according to a system of reciprocal labour-sharing (*seliu* or *magdangin*). Each household taking part reciprocates equally, with households taking turns to provide labour, and the host providing meals to the communal work party. Such traditions bind together Bajau communities.

Marriage in Bajau society normally involves the payment of bridewealth and dower gifts. Ideally, marriages are arranged by a couple's parents and senior kin through formal, and often prolonged, negotiations, sometimes involving the use of go-betweens (see 'Bajau customs and traditions'). The Bajau observe a traditional prohibition on marriage between cousins whose fathers are brothers. Families often look upon intermarriage as a way of extending or consolidating kin ties. Thus, in Bajau Laut society, for example, intermarriage among kin is likened to the mending of a fish net or to the closing (*magtiggup*) of bivalve shells. In instances of intermarriage between Iranun and Bajau families, the Bajau often adopt the Iranun practice of signifying status by exchanging marriage payments graded in amount by rank.

Bajau wooden gravemarkers (*senduk*). Column-like markers are for men, flat ones for women.

The Bajau Laut

The Bajau Laut (Sea Bajau), a small minority of Sama-Bajau speakers, refer to themselves as Sama Dilaut. Making their homes in boats and living in small, scattered flotillas along the east coast of Sabah, they subsisted in the past on fishing and inshore gathering, and by trading with shore villagers for manufactured goods and agricultural products.

Individual families formed anchor groups and their mooring sites were located over sheltered stretches of water, protected from the open sea by fringing reefs, islets, or coralline channels. The Bajau Laut were in the past protected by land-based patrons, usually village chiefs, who guaranteed their security and acted as trading agents, supplying them with agricultural produce in exchange for fish and other maritime commodities, including items such as *trepang* (sea slugs).

Very few of these original Sea Bajau remain and those now found in the Semporna district are usually newcomers from the southern Philippines. Development and pressure from growing populations threaten the coral reefs that the Bajau Laut once depended on for their livelihood. Opportunities for education and wage earning too have induced them to settle down or seek opportunities in coastal towns and cities. Even so, they preserve their identity as a separate community.

Boat races in Semporna also serve to display and promote the culture of the Bajau Laut.

ABOVE: A Bajau Laut village.

RIGHT: Bajau Laut children outside their houses built over the sea on Omadal Island, Semporna.

ABOVE RIGHT: Women husking rice in a wooden mortar.

Bajau customs and traditions

The Bajau of both the east and west coasts are heirs to a rich ritual and material culture that includes social traditions, boat building, woven crafts, dance and music. The rites of passage that mark transitions from one stage of a person's life to another are considered important events and are celebrated by the Bajau according to Islamic tradition. The ceremonies that accompany these rites, which vary in name and detail from one district and community to another, are often elaborate.

West coast Bajau women braiding processed pandanus leaves to be used for trimming handicrafts.

Maintaining culture

The Bajau form an adaptive and internally varied population. In Sabah, the extensive coastal zone is home to a great variety of peoples in addition to the Bajau, including Brunei Malays, Kadayan, Iranun, Tausug (or Suluk), Tidong and others. While the Bajau comprise the most populous of these peoples, they frequently live interspersed with other coastal groups and inland communities, forming in many areas long-standing social and economic relations. During the colonial period, the Bajau played an important role in the local administration of Sabah. Today, many Bajau on both the east and west coasts have moved into the political and economic mainstream, becoming successful political leaders, businessmen, employees and professionals—yet they still maintain a vibrant culture.

Rites of passage

Birth

The Bajau of the west coast observe birth and post-natal rituals for the well-being of the mother and to welcome the newborn into the world. After a child is born, the afterbirth (*tamuni*) is buried. Traditionally, among east coast groups, a sprouting coconut (*pangsutan*) was planted in the earth above the buried afterbirth. The palm that takes root from this coconut is believed to be mystically related to the child and so may not be felled or disturbed. The father of a newborn prepares a hanging cloth cradle (*buahan* or *rundangan*), and a ceremony (*magisi ni rundangan*, literally 'to fill the cradle') is held to mark the first time the child is placed inside the cradle.

Between seven and 40 days after birth, the infant undergoes a hair-cutting ritual (*gunting*). This is preceded by a weighing ceremony (*timbang*) for both mother and child. The mother, with the child in her arms, sits in a sarong sling suspended from one end of a horizontal beam suspended from the ceiling, while a bundle of firewood, coconuts, and rice, of equal weight, is balanced from the other end. The beam is then slowly rotated three times as a prayer is recited. A family observes this ceremony either to fulfil a promise or as thanksgiving (*nazar*). The mother observes a 40-day confinement period, during which time she receives special cleansing baths (*mandi nifas*) on selected days.

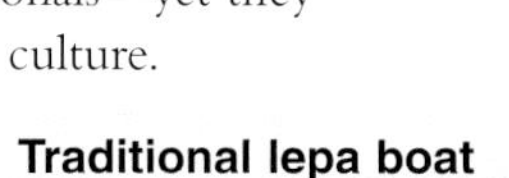

Weighing ceremony (*timbang*) for mother and child.

Traditional lepa boat

Throughout maritime Southeast Asia, the seafaring skills of the Bajau are legendary. Among the most striking boats constructed by the formerly nomadic Bajau Laut is the traditional *lepa*, some eight to nine metres long, and until recently the main type of fishing vessel used in the Semporna district.

Each boat traditionally housed a single family. Different sections of the *lepa* were associated with a gendered division of labour. The stern was associated chiefly with women's work, such as food preparation and cooking, while the bow was the site of masculine activities, such as hauling nets, manning sails and poling. Each boat had a lateral headside (*kokan*) where family members rested their heads when resting.

A *lepa* with carved bowsprit and roofed living quarters.

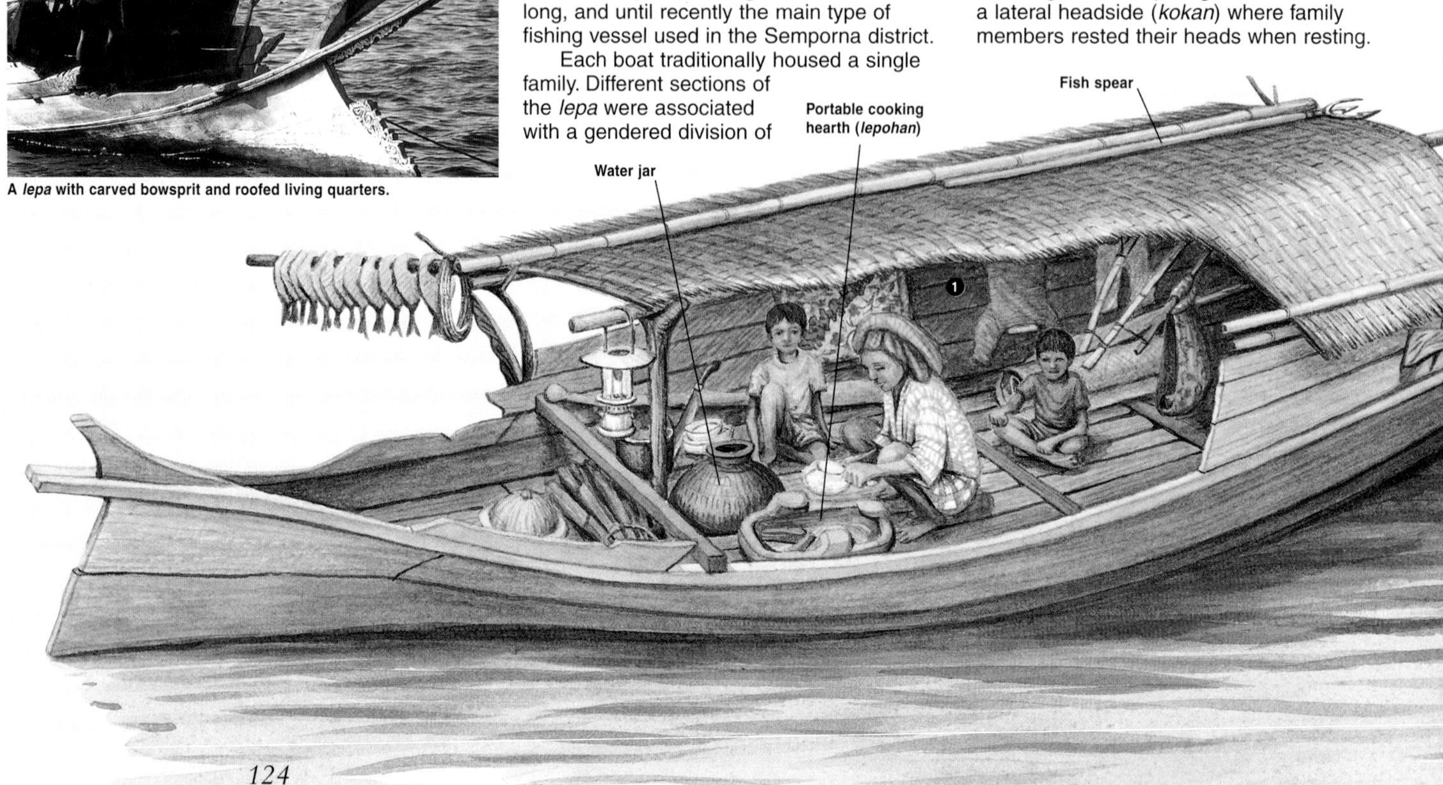

Adolescence

As in other Muslim communities, between the ages of seven and 16, boys undergo circumcision (*magislam*). Related households frequently share the expenses involved, circumcising a number of boys during a combined ceremony. The procedure is preceded by prayers, a thanksgiving feast (*kenduri*) and a village procession by kin, friends and neighbours in the boys' honour.

Young girls who have experienced their first menstruation (*sinukar*) are given a ritual cleansing bath (*mandi baligh*) by elderly women, which marks their transition to womanhood and attainment of marriageable age. Female circumcision is also performed in most Bajau communities, but not the Bajau Laut. In towns and urban areas, the circumcision is often carried out in a clinic or under the supervision of a qualified medical practitioner.

Marriage

Marriage ceremonies are perhaps the most colourful events in the social and cultural life of the Bajau. Not only do they join families together, but weddings provide the principal occasions on which families are able to display their material wealth and gain acknowledgment of status. The marriage process itself is spread over a period of time from several weeks to months, and is divided into stages. The marriage ceremony is opened by the formal presentation of bridewealth. In Semporna, among the formerly nomadic Sama Dilaut, the bridewealth was traditionally carried to the house or boat of the girl's guardian in a boat decorated with flying banners and accompanied by gong music.

At sunrise the next morning, after payment is received, the bride is bathed by her future mother-in-law. The formal wedding takes place at midday, officiated by an imam or village prayer-leader. The groom recites the marriage formula (*batal*) and is led to where the bride is sitting, screened off from view by a cloth partition. Forming the climax of the ceremony, the partition is opened, and the couple sit in state (*magsanding*) side by side. Among the Bajau of Kota Belud, buffalo form part of the bridewealth and are usually presented to the bride's family on the eve of the wedding.

Wedding outfits

In traditional Bajau weddings in Kota Belud, the bride and groom wear similar yellow jackets (*badu sepak*) with long flared sleeves split from the elbow. The bride wears a long handwoven tube skirt (*olos mogah*). Her attire includes long tapered silver, gold or brass finger decorations (*keku*); and a two-piece headdress (*serimpak*) containing an image of a boat, with hanging ornaments (*garigai*) at the side. The groom wears a traditional headcloth, tied into a headdress (*tanjak*), tight-fitting trousers (*suar*) and a silver tobacco pouch (*supu*) at his waist.

ABOVE LEFT: A Bajau bride is given a ritual bath on the morning of her wedding.

LEFT: The groom traditionally rode on a pony to the bride's home for the wedding ceremony. He was then carried into the house on the shoulders of two men, as his feet were not supposed to touch the ground.

RIGHT: The wedding dais (*pelamin*) is decorated with lengths of cloth (known as *simpangan*) made up of patches of fabric sewn together and often used as wall hangings and covered with mats (*tepo serisir*) made of appliquéd embroidered cloth sewn onto undyed pandanus.

Parts of the lepa

1. **Living quarters. The roof can be taken down when the boat is under sail.**
2. **The upper end of the bow (*tuja*) is finely carved.**
3. **The lower edge of the bowsprit (*jungal*) is also carved.**
4. **Raised poling platform.**

A Bajau Laut preparing a meal at sea.

***Tinduang* (food covers) for sale.**

Crafts

Bajau women of Kota Belud produce a variety of distinctive crafts, including finely woven headcloths (*kain podong*). In the Kudat area, the Binadan make a double-faced, richly embroidered headcloth (*kain pis*). Bajau women of Kota Belud also weave pandanus mats and baskets, as well as distinctive multi-coloured food covers (*tinduang*) which are sold at the weekly *tamu* market.

Traditional Bajau earthenware pottery, once produced in Kota Belud, is no longer made, but on the east coast, at Semporna, pottery-making is a continuing but declining cottage industry. Among the items made by local potters are portable earthenware hearths and cooking pots which seafarers and boat owners, including the once-nomadic Bajau Laut, carry aboard their boats for use at sea.

Entertainment and recreation

Special games, music and entertainment are provided during traditional weddings and festive occasions. A popular feature of Kota Belud weddings is the *sepak manggis* game, in which a decorated object (*manggis*) containing money and other novelties is suspended from a bamboo pole, the object being to strike the *manggis* by kicking a rattan ball at it. The *runsai*, an art form consisting of singing and dancing that employs a call and response pattern between male and female performers, is performed during festive occasions in Tuaran and Kota Belud. It is no longer practised by the Bajau of Semporna, although a variety of other song and dance forms still flourish, including, among the Bajau Laut, the traditional *magdaling-daling*. The east coast Bajau are also well-known for percussion and xylophone music.

Bajau percussion ensemble performing during a village festive occasion.

Murut society and traditions

The Murut were once a longhouse society who resided in southwestern Sabah. Many of the multi-room longhouses disappeared with the cessation of headhunting, and were replaced with smaller multi-family houses. Despite this, many aspects of their social life and belief system remain. The payment of bridewealth and its social exchanges are still important features of their social organization and lifestyle, although recent changes such as new economic opportunities and religious conversion, are making an impact on traditional Murut life.

Top: A traditional Murut longhouse. Many of these have been replaced with smaller dwellings consisting of three or four family units.

Above: Murut couple returning from the market.

Left: The Murut traditionally hunted with blowpipes.

The Murut population in Sabah was 94,000 in 2004. They speak a group of closely related languages.

Origins and history

The term 'Murut' (hill people) was used in the early 1900s to classify people living in the hilly regions of Sabah and Sarawak. In Sabah, they traditionally reside in the southwestern part of the state there are also two communities located on the east coast near the town of Tawau. Very little is known of the Murut before the British North Borneo Company was established in the state in 1881. While various theories on the origins of the Murut exist, they are believed by many to be the descendants of the earliest inhabitants of Borneo,

In pre-colonial Murut society, headhunting was a central feature of daily life. Unlike other Bornean groups that hunted heads for religious purposes, headhunting raids among the Murut were to settle feuds between longhouses. Such feuds would continue over several generations. The arrival of the British North Borneo Company changed the way of life for the Murut through the introduction of several policies, including the prohibition of headhunting and slave trading.

Kinship and residence

Historically, Murut settlements consisted of longhouses perched atop steep hills to provide defence against headhunting. Each longhouse consisted of several family rooms, sleeping platforms for guests, a central drinking area and, in the case of the Tagal Murut, a springy dance floor (*lansaran*). Many of the longhouses have been replaced with smaller multi-family or single family units with the cessation of headhunting. However, there is a central area either in the house or village that can accommodate large numbers of guests during feasts.

There are three important categories of kin for the Murut: the nuclear family, extended kin and affinal kin. Among the Tagal Murut a nuclear family and the man's parents often reside in the same dwelling. Usually, a father and his married sons occupy separate rooms in larger houses. This residence pattern reflects the obligations of bridewealth exchange wherein a man's father and relatives provide the items required for bridewealth payment and participate in feasts organized by the groom. The man, in turn, is obligated to stay with

Marriage and bridewealth

The payment of bridewealth and the obligations and social exchanges associated with it are the central feature of traditional Tagal Murut social life. A young man and his father initiate marriage by approaching the father of the prospective bride. The girl's father gives them a list of bridewealth items and they negotiate when and how bridewealth will be paid. Bridewealth consists of heirloom jars, cloth, gongs, gold items, cash and more recently, items such as television sets and chain saws. The bridegroom and his family are also obligated to provide items for the exchanges during the three-day feast marking the wedding. In addition to the payment of bridewealth, Tagal Murut are obligated to participate in further exchanges and feasts throughout their lifetime. These exchanges and feasts also require payment of heirloom property, prompting many Murut to remark of their bridewealth, 'we pay until we die'.

The Timugon Murut also have a social exchange which is an extension of bridewealth payment. In this ritualized rice and buffalo exchange, called *mansubak*, a man gives rice to a female relative who is not his sister. A man may initiate several exchange relationships, the only restriction being that he cannot initiate such a relationship with his brother's exchange partner. In the *mansubak* a man gives a sack of rice to his chosen exchange partner once a year for seven years. After the seven years the man calls a feast in which the husband of his exchange partner gives him a water buffalo.

Traditionally, bridewealth is rarely paid in one payment, and involves several instalments. Pictured here is a bridewealth exchange held during a funeral. Items range from heirlooms to modern electrical appliances.

Murut bride and groom in traditional dress.

Feasts

There are several events in a Tagal Murut's life that require a feast. These include marriage (*ahuot*), incorporation of children (*apasawang*), bridewealth payment (*bului*, *tinau*) and remembrance feast (*ilau pangimpayan*). A feast may also be held on other occasions such as the completion of a new house.

Several exchanges of goods occur in the course of a feast. In each exchange, the son-in-law and his relatives provide material goods whilst the father-in-law and relatives provide food and labour. The number of exchange partners (one of the son-in-law's relatives and one of the father-in-law's relatives) is represented by the number of jars that are filled with tapioca wine for drinking. Each jar represents one pair of exchange partners. On top of each drinking jar are eggs and cloth placed by the father-in-law's relatives. His exchange partner, one of the son-in-law's relatives, must exchange cash for these items in order to 'open' the jar. Exchanges are also made for the food that is consumed. The father-in-law's relatives provide hot drinks which they exchange for cash with the son-in-law's relatives. Rice and meat are exchanged for two pieces of cloth. Some feasts have additional exchanges—cash for fizzy drinks, cash for beer and food for a gold ring or cash.

RIGHT: An essential feature of Murut feasts is the exchange of goods between the parties involved, usually a man and his father-in-law.

LEFT: Before the drinking jar are opened, the son-in-law must exchange cash for items placed on the jars by the father-in-law.

his father and contribute to his household. When a second son marries, the first can set up his own room or house. This process continues, with the youngest son generally remaining with the father until his death.

The extended kin are distant relatives of an individual's parents. The Murut are obligated to assist anyone who is considered kindred. These obligations include participating in feasts, contributing labour for food production and helping with hospitality. Among affinal kin the most dominant kinship relationship is between a man and his father-in-law due to bridewealth payment.

Economic system

The obligations of bridewealth are a central feature of the Murut economic system. Traditionally subsistence hill rice cultivators, each family plants its own field and excess rice is used for feasts. Bridewealth obligations affect the assets of the nuclear family through economic exchanges between a man and his father. Because a man is dependent upon his father and father's siblings for bridewealth and continued assistance in feast exchanges, they can call upon his labour and food resources. Bridewealth payment also creates an economic relationship between a man and his father-in-law. Every year the father-in-law must help his son-in law prepare his rice field. In return, the son-in-law gives his father-in-law a gong, an heirloom jar or some other heirloom item that is used as bridewealth. During harvest time the son-in-law may harvest rice from his father-in-law's field for his own use. He brings some material item, such as a bolt of cloth, to exchange for the rice. When a man visits his in-laws, the latter give him some item of food. When the father-in-law visits his son-in-law, the latter gives him some material item.

Political system

In a traditional Murut village there is no formal decision-making body, such as a village council. The heads of households make decisions regarding the village through consensus. The village headman is the spokesman for the household heads. His right to lead the village comes from his extensive knowledge of *adat* (customary law) and his ability to lead. Although traditionally the post of headman was not inherited, often his son succeeded him. Today, under the state administration system, the headman is elected by the village. The government has also introduced an additional leadership position in villages, the chairman of the Safety and Development Committee (Jawatankuasa Kemajuan dan Keselamatan), to assist the headman to promote economic development.

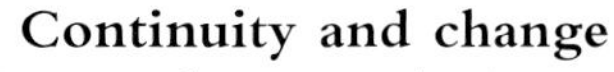

Baukan Murut woman in traditional beadwork blouse and skirt.

Continuity and change

Recent changes are having an impact on traditional Murut life. Many of them have resettled out of their traditional areas to seek economic opportunities. Younger Murut see bridewealth and traditional feasts as a barrier to the economic development of their families. Many prefer to pay labourers to help in their fields rather than rely on reciprocal labour among kin. Religious conversion has also had an impact on traditional exchanges, resulting in the reduction of bridewealth as well as a shift from traditional heirloom items to cash, making a Murut less dependent upon his father and his kin for payment and help with bridewealth feasts.

Murut Gong ensembles perform to welcome visitors and to accompany dance performances.

ABOVE: Murut women performing a traditional dance.

BELOW: A sprung dance floor made of timber logs (*lansaran*) is a feature of traditional Murut longhouses. Male performers bounce to reach trophies hung on the rafters.

Coastal and island groups of Sabah

In addition to the larger ethnic groups, Sabah has a distinct coastal and island population, most of whom are descendants of early settlers from the Southeast Asian region. Some of these ethnic groups inhabit Banggi and its neighbouring islands. Both the coastal and island communities have absorbed the practices of neighbouring groups, they have, at the same time, retained much of their rich and varied heritage, including traditional social systems and culture, which have distinguished them over the centuries and continue to do so.

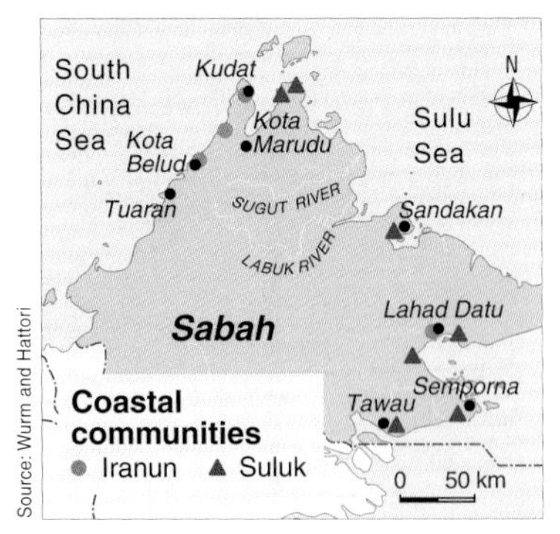

Origins

The coastal communities of Iranun and Suluk are mostly descended from settlers who came to Sabah as early as the 16th century. Historical accounts describe them as aggressive seafaring warriors, trading and raiding on the high seas around Borneo for slaves, maritime and forest products. Hence, the Iranun were often mislabelled 'Illanun' or pirate, a term sometimes shared by the Suluk. Part of the Iranun population in Sabah is descended from Maranao and Iranon refugees who fled from volcanic eruptions on Mindanao around 1630 and from later migrations. Others are descended from earlier waves of migration.

The presence of the Suluk people (known as Tausug in the Philippines) in Sabah dates back to the 17th century CE, when the domain of the Sultan of Sulu extended across the Sulu Archipelago, the east coast of North Borneo and Palawan. In the past, the Suluk were also referred to as Sooloos and Sulus to indicate their place of origin.

Below: Suluk village.

Bottom right: Many Suluk engage in traditional economic activities such as fishing and trading, others are civil servants and politicians.

Bottom left: Buffalo turning a press to extract sugarcane juice for members of the Iranun community.

Social organization

The Iranun and Suluk are Muslims and are distinguished by stratified traditional social systems, and a legacy of conferring hereditary and leadership titles that are still in use in Sabah. There are two main categories of real descent in Iranun and Suluk societies: the *datu* and the *sharif*. Both titles are hereditary: *datu* reflects aristocratic connections or royal lineage with historical links, while *sharif* (*sherif* among the Suluk) is a title for (putative) male descendants of Prophet Muhammad.

The bridegroom is ferried to the bride's house with his young attendant (inset) in a boat-shaped decorated palanquin (*usunan*).

Iranun marriage

Marriage in Iranun society is traditionally exogamous with regard to all first cousins on both parents' side and all other kin. Nowadays, marriages between first cousins occasionally do occur since they are permitted under Islam. Traditional courtship (*panganakan*) involves bride service (*pedsuor*), in which a young man, during his visits

Under a hierarchy of official authority institutionalized by the Sulu sultanate, the *panglima* were the appointed leaders or governors. The *orang kaya*, literally 'rich man', was the village headman, who by virtue of wealth had the means to exert local power and influence. The official titles of *panglima* and *orang kaya* are still used for appointed leaders in some Suluk villages. However, the power associated with the aristocracy in feudal society no longer exists other than in hereditary titles.

Cultural traditions

The Iranun are renowned for their woven textiles. Weaving using the traditional backstrap loom (*paga'ul*) is still practised by women in some Iranun villages. These textiles are traded with neighbouring

Iranun and Suluk classes and titles

Iranun	Suluk
***Datu* (male), *baih* (female)** Descendants of the rulers of the community in ancient times, and of the offspring of marriages between women from the *datu* class with original Muslim missionaries. Normally wear green clothes on ceremonial occasions. Graves of *datu* are also decorated with green cloth.	***Datu* (male), *dayang* (female)** Hereditary leaders with royal connections dating back to the Sulu sultanate. Male children inherit title through male lineage.
Sharif Hereditary title used by (putative) male descendants of Prophet Muhammad. Wear yellow or gold clothing on ceremonial occasions.	***Sherif*** Hereditary titles used by (putative) male descendants of Prophet Muhammad.
	Panglima Appointed leaders or governors.
	Orang kaya Village headman.

to the house of his future wife, is given work to undertake so that his future in-laws may ascertain his suitability as a husband.

Marriage is performed according to Muslim rites, and is endorsed with customary payment of bridewealth, consisting of water buffaloes and money, from the groom's family to the bride's. The amount of bridewealth is estimated according to the social strata of the couple, using a complex system based on the 19th-century *pikul* weight values which were used by the Chartered Company. In modern monetary values, the bridewealth for a bride from the *datu* class may be as much as RM20,000.

There are eight stages in an Iranun wedding. At the seventh stage, the bridegroom is carried to the bride's house with his attendant, usually a young boy, in an elaborate boat-shaped sedan chair (*usunan*) for the *edsanding* ceremony, where the bridal couple is presented seated on a dais. The higher the class of the groom, the larger and the more decorated the *usunan*. The arrival of a bridegroom of a *datu* class is announced by the firing of rifles.

Post-nuptial residence is determined by the status and strength of the newly-weds. Men who marry high-class women with powerful brothers tend to stay in their wives' villages, while influential men bring their wives and attract their brothers-in-law to their villages.

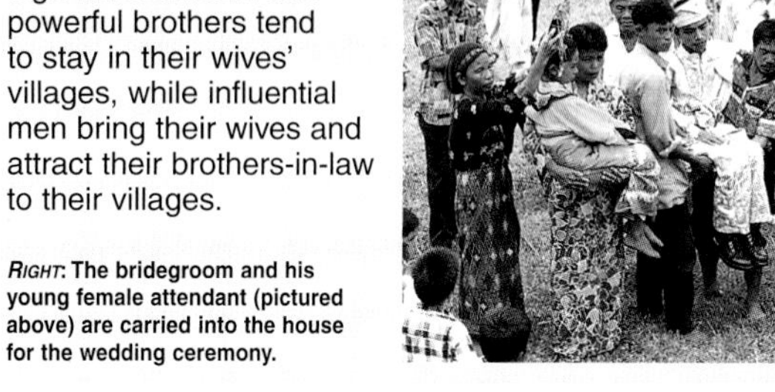

RIGHT: The bridegroom and his young female attendant (pictured above) are carried into the house for the wedding ceremony.

communities and have become part of the costumes of other groups. The long, striped *mogah* cloth worn by the Lotud Dusun and the Rungus in ritual ceremonies and dance is made by the Iranun. A unique needlework technique called *linangkit* amongst Dusunic and Bajau communities is believed to have derived from the Iranun *liangkitan*, which is a traditional form of seam binding and decoration on women's costumes.

The Iranun's oral traditions include a long epic poem, the *Darangen*, which recounts the exploits of a mythical hero named Bantogen who lived in Tempasuk in the land of Bambaran. The *Darangen* is believed by some to be the longest epic poem in Southeast Asia. The musical recitation of excerpts of the *Darangen* is called *tinubou*.

Suluk dancers performing the *daling-daling* dance attired in traditional costume and headdress (*maligai*).

In some Suluk villages on the east coast, remnants of Sulu culture continue to exist in a modified form, such as the modern *daling-daling* dance and song, which were traditionally performed at weddings, and the wooden xylophone (*gabbang*) that was frequently played as it is today at these occasions.

Island groups

ABOVE: An Ubian coastal dwelling.
INSET: Ubian children.

RIGHT: A Balabak man making a boat.

Island communities

Balabak · Bonggi · Kagayan · Ubian

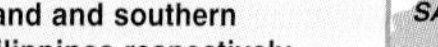

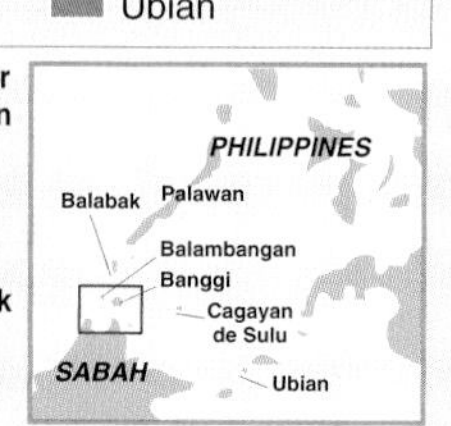

The Kagayan are named after their place of origin, Cagayan de Sulu Island in the southern Philippines; the Ubian originate from Ubian Island in the Sulu Archipelago; and the Balabak and Suluk from Balabak Island and southern Philippines respectively.

Six ethnic groups inhabit some 50 villages on Banggi, Balambangan, and other surrounding islands off the north coast of Sabah. These are the Bonggi, Balabak, Kagayan, Suluk, Ubian and Bajau (see 'Bajau society'). The only group whose population centre is located within this area is the Bonggi. The other population centres are in the Philippines. Several features distinguish the Bonggi from other groups in Sabah.

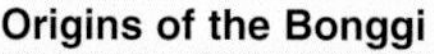

Origins of the Bonggi

The Bonggi claim to have lived on Banggi Island from time immemorial. Although the evidence is not conclusive, the Bonggi appear to have originated from the Palawan area more than 500 years ago.

Bonggi society

The Bonggi are a non-stratified society. The household is the primary economic unit, and is responsible for its own food supply. Marriages are normally conducted between geographically close villages. They tend to practise endogamy (marriage between people of the same blood or stock), and marriage is permitted between first cousins. Newly married couples traditionally lived with the bride's parents. The Bonggi also practise teknonymy (parents adopt the name of the oldest child).

The Bonggi have always lived in hamlets. Early settlers probably settled in hamlets along the coast at river estuaries, initiating a pattern that exists to this day. Later, with the arrival of other immigrants, the Bonggi were pushed into the interior. Today, they live in scattered homesteads inland and in fishing villages along the coast.

The Bonggi are mainly subsistence farmers practising swidden agriculture, and supplement their diet with fish. Some also cultivate copra as an additional source of income. Their staple crop is tapioca, not rice; unlike rice, tapioca requires little or no cooperation in terms of labour for harvesting the crop. Hence, little value is placed on cooperative work efforts.

Bonggi house built on tall stilts.

Bonggi house made of thatch.

Bonggi family grating tapioca, their staple diet.

Although the racial classification of the Bonggi is normally 'Dusun Banggi', their language is very different from the Kadazandusun and other Dusunic languages due to innovative adoptions which make their language complex and difficult for outsiders to understand. One feature not found in any other language in Sabah is the insertion of an extra consonant in words ending with 'm', 'n', or 'ng'. For instance, the Malay word *haram* (forbidden) is *arabm* to the Bonggi; *tahun* (year) is *toudn*; and *barang* (things) is *barakng*.

Riverine communities of Sabah

Adding to the multiethnic collage of Sabah are the inhabitants of the interior river valleys, who speak a variety of languages and dialects. The rivers are pivotal in the lives of these people who are collectively known as Orang Sungai (river people). Despite the influence of the outside world, the Orang Sungai's traditional world-view remains strong even as roads and modern communications media penetrate the isolated river valleys that have nurtured their culture for centuries.

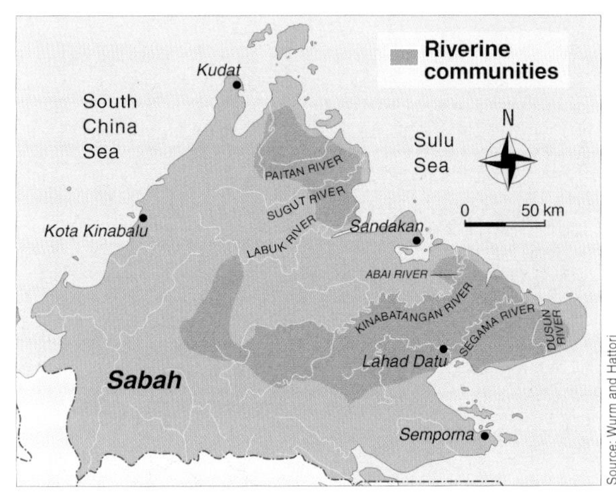

The Rumanau are among several groups who inhabit the Kinabatangan river valley.

Ethnic groups

The main riverine groups inhabiting the flood plains along the rivers of Sabah's east coast or the hillsides overlooking these rivers are the Labuk Kadazandusun in the Labuk River valley; the Tambanau along the Sugut, Paitan and Bengkoka rivers; and the Makiang, Kolobuan, Sinabu, Rumanau, Dusun Sehama and Ida'an in the Kinabatang and Segama river valleys.

Lifestyle and livelihood

The river is the Orang Sungai's compass, and their language expresses the concept of north, south, east and west in terms of the river's direction, such as 'upstream', 'downstream', 'away from the river', or 'toward the river'. The dugout canoe (*alud*) is the main mode of transportation on the rivers of Sabah's east coast. These canoes, each hollowed from a single log, vary in length from small one-man models some three metres long, to 10-metre craft capable of carrying a large family and their household goods. Traditionally, every Orang Sungai family owned at least one *alud*. Children learn to handle an *alud* at an early age.

To the Orang Sungai, the river is the main source of food and water as well as being the children's playground and the bathroom.

The riverine groups are rice farmers practising swidden agriculture on the forested hills near their homes. Harvesting is a group activity, with extended family and neighbours helping to bring in the crop and dry it for storage in bark bins in the family dwelling. Before the advent of sawn lumber and zinc roofs, the Orang Sungai built their dwellings from materials found in the forest. Tree trunks formed pilings to raise their houses off the ground, bamboo made a cool, springy floor and the leaves of the nipah palm or the garob tree provided thatch for the roof. Traditional housing was cool and cheap, important as many Orang Sungai moved location frequently due to shifting cultivation activities.

Visitors on a river expedition, accompanied by the Orang Sungai.

Social organization

The Orang Sungai do not have a longhouse tradition, preferring to live in separate, often isolated, single-family homesteads. The introduction of modern services such as roads, schools and clinics has begun to change this settlement pattern, as families cluster near available services. Villages are replacing individual homesteads in many areas.

Marriage is conducted in accordance with a bride-price system which obligates a man to provide his father-in-law with cash, merchandise and labour in return for his bride. The result has been a matrilineal residence pattern, with the newly-weds establishing their own nuclear family in or near the bride's father's house.

Adat and ilmu

Adat (customary law) governs every aspect of daily life. The Orang Sungai believe that trouble comes upon the world because of violations of *adat*, which requires the performance of rituals and offerings to offended spirits. *Adat* and omens determine when and where houses will be built and fields will be planted. *Adat* regulations surround not only the major events of birth and death, but also the daily routines of life, such as hunting and gathering, cooking and eating. *Adat* also prescribes penalties for social blunders and offensive behaviour.

The Orang Sungai are known for their powerful magic, *ilmu*. Male and female *bolian* are renowned as masters of the magic arts, and are frequently called upon to perform rituals related to healing, good harvests and protection from epidemic diseases. *Ilmu* works in tandem with *adat* to maintain balance in the Orang Sungai's world. The *ilmu* practitioner is able to discover which *adat* has been violated and then proscribes the ritual solution to the problem.

The Ida'an

The Ida'an are one of the most numerous Orang Sungai groups. They are perhaps the earliest indigenous inhabitants of Sabah's southeastern coast and are linguistically isolated from other indigenous groups. They also lay claim to Sabah's oldest written history. This document presents a legendary account of their beginnings and provides a defence for their claim to the lucrative collection of birds' nests.

The Ida'an live primarily in the area around Lahad Datu, along the lower Kinabatangan River, and the Segaliud and Suanlamba rivers that flow into Sandakan Bay. They divide themselves into three groups: the Ida'an (those who have converted to Islam), the Begak (those who are non-Muslim) and the Subpan (or Sugpan)—a group who migrated from central Kalimantan to the Danum and Segama rivers and who kept the remains of their dead above ground. They subsequently intermarried with the Dusun along the Segama River and have ceased to be a distinctive group.

The Ida'an document

The genealogy in this document lists reputed ancestors back some 25 generations to the primogenitors of the Ida'an. It was written in the Ida'an language in a Jawi-based script, and probably dates in its earliest form to the early 15th century CE. The document mixes legend with genealogy. Its legendary aspects, while distinct, have parallels with the oral literature of other Bornean ethnic groups. The legends featured here are selected highlights of the Ida'an genealogy.

1. Besai

The earliest progenitors of the Ida'an, according to the document, came from the Kinabatangan River. One ancestor, Besai, whose wife was childless, was told in a dream to search for a magical fruit, which could become a human being. The fruit would belong to the tiger if it fell on the ground, and to the crocodile if it fell into the water. After searching and waiting, the fruit fell beside him. He fought off the tiger that came to claim it and took it home. He wrapped it in leaves and bark, and after seven days and nights, the fruit burst open and human twins emerged.

2. Semurong Tegar Kun

A second ancestor, Semurong Tegar Kun, whose wife was also childless, was told in a dream to look for the egg of the garuda bird on top of the mountain. Upon finding it he took it home, and wrapped it in leaves and bark. After a week, the egg burst open to produce a human female child. One of the fruit twins, Teripo, and the egg-child, Dulit, married and became the founding parents of the Ida'an tribe.

3. Apoi

The document lists the descendants of Teripo and Dulit, the founders of the Ida'an tribe, with the lines of descent eventually becoming difficult to trace. In the fifth generation after Teripo, Apoi is born along with his dog-brother and deer-brother, the latter with a golden hide. The deer runs off into the jungle while Apoi is still young. Later, Apoi becomes a skilled hunter and one day he spots a golden deer. Together with his dog-brother, Apoi pursues the deer which leads them to a series of caves and tells them that he is their brother and that the caves would become Apoi's property to be passed on to his descendants. The deer then disappears. The caves that Apoi visited with his dog-brother eventually become the source of birds' nests, the treasured jewel of the Ida'an community.

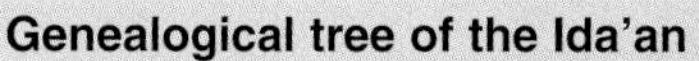

Genealogical tree of the Ida'an

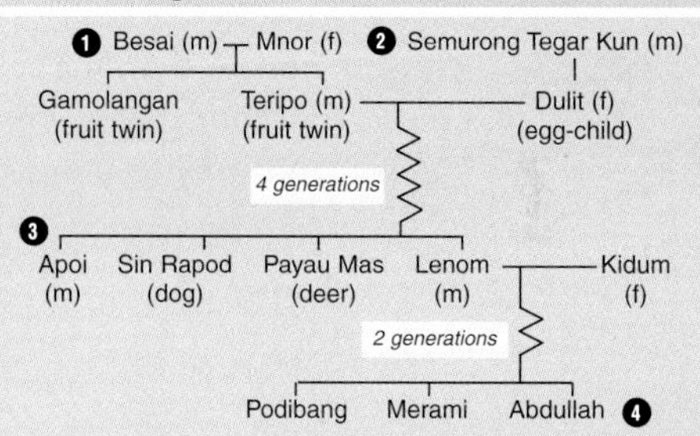

4. The first Muslim Ida'an

According to the document, it was in the eighth generation from Teripo that Abdullah converted to Islam. The conversion reputedly occurred in 1408 CE through the merchant-missionary activity of Machdom, who had previously introduced Islam to the Sulu Archipelago.

Birds' nest trade

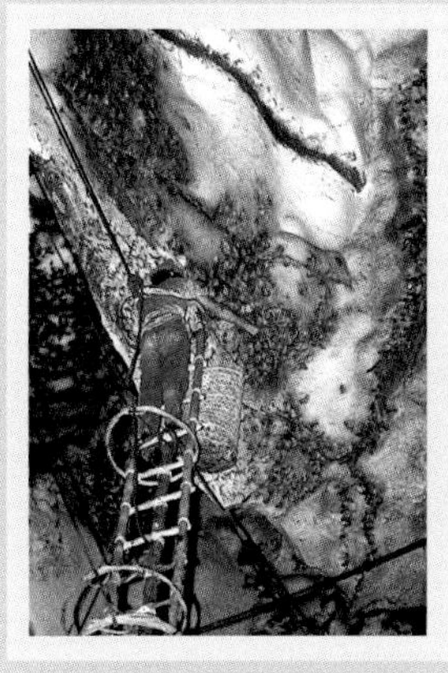

Suspended ladders made from bamboo and rattan are used to reach the swiftlets' nests on cave ceilings.

The legend of Apoi suggests that the Ida'an at one time were hunters. The Ida'an claim that about the same time that Islam was introduced around 1400 CE they began trading birds' nests. The earliest such mercantile activity possibly involved Arab traders and Chinese maritime merchants sometime after 1405 CE in Sulu. The birds' nest trade continued to flourish into the 19th century and still continues today.

The collection of nests is seasonal and is regulated by the Wildlife Department. Rights to collect the nests pass among the Ida'an from generation to generation along blood lines, with male and female heirs receiving equal portions. The exclusion of spouses from inheritance rights discouraged the Suluk, who in the 19th century had attempted to control the trade of the nests, from intermarrying with the Ida'an in order to gain access to collection rights. One function of the Ida'an document may have been to legitimize the rightful owners of harvesting rights. Until Sabah joined Malaysia, the British maintained a similar registry which the Ida'an continue to use as the basis for establishing legitimate collection rights.

The value of the nests has increased with demand outstripping supply. Many Ida'an still consider it their primary production activity, but its economic importance to them has diminished. Those nearer population centres pursue more diversified economic activities.

Non-indigenous peoples of Sabah

Amongst the heterogeneous population of Sabah are non-indigenous peoples comprising Chinese, Indians and other settlers who arrived in the 19th and 20th centuries. The British North Borneo Company that governed Sabah from 1881–1942 brought in large numbers of Chinese as part of its economic policy to open up the land in Sabah. The Indians are a small minority and were initially brought in as sepoys for the North Borneo Company's constabulary and clerical services. More recent migrants from neighbouring countries add to the state's cultural diversity.

A Chinese temple at Kudat.

The arrival of the Chinese

Historical records indicate that the Chinese had links with Borneo from as early as 518 CE. By the 15th century, trade between Brunei and China was flourishing and according to Brunei and Sulu annals, a Chinese colony on the Kinabatangan, Sabah's largest river, was established, presumably for the birds' nest trade. Chinese traders sailed up the Kinabatangan River to obtain these nests from the Gomantong Caves. The Sultan of Brunei at the time was said to have married the daughter or sister of Ong Sum Ping, the Chinese *raja* (ruler) of the Kinabatangan River. Ong was a Muslim and may have been responsible for the spread of Islam among the Orang Sungai in the area, who are predominantly Muslims.

The majority of the Chinese in Sabah today are descendants of immigrants brought in during British North Borneo Company rule. Before 1881 most of the traders who were plying their trade in the coastal areas and along the inland rivers of Sabah were either Hokkien or Teochew. Most of them came through the Straits Settlements or through the southern Philippines. After the establishment of the North Borneo Company in 1881, most of the new Chinese traders and businessmen came through Hong Kong. These traders were Cantonese and Hokkien, with some Teochew and Hailam. Also among these newcomers were Hakka agriculturalists who initially settled at Sandakan and Kudat, and founded the nucleus of two important early Chinese communities in Sabah.

Chinese labourers were also recruited to work in the tobacco and rubber estates that sprang up in Sabah between the 1880s and the 1910s. The number of Chinese labourers in the estates and mines reached its peak in 1920 when more than half of the estate population were Chinese.

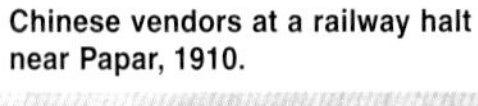

Chinese vendors at a railway halt near Papar, 1910.

Early Hakka immigrants in Sabah.

The Hakka Chinese of Sabah

The Hakka, who came from the Guangdong Province in southern China, are the most populous amongst the Chinese community in Sabah, a feature not found elsewhere in Southeast Asia. The Chartered Company recruited these people through the Basel Mission which had a large Hakka congregation in Hong Kong. In 1882 the first group of about 14 Hakka families landed in Kudat, the first capital. A second batch of a few hundred people arrived in 1886 and began cultivating coconuts. A third batch of Hakka contract settlers consisting of 107 families arrived in 1913 and settled at Kudat, Inanam, Menggatal and Telipok on the west coast and became a successful agricultural community, growing a variety of cash crops. The Hakka were also involved in coal mining and gold prospecting from the late 1880s to the 1930s.

The 'free passage' immigration scheme introduced by the Chartered Company administration in 1920 was popular among the Hakka who took the opportunity to bring in their relatives. As a result, there was a steady increase in the number of Hakka in Sabah. In the 1921 census, the Hakka community numbered 18,000, representing about 47 per cent of the Chinese population in Sabah. In 1931, the number of Hakka had increased to 27,424, or about 54 per cent of the Chinese population in the state. This resulted in the Hakka dialect emerging as the most widely spoken dialect in Sabah.

Chinese pottery jars, traded in Borneo for centuries, are heirlooms in longhouses and homes throughout Sabah.

Intermarriage between the Chinese and native women was fairly common. This had begun before Chartered Company days when early Chinese pioneers were roaming the coastal areas of Sabah. These marriages created a sub-category of indigenous people known as Sino-natives. This phenomenon was particularly common in the west coast of Sabah where, as early as the 1880s, there was a sizeable community of 80 Sino-native families on the Putatan River. The Sino-natives were formally acknowledged as an ethnic group in the 1951 census.

By 1931, the Chinese constituted 18 per cent of the total population. In 1938, stricter rules were placed on Chinese immigration, enabling only wealthier Chinese to enter Sabah. Many of them went into business and other commercial activities which established their economic power in today's commerce, agriculture and industry. The year 1946 marked the end of large-scale Chinese emigration into Sabah. In the 1960s, many Chinese came from the Peninsula, and a significant number came from Sarawak in the 1970s. By 1996, the Chinese population totalled about 270,000, the single largest ethnic group after the indigenous people.

Social organization

Since the first arrivals in the 1880s, the Chinese set up social organizations mainly to provide welfare and mutual help to their fellow countrymen. The early organizations were based on dialect affiliation or place of origin. As early as 1885, an association was established in Sandakan which catered for the Chinese who were from Guangdong province. In 1886, the Hakka in Sandakan established the first Hakka Association in Sabah. Many of these dialect group associations also opened places of worship, such as the San Sheng Kung Temple in Sandakan (1887) and the Tam Kung Chu Miao of the Hakka people in the 1890s.

In 1890, a new form of Chinese organization that was urban based emerged. The establishment of the Sandakan Chinese Chamber of Commerce marked the beginning of a new form of Chinese leadership institution.

The Chamber, whose membership comprised influential businessmen, was regarded by the colonial administration as the highest body of Chinese organization, and its views were sought on matters pertaining to the Chinese community. It was mainly through the Chamber's recommendations that Chinese members were appointed to government-initiated organizations and forums. Today, Chinese Chambers of Commerce are found in various towns, looking after the interests of the local Chinese communities.

The Chinese also organized schools for their children. Initially, most of the schools were privately owned and offered classical learning. In 1917, the Chung Hwa School was opened and conducted instruction in the modern Chinese syllabus.

About 30 per cent of the Chinese in Sabah are Christians. From the beginning, many of the Christian missions established schools for their members. Eventually, many of these mission schools became the backbone of education in the state.

After World War II, the Chinese in Sabah began to participate in local politics and political parties were formed to champion the interests of the community as well as to work with other political parties and races. Since 1963 the Chinese have entered politics and have become members of the Legislative Assembly. Some have been appointed as Cabinet Ministers.

Chinese shopkeeper at Mattungong Lama.

Above and above left: Like the Chinese communities elsewhere in Malaysia, those in Sabah celebrate the new lunar year with lion dances. Lion dance troupes in Sabah are often multiracial, with members from various indigenous groups.

The Indians of Sabah

During the North Borneo Company rule, sepoys were recruited for the constabulary, returning home after their tour of duty, and were replaced mainly by Sikhs and Pathans. Many Indians were also hired by the North Borneo Company to perform clerical duties and to fill supporting staff positions in the civil service. Some came as technical and medical personnel while others worked as station masters or overseers. Shortly after World War II, as Sabah was undergoing a reconstruction process, Indians were brought in as teachers, doctors, technicians and businessmen. In the 1960s, some Indians were brought in from Peninsular Malaysia under the Migration Fund Board schemes for estate work on the east coast of Sabah.

In 1911, the Indians and Ceylonese in Sabah numbered approximately 900, and in 1991 they numbered 9,310 or 0.6 per cent of the total population. After 1991 they were classified under the 'Others' category in the population census due to their relatively small population. Today, the Indian population includes recent migrants from Peninsular Malaysia who are active in the services sector.

During the North Borneo Company administration, the social life of the Indians was organized around their places of worship, and in the case of the Sikhs, at their temple, the gurdwara. The first gurdwaras were organized in the constabulary barracks. In 1924, a proper gurdwara was constructed in Jesselton (now Kota Kinabalu). Today, it is one of the oldest surviving buildings in the town.

After World War II, the Indians tried to organize themselves into some form of association, but this did not last very long. There is a Sabah branch of the Malaysian Indian Congress which acknowledges the presence and influence of Indians in the state. Deepavali, a Hindu festival, is a state public holiday.

Despite being a small community, the Indians have made significant contributions to the development of Sabah. Apart from joining the ranks of the professional and administrative sectors, many Indians, particularly the Sikhs, have also represented the state and the country in international sports competitions.

A Kadazandusun bride with her Chinese groom. Intermarriages between Chinese men and indigenous women are common in Sabah.

An Indian family in Sabah.

1. Menora, a Thai-influenced theatre performed in the northern Peninsular states, is a fusion of various cultural elements.

2. Intermarriages, increasingly common in Malaysia, promote ethnic integration and cultural accommodation.

3. Hamdolok, a theatrical performance, is derived from the Middle East. Pictured is a performance in the late 1970s.

4. Wayang Kulit Gedek features Malay and Thai traditions, with touches of modernity.

5. Zapin is a fusion of Middle Eastern and Malay traditions.

6. Creative mixes of cultural elements in fashion reflect a 'Malaysianized' style.

7. The Malay folk theatre of Mak Yong indicates foreign influences.

CROSS-CULTURAL INFLUENCES

Cross-cultural influences are an integral feature of the Malaysian way of life. Indeed, it is impossible to envision a Malaysian cultural landscape without the influences that since ancient times have shaped the life of the various communities that make up the nation. People from scores of ethnic groups call Malaysia home. Inevitably with such social diversification, the culture of the country becomes complicated and, at the same time, exciting.

The most obvious manifestation of cross-cultural influences is in racial mixtures. From the beginning of history, given the fact that the Malay Peninsula served as a bridge between east and west, it became the landing point of peoples from different parts of Asia. Racial mixtures were inevitable. With the opening up of trade routes, Westerners also found their way here, and the racial complexity became more complicated, with new racially mixed communities evolving.

Kuda Kepang, a hobbyhorse dance, was imported from Java.

Inevitably, within such a varied racial mosaic, inter-cultural and cross-cultural influences are evident in many aspects of Malaysian life. The traditional belief systems of the Malays were transformed by the arrival of Hinduism, Buddhism and Islam, all three religions laying down the foundation of what is today Malay culture. Customary practices related to enthronement and marriage ceremonies are perhaps the strongest remnants of the past. There are also areas in which religious accommodation has taken place, virtually giving rise to new traditions. The festivals and celebrations, manner of conduct and dressing, artistic and cultural expressions, and the kinds of food that Malaysians enjoy also, reflect inter-cultural influences.

The numerous languages and dialects spoken in the country continue to influence each other, giving rise to new encounters in language. An example of such fusion is Malaysian English or 'Manglish'. The national language, Malay, also reflects a considerable degree of enrichment through borrowing from other languages.

Changing times have increased interaction and cross-cultural exchange, particularly through the electronic media. Today, Malaysians enjoy the latest television programmes and films in diverse languages from around the world. The influences from these sources have been pervasive. Evidence is to be found in films, in particular, experimental films: multiracial and multilingual in character, they have had a considerable impact beyond Malaysian shores. Batik designing, the making of textiles and other handicrafts similarly represent an admixture of indigenous, foreign and modern elements.

All these cross-cultural influences will, in the long run, result in the creation of that ideal of politicians and social scientists alike—the single Malaysian *bangsa* (race).

Common identity and cultural fusion

Over the past 2000 years or so, Malaysia has experienced the impact of cultures from virtually every direction, resulting in the shaping and consolidation of indigenous traditions as well as the introduction of foreign cultural elements. Much of the present-day Malaysian culture is a fusion of various strands, some of which have been absorbed into the mainstream national culture, while others, although not totally indigenous, are nevertheless 'Malaysian' in character.

Malaysians from different ethnic and religious backgrounds acting in a drama on human values staged to promote inter-faith harmony and unity.

The Chitty community, having existed in Malaysia for so long, has been cut off from its roots and become a new community.

Cultural assimilation and ethnic mergers

Assimilation and fusion have taken place in interesting ways. The most significant development is that of the Malay community itself. The term 'Malay' is defined in the Federal Constitution as including those who profess the Islamic faith, speak Malay and who practise Malay customs. There is no requirement to belong originally to one of the Malay ethnic groups. Such a broadened base has had ramifications for ethnicity and ethnic relations as well as for cultural practices.

Apart from the national culture, thus defined as being based upon Malay traditions and incorporating compatible elements from the cultures of other ethnic groups in the country, there has been the development of 'new cultures' and even new communities through fusion and intermarriage. Indeed, since ancient times, the communities of the Peninsula, Sabah and Sarawak have been the result of movement and migration of people from various directions, and racial mixtures were inevitable.

The intermixing of ethnic groups has resulted in a varied Malaysian society, with communities such as the Jawi-Peranakan in Penang resulting from the fusion of South Asian Indian-Muslim and Malay cultures, the Chinese Peranakan (Baba) community in Melaka and Penang, the Eurasians, the Malay-Thai mixed Sam-Sam of Kedah, and the Chitties of Melaka. Contemporary Malaysian social and cultural environment is fluid, and such cultural exchanges and inter-community influences have affected the various communities' cultural manifestations, from behaviour and use of language to dress, food and celebrations.

Despite differences in religions, belief systems and cultures, Malaysian communities have found ways to accommodate the values of each other, taking what is universal in the various religions as a source of unity. Toleration is the keyword, even if one does not fully understand or appreciate the cultural and religious values of one's neighbours. Thus, the various festivals observed in Malaysia attract multi-racial participation.

Multi-dimensional fusion

Incoming influences have resulted in indigenous traditions undergoing changes without altogether losing elements of the past. Traditional Malay belief systems, particularly folk beliefs, represent a mixture of cultures. Upon the ancient animistic system of cosmology have been placed Hindu elements, including beliefs and mythology, and upon these, Islamic elements.

Popular legends still make references to Father Sky and Mother Earth (*Bapa Langit* and *Ibu Bumi*) as the progenitors of all that exists. Indigenous mythology still retains an important place in shaman rituals and the folk arts. Hindu myths and legends, including the popular epic *Ramayana*, find a place in the repertoire of traditional theatre forms—localized versions of the *Ramayana* are featured as the principal story in shadow play (Wayang Kulit), while Mak Yong dance theatre uses indigenous tales based upon adventures of mythological beings. Both art forms, as well as those involving shamanic processes such as Main Puteri, are the result of fusion between the earliest layer of beliefs

Folk theatre, such as Wayang Kulit (above left) and Mak Yong (above) reflect the influence of indigenous mythology and Hinduism.

Left: Bangsawan operatic theatre was the result of syncretism of East and West.

and Hindu customary practices. Islam, which began to spread across the Peninsula in the 14th century, modified these arts forms or reinterpreted them in its own colouring.

Folk literature genres, in both form and content, reflect borrowings from Asian and Middle Eastern traditions. Myths, epic cycles, stories of popular heroes (such as Raden Inu Kertapati) and stories of great Muslim figures and the cycles of animal stories (such as those of the wily mouse-deer, Sang Kancil) have all been suitably adapted and localized. Stories from the West have found a place in popular theatre genres such as Bangsawan. Modern Malaysian literature, particularly in Malay and English, also reflects international influences. Realist literature, developed in Malaysia since the 1950s, and theatre inspired by Western Absurdism and subsequent movements are two leading examples.

Syncretism and transformation

Certain imported traditions, such as those of the Chinese and Indian sub-groups, have retained their essential characteristics. At the same time, facets of the imported cultures show minor modification or drastic transformations when compared with identical or equivalent manifestations in their native countries. They are thus the result of localization, adaptation as well as fusion.

Certain Chinese and Indian festivals celebrated in Malaysia have died out altogether in their native countries. In other cases, minor festivals have grown into major ones, the Thaipusam festival being the most significant example. Originally a minor Chettiar festival in South India, in Malaysia it is no longer restricted to Chettiars or even to South Indians. Thaipusam is celebrated in Malaysia on a scale unmatched in its homeland, and has seen increasing participation by the local Chinese community as well as by others, including foreigners. Adaptation may also be seen in other festivals, including the Dragon Boat Festival, and some of the ceremonies commemorating the birthdays of resident spirits (*datuk kong*) at Chinese roadside shrines.

Language transformation taking place in Malaysia is another interesting phenomenon. Outside influences have come into the Malay language, just as Malay has influenced other languages. Certain Malay words such as 'kampong' and 'amok' have entered the Oxford English Dictionary as English words. Some Indian or Pakistani dialects spoken in Malaysia retain words or expressions no longer in use in their native lands.

Some festivals in Malaysia represent interesting examples of adaptation and syncretism, such as the Chinese Dragon Boat Festival (left) and the Hindu Thaipusam festival (below). Both attract multi-ethnic interest.

Several of the languages and dialects imported into Malaysia have also been influenced by Malay words and expressions. Malaysian English or 'Manglish' is an example of such an acculturation or fusion of languages. The result is not just the mingling or inter-borrowing of words, but the development of vibrant literatures in these fusion languages.

A unique heritage

Through these processes of change, development and adoption, the cultural face of the nation has been changing over the centuries. With such a heritage, Malaysia serves as an example of dramatic fusion of so many cultural traditions.

The indigenous artistic forms that have become associated with Malaysia include batik, *songket*, the traditional handwoven textile forms of the indigenous communities of Sabah and Sarawak, and woodcarving. While tradition is upheld in these forms, in the art of batik Malaysia has developed its own designs using traditional methods of production with imported materials, thus developing a unique variety of batik.

In the arts, many a modern Malaysian artist has worked within the tradition, drawing inspiration from traditional art forms while at the same time feeling at home in Western art forms such as modern painting or sculpture. There are outstanding efforts by Malaysian artists to use indigenous ideas, concepts and motifs, or even the various Malaysian festivals in creating fusion forms.

Fusion in the performing arts has resulted in a variety of art forms. Of the folk traditions the best known are Mak Yong and Wayang Kulit. Among the urban forms of artistic expression, Bangsawan operatic theatre incorporated cultural features from a variety of communities. On a more popular level, social dances such as the zapin of Johor and the joget gamelan of Pahang and Terengganu reflect a fusion between indigenous and imported traditions.

Hindustani films from Bollywood have had a considerable influence, too, ranging from food and dress to dance and music. Equally noticeable is the adoption of Western traditions in modes of dress and in forms of artistic expression, from language and literature to the visual arts, television and the cinema.

LEFT: Cross-cultural convergences are reflected in Malaysian arts and craft, such as oil paintings of Wayang Kulit puppets on batik and Chinese influenced vases with calligraphic motifs.

Multi-culturalism is also evident in music and dance genres. For instance, *gambus* musician Fadzil Ahmad has blended various ethnic musical elements.

Malaysia and world culture

Malaysia serves as a unique example of how peoples of diverse ethnic origins and cultures have come together to fuse into a nation. This has taken place without sacrificing too much of the originality of the various cultures, while making adjustments to the changing world. The process has been going on for the past several millennia. Having consolidated its national and cultural identity, Malaysia has begun making its contributions to the world.

A song presentation by Malaysians of various ethnic backgrounds.

Inter-ethnic harmony

Social and cultural consolidation in Malaysia has been made possible through attempts by each ethnic group to come to terms with the other communities, and as a result of the acceptance among the various communities of each other's religions, traditions and customs. The formation of Malaysia in 1963, bringing together the Peninsula, Sabah and Sarawak, saw the coming together of two almost separate worlds. Further adjustments were required, made more complicated by religious divergences. Harmony was achieved through acceptance and compromise. The process of accommodation of various cultures took form following the introduction, in 1971, of the National Cultural Policy, which recognizes the plurality and diversity of the multi-ethnic Malaysian society. The acceptance of Malay as the national language, and the acceptance of other languages, including Chinese, Tamil and the regional languages of Sabah and Sarawak into the mainstream, has assisted in integration. In ethnic relations and inter-religious harmony, Malaysia has achieved a fine balance that serves as a model for many countries of the world and, in particular, Muslim countries.

ABOVE: A Bajau craftsman demonstrates the art of basketry at a Sabah festival.

BELOW: Visitors at a Rungus longhouse get a first-hand look at their lifestyle and handicraft.

Tourism and national culture

The tourism industry has made a significant contribution towards the exposure of Malaysian culture to the rest of the world. Since Independence and particularly since the 1990s, tourism has attracted increasing numbers of visitors from a growing range of countries. Many elements in Malaysia's indigenous as well as 'fusion' cultures have attracted international attention, and in so doing have brought Malaysia global recognition.

Cultural organizations such as the Sarawak Cultural Village feature selected aspects of Malaysian culture, and crafts organizations such as the Craft Complex and the Central Market in Kuala Lumpur promote indigenous crafts from various parts of the

ABOVE: A visitor attempts a Bidayuh dance during the Gawai.

TOP: Performers at the annual World Rainforest Music Festival in Sarawak.

country. This has given some impetus to the development of crafts. In recent years, serious efforts have been made to revive the batik industry, to popularize the use of batik at home, and to export it to the rest of the world. All these efforts have resulted in some of the country's enduring traditions, particularly its textiles, crafts and food, gaining increased appreciation overseas.

Malaysian cultural troupes have, since the 1980s, presented dances and music as well as traditional theatre forms, such as Mak Yong and Wayang Kulit, in many countries. Malaysian painters, singers and film makers too, have begun to make an impact outside the country. A noteworthy step is the government's success in getting Mak Yong recognized by UNESCO as an item of Intangible World Heritage of Mankind.

On a more popular level, the tourism industry's initiative with its slogan 'Malaysia Truly Asia' has promoted a fusion of Malaysian culture—albeit a glamourized, watered-down version—in various parts of the world through visits by Malaysian troupes. Locally, the controversial annual cultural parade, Citrawarna (Colours of Malaysia), is the industry's attempt to reach out to the world. However, it is a long way from being taken seriously by the world. Some of the productions

Orang Asli dances are among a variety of Malaysian arts that are presented both locally and abroad to promote tourism.

held at Istana Budaya, the national theatre, particularly major foreign performances, have been designed to bring in tourists.

Malaysian popular music has received some international attention. International stars include Anita Sarawak and the late Sudirman. Siti Nurhaliza's concert in London's Royal Albert Hall in April 2005 represents the most recent effort to break into the world popular music scene. The nation's contribution to serious music is similarly limited, but not altogether absent. The World Rainforest Music Festival which takes place in Sarawak every July is an important event which is gaining international recognition. P. Ramlee's music has been performed by orchestras overseas, and a recording has been produced by the Tashkent Philharmonic Orchestra. In the film industry the influence of the rest of the world upon local films has been prominent, beginning with the first Malay film, *Laila Majnun*, produced in 1933. Malay films, including some featuring P. Ramlee, have received international awards over the decades. Since the late 1990s, major Malaysian films, such as *Puteri Gunung Ledang* and smaller private productions, such as *Sepet*, have generated considerable international interest by virtue of their content as well as quality.

Challenges

Some centuries-old artistic traditions have begun to be used to attract the tourist dollar through transformation or selective presentation, as well as in altogether non-traditional ways to the extent that in some instances they are no longer recognizable. The challenge is to make aspects of Malaysian culture available to tourists without loss of form or identity. Authenticity has the dual advantage of serving both as a means of preservation and promotion. While genuine tourists will get true representations of Malaysian culture, practitioners will be able to sustain their heritage.

Batik designed and produced in Malaysia for the international market.

Internationalization of traditions

Public universities have shifted their focus from Western traditions to Asian and regional traditions, thus allowing the performing arts and visual arts a common platform in their curricula. These courses attract foreigners who come to Malaysia principally for research and fieldwork. Many experts on aspects of Malaysian culture have been foreigners, since the days of Walter William Skeat and Sir Richard Winstedt. Malaysian academics, too, take an interest in such matters. A number of important publications by local specialists are becoming recognized the world over.

In addition, opportunities are increasingly available for the study of mother tongues and major foreign languages, particularly at tertiary level. In the forefront of such internationalization of Malaysia are the Chinese and Indian Studies departments in University of Malaya, and the university's language centre, where a dozen or more foreign languages are offered. Similar situations exist on a lesser scale in other institutions of higher learning. Universities and Dewan Bahasa dan Pustaka, the national language and literature agency, have also become well known for their efforts in the area of translation, mainly into the Malay language.

ABOVE LEFT: An American couple being blessed by an Iban headman after an elaborate traditional Iban wedding held at the Sarawak Cultural Village in Kuching, 2001.

LEFT: This British couple chose to get married Malay style in Malaysia, 2004.

Glossary

A

Adat: Traditional practice or customary law.
Adat perpatih: Matrilineal system of kinship.
Affinal: Related by marriage.
Akad nikah: Muslim solemnization of marriage.
Apok: Small pouch woven from pandanus leaves.
Austronesian: Previously known as Malayo-Polynesian; relating to the peoples and languages distributed from Taiwan to New Zealand, and from Madagascar to Easter Island.

B

Bajau: Second largest indigenous ethnic group in Sabah.
Bajau Laut: Sea nomads from the Sulu Archipelago living on the east coast of Sabah.
Baju Melayu: Traditional attire of Malay men: a tunic worn over trousers with a short sarong (*kain sampin*).
Balik kampung: To return to one's village of origin.
Bangsa: Race.
Bangsawan: Malay operatic theatre.
Baruk: Bidayuh round wooden building with conical thatch roof. The building is common property, and used for discussions, ceremonies and council meetings. Also known as *panggah*.
Batin: Orang Asli headman.
Belian: A shaman dance of the Orang Asli and Malays.
Bersanding: Sitting-in-state of a bridal couple.
Bhangra: Traditional Punjabi dance accompanied by a small ensemble.
Bharata Natyam: South Indian classical dance.
Bidayuh: Sarawak indigenous group formerly known as Land Dayak.
Bilek: Room or apartment in a longhouse.
Bilum: Sago pith images used in traditional Melanau curing rituals.
Bisaya: Indigenous people living in Sabah and northeastern Sarawak.
Bobohizan: Kadazandusun ritual specialists or priestesses. Known by different names in other Sabah languages.
Bomoh: Malay traditional medicine man, healer or shaman. Also known as *pawang*.
Bonggi: Indigenous people living on the island of Bonggi to the north of Sabah.
Borea: Theatre form said to derive from Shia Islamic passion plays.
Bridewealth: Payment in the form of money and/or property made by the groom to the bride and her family; bride price.
British North Borneo Company: A chartered company set up in 1881 to administer the territory of North Borneo.
Budi: Kindness; goodness.
Bulan puasa: The holy fasting month of Ramadhan in the Muslim calendar.
Bumiputera: 'Sons of the soil', referring to specific ethnic groups: Malays, Orang Asli, Melaka Portuguese, the Siamese of northern Malaysia, and the indigenous groups of Sabah and Sarawak.
Bungan: A syncretic religion incorporating elements of Christianity and paganism, which emerged in Kalimantan, Borneo, in the 1940s.

C

Carnatic: 'South Indian' (derived from Karnataka, South India); also Karnatic or Karnatak.
Chinese Peranakan: Localized Chinese in the Straits Settlements of Penang, Melaka and Singapore in pre-Independent Malaya; *peranakan* in Malay means 'local-born person or a person of mixed local and foreign parentage'. Also known as Baba-Nyonya and Straits Chinese.
Chitties: Descendants of Indian settlers in the Melaka Sultanate.
Consanguinity: Kinship characterized by shared ancestors.

D

Dalang: Puppeteer, originally from the Javanese for storyteller.
Datu: Hereditary title of aristocratic descent.
Dayak: Non-Muslim indigenous peoples of Sarawak: Iban, Bidayuh and Orang Ulu groups.
Dayong: Kayan male priests.
Dayung boris: Bidayuh priestesses.
Dikir Barat: A secularized form of Islamic religious chanting.
Dondang Sayang: Love songs; an elaborate form of *pantun* singing.

E

Endogamy: Custom of marrying within a community or clan.
Engkerumong: An Iban musical ensemble, including hanging gongs and drums.
Exogamy: Custom of marrying outside of a specific group.

G

Gambus: A lute fashioned after the Arabic *o'ud*.
Gawai: Iban ritual ceremonies or festivals; Sarawak harvest festival. Known by other names among other Sarawak native groups.
Gotong-royong: Cooperation or working together in groups in the form of mutual aid service.

H

Hamdolok: A theatre form derived from the Middle East.
Hantaran: Gifts exchanged between Malay bride and bridegroom.
Hoabinhian: From Hoa Binh, North Vietnam, refers to a stone tool industry and age distributed throughout Southeast Asia from about 13,000–3000 BCE.
Huaguan Siou: Paramount chief of the Kadazandusun communities of Sabah.
Huiguan: Chinese dialect group associations.

I

Iban: Largest indigenous group in Sarawak, formerly known as Sea Dayak.
Ida'an: Sabah indigenous group on southeastern coast known for their birds' nests trade.
Iranun: Coastal ethnic community of Sabah, formerly called Illanun.
Irau: Kelabit feast held in conjunction with a festival or ceremony, and involving the entire community.

J

Jawi-Peranakan: Local-born South Indian Muslims. Also known as *mamak*.
Joget: Malay dance genre.
Joget Gamelan: A court dance and music form that evolved in Pahang and Terengganu in the 19th century.

K

Kaamatan: Harvest festival celebrated by Sabah's indigenous rice-farming groups in May.
Kadazandusun: The largest indigenous ethnic group in Sabah, comprising both the Kadazan and Dusun peoples.
Kajang: Orang Ulu group of northern Sarawak.
Kampung: Village.
Karagattam: An impromptu dance seen during the Thaipusam festival; also the pot placed on the head during such a dance.
Kayan/Kenyah: Sarawak indigenous ethnic group settled in the northeastern highlands.
Kebaya: Malay woman's blouse,

usually worn with a sarong.

Kelabit: Sarawak indigenous ethnic group centred in the Kelabit Highlands.

Kenduri: Feast.

Kerajaan: Monarchy; government.

Keroncong: Melodious music involving the singing of love songs with origins in the 16th-century music of the Portuguese in the Moluccas and Batavia.

Klirieng: Poles used for storing burial jars in Sarawak.

Kompang: Frame drum.

Kongsi: Chinese publicly managed economic undertakings.

Kristang: Language of the Melakan Eurasians of Portuguese descent.

Kuda Kepang: Hobbyhorse made from plaited bamboo slats; form of dance originating from Java.

Kulintangan: A row of six to nine kettle gongs.

L

Lemambang: Iban priest-bard.

Longhouse: Long structure on stilts comprising common areas and separate family apartments.

Lun Bawang: Sarawak indigenous ethnic group centred in the northeastern highlands.

M

Magavau: Thanksgiving rituals.

Mahabharata: Hindu epic dealing with the conflict between the Pandawa and Korawa clans.

Main Puteri: A shamanistic healing ritual active in Kelantan.

Mak Yong: Ancient Malay dance theatre of Kelantan and Patani in present-day Thailand.

Manang: Iban shaman.

Marhaban: Literally, welcome; songs in praise of the Prophet Muhammad.

Masuk Melayu: Literally 'become Malay'; used to describe a convert to Islam.

Matrilineal: Descent through the female line.

Maulud: Celebrations marking the birthday of the Prophet Muhammad.

Melanau: Sarawak indigenous ethnic group.

Menora: A Thai-influenced dance theatre form.

Minangkabau: Matrilineal society originating from Sumatra.

Miring: Iban ritual to appease the spirits and mark commencement of Gawai.

Molong: Resource preservation concept used by nomadic Penan.

Moyang: Orang Asli ancestral spirits.

Murut: Sabah ethnic group centred in the southwest hilly regions.

N

Nasi: Cooked rice.

Natyasastra: The most important classical work on Indian performing arts, by Bharata.

Negritos: Also known as *Semang*; oldest aborigine group of Peninsular Malaysia descended from the Hoabinhians.

Ngajat: A dance of the Iban, Bidayuh, Orang Ulu and Melanau associated with bravery.

O

Open house: Custom of opening one's doors to all races during festive occasions.

Orang Asli: Indigenous, or aboriginal, peoples of Peninsular Malaysia.

Orang Sungai: Sabah ethnic group inhabiting interior river valleys.

Orang Ulu: A conglomeration of minority indigenous groups mainly centred in the northern interior of Sarawak.

P

Pandan: Plant of the genus *Pandanus*, leaves of which are used to make mats, baskets and bags.

Pantun: A poem of four (or sometimes more) lines with alternate rhyming lines.

Patrilineal: Descent through the male line.

Pelamin: Dais.

Pemanca: Paramount chief of the Kelabit people of Sarawak.

Penan: Hunter-gatherer indigenous group of Sarawak.

Penghulu: Village head.

Penyigar: Bidayuh ritualist.

Proto-Malays: Also known as Asli Melayu; Orang Asli group located in the southern part of Peninsular Malaysia.

Pua kumbu: Iban woven ritual blanket.

Q

Qipao: Cheongsam; traditional Chinese long fitting dress with a Mandarin collar and a slit in the skirt.

R

Rakyat: Subjects; citizens.

Ramayana: Literally 'Rama's wanderings', an Indian epic.

Rebab: Two or three-stringed lute.

Ronggeng: A Malay dance genre and the accompanying music.

Ruai: Gallery in a longhouse.

Rumah: House.

Rungus: Longhouse-dwelling indigenous people of northern Sabah.

S

Salong: Tomb hut in Sarawak, also known as *klirieng*.

Salwaar khamez: Long tunic worn over baggy trousers; traditional attire of Indian women, particularly Sikhs.

Sapeh: A lute of the Kenyah, Kayan, Kelabit and other Orang Ulu communities of Sarawak.

Sari: Traditional attire of Indian women; a long rectangle of fabric wrapped around the waist and draped over one shoulder.

Semangat: Soul, spirit, or universal vital energy.

Sembah: To pay homage to superior persons.

Senoi: Orang Asli group of upland Perak, Kedah and Pahang.

Sewang: Dance ritual of the Temiar (Orang Asli sub-group).

Sharif: Hereditary title of (putative) male descendants of the Prophet Muhammad.

Silat: Malay martial arts.

Sino-native: Sabah ethnic group with Chinese and Kadazan ancestry.

Sinseh: Chinese medicine man.

Sirih: Betel leaf.

Sogit: Ritual payment; compensation based on customary law in Sabah.

Songket: Gold thread cloth.

Suluk: Sabah coastal ethnic group descended from settlers from the Sulu Archipelago.

Sumazau: A dance of Sabah associated with the spirit world.

Sundatang: A wooden-based two-stringed guitar.

T

Thali: Sacred pendant worn by a Hindu woman as a symbol of marital status.

Tampang: Pyramid- or ingot-shaped tin ingot used as currency in some states such as Pahang, Perak and Selangor in the 1800s.

Tamu: Periodic or weekly market in Sabah.

Tandak: Social dance form that includes call and response singing.

Teknonymy: Change of name of parents after the birth of their first child, practised by the Kelabit of Sarawak and Bonggi of Sabah.

Tuai rumah: Iban longhouse headman.

Tuak: Sarawak rice wine, also known as *burak*.

Tunggu: Restitution or compensation based on customary law in Sarawak.

W

Wayang Kulit: Shadow play; puppet theatre using leather figures.

Wayang Kulit Gedek: Shadow play derived from the Thai form, performed in Kedah and Perlis.

White Rajah: Rulers of Sarawak from 1841 to 1941: namely, James Brooke, Charles Brooke and Vyner Brooke.

Wushu: Chinese martial arts.

Z

Zapin: Dance genre adapted from the Arabic version.

Melanau youth in masks during the Kaul.

Bibliography

Abbreviations

JMBRAS	*Journal of the Malaysian Branch of the Royal Asiatic Society*
MIH	*Malaya in History*

Abdullah, Munshi (1986), *Kisah Pelayaran Abdullah*, Petaling Jaya: Fajar Bakti.

Amir, J. (1989), 'Adat Resam Kaum Melanau', *Sarawak Museum Journal*, XL, 61 Pt. 2: 209–224.

Amster, M. (1999), 'Community, Ethnicity, and Modes of Association among the Kelabit of Sarawak, East Malaysia', PhD. Dissertation, Brandeis University.

Andaya, Leonard (2002), 'Orang Asli and the Melayu in the history of the Malay Peninsular', *JMBRAS*, LXXV 1.

Anderson, A. J. V. (1997), 'Sago and Nutrition in Sarawak', *Sarawak Museum Journal*, 25: 71–80.

Appell, G. N. (1978), 'The Rungus Dusun', in V. T. King (ed.), *Essays on Borneo Societies*. Hull Monographs on Southeast Asia, 7, Kuala Lumpur: Oxford University Press.

Asmah Haji Omar (1983), *The Malay Peoples of Malaysia and their Languages*, Kuala Lumpur: Dewan Bahasa dan Pustaka.

Attia Hosain and Pasricha, Sita (1967), *Cooking the Indian Way*, Bombay: Lalvani Publishing House, 4th impression 1970.

Baharon Azhar bin Raffiei (1973), 'Parit Gong: An Orang Asli Community in Transition', PhD Thesis, King's College, Cambridge.

Bala, P. (2002), 'Changing Borders and Identities in the Kelabit Highlands: Anthropological Reflections on Growing Up in a Kelabit Village near the International Border', Dayak Studies Contemporary Series, No. 1, The Institute of East Asian Studies, Universiti Malaysia Sarawak.

Banks, E. (1940), 'The Native of Sarawak', *JMBRAS*, 18(2), 49–54.

Bellwood, Peter (ed.) (1988), *Archaeological Research in South-eastern Sabah*, Kota Kinabalu: Sabah Museum and State Archives.

Benjamin, Geoffrey (1976), 'Austroasiatic Subgroupings and Prehistory in the Malay Peninsula', in P. J. Jenner, L. C. Thompson and S. Starosta (eds.), *Austroasiatic Studies*, Honolulu: University of Hawai'i Press, pp. 37–101.

Brewis, Kielo (1990), 'The Timugon', in Sherwood G. Lingenfelter (ed.), *Social Organization of Sabah Societies*, Kota Kinabalu: Sabah Museum and State Archives.

Buckley, C. (1963), *A School History of North Borneo*, London: Macmillan and Co. Ltd.

Carey, Iskandar (1976), *Orang Asli: The Aboriginal Tribes of Peninsular Malaysia*, Kuala Lumpur: Oxford University Press.

Cesar Adib Majul (1965), 'Political and History Notes on the old Sulu Sultanate', *JMBRAS* XXXVIII 1.

Clayre, I. F. C. S. (1971), 'The Kajang Kingdom', *Sarawak Gazette*, No. 1362: 120–122.

—— (1972), 'Punan Ba–Melanau Link with the Ulu Rejang', *Sarawak Gazette*, No. 1368: 23–25.

Cleary, M. C. and Eaton, P. (1992), *Borneo: Change and Development*, Singapore: Oxford University Press.

Clifford, M. L. (1968), *The Land and People of Malaysia*, Philadelphia and New York: J. B. Lippincott Company.

Datan, Ipoi (1989), 'A Brief Ethnography of the Lun Bawang of Sarawak', *Sarawak Museum Journal* XL(61) Pt. III: pp. 143–156.

Dentan, Robert Knox (1979), *The Semai: A Non-violent People of Malaysia*, New York: Holt, Rinehart & Winston.

Dentan, Robert Knox; Endicott, Kirk; Gomes, Alberto G. and Hooker, M. B. (1997), *Malaysia and the Original People: A Case Study of Development of the Impact on Indigenous Peoples*, Boston: Allyn and Bacon.

Evans, I. H. N. (1949), 'Dusun Customary Law in Kadamaian', *JMBRAS* 12(1): 31–37.

Freeman, Derek (1967), 'Shaman and incubus', *Psychoanalytic Studies of Society* 4: 315–344.

Freeman, J. D. (1955), *Iban Agriculture: A Report on the Shifting Cultivation of Hill Rice by the Iban of Sarawak*, London: Her Majesty's Stationery Office.

Golomb, Louis (1978), 'Brokers of Morality: Thai Ethnic Adaptation in a Rural Malaysia Setting', Asian Studies Programme, Honolulu: University of Hawai'i Press.

Gullick, J. M. (1989), *Malay Society in the Late Nineteenth Century*, Kuala Lumpur: Oxford University Press.

Hardaker, M. B. (1973), 'Tausug – a discussion of the language', *Borneo Research Bulletin*, Vol. 5 No. 1.

Harrisson, Tom and Harrisson, Barbara (1971), 'The Prehistory of Sabah', *Sabah Society Journal* IV, 1–292.

Hatton, Frank (1885), *North Borneo*, London: Sampson Low, Marston, Searle, and Rinnington.

Hood Mohamad Salleh (1978), 'Semelai Ritual of Curing', PhD Thesis, St. Catherine's College, Oxford.

Irwin, Graham (1955), *Nineteenth Century Borneo*, Singapore: Donald Moore Books.

Jamba, A. L. (1993), 'Mukah', *Sarawak Gazette*, Fourth Quarter Issue, 19-22.

Janowski, Monica (1991), 'Rice, Work and Community Among the Kelabit of Sarawak, East Malaysia', PhD Thesis, London School of Economics.

Khoo, Joo Ee (1996), *The Straits Chinese: A Cultural History*, Amsterdam and Kuala Lumpur: The Pepin Press.

Khoo Salma Nasution and Wade, Michael (2003), *Penang Postcard Collection 1899–1930s*, Penang: Janus Print and Resources.

King, Julie K. and King, John Wayne (eds.) (1984), *Languages of Sabah: A Survey Report*, Pacific Linguistics C-78, Canberra: Australian National University.

Kobkua, Suwannathat-Pian (1994), 'The Sam-Sams, A Study of Historical and Ethnic Assimilation in Malaysia', *Sojourn* 9(1): 135–162.

Laderman, Carol (1991), *Taming the Winds of Desire: Psychology, Medicine and Aesthetics in Malaya Shamanism*, Berkeley: University of California Press.

Leach, E. (1950), Social science research in Sarawak: A report on the possibilities of a social economic survey of Sarawak presented to the Social Science Research Council, London: HMO for the Colonial Office.

Lee Yong Leng (1962), *North Borneo: A Study in Settlement Geography*, Singapore: Donald Moore Press Ltd.

Lim, E. T. (Kelvin) (1992), *A Review of the Sago Processing and Other Related Research on Sago from 1980–1990*, Kuching: Department of Agriculture.

Lim Lin Lean (1983), *Population and Development: Theory and Empirical Evidence. The Malaysian Case*, Petaling Jaya: International Book Service.

Liu, James (1979), *Essentials of Chinese Literary Art*, Massachusetts: Duxbury Press.
Low, H. (1882), 'Journal of a trip up the Rejang', *Sarawak Gazette* 12: 52–54, 62–65, 72–73, 81–83, 93–96.
Luhat, H. O. (1989), 'Some aspects of Belaga Kajan ethnohistory', *Sarawak Museum Journal*, XL(61) Pt. III 49–57.
Merawin, H. T. (1994), 'Material Culture in Sarawak: the sago connexion', *Sarawak Museum Journal*, XLVII (68): 17–35.
Metcalf, P. (1975), 'A Berawan journey into death: mortuary ritual of a Central North Borneo People', PhD Thesis, Harvard University.
Miyazaki, K. (ed.) (1992), *Local Societies in Malaysia*, Institute for the Study of Languages and Cultures of Asia and Africa, Tokyo: Tokyo University of Foreign Studies.
Mohd Yaakub Hj Johari (ed.) (1991), *Issues and Strategies in Rural Development*, Kota Kinabalu: Institute for Development Studies.
Mohd Yaakub Hj Johari and Mohd. Ayub Amirdad (1992), *Population and Health Issues in Sabah*, Kota Kinabalu: Institute for Development Studies Sabah.
Moody, David (1984), 'Conclusion', in Julie K. King and John Wayne King (eds.), *Languages of Sabah: A survey report*, Canberra: Australia National University.
Moody, David and Moody, Marsha (1990), 'The Ida'an', in Sherwood G. Lingenfelter (ed.), *Social Organization of Sabah Societies*, Kota Kinabalu: Sabah Museum and State Archives.
Mooney, P. (1959), 'Melanau Sketches', *Sarawak Gazette*, No.85, 45–48.
Morris, H. S. (1953), *Report on a Melanau Sago Producing Community in Sarawak*, Colonial Office, London: HMSO.
—— (1993), 'Shamanism among the Oya Melanau', in R. L. Winzeler (ed.), *The Seen and Unseen: Shamanism, Mediumship and Possession in Borneo*, Monograph Series 2, Williamsburg: Borneo Research Council, pp. 101–129.
Nicholas, Colin (2000), *The Orang Asli and the Contest for Resources: Indigenous Politics, Development and Identity in Peninsular Malaysia*, Subang Jaya: Centre for Orang Asli Concerns. Reprinted by the International Work Group on Indigenous Affairs, Copenhagen, 2004.
Nicolaisen, I. (1976), 'Form and function of Punan Bah ethno-historical tradition', *Sarawak Museum Journal*, XXIV (45) (New Series): 63–83.
—— (1986), 'Pride and progress: Kajang response to economic change', *Sarawak Museum Journal*, XXXVI (57) (New Series): 75–116.
Norani Sidek (2004), *Keraian, Penyediaan, Sajian & Resipi*, Kuala Lumpur: Utusan Publications.
Ong, Kee Hui (1948), 'Sago Production in Sarawak', *Sarawak Gazette*, 212–215.
Ong Puay Liu (2000), 'Packaging Myths for Tourism: The Case of the Rungus of Kudat, Sabah, Malaysia', Unpublished PhD Thesis, University of Edinburgh, Scotland.
Passmore, Jacki (1991), *Asian Food & Cooking*, Kelvin Weldon Productions.
Piper, Madeleine (1988), 'The Idahan', in Peter Bellwood (ed.), *Archaeological Research in South-eastern Sabah*, Kota Kinabalu: Sabah Museum and State Archives.
Pollard, F. H. (1933), 'The Muruts of Sarawak', *Sarawak Museum Journal*, IV (II) No. 13: 139–156.
Raghavan, Ravec (1977), 'Ethno-racial Marginality in West Malaysia: The Case of the Peranakan Hindu Melaka or Malaccan Chitty Community', *Bijdragen tot de Taal-, Land- en Volkenkunde*, 133: pp. 438–458.
Rashid Abdullah (2000), 'The Sihan community', paper presented at the Workshop on Community Profiles of Ethnic Minorities, Kuching.
Regis, Patricia (1989), 'Demography', in Jeffrey G. Kitingan and Maximus J. Ongkili (eds.), *Sabah 25 Years Later: 1963–1988*, Kota Kinabalu: Institute for Developmental Studies.
Rousseau, J. (1990), *Central Borneo: Ethnic Identity and Social Life in a Stratified Society*, Oxford: Clarendon Press.
—— (1993), 'From shamans to priests: towards the professionalization of religious specialists among the Kayan', in R. L. Winzeler (ed.), *The Seen and Unseen: Shamanism, Mediumship and Possession in Borneo*, Monograph Series 2, Williamsburg: Borneo Research Council, pp. 131–150.
Rudolph, Jürgen (1998), *Reconstructing Identities: A Social History of the Babas in Singapore*, Aldershot: Ashgate.
Russell, A. Sue (1990), 'The Tagal', in Sherwood. G. Lingenfelter (ed.), *Social Organization of Sabah Societies*, Kota Kinabalu: Sabah Museum and State Archives.
—— (1999), *Conversion, Identity, and Power: The Impact of Christianity on Power Relationships and Social Exchanges*, New York: Oxford University Press of America.
Rutter, Owen (1929), *The Pagans of North Borneo*, London: Hutchinson & Co.
Saging, Robert Lian and Lucy Bulan (1989), 'Kelabit Ethnography: A Brief Report', *Sarawak Museum Journal* 61: 89–118.
Salfarina Abdul Gapor (2001), 'Rural Sustainability in Sarawak: The role of adat and indigenous knowledge in promoting sustainable sago production in the coastal areas of Sarawak', Unpublished PhD Thesis, University of Hull.
Sandin, B. (1985), 'Notes on Sian (Sihan) of Belaga', *Sarawak Museum Journal* XXXI (55) (New Series): 67–76.
Sather, Clifford (1993), 'Bajau', in David Levinson (ed.), *Encyclopedia of World Cultures (Vol. 5: East and Southeast Asia)*, Boston: G. K. Hall, pp. 30–35.
—— (1995), *The Bajau Laut: Adaptation, History, and Fate in a Maritime Fishing Society of South-Eastern Sabah*, Kuala Lumpur: Oxford University Press.
—— (2001), *Seeds of Play, Words of Power: An Ethnographic Study of Iban Shamanic Chants*, Kuching: Tun Jugah Foundation.
Saw Swee-Hock (1988), *The Population of Peninsular Malaysia*, Singapore: University of Singapore Press.
Sellato, B. (1994), *Nomads of the Borneo Rainforest: The Economics, Politics and Ideology of Settling Down*. (Translated into English by Stephanie Morgan), Honolulu: University of Hawai'i Press.
Sidhu, M. S. and Jones, G. W. (1981), *Population Dynamics in a Plural Society: Peninsular Malaysia*, Kuala Lumpur: UMCB Publications.
Singh, Balbir (1961), *Indian cooking*, London: Mills & Boon Ltd, 6th printing 1971.
Sullivan, Anwar and Regis, Patricia (1981), 'Demography', in Anwar Sullivan and Cecilia Leong (eds), *Commemorative History of Sabah, 1881–1981*, Kota Kinabalu: Sabah State Government.
Supriya Bhar (1980), 'Sandakan, Gun Running Village to Timber Centre, 1879–1979', *JMBRAS* LIII(1).
Tan Chee-Beng (1988), *The Baba of Melaka: Culture and Identity of a Chinese Peranakan in Malaysia*, Petaling Jaya: Pelanduk Publications.
Thambiah, S. (1995), 'Culture adaptation: change among the Bhuket of Sarawak, Malaysia', PhD Thesis, University of Hull.
Winstedt, Richard (1960), *The Malay Magician: Being Shaman, Shiva and Sufi*, London: Routledge and Kegan Paul.
Wong Tze Ken, Danny (1998), *The Transformation of an Immigrant Society: A Study of the Chinese of Sabah*, London: Asean Academic Press.
Wright, Leigh (1979), 'The Lanun Pirate States of Borneo: Their Relevance to Southeast Asian History', *Sabah Society Journal*, 6(4): 207–217.
Yong, L. L. (1970), *Population and Settlement in Sarawak*, Singapore: Asia Pacific Press.

Index

Picture Credits

A. Kasim Abas, p. 86, Melanau village; p. 88–89, headhouse; p. 103, longhouse. **Adam Ariel,** p. 1, Bidayuh woman; p. 3, Malay boys; p. 6, Chinese in Melaka, Indian Hindus; p. 9, performer; p.18, Chinese temple, *gopuram*, Eurasians; p. 37, family gathering; p. 43, *nasi lemak*; p. 52, *erhu* musician; p. 63, fire walking, bridal party; p. 69, nyonya kuih; p. 71, Festa Intrudo; p.73, Giant Buddha Temple, Kelantan temple, monks. **Ahmad Sarji,** p. 39, recipients of titles. **alt.TYPE/Reuters,** p.12, multiethnic performers. **Arkib Negara Malaysia,** p. 9, Royal Malay wedding; p. 16, Chinese immigrants; p. 34, women market traders; p. 35, FELDA settlement; p. 38, Sultan Ahmad and retinue; p. 39, village headmen and followers; p.46, Chinese market, physician, street vendors; p. 47, cobbler, rickshaw puller; p. 48, Loke Yew, p. 58–59, Indian labourers, Sikh Squadron; p. 59, migrants; p. 60, Indian family; p. 68, early Peranakan clothing. **Bala, Poline,** p. 98, Pemanca Ngimat Ayu and wife, view of Bario, farmer and wife; p. 99, elder dancing. **Bal Bahadur Rana,** p. 75, Dashera, Bhakta Bahadur. **BERNAMA,** p. 38, King and Queen at Parliament. **Brunton, John,** p. 32, Kelantanese house. **Blandoi, Joseph,** p. 94, Bisaya man and woman; p. 95 all photographs. **British Crown Copyright/MOD. Reproduced with the permission of the Controller of Her Majesty's Stationery Office,** p. 75, Gurkha soldiers. **Cadman, M. C.,** p. 128, Suluk village, fishing boat. **Chai Kah Yune,** p. 28, Malay court; p. 124–125, *lepa*, congregation in mosque. **Chia Oai Peng,** p. 53, pouring Chinese tea, *taiji*. **Chiew, George,** p. 57, longevity bun. **Chin, Jacky,** p. 11, Melaka court scene; p. 54, head shaving; p. 60, pre-wedding exchange; p. 72, Menora dancers. **Cross, Martin,** p. 44, *laksa* Kelantan; p. 45, Malay dishes (11), durian. **Cultural Centre, Universiti Malaya,** p. 135, Kuda Kepang. **EDM Archives,** p. 10, Pebble tools; p. 11, sea battle; p. 25, Semai dwelling; p. 29, British officials with Malay royalty; p. 35, houseboats, fishing boats, armed forces personnel; p. 36, portrait of Malay family; p.44, *pulut kuning berlauk;* p.46, tin mine workers; p. 47, metalware shop, traders; p. 48, street procession; p. 48, Chinese Chamber of Commerce committee; p. 55, lion dance; p. 68, Straits Chinese house, porcelain plate; p. 69, teapot, Straits Chinese publication, Tan Cheng Lock; p. 73, postcard. **Falconer, John,** p. 11, British High Commissioner with sultan; p. 21, Orang Asli in 1890s; p. 29, Malays in Penang; p. 76, war dance; p. 92, intertribal warfare; p. 97, Kayan hunters. **Federal Information Department, Sabah,** p. 108, census enumerators (2). **Fong, P. K.,** p. 78, Kelabit children, Punan Busang man; p. 82, Iban long-house; p. 93, gong and drum ensemble; p. 97, sapeh player; p. 99, Kelabit women dancing; p. 101, Penan dancer. **Foong, Thim Leng,** p.19, men playing flutes; p. 27, Temiar dance. **Foreign and Commonwealth Office,** p. 34, coffee plantation workers. **Gallery of Colour,** p. 44, making ketupat (4), *roti jala*; p. 52, masked man with 'lion'; p. 54, dragon dance; p. 55, joss paper offerings, dragon boat race; p. 56, *low sang*, dried sausages; p. 58, Chitties; p. 64, musicians, Kolattam dance; p. 65, goldsmith; p. 70, A Famosa; p. 74, chariot bearing statue, Sri Poyatha Vinayagar temple; p. 136, Chitties; p. 137, Dragon Boat festival; p. 140, Keropok maker. **Ghulam-Sarwar Yousof,** p. 33, Bangsawan, Mak Yong performer and scene; p. 134, Menora performance; p. 136, Mak Yong, Bangsawan. **Gocher, Jill,** p. 91, *pua kumbu* weaver. **Haks, Leo,** p. 29, estate workers. **HBL Network Photo Agency (M) Sdn Bhd,** p. 9, Orang Asli; p. 19, Chinese drummers; p. 24, Orang Asli settlement, Mah Meri bridal party, man with blowpipe; p. 25, Negritos dwelling, medicine man, Negritos family, men in forest, Proto-Malay cooking; p. 26, *moyang lanjut*; p. 44, *lemang*; p. 57, char koay teow, Penang laksa, Nyonya dancers, bridal couple; p. 91, man getting tattoed; p. 92, men in masks. **Heidi Munan,** p. 76, Bidayuh priestesses; p. 97, baby carrier. **Image Asia,** p. 91, *ngajat* dance; p. 136, Wayang Kulit. **Jabatan Muzuim dan Antikuiti Malaysia,** p. 10 iron tools. **Jacobs, Joseph,** p. 32, Kedah timber house, *rumah kutai*. **Kakoo, Serge,** p. 38, woman with attendants. **Kalvar, Richard,** p. 34, fishermen. **Kedit, Peter,** p. 87, *tibau* swing; p. 93, wine jars. **Koh, Deborah,** p. 51, tea ceremony; p. 54, baby's first month prayer; p. 56, popiah. **Lamb, A.,** p. 127, gong ensmble, lansaran dance floor. **Langub, Jayl,** p. 100, Penan chipping pith. **Lasimbang, Rita,** p. 119, hair cutting ceremony, bridal couple. **Lau, Dennis,** p. 78, Kayan and Kenyah settlement; p. 79, Melanau village, Bidayuh village, Sibu; p. 82, Gawai Dayak parade; p. 88, Bidayuh wedding; p. 90, Iban in traditional costume; p. 100, Penan with traditional hunting equipment; p. 101, Penan with blowpipe; p. 102, warrior dance, wedding; p. 105, new year prayers at temple; p. 112–113, *tamu* in Tuaran; p. 116, Kadazan farmer. **Lim Joo,** p12–13, Malaysian ethnic groups; p. 23, Jah Hut healing; p. 27, bamboo combs; p. 36, matrilineal system, solemnization of marriage; p. 42, spices and seasoning; p. 50, placing ancestral tablets at altar, *ren* character; p. 51, monks praying, Buddhist devotees; p. 53, Chinese dress; p. 54, Chinese New Year's Eve dinner (faces only); p. 80–81, ritual specialists at cleansing ceremony; p. 84–85, curing ritual; p. 86–87, healing rituals, *serahang*; p. 89, rice rituals; p. 94, gong musicians; p. 106–107, Pesta Kaamatan; p. 108–109, indigenous groups in traditional costume; p. 111, adat penalties (3); p. 114, appeasing ancestral spirits rituals; p. 119, cleansing universe rituals; p. 124, weighing mother and child; p. 131, Ida'an genealogy legends (3). **Majlis Adat Istiadat Sarawak,** p. 81, Datu Nellie Tangal, native law publications, people at dam site, jars; p. 82, priestesses reciting text; *paleh kemehing*, *paleh hingo*; p. 84, priestesses on swing. **Mandalan, Ravi,** p. 115, ritual sacrifice of fowls. **Mappae Japoniae,** p. 11, map. **Ministry of Culture, Art and Tourism,** p. 33, Malay headgear styles (all except royal *tengkolok*). **Muller, Kal,** p. 132, pottey jars. **Muzium Negara Collection/Tara Sosrowardoyo,** p. 10 figurine. **Muzium Negri Sembilan,** p. 36, bridal couple. **National Archives of Singapore,** p. 29, Chinese vendors; p. 68, Peranakan family, 1900s. **Natural History Publications (Borneo) Sdn Bhd,** p. 120, men with headgear; p. 121, man in woven jacket; p. 132, temple, Hakka immigrants; p. 133, shopkeeper. **New Straits Times Press (Malaysia) Berhad,** p. 8, *miring*; p. 10, Perak Man, Sarawak rock carvings, Tambun rock painting, Neolithic burial; p. 12, Penan man; p. 14, pre-Independence rally, multi-ethnic neighbourhood; p.17, census-taker with Orang Asli; p. 18, Hari Raya, women bearing wedding gifts, Chinese Peranakan wedding; p. 19, Bhangra; p. 20, Orang Asli family, woman and children, man with jungle plants, rock art in Gua Tambun, Negritos children, Senoi children, Proto-Malay man; p. 21, community hall, Orang Asli with Red Cross, queue at registration office, copper identity discs, *Timeless Temiar*; p. 23, Semai shaman, blessing of *tok batin*, midwife; p. 25, men building house; p. 26, children at *sewang*; p. 27, man playing *keranting*; p. 32, Minangkabau style roof; p. 33, wood-carver, Tarik Selampit performer; p. 34, rubber smallholder; p. 35, latex station; p. 40, *pokok sirih*, preparing *bubur lambak*; p. 41, *bubur* Asyura, midwife cutting infant's hair, *bunga telur* gifts, *bersanding*, children lighting oil lamps; p. 42, grilling *sate*; p. 43, preparing *dodol*, Malay cakes; p. 44, making *ketupat* and *dodol* the *gotong-royong* way; p. 49, Chinese women; p. 52, lion dance; p. 55, children during Wesak celebration; p. 56, *dim sum*, steamboat; p. 57, *nien gao*; p. 58, Chettiar; p. 59, rubber workers; p. 61, St Anne's feast; p. 62, Deepavali, cleansing in river; p. 63, head shaving; p. 65, flower stall, *kolam* drawing; p. 73, Songkraan; p. 79, longhouse at Baleh River; p. 90, child dancing, Iban fishing; p. 98, beaded women; p. 99, computer class; p. 100, hunters at shelter; p. 101, child with hornbill, woman and children; p. 103, Berawan women; p. 109, Dusun woman; p. 112, Murut drinking *tapai*; p. 115, blessing of Huguan Siou; p. 123, boat race; p. 125, percussion ensemble; p. 130, river expedition; p. 134, Hamdolok, Malaysianized fashion; p. 137, oil painting of Wayang Kulit puppets, vases, Thaipusam, gambus musician. **Nicholas, Colin,** p. 12, Orang Asli; p.23, Semai wedding. **Noeb, Jonas,** p. 81, gongs, jars. **Noeb, Leo Mario,** p. 83, gong beaters, priestesses placing offerings. **Nomachi,** p. 123, women husking rice. **Noraini Sidek,** p. 43, crisps. **Ong Puay Liu,** p. 120, Rungus bridal couple, bride presents brass box to in-laws; p. 121, woman weaving, playing *sundatang*, woman with brass coils. **Penang Museum,** p. 32, *tekat* embroidery; p. 44, filling *ketupat*. **Perusahaan Otomobil Kedua Sdn Bhd,** p. 8, Malay, Chinese and Indian men. **PETRONAS,** p. 15, children in field. **Phelan, Peter,** p. 110, Native Courthouse in Sapulut, Native Chief beside oath stone, inauguration of oath stone; p. 111, district and native chiefs in courthouse. **Picture Library Sdn Bhd,** p. 4, Baba-Nyonya couple; p. 6, Orang Asli; p.7, *rebana ubi* drums, kite-flying; p. 17, electronics workers; p. 32, Melaka house, printing batik; p. 33, Wayang Kulit puppeteer; p. 34, women drying fish; p.42, traditional Malay dishes; p. 47, clog maker, mason; p. 48, graduates; p. 52, calligrapher, p. 53, folk dance; p. 55, All Souls Day, child with lanterns, offerings to hungry ghost king; p. 56, *yee sang*, p. 59, bread vendor; p. 65, jasmine and Kanakambaram flowers; p. 66, tandoori chicken, meat curries and korma; p. 67, spices; p. 103, Orang Ulu fishing; p. 107, horsemen; p. 108, west coast Bajau; p. 122–123, Bajau of Kota Belud. **Pinsler, Ronni,** p. 48, Khoo Kongsil p. 50, altar. **Pos Malaysia Berhad,** p. 142, ethnic groups. **Radin Mohd Noh Saleh,** p. 10, pottery, tomb-temple; p. 11, cultural museum; p. 28–29, Malay chiefs; p. 32, Istana Kenangan, Bugis-style house, Pahang house, Selangor house; p. 73, Wat Uttamaran. **Rashid Esa,** p. 22, offerings, worship house, Hari Moyang, *tok jenang*; p. 23, ancestor spirit hut; p. 26, moyang naga, masks, *moyang harimau berantai*, making a blowpipe (all), Saia Anak Tippit, quivers and blowpipe casings; p. 27, girl with painted face, woman weaving mat, baskets, *apok* pouches, rattan bracelets, Mah Meri man and woman in traditional costume. **Regis, Patricia,** p.106, Rungus longhouse; p. 109, Bonggi, Tagal Murut; p. 113, Lotud priestesses, male priest performs Rungus rice rituals; p. 114, Kadazandusun priestesses with wide-brimmed hats, male ritual specialist, priestesses and ritual specialists; p. 115, ritual paraphernalia, Odun Piduru, priestesses praying in the rain; p. 116, Kwijau ritul specialists; p. 117, Lotud elder dancing, girl weaving, women elders; p. 118, Papar priestesses, male shamans, rice offerings, rice seedlings; p. 119, priestesses in death ritual, Kadazandusun priestess, Papar *bobohizan*, Lotud *tantagas*; p. 122, Bajau fisherman, woman harvesting rice, grated cassava; p. 123, Bajau Laut children; p. 124, women braiding leaves; p. 126, longhouse, couple returning from market, bride-wealth exchange (9); p. 127, Baukan Murut woman, feasts (2); p. 128–129, Iranun marriage (4), buffalo turning sugarcane juice press, island groups (6); p. 120, priestess at rice hut; p. 121, family in *apad*; p. 130, Rumanau women, fishing. **Ritchie, James,** p. 76, Penan; p. 81, Dayung reciting; p. 86, preparing sago pith; p. 88, skulls; p. 89, women dancing; p. 92, Iban in warrior costume, wooden figures, miring ceremony; p. 94, farmer and family; p. 96, women with earrings, women with tattoos; p. 98, bamboo flute band; p. 99, Lun Bawang in traditional costumes; p. 100, Penan on fishing trip; p. 101, girl weaving basket; p. 102, Sekapan chieftain; p. 103, Punan Busang in boat, Punan Busang man, Saiban women; p. 104, Eurasian, Indian and Javanese girls (3); p. 105, Indian family, stilt walking, Ching San Yen temple. **Sabah Museum,** p. 132, Chinese vendors. **Salfarina Abdul Gapor,** p. 86, *cherindak* hats. **Sather, Clifford,** p. 85, Iban *manang*; p. 115, Bajau spirit medium; p. 123, Bajau Laut village; p. 125, bride in bath. **Sarawak Museum,** p. 7, Iban in traditional attire; p. 15, Kayan midwife; p. 30, Gua Hitam; p. 47, Chinese medical shop; p. 76, Kelabit headman with son, Dayak men drinking, Chinese and Malays; p. 78, government officers in longhouse; p. 79, Teochew Association band, Malays; p. 84, Orang Ulu shaman; p. 85, Melanau shaman, *bilum*, curing session; p. 88, long drums; p. 89, ritualists dancing; p. 90, Iban woman in traditional dress; p. 92, trophy skulls, medicine box; p. 93, ritualist conductig rites, hornbill effigees, headman makes offering, preparing death hut; p. 98, Kelabit man trimming hair; p. 99, drinking rice wine; p. 101, Penan with blowpipe; p. 102, ritual pole, *save*'; p. 103, Beketan, Tanjong, Punan Bah, Kejaman, Lisum, Sihan; p. 104, Foochow settlement, rickshaw puller, noodle maker; p. 105, Chinese family, dragon dance. **Seling, Ding,** p. 97, child naming ceremony. **Seth Yahya,** p. 30, *budi* and etiquette, reverence towards elders; p. 40, Khatam Qur'an; p. 43, *belacan*; p. 59, news vendor. **Shekar, S. C.,** p. 47, fishermen; p. 56, popiah vendor; p. 57, claypot rice, cook frying, dumplings; p. 60, honouring elders; p. 64, Bharata Natyam, dance drama; p. 74, Chitty family, Chitty with portrait. **Sheppard, Mubin,** p. 32, songket weaver; p. 33, royal *tengkolok*; p. 37, wedding procession; p. 134–135, Mak Yong. **Sindon, Gerald Oscar,** p. 80, headman's court. **Smith, Ravi John,** p. 13, Rungus lady; p. 52, Chinese opera. **Solness, Peter,** p. 13, Rungus women. **Star Publications (M) Bhd,** p.14, schoolchildren in National Day parade; p. 15, national service, 'open house', Deepavali celebrations; p. 18, Chitty newly-weds; p. 22, shaman in ritual; p. 26, carvers; p. 31, reciting verses, women praying, *gotong -royong*; p. 33, Kuda Kepang; p. 36, boy kissing hand of elder; p. 40, family at Hari Raya, receving duit raya, shopping; p. 43, nasi tomato; p. 44, family at Hari Raya; p. 49, OCBC branch, Khoo Kongsi shophouses; p. 50–51, Taoist devotees carrying float; Buddhist devotee, Monk, man praying, Chinese medium; p. 52, school orchestra; p. 53, wushu exponents; p. 56, Yut Kee coffee shop, chicken rice, wantan mee; p. 57, bak kut teh, lok lok; p. 59, Gujerati wedding; p. 60, horoscope reading; p. 61, Mariamman Thirunal festival, Sikhs praying, donating to charity, family worshipping, serving food to the public; p. 62, Bhangra, Thaiponggal, kavadi bearer; p. 63, bathing of diety, ear piercing; p. 66, nasi kandar vendor, *mamak* mee, *thosai*, *briyani*; p. 67, *teh tarik*, mamak eateries, naan, stringhoppers, vadai, sweetmeats; *murukku*; p. 68, altar in Peranakan home; p. 69, wash stand; Good Friday; p. 72, Loy Krathong, dance by Thais; p. 73, novice monks and nuns; p. 75, Chitty bride, security guards, Gurkhas Association, Bal Bahadur Rana; p. 77, Kayan wedding; p. 78, Bidayuh girls dancing; p. 82, Gawai opening ceremony, beauty pageant; p. 83, shaman leading ritual, p. 87, martial arts, hut with offerings; p. 96, egg chant ceremony; p. 97, shamans make offerings; p. 105, mayor at temple; p. 106, Murut with brew; p. 107, Dusun priestess and ritualist; p. 112, procession, stilt game, traditional crafts; p. 113, cutting rice stalks; p. 134, Wayang Kulit Gedek; p. 136, Malaysians in drama; p. 138–139, music festival; p. 138, song session, Bajau craftsman, visitor at Gawai; p. 139, Orang Asli dancers, batik design, American couple, British couple. **Syed Ahmad Jamal,** p. 32, kris. **Tan Hong Yew,** p. 6–7, map; p. 37, marriage in *kampung*; p. 70–71, Festa San Pedro procession; p. 76–77, Gawai Kenyalang; p. 78–79, Sarawak map; p. 90–91, Iban longhouse; p. 110–111, court hearing; p. 120–121, longhouse. **Teo, Albert C. K.,** p. 126, Murut bridal couple. **Tettoni, Luca Invernizzi,** p. 79, traditional Iban longhouse, p. 88, headhouse; p. 89, priestesses in rice field, p. 90, chiefs in ceremonial dress; p. 97, woman making hat; p. 102, penghulu and followers; p. 104, meeting, merchant with native artefacts; p. 141, Melanau masks. **TheimageAsia.com Centre,** p. 66, banana leaf cuisine. **Tommy Chang Image Productions,** p. 7, Kadazandusun ritual; p. 9, wedding; p. 108, Ludayeh bride and family; p. 109, Dusun Tindal, *tamu*; p. 113, Unduk Ngadu; p. 116, Sino-natives; p. 117, flautist; p. 118, offerings before harvest; p. 122, houses on stilts; p. 123, gravemarkers; p. 124, Bajau preparing meal, lepa with carved bowsprit; p. 125, *tamu*, wedding, groom on pony; p. 126, Murut hunting; p. 127, women dancing; p. 131, collecting birds' nests; p. 133, new year celebrations (2), Indian family; p. 138, visitors at Rungus longhouse; p. 148, Semporna fisherman. **Usahasama Seri Cemerlang Sdn Bhd,** p. 41, blessing of newly-weds. **Vani,** p. 57, curry mee; p. 59, office workers; p. 63, ceremony for pregnant woman, after birth purification rite, puberty rite, wedding; p. 64, lighting oil lamps, clay pots, pot in marriage ceremony; p. 65, men in traditional attire (2), women in sari and khamez (2), children in costume, bride with hair decoration; p. 66, betel quid; p. 67, making roti canai (all); p. 134, intermarriage. **VirtualMalayasia.com,** p. 5, Chitty boys; p. 57, mooncake; p. 70, girls with painted faces, folk dance, parade; p. 112, buffalo race. **Waks, Leo,** p. 35, rice farming. **Werner, Roland,** p. 24, 1960s Mah Meri wedding. **Wong Leck Min,** p. 54, Chinese New Year's Eve dinner. **Yahaya Ismail,** p.106, Murut men; p. 107, Cocos Islanders; p. 129, Suluk dancers; p. 133, Kadazandusun bride and Chinese groom. **Yayasan Budi Penyayang Malaysia (*The Nyonya Kebaya: A Century of Straits Chinese Costumes* by Datin Seri Endon Mahmood),** p. 68, models wearing sarong *kebaya*. **Yayasan Warisan Johor,** p. 134–135, Zapin dance.